Rev. Joseph Smale

Photograph courtesy of the First Baptist Church Los Angeles Archives.

STUDIES IN EVANGELICAL HISTORY AND THOUGHT

Joseph Smale

God's 'Moses' for Pentecostalism

STUDIES IN EVANGELICAL HISTORY AND THOUGHT

STUDIES IN EVANGELICAL HISTORY AND THOUGHT

Joseph Smale

God's 'Moses' for Pentecostalism

Tim Welch

Foreword by Allan Heaton Anderson

Copyright © Tim Welch 2013

First published 2013 by Paternoster

Paternoster is an imprint of AuthenticMedia
52 Presley Way
Crownhill
Milton Keynes
MK8 0ES

19 18 17 16 15 14 13 7 6 5 4 3 2 1

The right of Tim Welch to be identified as the Author of this Work has been asserted by him in accordance with the Copyright, Designs and Patents Act 1988

All rights reserved. No part of this publication may be reproduced, stored in a retrieval system, or transmitted in any form by any means, electronic, mechanical, photocopying, recording or otherwise, without the prior permission of the publisher or a license permitting restricted copying. In the UK such licenses are issued by the Copyright Licensing Agency, 90 Tottenham Court Road, London W1P 9HE.

British Library Cataloguing in Publication Data
A catalogue record for this book is available from the British Library

ISBN 978–1–84227–781–2

Typeset by Anthony Cross
Printed and bound in Great Britain
for Paternoster
by Lightning Source, Milton Keynes

STUDIES IN EVANGELICAL HISTORY AND THOUGHT

Series Preface

The Evangelical movement has been marked by its union of four emphases: on the Bible, on the cross of Christ, on conversion as the entry to the Christian life and on the responsibility of the believer to be active. The present series is designed to publish scholarly studies of any aspect of this movement in Britain or overseas. Its volumes include social analysis as well as exploration of Evangelical ideas. The books in the series consider aspects of the movement shaped by the Evangelical Revival of the eighteenth century, when the impetus to mission began to turn the popular Protestantism of the British Isles and North America into a global phenomenon. The series aims to reap some of the rich harvest of academic research about those who, over the centuries, have believed that they had a gospel to tell to the nations.

Series Editors

David Bebbington, Professor of History, University of Stirling, Stirling, Scotland, UK

John H.Y. Briggs, Senior Research Fellow in Ecclesiastical History and Director Emeritus of the Centre for Baptist History and Heritage, Regent's Park College, Oxford, UK

Timothy Larsen, Professor of Theology, Wheaton College, Illinois, USA

Mark A. Noll, McAnaney Professor of History, University of Notre Dame, Notre Dame, Indiana, USA

Ian M. Randall, Director of Research, Spurgeon's College, London, and Senior Research Fellow, International Baptist Theological Seminary, Prague

To my dear wife and best friend
Rachel
and our three precious and delightful children
Susannah, Frazer and Emelia
with love and deep appreciation

Contents

Foreword by Allan Heaton Anderson ....

Acknowledgements ....

Chapter 1
Introduction 1
Introduction 1
Significance for Pentecostal and Baptist History 3
   Accuracy of Facts 4
   The Spurgeonic Roots of Pentecostalism 7
   'Organisation' versus 'Freedom' 8
Methodologies 9
   Smale Relatives 10
   Baptist Archives 11
   Secular Newspapers 13
   Pentecostal Documents 14
   Other Sources 15
   Narrative Analysis Using Data Triangulation 16

Chapter 2
Smale's Spiritual and Pastoral Formation (1881–92) 19
Family and Conversion 19
   Wesleyan Revival Roots in Cornwall and Somerset 22
Training: The Pastors' College, London (1887–90) 25
   Spurgeonic Strand: Word and Spirit 28
   Spurgeonic Theological Education 29
      TRAINING OPPORTUNITIES FOR ALL 30
      A BROAD BASED EDUCATION 31
      APPLIED THEOLOGY 33
      PREACHING 34
      EVANGELISM 37
   Distinct Pneumatology 39
      THE PASTOR'S NEED FOR HOLY SPIRIT POWER 39
        A Felt Need for God the Holy Spirit 40
        A Practical Experience of God the Holy Spirit 41
      THE CHURCH'S NEED FOR REVIVAL 43
        Practical Signs of Revival 44
   College Assessment 46
Smale's First Church: Park Road Baptist Church, Ryde, Isle of Wight 46
   Shared Platforms 48
   Bible-Based Preaching 50

Innovations 51
Social Concerns 53
Farewell Reflections 55

Chapter 3
Smale's Preparation for Revival (1893–1904) 57
The Lone Star Baptist Church, Prescott, Arizona (1893–97) 57
  'Spiritually faithful during these years of testing' 59
    EVANGELISM AND MISSION 59
    CONTEMPORARY INNOVATIONS 60
    LECTURE TOURS 61
    THE ARIZONA BAPTIST ASSOCIATION 61
  Marriage to Helena Dunham 62
First Baptist Church Los Angeles, California (1897–1905) 63
  'The great factors promoting a revival' 68
  'The power of the Spirit in action' 69
  'A spirit of unity has been happily manifest' 70
  Pentecostal Prayer Union of Southern California 70
  The Centennial Conference at First Baptist Church Los Angeles 71
Evidence of Schism at First Baptist Church Los Angeles 72
  Analysis of Historical Qualitative Data using 'Transformational Logic' 73
  Smale's Conflict-in-Context 75
    ENGAGEMENT, RESIGNATION, MARRIAGE AND SEPARATION 75
    A VOTE OF CONFIDENCE 78
    'BUNCH OF COINCIDENTS SETS BAPTISTS AGOG'
    18 SEPTEMBER 1902) 79
    'PASTOR SMALE'S TRIAL BUT BEGUN' (19 SEPTEMBER 1902) 80
    'PASTOR AND HIS FOES BOTH SCORE' (20 SEPTEMBER 1902) 80
    'CHURCH TRIAL WON BY PASTOR SMALE' (23 SEPTEMBER 1902) ... 83
    'SMALE'S ASSISTANT ABOUT TO RESIGN' (26 SEPTEMBER 1902) 84
    'SWAY OF SMALE MUCH EXTENDED' (9 OCTOBER 1902) 85
    'OBJECTIONS MADE TO PASTOR SMALE' (5 FEBRUARY 1903) 87
Smale's 'Scanning' and the Role of the 'Inner Teacher' 89
  *Reappraisal of Smale's Tour to the Holy Land and Welsh Revival
  (1904–05)* 91
  Smale's Return to Los Angeles: Prepared for Revival 94
  First Baptist Church Los Angeles Welcome Smale Home: Context for Revival ... 96
  'The Transforming Intuition of Christ' 98

Chapter 4
Pentecostalism's 'Moses' (1905–06) 99
William Seymour and Joseph Smale: Towards a 'Promised Land' 99
Fifteen Weeks of Daily Prayer and Praise Meetings 101
  Week One: Sunday 28 May–Saturday 3 June 102

Weeks Two and Three: Sunday 4 June–Saturday 17 June 103
Week Four: Sunday 18 June–Saturday 24 June 106
Weeks Five and Six: Sunday 25 June–Saturday 8 July 109
Weeks Seven and Eight: Sunday 9 July–Saturday 22 July 111
Weeks Nine and Ten: Sunday 23 July–Saturday 5 August 112
Weeks Eleven and Twelve: Sunday 6 August–Saturday 19 August 113
Weeks Thirteen and Fourteen: Sunday 20 August–Saturday 2 September 115
Week Fifteen: Sunday 3 September–Saturday 10 September 119
Deacon Dozier's Opposition: Wednesday 6 September 1905 119
Smale's Resignation: Sunday 10 September 1905 121
Reappraisal of Bartleman's Account 122
   Smale versus Dozier: The Core Issues 126
   The Board of Deacons Respond..129
First New Testament Church Los Angeles (1905–06)..131
   Smale's Advocacy through Organization 133
   Smale's Advocacy through Demonstration of the Spirit's Power 138
     'THAT NEVER TO BE FORGOTTEN NIGHT'
     (MONDAY 9 APRIL 1906) 141
     'THE GIFT OF TONGUES' (EASTER SUNDAY 15 APRIL 1906).............143
     'HEAVEN TOO IS COLOR BLIND' (JUNE 1906).....................................146
   Smale's Advocacy through Identification with 'The Holy Rollers' 147
     IMPLICIT AMBASSADORIAL SUPPORT 148
     EXPLICIT AMBASSADORIAL SUPPORT 152
   Smale's Advocacy through Publication 156

Chapter 5
Smale's Pentecostal Life and Service **159**
A Plethora of Pentecostalisms 160
The Shape of Smale's Preaching 161
   A Four-Fold Gospel..163
   Word and Spirit – Without the Play 165
   Word and Spirit – At Play..166
   Smale's Rhetoric...168
     TRUE WORSHIP OF A TRIUNE GOD 171
     SANCTIFICATION: AS A DISTINCT WORK OF GRACE.....................173
     THE BAPTISM OF THE HOLY GHOST 176
The Shape of Smale's Ecclesiology..181
   Pentecostal Identity..183
     THE HEADSHIP OF CHRIST AND HOLY GHOST
     ADMINISTRATION..184
     INTENSELY SPIRITUAL IN CHARACTER...186
     NEW TESTAMENT CHURCH PRACTICES...190
        Church Membership 190
        Church Finances 193

The Shape of Smale's Missiology 194
   A Chinese Mission 195
   A Spanish Mission.. 196
   Door to Door Tract Distribution 196
   Christmas Day 1905 196
   City Tent Work... 197
   The Bible and Missionary Training School 198
   China New Testament Mission 199
   A German Missionary: A.H. Bach 201
   China Centenary Missionary Conference... 204
Smale's Withdrawal from Pentecostalism 210
   Circumstantial Reasons for Retreat: Smale and Keyes 210
   Theological Reasons for Retreat: Tongues and Disunity 213
Summary.. 215

Chapter 6
Conclusion 219
Smale's Post-Pentecostal Phase (1909–26) 219
   Familial Circumstances: Divorce and Bereavement 219
   Marriage to Esther Hargrave 220
   Conflict: Hitherfield Road Free Church, London (1912–13) 222
   Mission Entrepreneur: Spanish Gospel Mission 224
   Independent Pastor: Unity Chapel, Bristol (1913–15) 225
   Bible Teacher: Grace Baptist Church, Los Angeles (1915–26).................. 228
A Baby Daughter: Esther Grace Smale 232
Final Assessment 233
   The 'Moses' Idiom 235

Appendix 1
Joseph Smale Timeline 239

Appendix 2
The Logic of Transformation 242

Appendix 3
'The gift of tongues is not for every Christian' 246

Bibliography.. 248
General Index.. 267

Foreword

It has really been a privilege to have worked over several years with Tim Welch on his Joseph Smale PhD, and now to write the Foreword to this book. Tim was a doctoral supervisor's dream student. Once he had grasped his subject, he leapt into it with an insatiable curiosity and determination and made transatlantic (and transcontinental) crossings to pursue his goal – it seemed he would not leave any stone unturned on this 'Smale Trail'. The result is this volume, a compelling account of a most significant, if neglected, character in the events of the Pentecostal Revival that began in Los Angeles at Smale's instigation in 1905, and not, as is commonly thought, in 1906. What this book supports is a far more complex account of the beginnings of Pentecostalism than that often told by historians of Pentecostalism. About a quarter of early American Pentecostal leaders were or had been Baptists, second in number only to Methodists. They included Jennie Moore, the future wife of the leader of the Azusa Street Revival William Seymour, the Bishop of the Church of God in Christ Charles H. Mason, and the first chairman of the Assemblies of God, Eudorus N. Bell. And, of course, the vast majority of classical Pentecostal and independent Charismatic churches worldwide practise believers' baptism by immersion, another Baptist contribution to Pentecostalism that is often overlooked. But the importance of this particular study is its meticulous chronological account of the events in Los Angeles preceding and immediately following the Azusa Street Revival, and, in particular, the catalytic role played by Smale and his ministry at the First Baptist Church and then, after his resignation, at his New Testament Church in the Burbank Hall.

Pentecostalism did not arise in a vacuum, but was deeply moulded by several factors in nineteenth-century Evangelicalism, in which Smale with his Spurgeonic background was thoroughly immersed. Revivalism, with its focus on an emotional and personal encounter with God through the Holy Spirit, was part of the very fabric of Evangelical experience. During the late nineteenth and early twentieth centuries, radical Evangelicals, especially premillennialists nurtured in the schools of J.N. Darby and D.L. Moody, were expecting a new, worldwide revival to precede the second coming of Christ. This was part of the driving force behind the various revivals erupting around the globe during the first two decades of the twentieth century in parts of North America, Chile, India, China, Korea, Estonia, Latvia, Nigeria, Uganda, and Madagascar, to name but a few.

Pentecostalism did not appear 'suddenly from heaven'. Discontinuity is often assumed in Pentecostal historiography, particularly through the influence of 'latter rain' teaching, which referred to the 'former' and 'latter rain' spoken of by Hebrew prophets as pointing to two separate outpourings of the Spirit.

This suggested an historical gap between the first and the twentieth centuries, when 'signs and wonders' were restored to a prodigal church. However, signs and wonders, including healing, miracles and glossolalia, were always part of the expectations that would accompany mission work in Catholic, Orthodox, and radical Evangelical circles. There are historical precedents for everything the Pentecostals did and this history is in continuity with the revival movements of the past. Miracles were referred to in the western and eastern Church Fathers, during medieval Catholic missions – and it was only Lutheran and Reformed Europe that introduced the denial of the possibility of contemporary miracles. Catholics charged Protestants with practicing a form of deism where, in effect, God had withdrawn to become an absent and inactive deity.

Yet many nineteenth and early twentieth century Evangelicals like Joseph Smale were aware of the enormous gap between what they read in the New Testament and their own practices – and how much more effective they would be if they could have the same power that marked the ministry of the first apostles. Their efforts had been met with few converts, and on the mission field their most significant achievements were the medical and philanthropic activities they had engaged in. In these circles there was a conviction that a great, worldwide outpouring of the Spirit would result in the restoration of miraculous power to the Church's mission, so that the nations could be reached for Christ before the impending end of the ages. The nineteenth century had seen a whole series of Evangelical revivals resulting in an unprecedented missionary movement, the birth of new Evangelical denominations, and the holiness and healing movements. Many of these revival movements defined what we mean by Evangelicalism today and had a profound influence on the emergence of Pentecostalism and its global expansion in the twentieth century. These revivals introduced a new method of evangelism characterised by emotion, large and long nightly services indoors or outdoors, often led by lay people, that brought Evangelical faith and, often, profound moral change to communities.

This was taken a step further when radical Evangelicals, including some in A.B. Simpson's Christian and Missionary Alliance, began to expect the restoration of the gift of tongues for the speedy and effective preaching of the gospel to the nations. It was only with the introduction of 'initial evidence' that people like Simpson, Pandita Ramabai, and Smale himself, were to withdraw from the excesses of Pentecostalism. The stage was set for this doctrine to become the hallmark of early American Pentecostalism. Former Methodist maverick preacher Charles F. Parham's linking tongues with Spirit baptism was the radically new idea that caught fire in the early twentieth century. But the first Pentecostals believed that they alone had the 'apostolic mission' that would return the power of the Spirit lost since the 'Dark Ages'. It was this intransigence, not the manifestations of revival, which upset Smale, as these pages show.

The seamless web of Evangelical expectations in history means that instead of a sudden new start in 1901 or 1906, there is a continuation and growth of ideas that have their origins much earlier. The first Pentecostals, like Smale himself, tended to come from one or other of these radical Evangelical groups. The Welsh Revival in particular played a major role in the Evangelical expectations of a worldwide revival in the early twentieth century. All held a conviction that the second coming of Christ was imminent and that this worldwide revival would usher it in. They were conditioned by a movement reacting to rationalism and secularism, a response to modernity that focused on personal spirituality, emotional release and divine intervention in human affairs – even if it used modernity's tools to formulate and justify this reaction. The idea grew that there would be a great outpouring of the Spirit throughout the world before the Second Coming of Christ – and, it was hoped, at the beginning of the twentieth century.

Although the Azusa Street Revival was the most significant North American centre of early Pentecostalism, it was neither the only one nor the earliest. The events in Smale's congregation were a case in point. Various revivals occurred within a few years of each other in different parts of the world during the late nineteenth and in the first decade of the twentieth century. These revivals had decidedly Pentecostal characteristics, with gifts of the Spirit like healings, tongues, prophecy, and other miraculous signs. They were conscious and deliberate attempts by ordinary people to adapt revivalist Christianity to their own local contexts, thereby giving expression to their desire for a more satisfying and relevant religious life. Smale's brief visit to the Welsh Revival and his beginning revival meetings in the First Baptist Church were as much a part of these movements as anywhere else. There were precedents laid down by earlier revivalists that were to mould the expectations of Smale and the first Pentecostals. Many of these expectations were nurtured in the holiness and healing movements, the soil out of which Pentecostalism grew and without which it would not have survived. Some of these revivals occurred many years before the events of 1905–06. The 'American Pentecost', the Cane Ridge Revival, occurred in 1801; in Britain the movement under the Scottish Presbyterian Edward Irving resulted in the Catholic Apostolic Church in the 1830s; the revival in Russia and Armenia in 1855 with people speaking in tongues resulted in a group called 'Pentecostal Christians' who formed congregations there that predated Pentecostal denominations in origin by fifty years; in South India in 1865 a revival under the Tamil evangelist Arulappan included Pentecostal manifestations. Keswick leader F.B. Meyer visited Estonian Baptist congregations in 1902 and reported approvingly of the 'marvellous manifestations' of the Spirit that were frequent occurrences, and of the gift of tongues being heard 'quite often in the meetings', accompanied by interpretations about the imminent coming of Christ. The Mukti Mission near Pune, India, under Pandita Ramabai witnessed another revival from 1905–07. What Smale achieved was to make these expectations thoroughly Baptist and in keeping with his own thoroughly Baptist credentials. In this respect he was many decades ahead of his time. Tim Welch shows us how important Smale was in creating space for the Azusa Street Revival. It might even be said that without Smale Azusa Street might never have happened.

The precedents in the nineteenth and early twentieth centuries illustrate that the soil preparing the way for the emergence of Pentecostalism was not only found in the western world. The revival movements were in many respects revolutionary, paving the way for momentous change within the church, society, and nations, and, in particular, creating a heightened awareness of personal dignity and identity. These forces were affected by political forces geared towards independence from colonialism that characterized the early twentieth century. The numerous independent churches and movements that emerged were preceded by the revival events that not only served to further 'spiritual' concerns, but also possessed far-reaching implications for political action, patriotic fervor, and social activism. These various revivals were not primarily movements from the western world to foreign lands but, more significantly, they were movements within these continents themselves. In most cases the revivals were led by local leaders. It can be argued that the revivals independent of western Pentecostalism in Korea, China, India, Chile, Nigeria, and the Ivory Coast were not specifically Pentecostal revivals, but this depends on how 'Pentecostal' is defined. If the charismatic practices of healing, prophecy, speaking in tongues, other physical manifestations, and emotional prayer meetings are characteristics of Pentecostalism, then these revivals demonstrate that Pentecostal origins are complex and varied, polycentric and diffused. The revival that began in the First Baptist Church in Los Angeles under Joseph Smale is a splendid illustration of this, and nowhere is this better demonstrated than in this book. This story deserves to be told, and I am delighted that it is now made available to the wider reading public.

Allan Heaton Anderson,
Professor of Mission and Global Pentecostal Studies,
University of Birmingham,
February 2013.

Acknowledgements

During a lecture in 2002, Professor Allan Anderson referenced a person called Joseph Smale, who was British, Baptist and trained at Spurgeon's College, London. This was my *kairos* moment! My personal journey (which colloquially became known as the *Smale-Trail*) to discover more about Smale had begun. I remain profoundly grateful for Allan's expertise as my doctoral supervisor, for his friendship and encouragement along the way, as well as his willingness to write the foreword to this book.

Alongside Allan, I also pay tribute to the impact of Mark Cartledge and their joint leadership of the Centre for Pentecostal and Charismatic Studies at the University of Birmingham. They and fellow students helped to sharpen my thinking and research, while providing many international perspectives and friendships within a very special cohort.

Starting as an 'outsider' to the field of Pentecostal scholarship, I soon became the beneficiary of many practical expressions of welcome, insights, and primary materials. Cecil M. Robeck, Jr, deserves particular mention, because in my first few years of research he graciously gave me sight of his unpublished manuscript concerning Smale and inspired me to keep digging, aware that Joseph Smale's story required fuller exploration. Similarly, Darrin Rodgers, Director of the Flower Pentecostal Heritage Center (Springfield, Missouri), discovered and sent me a copy of Smale's book of revival sermons, *The Pentecostal Blessing*, as well as offering me regular support and encouragement thereafter. The late Desmond Cartwright also provided valuable connections and significant Smale-related documents along the way.

Reflecting on the various challenges of the S*male-Trail*, I am overwhelmed by the number of individuals from around the world who have enabled me to complete this project. Although space does not enable each name to be repeated here, my gratitude for every contribution remains deep.

This is, however, my opportunity to recognise the loving and prayerful impact of my parents, Bernard and Jean Welch, and my father and mother-in-law, Morris and Gwyneth Bird. Similarly, I thank God for Robert and Beth Amess, who mentored me during my early days of ministerial formation at Duke Street Baptist Church, Richmond. Robert also served as Chair of Governors at Spurgeon's College, and his word and Spirit emphasis has been immensely influential, coupled with his contagious love of church history and its relevance for ministry contexts today.

Appreciation is also expressed to the following scholars, librarians, archivists and friends who have assisted my research at various points over the past decade: David Bebbington (University of Stirling); George J. Fogelson (Los Angeles Public Library); Susan Mills and Emma Walsh (Angus Library,

Regent's Park College, Oxford); Judy Powles (Spurgeon's College, London); Gary Tiedemann (Centre for the Study of Christianity in China); Deborah van Broekhoven and Betsy Dunbar (American Baptist Historical Society, Atlanta, Georgia); Grace Yoder (Asbury Theological Seminary, Wilmore, Kentucky); Helen Taylor, Joann and Dick Looney, Karen Carmen (First Baptist Church Prescott, Arizona); Ernestine and Paul Rotcher, Sandy and Richard Rogers (First Baptist Church Los Angeles); Michael Matthews (Hitherfield Road Baptist Church, Streatham, London); Connie Au (Hong Kong Christian Council); Matthew Hill and Helena Stevens (Spanish Gospel Mission); Alan Linton (Bristol); Susan Maria Farrington (Wiveliscombe); Daphne Beauchamp (Richmond); Steve and Rachel Cole (Tonbridge); Martin Light (Isle of Wight); Roger and Sheena Marx (Richmond); Marjorie Waller (Richmond); Fred and Viv Hughes (Cheltenham); and Theo and Pam Welch (Cambridge).

I also wish to pay tribute to the immeasurable support I have received from countless individuals within the church communities where I have been privileged to serve: Duke Street Baptist Church, Richmond; Claremont Baptist Church, Shrewsbury; Jersey Baptist Church, St Helier; and now Cambray Baptist Church, Cheltenham.

Having been afforded the opportunity to incorporate several significant photographs, I acknowledge the kind permission given by: the California Historical Society; First Baptist Church Prescott; First Baptist Church Los Angeles; Paula Hinkel; Hitherfield Road Baptist Church, London; the Isle of Wight County Record Office; Alan H. Linton; Los Angeles Public Library, Spurgeon's College; and the Wiveliscombe Book Group Archive.

In terms of encouragement to get the *Smale-Trail* to publication, I owe a debt of gratitude to all the scholars who read this manuscript and offered their helpful comments and generous commendations, namely Mike Parsons (Commissioning Editor at Paternoster), William K. Kay, Peter J. Morden, Cecil M. Robeck, Jr, and Anthony R. Cross. Anthony's willingness to critique my final drafts has been invaluable. While deeply appreciative of every contribution, I happily confirm that I take full responsibility for all facets of this finished work.

Penultimately, a special word of acknowledgement is reserved for the descendants of Joseph Smale, in particular his two grandsons, the Rev. Dr George L. Wood and the Rev. Dr H. Stanley Wood. Their warm and generous receptivity to this research has been pivotal to the success of this project, their patience with my repeated correspondence has been unstinting, and their warm hospitality on my two research trips to Los Angeles memorable indeed. I trust George and Stan (and other members of the Wood/Smale family) will enjoy this work in memory of their inspirational grandfather.

Finally, as stated in the dedication, deepest appreciation of all goes to my own family for their constant love and support. Rachel, my wife, and our three children Susannah, Frazer, and Emelia have made countless sacrifices to enable the *Smale-Trail* to reach publication, and for that I will be forever grateful.

Acknowledgements

Juggling the demands of church ministry and academic work it has been their persistent encouragement and belief in me which has given me the strength to complete this book. To all four of them I pledge my love and devotion. I am, among all people, most richly blessed.

To God be the glory!

Tim Welch
Cheltenham
February, 2013

CHAPTER 1

Introduction

Introduction

Pastor Joseph Smale, described by Frank Bartleman as the 'Moses' of Pentecostalism, immediately caught my attention with the discovery that he had also trained at Spurgeon's College, London, albeit 100 years before me! Therefore, my exploration into the life and ministry of Smale is unashamedly from a similar Baptist background which has undoubtedly shaped many of my presuppositions within the spheres of research undertaken. Being aware that any qualitative investigation requires recognition of 'a cacophony of voices speaking with various agendas',[1] it is imperative that my personal experiences and feelings are considered as valid as any of the multiple 'voices' under consideration.

My initial assumptions were based on the recognition that present-day British Baptists were, and predominantly still are, ignorant of Smale's past existence, ministry and involvement as an early pioneer of Pentecostal-Charismatic Christianity. This is particularly surprising given the subsequent prolific growth of the Pentecostal movement globally throughout the twentieth and into the twenty-first centuries. Such omissions can best be interpreted because of the following three factors.

Firstly, Smale's catalytic role in the chain of events leading to the Azusa Street Revival in Los Angeles in 1906 naturally forms part of the Pentecostal storyline and, therefore, by definition, is located outside the domain of Baptist historiography. Secondly, as far as the Baptist archives at Spurgeon's College, London, and Regent's Park College, Oxford, were aware Joseph Smale had left Britain in 1893 for ministry in Arizona, and then his subsequent churches were listed up until 1913, but with nothing else recorded about his life and ministry thereafter. Whereas former pastors usually have their obituary printed in the official Baptist Union of Great Britain handbook the year after death, the fact that Smale had left his home country and later the Baptist denomination offers sufficient explanation why such an omission occurred in his case.[2] Thirdly, the late Douglas McBain, a leading proponent of Charismatic Renewal within the Baptist denomination in Britain over the past forty years, unwittingly made a similar omission concerning Joseph Smale in his detailed account of the history of renewal among British Baptists. When charting the early days of the modern

---

[1] B. Roberts, *Biographical Research* (Open University Press, 2002), p. 168.
[2] J. Powles, Spurgeon's College Librarian/Archivist, email 12 February 2003.

Pentecostal movement at Azusa Street McBain makes no mention of Smale or First Baptist Church Los Angeles, simply because he was not aware of Joseph Smale's existence.[3]

Even Spurgeon's College, which historically since inception[4] has maintained a vibrant interest in equipping students to minister in the power of the word and the Holy Spirit, has not registered the fact that Joseph Smale was one of their former students from 1887–90, before going on to accomplish this significant 'Moses' pioneering role towards the 'Promised Land' referred to in the context of this book as Pentecostalism. Within spheres of academic and ministerial formation at such institutions as Spurgeon's College, where a keen interest in revival movements of Charismatic and Pentecostal Christianity is regarded as a necessity in the modern milieu, Smale's story deserves to be discovered.

Significantly, just as the research for this book commenced in 2002, so Baptist historian Ian Randall wrote a chapter about 'Baptists and the Shaping of Pentecostalism',[5] in which Joseph Smale and his pivotal role in Los Angeles was succinctly described in a paragraph.[6] Although brief, Randall's reference to Smale signified an important growing Baptist awareness, from a British perspective at least, of the early days of Pentecostalism and the impact of a Baptist heritage for at least ten of the forty-five Pentecostal leaders who joined the movement before 1914.[7] Douglas Jacobsen accordingly notes how each participant in the Pentecostal movement, Baptist or otherwise, was important because they 'brought his or her own set of perceptions and theological insights to the work of theologically making sense of Pentecostalism'.[8]

Inevitably the Baptistic roots of Pentecostalism that have gained most prominent attention are the early North American Pentecostal leaders E.N. Bell (1866–1923), who became the first general chairman of the Assemblies of God, and C.H. Mason (1866–1961), co-founder and long time leader of the Church

---

[3] D. McBain, *Fire Over the Waters: Renewal among Baptists and Others from the 1960s to the 1990s* (Darton, Longman and Todd, 1997), pp. 12-13; also personal email correspondence and telephone conversations, November 2002–March 2003.

[4] Originally known as 'The Pastors' College', which C.H. Spurgeon founded in 1856. Bebbington clarifies that it was only 'for the first fifteen years of the institution's existence, [that] the apostrophe in its title, Pastors' College, was placed before the *s*'. D.W. Bebbington, 'Spurgeon and British Evangelical Theological Education', in D.G. Hart and R.A. Mohler, Jr (eds), *Theological Education in the Evangelical Tradition* (Baker Books, 1996), p. 220.

[5] I.M. Randall, '"Days of Pentecostal Overflowing": Baptists and the Shaping of Pentecostalism', in D.W. Bebbington (ed.), *The Gospel in the World* (Paternoster Press, 2002), pp. 80-104.

[6] Randall, '"Days of Pentecostal Overflowing"', p. 82.

[7] See also R.M. Anderson, *Vision of the Disinherited: The Making of American Pentecostalism* (Oxford University Press, 1979), p. 103.

[8] D. Jacobsen, *Thinking in the Spirit: Theologies of the Early Pentecostal Movement* (Indiana University Press, 2003), p. 17.

of God in Christ. Both attended Baptist theological institutions; Bell the Southern Baptist Theological Seminary from 1900–02, and Mason the Arkansas Baptist College in 1893. Another early Pentecostal leader with Baptist roots was Charles Price Jones (1865–1949), latterly 'Senior Bishop' of the Church of Christ (Holiness), USA. Having established a network with C.H. Mason in revivals and church planting that arose from a convention held at the Mt. Helm Baptist Church, Jackson, Mississippi, in 1897, Jones was later to accompany Mason to Azusa Street for his Holy Spirit baptism.[9]

While Baptist historians may be excused for not realising the significance of Pastor Joseph Smale, Pentecostal historiography has for over a century included Smale in their storyline, even though superficially. From the emergence of Pentecostalism in Los Angeles, Smale has been recognised as one of many catalysts involved in the chain of events that led up to the 1906 Azusa Street Revival. However, an in-depth biographical assessment of Smale's unique contribution has, to date, never been attempted. In defence of Pentecostal scholars, the primary reason why Smale has escaped the attention allotted to characters such as Bell, Mason and C.P. Jones is probably integrally linked to his peculiar 'Moses' role and designation. Given that, although Smale initially anticipated the fullness of Pentecostal blessing in a localised revival that would ripple out to encompass the world, he very quickly withdrew himself and his First New Testament Church from the expressions of Pentecostalism that were emerging at Azusa Street and elsewhere. The consequence of such disaffection with the Pentecostal movement by late 1906 caused Smale to recalibrate his theological and ecclesiological position as an independent non-denominational pastor and church. Consequently, although he still viewed himself as an exponent of Evangelical and Pentecostal Christianity, he consciously disassociated himself from the radical Pentecostals of the Apostolic Faith. Reasons such as these, therefore, explain why Smale has not previously been identified by Pentecostals as one worthy of scholarly attention.

Significance for Pentecostal and Baptist History

The underpinning contribution of this study is that in spite of his premature withdrawal from Pentecostalism, Joseph Smale participated in some quite remarkable phenomena which contain pertinent factual data that merits inclusion as integral background to the Azusa Street Revival. Furthermore, the accumulative practical and theological criteria which ultimately prompted Smale's decision to extricate himself from the movement have remained a neglected aspect of study, to the detriment of Pentecostal research. These can best be summarized within the following three categories.

---

[9] D.T. Irvin, 'Charles Price Jones: Image of Holiness', in J.R. Goff and G. Wacker (eds), *Portraits of a Generation: Early Pentecostal Leaders* (University of Arkansas Press, 2002), p. 39.

Accuracy of Facts

The historical challenge is, as ever, to dig beneath the surface of all documentary materials available in order to be able critically to expand the paradigms of previous narratives, namely those standardized accounts of the events leading up to the Azusa Street Revival as published by the 'official' Pentecostal historians, such as Frank Bartleman,[10] B.F. Lawrence,[11] C.W. Shumway,[12] and others.

The importance of this original research is that most subsequent Pentecostal histories have tended simply to concentrate upon the following five aspects of Smale's life and ministry, as initially recorded by Pentecostal journalist Frank Bartleman. First, news of the 1904 Welsh Revival caught the interest of Joseph Smale resulting in his visit to meet Evan Roberts and witness the revival firsthand. Secondly, returning to Los Angeles, Smale communicated accounts of the Welsh outpouring and prophesied that Los Angeles would soon be shaken by a similar mighty Pentecost. Thirdly, in anticipation Smale initiated home prayer meetings and nineteen weeks[13] of daily prayer meetings seeking the revival to come to LA. Such was Smale's openness to the work of the Holy Spirit. Fourthly, the board of Smale's own church (First Baptist Los Angeles) complained, and so Smale resigned his pastorate and established the First New Testament Church Los Angeles. Finally, Smale's new church witnessed speaking in tongues for the first time on Easter Sunday 1906, spoken by Jennie Moore, who later married William Seymour.

Pentecostal historiography is indebted to Bartleman for his legacy in recording the early days of the Azusa Street Revival, in his work *How 'Pentecost' Came to Los Angeles*.[14] The surprise, however, is that little has been added to Bartleman's portrayal of Smale over subsequent years, other than a repetition of these five core details. Therefore, apart from Bartleman's classic text, Smale typically occupies, on average, just one page of the Azusa Street history as retold by scholars of Pentecostalism, including R.M. Anderson,[15]

---

[10] F. Bartleman, *Azusa Street: The Roots of Modern-Day Pentecost* (Logos International, 1980).

[11] B.F. Lawrence, *The Apostolic Faith Restored* (Gospel Publishing House, 1916).

[12] C.W. Shumway, 'A Critical History of Glossolalia' (PhD diss., Boston University, 1919).

[13] Nineteen weeks according to C.M. Robeck, Jr, 'Joseph Smale', in S.M. Burgess and E.M. Van der Maas (eds), *New International Dictionary of Pentecostal and Charismatic Movements* (Zondervan, 2002), p. 1074; but fifteen weeks according to First Baptist Church Los Angeles minutes.

[14] F. Bartleman, *How 'Pentecost' Came to Los Angeles – How It Was in the Beginning* (Private Publication, 1925).

[15] R.M. Anderson, *Vision of the Disinherited: The Making of American Pentecostalism* (Oxford University Press, 1979), pp. 64, 70.

Vinson Synan,[16] Walter Hollenweger,[17] and Edith Blumhofer.[18] These details have been consistently handed down, seemingly with minimal critical investigation or challenge. Their concurrent view being that the Welsh Revival was the catalyst for raising expectations in Los Angeles for a similar outpouring of God's Spirit. Blumhofer regards Smale's response as 'representative of the reactions of many American evangelicals who saw in Wales an event that they believe confirmed the restoration in their day of New Testament experience'.[19] The practical outworking of Smale's response back in Los Angeles received further recognition a decade later when, in an article printed in *Confidence*, Bartleman referred to the prayer meetings Smale had started as having a formative effect on the events at Azusa Street.[20]

Besides Bartleman's account, a more recent article by Cecil Robeck also demands specific reference as it has informed numerous enquiries and writing concerning Smale, as a respected first-stop for information within *The New International Dictionary of Pentecostal and Charismatic Movements*.[21] However, the tendency for some naively to transfer erroneous details from generation to generation can be illustrated in the 2004 CD production of *The Apostolic Faith* papers.[22] In addition to the thirteen original Azusa Street papers, the producer Tony Cauchi has included six 'short biographies of the principal participants' at Azusa Street; namely, Frank Bartleman, Florence Crawford, William Durham, Lucy Farrow, Charles Parham, and Joseph Smale. According to Cauchi's research, which relies heavily upon Bartleman and Robeck's 'Smale' article, these six facts presented in Smale's résumé are simply incorrect; some, of course, more vital to Pentecostal history than others.

First, Cauchi states that 'At 21 years of age he entered the Baptist ministry' – whereas Smale was twenty. He claims that 'In 1895 Smale moved to the Los Angeles area, where he became pastor of First Baptist Church', but actually it was in 1897. Thirdly, 'When news of the Welsh revival reached California Smale was so hungry for revival that he travelled to Wales in 1905 to see the revival firsthand'. However, this study will demonstrate the truth that Smale was burnt out, and travelled to Wales only at the end of a long sabbatical trip to the Holy Land amidst circumstances that appear far more providential.

---

[16] V. Synan, *The Holiness–Pentecostal Tradition: Charismatic Movements in the Twentieth Century* (Eerdmans, 1971), p. 86.

[17] W.J. Hollenweger, *The Pentecostals* (SCM Press, 1972), p. 22.

[18] E.L. Blumhofer, *Restoring the Faith: The Assemblies of God, Pentecostalism, and American Culture* (Univesity of Illinois Press, 1993), pp. 57, 59.

[19] Blumhofer, *Restoring the Faith*, p. 57.

[20] F. Bartleman, 'With Other Tongues', *Confidence* 9.4 (April, 1916), p. 64.

[21] C.M. Robeck, Jr, 'Joseph Smale', in Burgess and Van der Maas (eds), *New International Dictionary*, pp. 1074-75.

[22] T. Cauchi, 'The Apostolic Faith; Biographies on Principal Participants, Joseph Smale', CD-ROM (www.revival-library.org, 2004).

According to Cauchi, 'The highlight of the trip was a personal meeting with Evan Roberts', and while Roberts did correspond with Bartleman, there is no evidence that Evan Roberts and Smale ever met other than Bartleman's ambiguous reference that Smale 'had been in touch with the [Welsh] revival and Evan Roberts'.[23] Cauchi maintains that 'Smale began 19 weeks of protracted meetings in anticipation of a similar outpouring of the Holy Spirit' – Faupel quotes this as a '16 week revival in his church'[24] – but these comments contradict the church records and newspaper accounts that the meetings lasted for a fifteen week period. Finally, that 'Smale was confronted by the church board [at First Baptist] but refused to lay down his passion for revival' is also inaccurate as only one church deacon opposed Smale! The interview with Smale in the *Los Angeles Times*[25] illustrates the problem with the impression that has been perpetuated by Bartleman's history that the whole diaconate reacted against him, resulting in his forced resignation and the establishment of First New Testament Church.

Another detail to be reinterpreted is the statement that 'Smale was married to Esther Isabelle.' Simply stated like this in any summary is misleading, because actually Smale did not marry Esther Isabel until 1911, and she was, in fact, his third wife. Of impact historically to Smale's ministry at First Baptist was the fact that he remained separated from his second wife all through the decade 1900–10. That personal detail may appear surplus to requirement within a Pentecostal history, except for its contributory factor to much of the conflict within the First Baptist Church and subsequent developments.

However, even within the brief schema outlined above there are numerous inaccuracies that have inadvertently been perpetuated by scholars over the century. Nigel Scotland's historic overview identifying the origins of the Charismatic Movement at least succeeds where McBain had earlier failed,[26] in that he recognises Smale as the catalyst linking the Welsh and Los Angeles Revivals. However, Scotland's error in recording 1904 as the year that Smale returned with the Pentecostal fire is then incorrectly quoted by Keith J. Hacking, who in turn propagates further inaccuracies with a presumptive reference to Smale being 'an American Baptist minister'.[27]

Similarly, Noel Gibbard's work on the rippling impact of the Welsh Revival provides details pertaining to Smale's pivotal influence, yet without any critical evaluation of Bartleman's account on which Gibbard draws heavily for his primary evidence. This in turn illustrates how compelling Bartleman's account has been in perpetuating a number of generalizations as well as some wholly

---

[23] Bartleman, *Azusa Street*, p. 13.
[24] D.W. Faupel, *The Everlasting Gospel* (Sheffield Academic Press, 1996), p. 193.
[25] 'Baptist Boil Still "Biling"', *Los Angeles Times* 12 September 1905, p. II.10.
[26] N. Scotland, *Charismatics and the Next Millennium* (Hodder & Stoughton, 1995), p. 5.
[27] K.J. Hacking, *Signs and Wonders Then and Now* (Apollos, 2006), p. 34.

flawed notions. For instance, according to Gibbard, 'it was not until the Azusa Street meetings that Joseph Smale spoke in tongues'.[28] Included in synopses such as Gibbard's portrayal, mythologies surrounding Joseph Smale have been allowed to develop unchallenged. This study aims to correct such errors by providing a critical account of Smale's life and theology.

The one exception to these criticisms of literature regarding Joseph Smale is Cecil Robeck's recent publication, *The Azusa Street Mission and Revival*.[29] Unanimously appreciated by other Pentecostal scholars as the world's leading authority on Azusa Street, Robeck has provided the first and most comprehensive account of Smale's involvement leading up to, and during, the revival in Los Angeles in 1906. The timing of Robeck's 2006 work, along with his personal encouragement in 2004 that I should pursue the *Smale-Trail*[30] to discover the actual facts behind the Smale persona, has been immensely influential. Consequently, many of the paradigms for Smale's ministry connections with early Pentecostalism and the Los Angeles Church Federation are indebted to Robeck's innovative research in this field.

The Spurgeonic Roots of Pentecostalism

A unique theme surfaced while pursuing the background to Smale's ministerial formation and earlier pastorates. Intrinsically embedded in his teaching prior to Azusa Street is a root of Pentecostalism previously unidentified, let alone analysed; namely, the influence of the nineteenth-century Baptist preacher Charles Haddon Spurgeon on Joseph Smale.

Spurgeon's pneumatology pervaded the training of young pastors at his College in South London through college lectures and published sermons.[31] It charts a dominant influence that can be traced back to Smale's own formation at the College and beyond. For through both the Pastors' College and Spurgeon's personal acquaintance with Smale, Spurgeon created a hunger for Holy Spirit power as the prerequisite for the fulfilment of Acts 2:17-21. Helpfully, there are numerous sermons by Spurgeon which enable analysis of these non-Wesleyan roots of Pentecostalism, for what both Spurgeon and Smale anticipated would herald 'a season of glorious disorder'.[32]

---

[28] N. Gibbard, *On the Wings of the Dove: The International Effects of the 1904–05 Revival* (Brynterion Press, 2002), p. 55.

[29] C.M. Robeck, Jr, *The Azusa Street Mission and Revival: The Birth of the Global Pentecostal Movement* (Nelson, 2006).

[30] I am indebted to C.M. Robeck, Jr's endorsement of this research and his generous encouragement. The 'Smale-Trail' is a personal phrase that I use colloquially with reference to my doctoral research into the life and ministry of Pastor Joseph Smale.

[31] This will be explored in the next chapter.

[32] C.H. Spurgeon, 'The Pentecostal Wind and Fire', *Metropolitan Tabernacle Pulpit* 27.1619, 18 September 1881, p. 104.

Therefore, this study argues that Smale's role was more pivotal than simply the fact that he told his people about the Welsh Revival and encouraged them to pray for a Pentecost of their own. As important as these steps were, important precursors must be recognised given that Smale was preaching and encouraging prayer for a move of the Spirit ever since he began his pastorate at First Baptist Church Los Angeles in 1897.[33] The significance of this analysis will consequently extend beyond a biographical portrayal of Smale, identifying the Spurgeonic factors that shaped his pneumatology before and after Azusa Street. Given that much of his teaching in subsequent years focused on the inter-relationship between earthly and heavenly aspects of Christian experience, there are some conclusions which are equally applicable to both historical research and to contemporary Baptist-Pentecostal-Charismatic discussions.

'Organisation' versus 'Freedom'

It is instructive to observe how similar tensions which overshadowed Smale's life and ministry, as he sought a more Pentecostal form of ministry, were also familiar to other Baptists who likewise had to undergo a metamorphosis from old structures of organisational and denominational life into new forms of Pentecostal freedom. This can be seen prior to Smale's revival experiences, where from 1898 C.P. Jones' promotion of holiness doctrines met with increased resistance with Baptists in the Southern United States, as Jones sought to untangle Baptist denominational identity from the sanctifying work of the Spirit to realize the unity of the church.[34] Drawing together some of the transatlantic Baptist-holiness strands, Jones noted in a short article dated around 1907 that

> As we now stand we might be called 'Higher Life Baptists,' our doctrine differing very little from that advocated by A.J. Gordon, F.B. Meyer, Evangelist Torrey, Chas. H. Spurgeon and others. Only like the Christians ... we believe that we ought to HONOR THE NAME of Christ as it is honored in the New Testament and not put human nicknames on Christ's bride, since there is only one name by which we may be saved.[35]

Another significant example comes from Sweden and shows that former Baptist pastor Lewi Pethrus had to face similar issues having become a Pentecostal in 1907. David Bundy comments how 'in 1913 the Swedish Baptist Convention expelled Pethrus and his entire congregation from the convention

---

[33] J. Smale, *Our Church Quarterly* (First Baptist Church Los Angeles, December 1897), p. 1.

[34] D.T. Irvin, 'Charles Price Jones: Image of Holiness', in Goff and Wacker (eds), *Portraits of a Generation*, p. 39.

[35] C.P. Jones, *The Gift of the Holy Ghost in the Book of Acts* (National Publishing Board of the Church of Christ [Holiness], 1996), p. 40.

because they practiced open communion but in reality because of their Pentecostal theology and liturgy'.[36] Significantly, Pethrus attempted to contact Smale during the Swedish denominational debacle,[37] presumably because Smale represented someone who possessed valuable insights following his earlier experiences in Los Angeles. The evidence of such Pentecostal-Charismatic church history over the past century indicates that 'organization' versus 'freedom' issues very quickly become highly charged matters of debate and schism, irrespective of geography or denomination.

Emerging from the Smale primary materials discovered are clear insights into the 'organized-freedom' patterns he established during the inception of First New Testament Church. There is a clarity attached to these plans and convictions as Smale was starting a church from scratch, with the sole purpose of creating an organisation in which the Holy Spirit was encouraged to exercise perfect freedom. Although discredited by Bartleman and others, Smale's model can be regarded as a *via media* by which he sought to construct a model of church life and practice based upon firm ecclesiological convictions.[38] This was a significant church model based around prayer, global mission and preaching, revealing patterns for all who continue to attempt mediation between Reformed and Pentecostal-Charismatic constituencies, such as evidenced within the World Alliance of Reformed Churches' dialogue with Classic Pentecostal Churches, 1996–2000.[39] Furthermore, recent indications suggest that these themes are prompting ongoing academic research and comment, as exampled by Calvin College's Professor James K.A. Smith's recent article exploring the experiential and theological embodiment of being 'Reformed-Charismatic' and 'Pentecostal Calvinist'.[40]

Methodologies

The central aim of this study has been to accumulate all extant sources pertaining to the life and ministry of Joseph Smale to enable an accurate analysis of his life and ministry. Given the superficial knowledge of Smale's background and decisions, as outlined above, the priority was initially to

---

[36] D.D. Bundy, 'Lewi Pethrus', in Burgess and Van der Maas (eds), *New International Dictionary*, p. 986.

[37] Letter from Bartleman to Pethrus, 9 July 1913. I am indebted to Desmond Cartwright for providing a copy of this letter.

[38] See ch. 5 below.

[39] World Alliance of Reformed Churches, 'Word and Spirit, Church and World Report', Pentecostal-Reformed Dialogue, http://www.warc.ch/dt/erl1/20.html; accessed 1 August 2006.

[40] J.K.A. Smith, 'Teaching a Calvinist to Dance: In Pentecostal Worship my Reformed Theology Finds Its Groove', *Christianity Today* 52.5 (May, 2008), pp. 42-45. See also Smith's development of this in his *Thinking in Tongues: Elements of a Pentecostal Worldview* (Eerdmans, 2010).

discover whether or not any primary materials had actually survived, especially in the form of sermons, church magazines/bulletins, church records, journals, newspaper reports, and the like.

Then, because the theoretical and methodological questions that underpin investigation into characters of history requires more than a simple retelling of biographical facts, the challenge has been to detect something of the subject's 'voice', his reasoning, motives, and behaviour, which may have been lost over the passage of time, if ever recorded properly at all. Also, as modern historiography encourages any medium possible that can help to unlock the past and enhance historical understanding, the discovery of some photographs has informed the narrative further by providing images of people and locations which have, up until now, simply been names in the story.[41]

In order to achieve a more accurate reconstruction of Smale's life and influence in a way which enables his own theological insights to permeate the details of his life, it was deemed necessary to discover answers to basic questions such as: who in particular was influencing Smale? What was he reading? With whom did he associate, looking both at his time in England as well as North America? Which meetings and conferences did he organise and attend, and to what effect? All such queries were incorporated in this one overarching research question: what were the contributory factors in Joseph Smale's life that caused him to find significance as God's 'Moses' for Pentecostalism? These questions then controlled investigation for original data covering every phase of Smale's life and ministry. This search was appropriately organized in five directions, with the following results.

Smale Relatives

The first initiative was to locate any surviving relatives of Joseph Smale, whether in the United Kingdom or North America, who might possess valuable oral history and the tantalising possibility that some documentary sources may have survived in family archives. After searching for six months, with the assistance of George Fogelson,[42] contact was eventually made with one of Smale's relatives, namely his grandson, George Wood, based in California.[43] A

---

[41] E.g., the photographs of the interior at First Baptist Church Los Angeles, 1897; and Burbank Theatre, 1905.

[42] I am indebted to George Fogelson (Los Angeles Public Library researcher) for his local Californian expertise in helping to locate Smale's grandson, George Wood, and for the interest he has shown in my research.

[43] I later discovered that Cecil M. Robeck, Jr, had already established contact with Stan and George Wood, having, in fact, previously interviewed their mother, E. Grace (Smale) Westberg about Joseph Smale a decade earlier. Personal interview with C.M. Robeck, Jr, at the Society for Pentecostal Studies Conference, Marquette University, Milwaukee, 13 March 2004.

telephone call with George confirmed a number of important details that Smale's daughter, Esther Grace, had in fact died in September 2000, leaving two sons from her first marriage, Stanley and George Wood. Unfortunately for research purposes it became apparent that the majority of family Smale memorabilia, including sermons, pamphlets and personal items had not survived.

However, an assorted collection of preserved papers and photographs have generously been made available to me by George and Stan, including some photographs, a journal of Smale's trip to China in 1907 to establish the China New Testament Church, and bulletins that Smale wrote during his years at First New Testament Church Los Angeles. These include three copies of a periodical that Smale self-published, entitled *Truth: Earthly & Heavenly*, which provide valuable insights into his developing dispensational notions after 1909. George Wood also recorded an interview with his mother in the last decade of her life, quizzing her on early recollections of her father. But given that Smale died in 1926 when she was still a child has meant that only the briefest of memories have been passed on orally. Nonetheless, these possess valuable biographical importance in piecing together as much of the narrative of Smale's life as possible. Family details that would never be known otherwise have been preserved orally, such as Smale's musical ability to sing solos, particularly as C.H. Spurgeon's soloist, and the fact that Joseph and Esther Smale had a son while pastoring Unity Chapel in Bristol, England (1914), although this son tragically died at birth. The support of the Smale family to this research enterprise cannot be underestimated; especially the inherent benefit that Smale's grandsons have both obtained doctorates and each has extensive experience of Christian ministry and mission. Consequently they have both understood the nature of this research.

Baptist Archives

With Smale's life and ministry encompassing significant phases either side of the Atlantic, it was necessary to search for primary materials at all the various college and church archives to which he was connected. Starting in Britain, where Joseph Smale sat under the tutelage of Spurgeon, it was vital to discover what College records from 1887–90 still existed. As noted already, the Spurgeon's College librarian, Judy Powles, acknowledged that their records for that era are minimal,[44] but she confirmed that Smale started at the College in 1887, coming from Spurgeon's church, the Metropolitan Tabernacle. It lists his pastorates up to 1913 and then his date of death. But, as already mentioned, no obituary was printed in the *Baptist Union Handbook* the following year. Delving deeper within the College Heritage Room archives has since revealed a

---

[44] J. Powles, Spurgeon's College Librarian/Archivist, email 12 February 2003.

number of references to Smale's training and assessment, as well as two photographs of him as a young student (see Figures 5 and 6).

Similarly, The Angus Library at Regent's Park College, Oxford, has only the briefest record, listing Smale's different churches, but again with no memoirs held for him as they are for some other Baptist ministers. This realised, and finding no reference to Smale in any old British Baptist magazines of the Metropolitan Tabernacle or *Baptist Times and Freeman* newspapers during his time in Britain before emigrating in 1893, the value of The Angus Library to this study has been primarily in the wealth of writings by Spurgeon providing the opportunity for analysis of Spurgeon's pneumatological emphases that permeated his ministerial students, among them Joseph Smale. Chapter 2 utilises these archives, with illustrations of the distinct Spurgeonic influence that impacted Smale so significantly, supporting the view, as David Bundy comments, that Smale contributed a distinctive 'Spurgeon-Baptist' analysis that was not typical of Southern Baptists in the at the beginning of the twentieth century.[45]

With regards to Baptist archives in the USA, the bulk of documentary evidence involving Joseph Smale has been located through The American Baptist Historical Society.[46] Discovered here was a mixture of Arizona Baptist Association Minutes, Los Angeles Baptist Association Minutes, church records, annual reports, and copies of *The Pacific Baptist* magazine containing two of Smale's published sermons.[47] Each item has provided part of the emerging larger picture, clarifying the critical stages between his pastorates in Arizona and California, and demonstrating Smale's developing network with widening aspects of ministry pre-1906.

First Baptist Church Prescott possesses no remaining documents from Smale's time in Arizona, presumably because these were the early days of the town, as well as the church. However, the bulk of Smale's life and ministry surrounding the 1905–06 revival in Los Angeles has been located in the First Baptist Church Los Angeles archives. Thanks to the help of their church archivist, Ernestine Rotcher, the most significant finds are contained within the church records minute books. These hand-written accounts dating from 1900 to 1906 provide detailed descriptions of all the background troubles within First Baptist Church life that ultimately proved so definitive for Smale and the emerging revival movement. The church clerks who penned the records during these turbulent years, R.G. Haskell and H.S. Keyes, were both very supportive of Smale, even amid the troubles, and wrote with a bias that must be weighed

---

[45] Personal interview with David Bundy, at the Society for Pentecostal Studies Conference, Marquette University, Milwaukee, 13 March 2004.

[46] Details about the American Baptist Historical Society can be located at http://www.baptisthistory.us.

[47] I am grateful for the assistance of Betsy Dunbar for trawling through the archives at the American Baptist Historical Society and discovering these materials.

against other accounts discovered in the secular press. Recognising this tension, they have still provided a valuable mix of factual information and useful descriptions of Smale's personality and the atmosphere at various key points of church life which provide useful background to chapters 3 and 4.

In addition to the written documentary evidence, the discoveries of three previously unpublished photographs from the First Baptist Church Los Angeles archives are valuable additions in their own right. Robeck has included one portrait of Smale in his recent work,[48] but the other photographs have yet to be seen by a wider audience. Their particular importance show Smale with his board of deacons around 1900, and Smale standing on the platform of First Baptist Church Los Angeles revealing the internal features of the sanctuary which was the venue for the fifteen weeks of protracted prayer gatherings for revival.

Secular Newspapers

The supply of materials has ultimately determined the extent to which various periods of Smale's ministry can be adequately examined. Following numerous research visits to the Isle of Wight, Prescott, and Los Angeles, over 150 newspaper accounts concerning Smale have been discovered, assisting the presentation of a more accurate biographical framework for Smale's life and ministry. However, it should be noted that the degree of publicity Smale received in local papers varied across the phases of his life in accordance with his public standing in each community and the interest generated by the churches he served. So, for instance, the Isle of Wight news was conveyed by two main newspapers, the *Isle of Wight Observer* and the *Isle of Wight County Press*, and in Prescott, Arizona, again by two papers, the *Arizona Weekly Journal-Miner* and *The Arizona Republican*.

Los Angeles was served by at least eight daily newspapers at the time when Smale and his ministry had reached the greatest prominence. A plethora of information has been located especially within the *Los Angeles Times*, thanks to regular columns reporting news from the local church scene. Included weekly was a section entitled 'At the Churches Yesterday'. Herein were frequently printed synopses of Smale's sermons from the previous day, along with those of other leading churchmen in the city, all of which has boosted the opportunities for accurate qualitative analysis in identifying themes and developments in his preaching.

Besides these regular reports, Smale was a high profile figure in Los Angeles society amidst a prestigious membership at First Baptist Church. Therefore, for the period this book is particularly focusing on where pertinent background to the 1905–06 Revival is required, there are plenty of accounts in the secular press containing all the church business, including church

---

[48] Robeck, *Azusa Street*, p. 58.

squabbles, decisions taken, and Smale's responses. Indeed, such journalistic attention to detail has proven essential corroboration to the documentary evidence available in the church records. Numerous examples are given in chapter 3 illustrating how every stage and participant in the proceedings at First Baptist Church tallies precisely with the church minutes in question.

Interestingly, by the later phases of Smale's ministry in England and then upon his return to the USA, the secular press attention in local church life *per se* had noticeably declined. Whether this was a feature of increased attention to First World War matters and ground shifts in society diminishing the impact of the Christian church is not analysed within the parameters of this work. The point at stake is the tangible reduction in material available concerning Joseph Smale from secular sources in Britain and the USA for the years 1911 to his death in 1926. The resulting conclusion is that Smale's public profile, therefore, decreased over his later years, enabling a knowledge of where he was serving via the occasional advertisement or notice, but no more than that. Hence, during these latter years, a greater proportion of the Smale narrative is only obtainable from church source materials. Inevitably this appraisal concurs with the 'Moses' motif that somehow Smale stopped short of reaching greater success as a Pentecostal pioneer, although the other church documents discovered reveal that Smale was still serving his church and mission enterprises long after they were established, right up until his death.

Pentecostal Documents

Having already stated that Pentecostal archives possess limited documentary material pertaining to Smale, it is necessary to add one caveat in order to highlight where a small number of papers are located, and the generous spirit in which these materials have been willingly shared to aid this study. Asbury Theological Seminary obtained a small collection of Smale papers, including eleven Sunday bulletins for First New Testament Church (dated between 1906 and 1908), and copies of two sermons preached by Smale.[49]

While indicating the scarcity of such source documents connected with Smale, reference must be made once again to the importance of Cecil Robeck's personal collection of Azusa Street primary materials. His willingness to share some of his information regarding Joseph Smale[50] was a vital catalyst enabling my search to head off in fruitful directions. However, while many of Robeck's insights regarding Smale are now in the public domain with his 2006 publication, the fact that this book has been intentionally printed without footnotes or endnote references inevitably precludes the sources being located.

---

[49] See the Bibliography for precise details and locations of all the Smale documents discovered, including those archived at Asbury Theological Seminary.

[50] Personal Interview with C.M. Robeck, Jr, at the Society for Pentecostal Studies Conference, Marquette University, Milwaukee, 13 March 2004.

Further patience is required while awaiting the publication of Robeck's Azusa Street *magnum opus*, which hopefully will be complete with references. Meantime this study identifies all the Smale sources discovered throughout the research for this project, providing additional original material.

The Flower Pentecostal Heritage Center has also contributed to this research, initially with a handful of newspaper pieces about Smale's involvement in Los Angeles, including the famous 'Rolling on Floor in Smale's Church' article.[51] However, in November 2007 the greatest surprise occurred with an email from the Director of the Flower Pentecostal Heritage Center, Darrin J. Rodgers, informing me that he had just obtained a copy of Smale's published sermons, *The Pentecostal Blessing*.[52] The timing of this find was impeccable. While I had been aware of the book's existence through advertisements in First New Testament Church bulletins, it had been an on-going frustration not to be able to trace a copy.

Other Sources

The trawl for materials has obviously necessitated approaching numerous institutions and personnel, many of whose names and contributions are noted in the acknowledgements. Photographic collections held in the Los Angeles Public Library, as well as the California Historical Society, yielded some important finds, a few of which appear in this book. Yale Divinity School possess a copy of Smale's 1907 booklet, *Apostolic Journey in the 20th Century: Relating to the facts that led the First New Testament Church of Los Angeles to establish a Gospel Mission in Southwest China*, recording his pioneering visit to China. This, along with the copy of Smale's handwritten journal, kindly provided by Stan Wood, provide numerous insights into Smale's objectives and experiences as he attempted to deploy a Chinese and Pentecostal extension of their home church in Los Angeles.

Limited space prevents accounting for every discovery and helpful source along the *Smale-Trail*. Needless to say, much biographical data has been obtained through extensive searches online and via public records offices in Britain and the USA. Other church and mission information has been gleaned from significant individuals, such as British Pentecostal archivist Desmond Cartwright, who on numerous occasions has pointed me in the right direction. His expertise as a conduit of so much useful information helped in making the links between Smale and the founding of the Spanish Gospel Mission, the role

---

[51] 'Rolling on Floor in Smale's Church', *Los Angeles Times* 14 July 1906, p. II1.

[52] Darrin J. Rodgers' kindness in contacting me regarding his discovery of Smale's book, *The Pentecostal Blessing*, will remain one of the high landmarks of this research. His generosity in sending me a copy with exclusive use for one year is duly acknowledged, with deep appreciation.

of G.H. Lang in Bristol, and Lewi Pethrus' connection with Smale acknowledged above.

Narrative Analysis Using Data Triangulation

Finally, a statement about how all this data has been processed is important in view of checking the validity of methods adopted. In order to adequately respond to the 'realism' versus 'constructionism' debate raised by sociologists engaging in biographical research,[53] the following methods have been selected in this study for their pragmatic qualities.

a) All biographical data has been consistently presented in chronological order, thus at one level allowing the facts of the Smale story to be constructed within a coherent narrative.

b) The authenticity of all primary materials sourced from the various contexts outlined above is checked with caution, acknowledging that implicit agendas are present in all narrative forms.

c) To formulate as accurate a portrayal as possible, the basic framework originally available in Frank Bartleman's account of Azusa Street (as the principal narrative) is triangulated with, and against, all available 'church records' and 'secular newspaper' accounts discovered. Such 'data triangulation'[54] provides ample opportunity to critique Bartleman's account accordingly. By broadening the framework to enable other, previously unknown, 'voices' to provide their evidence will, by definition, test the accuracy and objectivity of the prototypical Bartleman account. Although at times a 'messy' science[55] involving multiple perspectives to be checked and interpreted, this at least provides a consistent axis for analysis of Smale's emergent theological positions to be considered.

d) Close attention to the 'realism' of details and voices evident within the primary data has naturally facilitated the formal apportionment of material into connected themes and patterns. In part this is an intuitive process, notwithstanding sincere attempts to maintain objectivity. But the fact the 'plot' is already well defined within Pentecostal history has ensured that further narrative analysis concerning Smale's meaning and self-understanding is well

---

[53] Roberts, *Biographical Research*, p. 7.

[54] G. McCulloch, *Documentary Research in Education, History and the Social Sciences* (Routledge Falmer, 2004), p. 129. Also, L.A. Guion, 'Triangulation: Establishing the Validity of Qualitative Studies', University of Florida, http://www.rayman-bacchus.net/uploads/documents/Triangulation.pdf, accessed 4 September 2004.

[55] Roberts, *Biographical Research*, p. 174.

established as a 'construction' within this historical and theological framework, thus avoiding the dangers of reconstructing 'myths'.[56]

Certainly within Pentecostal historiography, scholars such as Spittler[57] and others have long affirmed the merit of using biography as a valuable tool for uncovering and corroborating much more of the Pentecostal storyline. In this regard, Robeck, following David Nelson Duke, advises that the following helpful pointers should be taken into account in order to avoid the dangers of hagiography:

1) The biography must be critical with renewed objectivity.
2) It must provide more than a mere chronology of events.
3) It needs to take seriously the original *Sitz im Leben* of the figure involved.
4) The work should probe the subject's self-understanding.
5) Recognition of the genera of each source used should be recorded, assessing its particular strengths and weaknesses.[58]

With those criteria in mind, the factors evident in Joseph Smale's life which contributed to him finding significance as God's 'Moses' for Pentecostalism are presented in four phases (chapters) in this work: namely, his spiritual and pastoral formation; his preparation for revival; his catalytic role within the Los Angeles revival of 1905–06; and the outworking of his developing pneumatology, as evidenced in his Pentecostal preaching, ecclesiology and missiology (1905–09). Although the quantity of data regarding Smale's later life and ministry from 1909 to 1926 is not plentiful, a brief overview of these latter years is also incorporated in the final chapter, enabling this book to represent a comprehensive account of Smale's life story. To assist a cursory understanding of Smale's life and ministry, a bibliographical overview is provided within a timeline presented in Appendix I.

The conclusions prove Bartleman's 'Moses' motif for Smale to be an appropriate epitaph in terms of Pentecostalism. However, the biographical approach raises a far broader set of pneumatological questions than simply the phenomena of 'baptism in the Spirit' and 'glossolalia' which were highlighted by Bartleman as the crux of his criticisms concerning Smale. Reasons why

---

[56] Roberts, *Biographical Research*, pp. 115-33. Chapter 7, 'The Narrative Analysis of Lives', approaches the study of lives, linking 'story' to an understanding of the 'self' or 'identity'.

[57] R.P. Spittler, 'Suggested Areas for Further Research in Pentecostal Studies', *Pneuma* 5.2 (Fall, 1983), p. 49.

[58] C.M. Robeck, Jr, 'The Use of Biography in Pentecostal Historiography', *Pneuma* 8 (Fall, 1986), p. 79. See David Nelson Duke, 'Theology and Biography: Simple Suggestions for those who wish to write biography', *Perspectives in Religious Studies* 3 (1986), pp 137-49.

Smale extracted himself from the Pentecostal movement requires careful consideration in light of contemporary ecumenical dialogue and understanding between Reformed, Baptist and Pentecostal-Charismatic constituencies. In particular, the debate focuses around the nature of freedom and organization, and the extent to which the Holy Spirit relates to both. Intrinsic to the arguments contained within this study is the importance of the narrative and accompanying analysis of Smale's life and ministry, offering a unique element of the Azusa Street history – prior, during and subsequent. To that end, even a century later, Joseph Smale 'being dead, still speaketh'.

CHAPTER 2

Smale's Spiritual and Pastoral Formation (1881–92)

Family and Conversion

The English Census records of 1861 and 1871 show that Joseph was the youngest child of John and Ann Smale, residing in the village of Hampton in the Parish of Stokeclimsland, near Launceston, Cornwall. His father John Smale (1826–81) was a copper and tin miner,[1] and his mother Ann (*née* Stephens, 1831–1911) officially classified as a 'dressmaker',[2] and later 'charwoman'.[3] Joseph's siblings were Elizabeth Stephens (b. 1851), Samuel (b. 1855), Ebenezer (b. 1859) and Mary Hannah (b. 1862). Together with Joseph (b. 7 July 1867) the indication is that all five children received local education up until the age of at least fourteen.[4]

Opportunities for the family were such that Samuel followed in his father's footsteps as a Cornish tin miner, Elizabeth Stephens was married by the age of twenty-one,[5] Ebenezer became a steward on a steam ship,[6] and Mary Hannah found employment as a dressmaker.[7] Inevitably there is limited information about the Smale family, given their 'working class' status of the latter nineteenth century. However, from census records it is possible to trace a move that the family made sometime during the 1870s, when they relocated to Abbotsfield cottages in Wiveliscombe, Somerset.[8]

These cottages (see Figure 2), built in 1875, provide the explanation for the family's move from Cornwall to Somerset. A wealthy businessman, Lukey

---

[1] 1861 English Census: Reference – RG9/1521; Place: Launceston – Cornwall; District: 7; Folio: 85; p. 2. Also Joseph Smale birth certificate, General Register Office reference: 1867; Quarter - September; District – Launceston; Volume 5c; p. 27; Entry No. 222.

[2] 1861 English Census: Reference – RG9/1521; Place: Launceston – Cornwall; District: 7; Folio: 85; p. 2.

[3] 1871 Cornwall Census – Parish: Stokeclimsland; District: 7; Schedule: 034.

[4] 1881 English Census: Reference – RG11/2359; Place: Wiveliscombe – Somerset; District 4; p. 2.

[5] Marriage registered June 1872; District: Tavistock, Cornwall; Volume 5b; p. 661.

[6] 1891 English Census: Reference – RG12/1748; Place: Calstock – Cornwall; District 5.

[7] 1881 English Census: Reference – RG11/2359; Place: Wiveliscombe – Somerset; District 4; p. 2.

[8] 1881 English Census: Reference – RG11/2359; Place: Wiveliscombe – Somerset; District 4; p. 2.

Collard, had constructed an 'expensive new mansion',[9] named Abbotsfield House, overlooking the town of Wiveliscombe.[10] Collard simultaneously built a row of six cottages for his new staff, hence providing Ann Smale with employment and the necessary family accommodation for the family's next phase of life.

Figure 2: Abbotsfield Cottages, Wiveliscombe, 1907

Figure 3: Wesleyan Chapel, Wiveliscombe (built 1845).
Photograph courtesy of Wiveliscombe Book Group Archive.

---

[9] S.M. Farrington, *Wiveliscombe: A History* (Colden Publications, 2005), p. 25.
[10] Abbotsfield House and cottages remain to the present day for residential occupancy. I am indebted to Susan Farrington for her insights into the life and history of Wiveliscombe.

Figure 4: Joseph Smale's school: Wiveliscombe Board School.
Permission to use photograph has neither been granted nor refused as
Somerset Record Office were unable to contact the depositor
(SCRO DD\R1/20)

1881 was certainly a seminal time in Joseph Smale's life, being his fourteenth year, for reasons which provide an important framework for the commencement of the period under investigation in this chapter. On 30 January his father John, aged fifty-five, died of pneumonia with Joseph present at the death.[11] By this time the only family members remaining in the family home were his mother, sister, Mary Hannah, and Joseph as he continued his education as a 'monitor' at the Wiveliscombe Board School in Somerset where he attended (see Figure 4).[12] Later on that year the most significant event in Smale's spiritual formation occurred, namely his Christian conversion. He referred to this during his ordination in 1890, stating that 'his call to the ministry took place from the time of his conversion'.[13] Smale is reported in the *Isle of Wight County Press*, testifying that

> he was converted when fourteen years of age in a Wesleyan chapel, by a Baptist preacher, in West Somersetshire, on the 4th September 1881.[14]

Whereas the church reference may only be presumed to be the Wesleyan chapel in his home town of Wiveliscombe (see Figure 3),[15] the *Isle of Wight Observer*

---

[11] John Smale death certificate, General Register Office reference: 1881; Quarter - March; District – Wellington; Volume 5c; p. 263; Entry No. 225.
[12] 1881 English Census: Reference – RG11/2359; Place: Wiveliscombe – Somerset; District 4. The school had been established by public finance following the 1870 Forster Education Act for children of all denominations between the ages of five and twelve, see Farrington, *Wiveliscombe*, p. 86.
[13] 'Baptist Ordination at Ryde', *Isle of Wight County Press* 17 May, 1890, p. 6.
[14] 'Baptist Ordination at Ryde', p. 6.

provides the name of the Baptist preacher who impacted Smale's life that September day in 1881, as being a Mr Tipton from Taunton, apparently 'well-known as the compiler of several services of song'.[16] Unfortunately, no other detail about Mr Tipton has been discovered, apart from an example of one of his 'services of song' entitled 'For the Master's Sake'.[17]

However, what must be registered as particularly significant for this biographical and theological survey are Smale's early connections in Cornwall and Somerset with the British brand of Wesleyan-Methodism that encompassed doctrinal, ecclesiastical and worship roots of holiness life and teaching.

Wesleyan Revival Roots in Cornwall and Somerset

As we have already noted, the principal thrust behind Smale's unique role within the emergence of Pentecostalism concerns his Baptist-Spurgeonic roots. Yet this opportunity to use biography as a means of analysing Smale's emerging theology provides the opportunity also to inspect the religious culture and background of his earliest years which may be regarded as a contributory factor in Smale's spiritual formation.

Contextually, Smale's formative years spent in Cornwall and Somerset were the loci of 'a rhythm of revival' among Wesleyan Methodists throughout the nineteenth century.[18] That rhythm began with a 'Great Revival' which impacted the widespread tin mining areas of Cornwall, beginning in the Methodist chapel at Redruth in 1814. Eyewitness accounts report how 'The doors [of the chapel at Redruth] were scarcely closed for eight successive days. It spread with amazing rapidity through the Redruth circuit and their number soon increased from 1,980 to 4,000.'[19]

Indeed, the ripple effects of this revival across the county established many new churches around that time, including the Wesleyan chapel in Stokeclimsland built in 1816.[20] David Bebbington describes how 'supplication

---

[15] This recognises that an active Wellington Methodist Circuit existed in 1881, linking Taunton, Wellington, and Wiveliscombe, ably serviced by the Bristol and Exeter Railway branch lines; see H.W. White, 'Methodism Hereabouts', a paper presented to the Wiveliscombe Historical Society, 15 February, 2005, p. 4.

[16] *Isle of Wight Observer* 17 May, 1890, p. 8.

[17] *The Bridgewater Mercury* 2 March 1892, http://dbown100.tripod.com/Temp.html, accessed 9 March 2005.

[18] D.W. Bebbington, 'Culture and Piety in the Far West: Revival in Penzance, Newlyn, and Mousehole in 1849', in K. Cooper and J. Gregory (eds), *Revival and Resurgence in Christian History* (Boydell Press, 2008), pp. 225-50.

[19] 'Revival in Cornwall', letter from George Russell to Isaac Clayton, 7 July, 1815, in R. Davies, A.R. George and G. Rupp (eds), *A History of the Methodist Church in Great Britain*, Volume 4 (Epworth Press, 1988), p. 349.

[20] See the following, accessed: 8 September 2008. http://www.genuki.org.uk/big/eng/Cornwall/Stokeclimsland/index.html#ChurcHistory

for revival became a deeply rooted feature of Methodist spirituality in the area' and consequently 'memories of the Great Revival in particular lingered as a paradigm for what Methodism should ideally be about'.[21] Such spirituality manifested itself in the 1814 Revival amidst 'scenes of agony, with people "on their knees for six, twelve, or twenty hours, without intermission, crying aloud for mercy".'[22] Similar episodes were repeated periodically through the nineteenth century in Cornwall indicating a heightened spirituality noticeably among the poor.[23] In fact the patterns and phenomena of those Cornish Wesleyan revivals bear striking resemblance with Smale's own later experiences of spiritual life and revival in Los Angeles which were also noted for their deep emotional component.

> The services went on quietly for several nights & then suddenly the people were roused as though a bomb had fallen. Moans and groans, lamentations & strong crying & tears burst on every side. The scene might almost be described as one of weeping & gnashing of teeth.[24]

Not surprisingly in light of these rhythms of revival, the growth of the Wesleyan chapel in Smale's village of Stokeclimsland required further expansion, such that major building works were carried out during his early childhood in 1869.[25] Given the close knit community within his village, comprising a population of 2,422 in 1871,[26] the necessity for church growth would have been noted by all families in the locality. Although there are inevitable and unanswerable questions regarding the extent to which the Smale family were directly impacted by this Cornish Methodist revivalist spirituality, it certainly appears credible to recognise that Joseph Smale's earliest years were spent in a local culture that imbibed 'characteristics of spontaneity' with 'conscious planning'.[27]

Moving on to examine the religious milieu in the Somerset town of Wiveliscombe and district where the Smale's moved in the 1870s, similar patterns are revealed to those just described in Cornwall. Prior to the Smales' relocation some great revivals are recorded, notably in 1850, 1859, and 1863, where 'scores of conversions' added hundreds to the Methodist churches, resonating with eyewitness accounts. For instance,

---

[21] Bebbington, 'Culture and Piety', p. 234.
[22] Bebbington, 'Culture and Piety', p. 234, quoting John Riles.
[23] Davies, George and Rupp (eds), *History of the Methodist Church*, IV, p. 558.
[24] Davies, George and Rupp (eds), *History of the Methodist Church*, IV, p. 559.
[25] See the following, accessed 10 February 2009.
http://www.genuki.org.uk/big/eng/Cornwall/Stokeclimsland/index.html#ChurchHistory
[26] See the following, accessed 8 September 2008
http://www.genuki.org.uk/big/eng/Cornwall/Stokeclimsland/index.html#ChurchHistory
[27] Bebbington, 'Culture and Piety', p. 237.

A holy awe rested on many of the villages, so that mockers were silenced, and the enemies put to shame ... Some of the Old Lights say that this revival was attended by some remarkable psychic phenomena. These were the halcyon days of the circuit, and from that revival came the men who for 40 years remained the stalwarts of the cause.[28]

The 1851 Religious Census, informs us that the numbers attending the Wiveliscombe Wesleyan chapel, formed in 1845,[29] on the designated Sunday were seventy-five at morning worship (plus forty children 'downstairs'); eighty in the afternoon (plus forty-five children); and 184 in the evening congregation.[30] Unpacking these statistics further in a broader context, the annual returns for the Taunton Methodist Circuit describe 1850 as having experienced 'a revival of God's work' where 'many conversions were recorded'.[31] One local preacher reported that 'at one church he did not attempt to preach lest he interfered with the work of the Holy Spirit'.[32]

As with Cornish Methodism, a discernible rhythm of revival in the Wiveliscombe area repeated itself every few years, significantly encompassing other denominations. For instance, the Wiveliscombe Congregational Church records describe 1860 as another 'Year of Revival':

> The services with but a few exceptions were crowded, religious feeling in the town was intense, the influence extended to the neighbouring villages, and many were saved of the Lord.[33]

By 1863 there was a further revival among the Circuit of Wesleyan chapels with forty conversions reported.[34] At the close of the decade, daily prayer meetings were arranged at the Congregational church 'on account of a great awakening having taken place. Upwards of 150 persons attended every evening. Many were soundly converted.'[35] Similarly in Watchet, a town ten miles from Wiveliscombe, a revival there in 1869 lasted three months with 150

---

[28] L.H. Court, *The Romance of a Country Circuit: Sketches of Village Methodism* (Henry Hooks, 1921), p. 32. In this work, Court provides numerous examples of revivals, preachers and conversions impacting many villages in West Somerset.

[29] A Brief History of the Wellington Circuit: 'Wiveliscombe' (Methodist Union, 1932).

[30] White, 'Methodism Hereabouts', pp. 5-6.

[31] Taunton Methodist Circuit Historical Notes (Somerset Record Office, D\N\tmc/7/2/1), p. 15.

[32] Taunton Methodist Circuit Historical Notes, p. 15.

[33] A. Kelly, 'Wiveliscombe Congregational Church: A Brief History', http://www.wiveliscombe-congregational.org.uk/history.htm, accessed: 19 July 2008.

[34] Taunton Methodist Circuit Historical Notes (Somerset Record Office, D\N\tmc/7/2/1), p. 18. Unfortunately these notes do not continue beyond 1871.

[35] Kelly, 'Wiveliscombe Congregational Church'.

converted.[36] This work of God was attributed to 'the earnest prayers of the Methodists in the town and to the unity with which both Wesleyans and Bible Christians followed the lead of the Holy Spirit'.[37]

This brief overview describing the spiritual climate of life in Cornwall and Somerset, in which Smale developed as a person, links to an implied understanding that spiritual formation is an amalgam of personal life experiences within a local culture. It will become increasingly apparent in the later chapters that Smale's life and ministry did not suddenly embark on a Pentecostal phase in 1905. Rather, as we have seen, he was brought up in such an atmosphere permeated by nineteenth-century Wesleyan piety.

Training: The Pastors' College, London (1887–90)

Information gleaned from accounts of Joseph Smale's ordination contain the only personal references we have regarding his Christian experience prior to the commencement of his training at the Pastors' College founded by C.H. Spurgeon. Following conversion in 1881, Smale required patience, finding that he

> could not get away from the idea that his life work was the preaching of the Gospel, and it was his constant prayer that God would reveal his mind, and he had proved that 'to wait on the Lord,' was no vain thing.[38]

Given the clarity of his call to Christian service it is not surprising that, aged sixteen, Joseph Smale began to preach as 'the way was opened up for him to begin public speaking'.[39] By his own admission, although he lacked training in those early years of service, Smale's preaching of the gospel had been blessed here and there, the Lord 'sealing with His approval the word preached, by the salvation of many souls'.[40]

Wishing for 'an educational course', Smale's motivation was a felt-need to be 'better prepared for such Holy work, and [so] he sought admission to the Metropolitan College'.[41] Following the second interview with Spurgeon himself, Smale was then informed personally of Mr Spurgeon's 'pleasure to receive him'[42] as a student of the Pastors' College. Consequently, a two-year

---

[36] Court, *Romance of a Country Circuit*, p. 32.
[37] Court, *Romance of a Country Circuit*, p. 32.
[38] 'Ordination Services at Park Road Baptist Chapel, Ryde', *Isle of Wight Times & Hampshire Gazette* 15 May, 1890, p. 4.
[39] 'Baptist Ordination at Ryde', *Isle of Wight County Press* 17 May, 1890, p. 6.
[40] 'Baptist Ordination at Ryde', p. 6.
[41] 'Baptist Ordination at Ryde', p. 6.
[42] 'Baptist Ordination at Ryde', p. 6.

(plus[43]) theological training course began in 1887 with Joseph Smale aged twenty-one (see Figure 5). He was about to enter what he later described as his 'veritable *alma mater*'.[44]

I believe that Smale's choice of college, as well as insights into college life and lectures, particularly, though not exclusively, those gleaned from the 1880s, can tell us much about his formation as a minister. Spurgeon's own personal involvement in the life of the College and with his students forged indelible convictions in the life of his prodigies. For Joseph Smale this was to form the foundations and framework for his ministry over the subsequent four decades, both in Britain and the USA, as Spurgeon's College helped shape the foundational elements of Smale's ecclesiology, missiology, and pneumatology.

Figure 5: Joseph Smale as a new student at The Pastors' College, 1887.
Photograph courtesy of Spurgeon's College Archives.

Given the explicit intention of his training college to produce preachers who would in turn bless other churches around the world,[45] Spurgeon developed a

---

[43] Smale's College career lasted about thirty months. Bebbington explains that the two year training course at the Pastors' College was the general rule, in contrast with four or five years at the other British Baptist colleges. See D.W. Bebbington, 'Spurgeon and British Evangelical Theological Education', in D.G. Hart and R.A. Mohler, Jr (eds), *Theological Education in the Evangelical Tradition* (Baker Books, 1996), p. 229.

[44] 'Baptist Ordination at Ryde', p. 6.

[45] I. Murray, 'Introduction' in C.H. Spurgeon, *An All-Round Ministry* (Banner of Truth Trust, 1960), p. vii. By 1891, 845 students had been trained and sent to work as

philosophy of training that maintained integral links between classroom lectures and the thriving church work at the Metropolitan Tabernacle. As such, students were eye-witnesses of church growth far beyond the expectations of many in their denomination and generation.[46] Explaining this in his own words, Spurgeon wrote of the necessity of this formative experience for every student.

> It is a grand assistance to our College that it is connected with an active and vigorous Christian church ... It is a serious strain upon a man's spirituality to be dissociated during his student life, from actual Christian work, and from fellowship with more experienced believers ... Through living in the midst of a church which, despite its faults, is a truly living, intensely zealous, working organisation, they gain enlarged ideas, and form practical habits.[47]

Additional to such practical exposure to local church life, there were inevitably other more implicit Spurgeonic influences at work in Smale's training from its outset. Present in his larger than life personality was Spurgeon's independent spirit that had enabled him to proceed into a pulpit ministry without any formal training, thus developing his own style, 'strongly doctrinal and probingly experiential'.[48] The Spurgeonic profile that Bebbington presents[49] is a succinct endorsement, in terms of this study, as to why Spurgeon (via Smale) should be recognised as a legitimate antecedent of Pentecostalism. He advised his students to shun

> the foolish affectation of intellectualism ... he was happy to court controversy ... he recommended that his students should adapt their pulpit style ... to go up to the level of a poor man but down to the level of an educated person. Spurgeon professed a version of egalitarianism that made him seem the champion of the common man.[50]

Smale was in many respects to typify these and other Spurgeonic characteristics.[51]

---

pastors, missionaries and evangelists, breaking new ground and forming new churches at home and abroad.

[46] See chapter 23, 'Revival at New Park Street', for instances of church life and growth at the Metropolitan Tabernacle, in C.H. Spurgeon, *Autobiography: Volume 1. The Early Years* (Banner of Truth, 1962), pp. 329-44.

[47] C.H. Spurgeon, *Autobiography: Volume 2. The Full Harvest* (Banner of Truth, 1973), p. 98.

[48] D.W. Bebbington, *The Dominance of Evangelicalism: The Age of Spurgeon and Moody* (IVP, 2005), p. 40.

[49] Bebbington, *Dominance of Evangelicalism*, pp. 40-45.

[50] Bebbington, *Dominance of Evangelicalism*, pp. 42-43.

[51] Bebbington helpfully categorizes the distinctive features of Spurgeon's personal impact by examining the theological, social and educational distinctives of the Pastor's

Furthermore, Spurgeon's openness to signs and wonders is worth stating, given his own experience in childhood when he was prophesied over that one day he would preach the gospel to great multitudes.[52] Other instances are also recorded during sermons, whereby he spoke out 'words of knowledge' to members of his congregation.[53] However, as we will see, on other occasions Spurgeon was critical and suspicious of manifestations of power, so it is uncertain what he himself would have made of Smale's embrace of the phenomena in Los Angeles before and during the Azusa Street Revival.

Spurgeonic Strand: Word and Spirit

It is my conviction, reflected in an array of sermons and college materials, that from the outset of his formal college education, Joseph Smale studied in an environment that was evidently desirous for Holy Spirit power and earnest for firsthand experience of revival, and all this within the scope of expository ministry of the word.

Herein exists one of the major factors why Joseph Smale's contribution to the study of Pentecostalism requires further study. Multiple roots of Pentecostalism, Wesleyan and non-Wesleyan, have been identified and analysed in depth,[54] but the contribution of Smale, with his distinct Spurgeonic influences, provides a contributory factor of a different theological complexion to the events as they unfolded in Los Angeles in 1905–06.

To that end, Smale was a product of what will be depicted in this study as a distinct strand of 'word *and* Spirit' theology and praxis. Following Spurgeon's strong Calvinistic emphasis, Smale stated at ordination 'some particulars of his doctrinal convictions, saying that he was not ashamed to avow himself a Calvinist and a believer in the doctrine of grace'.[55]

However, their Calvinism was not akin to other non-Wesleyan Evangelicals who exercised 'Reformed Pentecostal Theology',[56] to use Edith Blumhofer's phrase. By that, Blumhofer refers to the Reformed antecedents of Pentecostalism, including various teachers from the British Keswick tradition, typically Baptists, Congregationalists, and Presbyterians, including such

---

College. See Bebbington, 'Spurgeon and British Evangelical Theological Education', pp. 221-34.

[52] Spurgeon, *Autobiography*, I, p. 27.

[53] Spurgeon, *Autobiography*, II, p. 60.

[54] See D.D. Bundy, A. Cerillo and G. Wacker, 'Bibliography and Historiography', in S.M. Burgess and E.M. Van der Maas (eds), *New International Dictionary of Pentecostal and Charismatic Movements* (Zondervan, 2002), pp. 382-417.

[55] *Isle of Wight Observer* 17 May, 1890, p. 8.

[56] Bundy, Cerillo and Wacker, 'Bibliography and Historiography', p. 400.

characters as R.A. Torrey, Albert B. Simpson, and D.L. Moody.[57] That group held convictions such as

> the need for a Holy Spirit baptism as separate from conversion; belief in sanctification as a progressive overcoming of sin and not the instantaneous eradication of the sinful nature; advocacy of the premillenial return of the Lord, and healing in the atonement.[58]

Spurgeon, on the other hand, did not emphasise a secondary experience of baptism in the Holy Spirit, but nonetheless developed a distinct pneumatology which will be explored in more detail later in this chapter. Significantly, he was never invited to participate in the Keswick Convention from 1875, perhaps for theological reasons as well as a consequence of the Downgrade controversy in which he was embroiled. To that end both he and the Pastors' College were increasingly isolated from the holiness spirituality that emerged within the 'Keswick idiom'.[59]

Spurgeonic Theological Education

Due to Spurgeon's prolific writing ministry through lectures, sermons, as well as editing the monthly journal, *The Sword and the Trowel*, there are plenty of archival insights into the training of a student, such as Smale, at the Pastors' College.[60] The College had been informally established in 1856, as an extension of church-based ministry, to equip any promising preachers within Spurgeon's church, the Metropolitan Tabernacle, that 'they might become ministers of the cross of Christ'.[61] In Spurgeon's own words, he was adopting the training pattern of the Lord, as well as the Reformers, who then 'multiplied themselves in their students, and so fresh centres of light were created'.[62] But what of the distinctive elements that made Spurgeon's pattern of theological education different to other institutions of the day? Dr John Campbell,[63] a sympathetic outsider who visited the College in 1882, made the following observations:

---

[57] E.L. Blumhofer, *The Assemblies of God: A Chapter in the Story of American Pentecostalism:* Volume 1. *To 1941* (Gospel Publishing House, 1989), pp. 50-64.

[58] Bundy, Cerillo and Wacker, 'Bibliography and Historiography', p. 400.

[59] D.W. Bebbington, *Evangelicalism in Modern Britain: A History from the 1730s to the 1980s* (Unwin Hyman, 1989), p. 151.

[60] The terms 'Metropolitan College', 'The Pastors' College' and 'Spurgeon's College' are used interchangeably throughout this chapter.

[61] Spurgeon, *Autobiography*, II, p. 97.

[62] Spurgeon, *Autobiography*, II, p. 96.

[63] Dr John Campbell was a Congregational minister, and edited the *British Banner* magazine.

[The Pastors' College] is a thing by itself, there is nothing to be compared with it in these islands. It shows the founder to be ... a singular ecclesiastical originality. Not satisfied with things as now existing in colleges, and guided by strong instincts, he determined in a happy hour to create something for himself. His habit has been ... to do things in a new way.[64]

Such reproduction of core 'strong instincts', to use Campbell's phrase, were propagated within the College by the 'family-feel' that Spurgeon naturally gave the student body. Having started with just one student (Thomas Medhurst), Spurgeon 'began to look about for "another to be my dearly-beloved Timothy"'.[65] By the time Smale started as a student, thirty-one years after the College's inception, this project of theological education had developed a unique brand of pastor, modelled and taught by Spurgeon along with the tightly-knit group of four professors that Spurgeon had gathered around himself. Indeed, Smale's Principal, David Gracey, was one of those former students of the College who 'left their mark upon the age ... as teachers of others',[66] having assimilated the College ethos that all academic studies should be 'relevant to the task of communicating the gospel' to 'the masses'.[67]

Drawing on the major biographies of Spurgeon's life and ministry, as well as College records, some of those distinctive values of Spurgeon's College life will briefly be enumerated in order to appreciate the strands of theological and ministerial formation which prepared Joseph Smale for a life time of ministry.

TRAINING OPPORTUNITIES FOR ALL

Lack of finance was not regarded as a legitimate reason to preclude training for anyone who had the call of God upon their life, with an irresistible urge to preach the gospel.[68] In fact, it was for poorer students such as Smale that the Pastors' College was established. This is substantiated by the family account passed on to Smale's grandson, George Wood, that his grandfather was sponsored through his full-time education by Spurgeon himself.[69] As we have already noted, Spurgeon's view of ministry differed from other institutions, as expressed in the sentiment that

---

[64] The Pastor's College, *Annual Report* (1882), p. 17.
[65] Bebbington, 'Spurgeon and British Evangelical Theological Education', p. 221.
[66] Spurgeon, *Autobiography*, II, p.109.
[67] I.M. Randall, *A School of the Prophets: 150 years of Spurgeon's College* (Spurgeon's College, 2005), p. 4.
[68] J.C. Carlile, *C.H. Spurgeon: An Interpretative Biography* (Religious Tract Society, London, 1933), p. 171.
[69] Personal interview with George Wood (Joseph Smale's grandson), Los Angeles, 15 March 2004.

> No college at that time appeared to me to be suitable for the class of men that Providence and the grace of God drew around me. They were mostly poor and most of the colleges involved necessarily a considerable outlay to the student.[70]

Yet convictions regarding God's calling for pastoral training were not purely a matter of finances. Countering the charge that he was organising 'a parson manufactory', Spurgeon set out a robust defence that he would naturally gravitate to being 'a parson killer', dissuading many candidates away from ministry, as 'duty to the churches has compelled (him) to judge with severe discrimination'.[71] However, Spurgeon's emphatic 'egalitarian understanding of the role of the college',[72] that God could take and use the poor, the uneducated, the local, to go anywhere and be world changers for Christ in the power of the Holy Spirit, is a theme which connects directly to the quarters from whence Pentecostalism emerged in the early-twentieth century. These were Smale's roots, although admittedly the impact of the Pastors' College transferred these values to students in an organised setting, via tutors; while Azusa Street and the emergence of Pentecostalism released a generation who relied primarily on the power of the Holy Spirit without the necessity for elements of human training and systems of institutional organisation in place.

A BROAD BASED EDUCATION

A broad range of academic studies were introduced to the curriculum to improve the lack of education which hampered many of the student pastors. Keen to neither undervalue nor overvalue education, the Pastors' College still needed to train students to preach with interest and relevance for 'the vast masses of the East End of London and for those pulpits where scholarship and piety were both required'.[73] As the case of Smale illustrates, he did go on to occupy diverse pulpits, both in a provincial town such as Ryde, as well as the prestigious First Baptist Church of Los Angeles. Perhaps this in itself is a tribute to the training he received, and the balanced curriculum on which Spurgeon insisted.[74]

---

[70] Carlile, *Spurgeon*, p. 171.

[71] Spurgeon, *Autobiography*, II, pp. 100-101.

[72] Bebbington, 'Spurgeon and British Evangelical Theological Education', p. 225.

[73] M. Nicholls, *C.H. Spurgeon: The Pastor Evangelist* (Baptist Historical Society, 1992), p. 77.

[74] C.H. Spurgeon, 'What we aim at in the Pastors' College', *The Sword and the Trowel* (May, 1887), pp. 205-11. The College curriculum included: a knowledge of the scriptures, studying whole books and making the best use of commentaries/exposition; the study of doctrine; the history of the church and the history of the nations; the rudiments of astronomy, chemistry, zoology, geology and botany; mental and moral science, metaphysics and casuistry; mathematics; Latin, Greek and Hebrew; composition and style; poetry; practical oratory; the conduct of church work.

In Smale's case, it was a measure of these expansive foundations put in place at the Pastors' College that, given his humble beginnings, enabled him to adapt to the challenges of crossing cultures and continents with the gospel. Of course, students and mentors alike would ultimately attribute even the value of their general education to be subservient to the primary work and teaching of the Holy Spirit for ministry.

Stressing that tension between studies and spirituality further, College life required hard work and strict discipline in all classes. Whether 'Logic and Metaphysics with Professor Fergusson, or under Professor Marchant with Caesar and Xenophon, or taking … loftier flights in the pleasures of Tacitus and Plato, not forgetting Theology, Greek New Testament, and Hebrew, with Principal Gracey',[75] all academic pursuits, however useful for a general education, were ultimately considered secondary to the need 'to seek for greater spiritual strength'.[76] Spurgeon expounded this stating that, besides academics, the

> development of a man of God requires more self-knowledge, more faith, more fire, more communion with God, more likeness to Christ, more absorption into the designs of the Eternal.[77]

Once a week students were required to participate in College debates. Discussions were opened by students who took turns to present a given subject, 'speaking impromptu before the principal propounded the official line'.[78] All debates, recorded in the Discussion Minute Book, confirm that Smale was required to open the debate on two occasions during his time at the college:

> October 25 1888: 'Will the Lord's coming be personal and premillennial?'
> November 14 1889: 'Ought Capital Punishment to be abolished?'[79]

Smale's contributions in both sessions provide helpful insights into his emerging views and powers of rhetoric. In the first debate, he provides a full and detailed defense as to his premillennial convictions, quoting scripture and three succinct points, including consequent implications for missionary zeal.[80]

---

[75] Anonymous, 'Impressions of one who has just left the College', *Annual Report of the Pastors' College* (1888), p. 325.

[76] C.H. Spurgeon, 'The Student's Progress', *Annual Report of the Pastors' College* (1886), p. 330.

[77] Spurgeon, 'The Student's Progress' (1886), p. 330.

[78] Bebbington, 'Spurgeon and British Evangelical Theological Education', p. 230.

[79] The Pastors' College, *Discussion Minute Book* (1888–1889).

[80] The Pastors' College, *Discussion Minute Book* (1888–1889), 25 October 1888. Smale immediately identified himself as a pre-millennialist, stating three points:

This discussion continued for several weeks. However, placed in the deep end for the second debate on capital punishment, Smale appears hesitant, acknowledging 'he had not bestowed upon it much serious thought' though 'on the authority of scripture he was opposed to abolition'.[81]

One further reason behind the College's successful work of ministerial formation in students like Smale requires comment here, as a bridge to the next point. It was the personal involvement of the President, Spurgeon himself, in the aspect referred to above as 'the conduct of church work'. Professor Fergusson described 'the value and potency' of Mr Spurgeon being around and involved in College life as the 'chief success' behind all the subjects studied.[82] It was particularly on Friday afternoons that students had the opportunity to engage with the model pastor himself in Spurgeon's lectures that encompassed the practicalities of applied ministry and theology.

APPLIED THEOLOGY

Fundamentally, the teaching of every subject was for the express purpose of equipping students for church based or church planting ministry. On these Fridays, Spurgeon would spend 'two very happy hours together' with his students.[83] Setting out the rationale behind the series *Lectures to my Students*, Spurgeon explained the training to be intentionally 'colloquial, familiar, full of anecdote, and often humorous'.[84] In the words of one former student, these sessions proved a very fitting climax to the week for students who were 'weary with sterner studies'.[85] Writing anonymously, another former student

---

'(1) Because Anti-Christ was to have his day before Christ came to reign 1000 years. The Jews were to return to their own land and Anti-Christ was to make himself manifest, who was to be a "man of sin", not a system ...

(2) The last day spoken of in Jn. VI, 39-40 was a dispensational day. In the world's history there were dispensations analogous to the days of creation ... we are in the 6th Day or Gospel Dispensation, and the rest was the 7th or Millennial Day, answering to the Day of Rest. This did not take place till the Lord came and caused the resurrection of the dead in Christ.

(3) The character of the Millennial Dispensation was Theocratic. Christ was to sit upon the throne of David and He had not yet done so ... So far from this steady bending or tending to repress missionary zeal, the most devoted workers held it, such as Hudson Taylor, Moody, George Müller and Gratton Guinness.'

[81] The Pastors' College, *Discussion Minute Book* (1888–1889), 14 November 1889.

[82] A. Fergusson, *Annual Report of the Pastors' College* (1886), p. 310.

[83] C.H. Spurgeon, 'President's Note', *Annual Report of the Pastors' College* (1888), p. 316.

[84] C.H. Spurgeon, *Lectures to my Students* (Baker Book House, 1984), First Series, p. v. *Lectures to my Students* is comprised of two series of lectures in one volume, both individually, not consecutively paginated.

[85] Spurgeon, *Lectures to my Students*, First Series, p. v.

highlighted how Spurgeon's practical teaching 'fired their hearts' enabling him and his contemporaries to never forget 'the great end of student life'.[86]

It is beneficial to grasp a sense of these important formative afternoon sessions, as hundreds of students such as Smale were helped to mature in many areas, especially preaching and evangelism. Following each class, students were then issued with their preaching 'appointments for the next Lord's Day',[87] and allowed the opportunity for private counsel with Mr Spurgeon before tea and an evening prayer meeting for the students.[88] Without stopping to analyse these major areas of applied theology in detail, the following two sections will suffice briefly to illustrate the importance of these distinctive Spurgeonic influences that Smale received as a student, each of which can be traced throughout later stages of Smale's life and ministry.

PREACHING

The fact that Spurgeon's *Lectures to my Students* is still in print today is ample evidence that a wealth of practical wisdom and help for preachers was appreciated by Smale and his contemporaries, as well as by many subsequent generations. Desmond Cartwright believes this book containing Spurgeon's lectures has remained a favourite book of Elim Pentecostal pastors in the UK to the present day.[89] Bibliocentric in every dimension, Spurgeon pragmatically taught far-ranging dimensions to increase the effective ministry of the word, covering aspects such as selecting a text,[90] use of the voice,[91] boldness,[92] the use of anecdotes and illustrations, etc., typically conjoining the spontaneous with conscious planning.[93]

---

[86] Anonymous, 'Impressions of one who has just left the College', *Annual Report of the Pastors' College* (1888), p. 325.

[87] Spurgeon, *Autobiography*, II, p. 109.

[88] C.H. Spurgeon, 'The Student's Progress', *Annual Report of the Pastors' College* (1886), p. 326.

[89] Personal interview with Desmond Cartwright, Cardiff, 26 October, 2004.

[90] Spurgeon, *Lectures to my Students*, First Series, pp. 84-101.

[91] Spurgeon, *Lectures to my Students*, First Series, pp. 117-35.

[92] Spurgeon, *Lectures to my Students*, First Series, p. 36.

[93] Spurgeon, *Lectures to my Students*, First Series, pp. 31-53.

Figure 6: Spurgeon's students 1888.
Joseph Smale is seated, front row, second from the left.
Photograph courtesy of Spurgeon's College Archives.

Looking at patterns within Smale's sermons over the course of his later ministry,[94] there are some noticeable similarities which, unsurprisingly, confirm the impact of Spurgeon's influence upon him. The only period where the style and content arrangement of Smale's sermons is not consistent with Spurgeon's model is the phase immediately before and after Azusa Street, c. 1905–07. Explaining this briefly for now, it was during this Pentecostal phase of ministry after Smale had just returned from witnessing the Welsh Revival firsthand, that he preached using themes rather than specific Bible texts, as had been his norm. It is far more anecdotal, relying upon the Holy Spirit to prompt preacher and people, in some cases deleting the sermon from the service altogether in favour of experiential responses among the congregation.[95]

Otherwise, regarding sermon arrangement, Smale preached in the mould of students who had sat under Spurgeon's ministry and instruction. Using a title and/or a text, along with an interesting introduction to grab the attention of

---

[94] Smale's sermons will be analysed further in chapter 5.
[95] First Baptist Church Los Angeles, *Church Records* IX, 31 May 1905.

hearers, Smale likewise would typically break down his sermon into three major points, each giving rise to numerous sub-points.[96] But that only explains the content of those messages recorded in print. Unfortunately we have no clues about aspects of Smale's persona or any idiosyncratic habits he may have employed while preaching.

Therefore, relying on what we do know, it would be beneficial to develop doctrinal insights into elements Smale was taught regarding the imperative work of the Holy Spirit in connection with preaching.[97] Given the absolute necessity of the Holy Spirit as the prerequisite for any preaching, Spurgeon delineated the role of the Spirit within the preacher in numerous respects, including: he is the Spirit of knowledge; the Spirit of Wisdom; the Spirit that touches the lips in utterance, as 'a live coal from off the altar' provides the power of divine energy; the Spirit of God that acts as an anointing oil with regard to the 'entire delivery'; the Spirit to produce the 'actual effect from the gospel' leading to conversions. Elsewhere in this lecture, Spurgeon elaborated upon the Spirit's work for matters of church oversight and guidance, and warned that all too often the Holy Spirit is absent.[98]

Reaffirming the teaching of Spurgeon above, Pastor T.I. Stockley addressed the 1888 Pastors' College Association which Smale, in all likelihood, attended, stating the need for every preacher was to abide in Jesus in absolute dependence and loving communion, because 'the Holy Ghost is within us as a mighty, quickening power. He inspires the hearers too, and so there is a Pentecost; for true success in the ministry is given according to the measure in which the Holy Spirit is really trusted.'[99]

This slant on a Pentecostal experience challenges the filters that condition a Baptist, word-centred ministry. Acts 2, for example, may simply be interpreted with the focus upon the preached word, namely, Peter's sermon with its unction and power. The evidence of that Holy Spirit power is measured by the response of the crowd to such preaching. Noting this here, it is important to appreciate the paradigms that were the dominant forces controlling Smale's later ministerial conduct. This may also explain part of the reason why Smale refused to join the Pentecostal movement as it developed from 1906 onwards.

One further factor in Smale's education as a preacher needs to be mentioned here, as Smale was a product of the year group caught up at the time of the Downgrade Controversy. The theological controversies that raged during 1887–88, were a significant backdrop for all the students at the Pastors' College

---

[96] J. Smale, see numerous examples contained within his published sermons.

[97] Spurgeon, *Lectures to my Students*, Second Series, pp. 1-22.

[98] Spurgeon, *Lectures to my Students*, Second Series, p. 16.

[99] T.I. Stockley, 'Our Spiritual Life – Its Influence upon our Preaching', Pastor's College Association (1886), p. 590.

during that period. Bebbington explains that this controversy occurred because 'something of the incisiveness of Evangelical theology had been lost'.[100]

In the public domain, Spurgeon fronted the attack against denominations that were veering towards modern, liberal thinking, with a series of articles published in *The Sword and the Trowel*. In the privacy of College lectures, one lecturer observed that the effect of the Downgrade Controversy

> created an intense desire for efficiency in preaching the Old Gospel ... The noise of the Down-Grade battle has led our students to seek for increased assurance and certainty in preaching the Gospel ... The coming struggle is increasing among our students an intense spirit of consecration to the person of the Lord Jesus ... The coming struggle is fostering among our students a spirit of complete reliance on the Holy Spirit's help for true success.[101]

These insights, of one so close to the student body, are worth noting as they constitute strands that inevitably participated in Smale's applied theology and preaching formation, not least Spurgeon's decision to withdraw from the Baptist Union.

EVANGELISM

Besides Spurgeon's desire to create 'good expositors',[102] he also passionately believed that pastors should be able to fulfil the role of evangelists as 'soul-winning ministers'.[103] To this end Joseph Smale excelled, both prior to his arrival at the Pastors' College,[104] and also in each of his pastorates as this book will show. For now, to limit the evidence to his second church only, while at Prescott in Arizona, Smale led evangelistic teams in their covered wagons, 'sleeping at night by the roadside and feeding our horses with a nosebag'.[105] On another occasion, Smale is recorded as holding 'street meetings during the session' of some Association Meetings of the Baptists of Arizona.[106] Certainly the church growth in all of Smale's churches – at Ryde, Prescott, and Los Angeles – would indicate a consistent zeal for evangelistic outreach. Added to which, Smale's ability to plant new churches and initiate new mission work[107] is also indicative of the direction Spurgeon's College pointed their new pastors.

---

[100] Bebbington, *Evangelicalism in Modern Britain*, p. 145.
[101] A. Fergusson, *Annual Report of the Pastors' College* (1888), pp. 317-20.
[102] C.H. Spurgeon, *The Sword and the Trowel* (November, 1888), p. 571.
[103] Spurgeon, *The Sword and the Trowel* (November, 1888), p. 570.
[104] See above on his preaching success as a teenager following conversion.
[105] R.A. Windes, unpublished letter, 1897. Prescott Baptist Church, Arizona Archive.
[106] Windes, unpublished letter, 1897.
[107] E.g., church plants at First Baptist Church Los Angeles, First New Testament Church Los Angeles, China New Testament Mission, and Spanish Gospel Mission. Further details of each of these will be given in subsequent chapters.

As students, they were encouraged by their President to be effective in conversions by various means, whether writing 'to produce readable tracts'[108] or especially by speaking the living word. Once again, whatever the means employed, the source of true evangelistic power may be identified in a clear word and Spirit formulation. Spurgeon's Friday afternoon lecture series elaborated on some of the dynamics of church work,[109] with spiritual conversion in mind. In the spirit of the Friday lectures mentioned above, topics included far reaching encouragement that 'not only must *something* be done to evangelize the millions, but *everything* must be done, and perhaps amid variety of effort the best thing would be discovered. "If by any means I may save some" must be our motto'.[110]

Spurgeon's entrepreneurial vision for evangelistic strategies within the conduct of church life was not only embraced by Smale in his College studies, but also in his later pastorates. Later chapters describe some of the innovations Smale introduced during his pastorates to illustrate the point being made here, that there is a direct relationship between methodologies Smale acquired at the Pastors' College and efforts he employed for outreach in each of his church pastorates.

Furthermore, the element of reproducing the necessary skills in the lives of other Christians was also a key component in Smale's expanding influence upon the discipleship of young Christians, being challenged themselves to engage in evangelism. One such talk that Smale presented, entitled 'Lessons in Personal Work',[111] encouraged a young people's session of the 'Los Angeles Baptist Association' with the example of 'an unlettered, rugged man like Peter that three thousand in one day were won to give undying devotion to the crucified Nazarene'.[112] Typical of his training and similar convictions to Spurgeon's, Smale correlates the work of the word and the Spirit in the personal work of evangelism. 'Young people, you must know your Bible in dealing with a soul,' he categorically states, before going on to advocate a direct presentation of Christ crucified as 'a vicarious offering'. The concluding point of the talk balances the power of the word with the required power of the Spirit to accomplish God's work. In the printed synopsis of this talk, Smale's theology of the Holy Spirit is unequivocal at this early stage of his ministry,

---

[108] C.H. Spurgeon, 'What we aim at', *The Sword and the Trowel* (November, 1888), p. 571.

[109] C.H. Spurgeon, 'The need of Decision for the Truth', 'Open Air Preaching', 'On Conversion as our Aim', all in *Lectures to my Students*, Series 2, pp. 39-53, pp. 76-95 and pp. 179-192 respectively.

[110] Spurgeon, 'Open Air Preaching', *Lectures to my Students*, Second Series, p. 75 (italics original).

[111] J. Smale, 'Lessons in Personal Work', *Pacific Baptist* 22.43 (26 Oct 1898), p. 8.

[112] Smale, 'Lessons in Personal Work', p. 8.

and warrants exact quotation for both its pragmatism and sense of balance between human methods and Spirit controlled action.

> It must not be to use the Lord, but to let the Lord use us. God is not our servant, but we are His, and we must therefore be under the direction of the Holy Spirit. And our first, middle and last word must be, 'Lord, what would'st Thou have me to do.' Be definite in your work and methodical, but let your definiteness and methods be the creation of the Holy Spirit.[113]

One other point of interest arises from this particular talk in 1898, reaffirming the causal link between Spurgeon the mentor and Smale the disciple, even eight years after Smale had left the College. In this one talk Smale uses three separate illustrations and anecdotes from Spurgeon to emphasise his preaching points.

Distinct Pneumatology

An overall summary of the pneumatological influences Smale received as a student at the Pastors' College may be presented by paying close attention to Spurgeon's influential teaching on the subject. This must be understood within the ethos of Spurgeon's College which 'made a substantial contribution to the spread of revival' right through to the Welsh Revival and beyond, by maintaining 'a spirit of prayer for an awakening' and 'providing the personnel for overseas mission'.[114]

Two areas in particular will be highlighted: the pastor's need for Holy Spirit power; and the church's need for revival. These are formulated from selected sermons and articles delivered and printed in the latter phase of Spurgeon's lifetime. Careful observation of both the content and 'heartbeat' of his messages, each section reveals aspects of Spurgeon's teaching emphasis for students, including Smale, during their formative student days in South London.

THE PASTOR'S NEED FOR HOLY SPIRIT POWER

Joseph Smale, along with his contemporaries, was the beneficiary of the latter years of Spurgeon's thinking and preaching. Consistently, Spurgeon had promoted the essentials of Holy Spirit empowerment as the paramount prerequisite for effective ministry as pastors and preachers of the word. Listing just a few, this can be illustrated by a cursory glance at some of the titles Spurgeon gave to some of his sermons over those years: 'Our Urgent Need of the Holy Spirit' (7 January, 1877); 'The Pentecostal Wind and Fire' (18 September, 1881); 'The Personal Pentecost and the Glorious Hope' (13 June,

---

[113] Smale, 'Lessons in Personal Work', p. 9.
[114] N. Gibbard, *On the Wings of the Dove* (Brynterion Press, 2002), p. 221.

1886); 'The Holy Ghost – The Need of the Age' (13 March, 1887); and 'Filling with the Spirit, and Drunkenness with Wine' (26 May, 1889).

These themes, integral to ministerial formation at the Pastors' College, were reiterated by the President in various sermons, conference talks and articles, as well as his Friday afternoon lectures to the students, considered by many to be a lifeline of encouragement after the rigours of the week's study.[115] Thematically, they can be evaluated under the following categories.

A Felt Need for God the Holy Spirit

'Do you not see your need of an extraordinary power?',[116] Spurgeon asked his students at the 1889 annual conference held at the College. His challenge on that occasion was for students to discover the power available to preachers and the essential conditions for obtaining it. In the address lasting one and a half hours, which Smale as a final year student in all probability attended, Spurgeon encouraged simplicity of heart, because 'the Lord pours most into those who are empty of self'.[117] Rejecting dependence upon human wisdom, Spurgeon promoted humility of mind, complete subordination to God and a deep seriousness of heart[118] as necessary preparation for the Spirit's anointing.

Such appeals counter any erroneous assumptions that it was purely word-centred ministry that emanated from the Pastors' College during those days. Their President had a far more developed understanding of the work of the Holy Spirit as the only power source available to meet the needs of pastor and people. Drawing on Ezekiel chapter 37's vision of the valley of dry bones in one sermon, Spurgeon exhorted 'God's people to deal with the Holy Spirit as he should be dealt with',[119] because 'only the Holy Spirit can quicken dead souls'.[120] In Spurgeon's estimation, the Spirit is never to be regarded as merely an 'it' or an 'influence',[121] rather the antidote for human need as each believer honours, worships, adores and looks to the Holy Ghost for help.[122] Smale clearly embraced this teaching as foundational for his own ministry, and testified to the necessity he had of the Spirit's help at times of need. One

---

[115] Anonymous, 'Impressions of one who has just left the College', *Annual Report of the Pastors' College* (1888), p. 325.

[116] C.H. Spurgeon, 'The Preacher's Power and the Conditions of Obtaining it', *The Sword and the Trowel* (June, 1889), p. 257.

[117] C.H. Spurgeon, 'The Preacher's Power and the Conditions of Obtaining it. Continued', *The Sword and the Trowel* (July, 1889), p. 349.

[118] Spurgeon, 'The Preacher's Power and the Conditions of Obtaining it. Continued', pp. 350-52.

[119] C.H. Spurgeon, 'Come From The Four Winds, O Breath' [preached 15 May 1890], *Metropolitan Tabernacle Pulpit* 38 (1892), p. 110.

[120] Spurgeon, 'Come From The Four Winds, O Breath', p.111.

[121] C.H. Spurgeon, 'Filling with the Spirit, and Drunkenness with Wine' [preached 26 May 1889], *Metropolitan Tabernacle Pulpit* 35 (1889), p. 586.

[122] Spurgeon, 'Filling with the Spirit, and Drunkenness with Wine', p. 587.

instance to mention, leads appropriately on to the next section, by virtue of the fact that his need was met by a vivid experience of the Holy Spirit's power. Writing at the time of moving from Arizona to California, Smale explains that

> All my strength seemed to go from me when I was telegraphed for, to come to your assistance, and as I tremblingly obeyed, I must record the fact to the praise of God. I had no sooner entered the thick and felt shadows than a sudden joy thrilled and energised me in making the sweet discovery that Jesus was in the midst of that cloud.[123]

On the basis of that experience, Smale proceeded to urge the church members to seek 'a full indwelling of the Holy Spirit'.[124]

A Practical Experience of God the Holy Spirit

Similarities between Smale's emphasis and Spurgeon's exist in their characteristic and consistent connection of teaching to the 'practical purposes' of sermon preparation and preaching, stating that, as pastors, 'we are nothing without the Holy Spirit'.[125] By stressing the 'practical', the stress of his teaching was for hearers to understand and rely on what Spurgeon describes as the 'operations of the Holy Spirit'.[126] While not claiming fully to comprehend the mysteries of the Spirit's working,[127] Spurgeon does, however, specify the provision of divine 'endowment' as the spiritual qualification prior to doing anything for Christ.[128] Using points from another sermon to exemplify this, Spurgeon sought to guide his audience to actively seek a greater power for service through the Spirit's operations. 'The minister studies his text; but does he ask for a baptism of the Holy Ghost?'[129] is the challenge presented, as power must accompany the word preached, and that means, by definition, the 'power must first be in the man who speaks that word'.[130]

Analysing the necessity for Holy Spirit power further, Spurgeon uses alliteration to display his own pneumatological convictions, which neatly fit with later practice at Azusa Street and beyond, namely that the Spirit provides *miraculous power* – as he did for those in 'olden times', who, having received the Spirit of God, went forth to do great signs and wonders in the name of

---

[123] J. Smale, *Church Quarterly* (First Baptist Church Los Angeles, Dec 1887), p. 1.

[124] Smale, *Church Quarterly* (First Baptist Church Los Angeles, Dec 1887), p. 1.

[125] Spurgeon, 'Come From The Four Winds, O Breath', p.110.

[126] For two examples, see C.H. Spurgeon, 'A Message from God to His Church', in *Sermons on Revival* (Zondervan, 1958), pp. 7-16; and 'The Outpouring of the Holy Spirit', in *Power for You* (Whitaker House, 1996), pp. 7-30.

[127] Spurgeon, 'The Outpouring of the Holy Spirit', p. 12.

[128] C.H. Spurgeon, 'Witnessing better than Knowing the Future' [preached 29 August 1889], *Metropolitan Tabernacle Pulpit* 39 (1893), p. 498.

[129] Spurgeon, 'Witnessing better than Knowing the Future', p. 498.

[130] Spurgeon, 'Witnessing better than Knowing the Future', p. 498.

Christ.[131] Secondly, there is *mental power*, well beyond our education, that is freely available for those who will be led into truth. Typical of the preacher, Spurgeon describes how 'the Holy Spirit takes the fool, and makes him know the wonders of redeeming love'.[132] Thirdly, the scope of the Spirit's work is to be experienced within the realm of *moral power*, which according to Spurgeon incorporates inner and outward qualities, as the Spirit 'imparts dauntless courage, calm confidence, intense affection, zeal, deep patience, much-enduring perseverance'.[133]

No wonder Spurgeon elsewhere describes the realities of Holy Spirit power at work as a 'Pentecost [to be] repeated in the heart of every believer'.[134] He also identifies the alternative danger of neglecting the work of the Spirit, using more graphic descriptions, to show the necessity of the Spirit's work as intrinsic to make everything alive.

> We can preach as machines, we can pray as machines, and we can teach Sunday-School as machines. Men can give mechanically, and come to the communion-table mechanically: yes, and we ourselves shall do so unless the Spirit of God be with us.[135]

However, it has to be noted that the wider context of Spurgeon's teaching during the latter half of the nineteenth century in Britain was not so much concerned with pneumatological contests, but the task of seeing the Christian church reverse the declining spiritual tide. To that end he was quite scathing about the various forms of holiness teaching that promoted perfectionism during the latter nineteenth century.[136] It was, for Spurgeon, a further reason for the needs of the age to be met through activism by a 'continual manifestation of

---

[131] Spurgeon, 'Witnessing better than Knowing the Future', p. 497.

[132] Spurgeon, 'Witnessing better than Knowing the Future', p. 497.

[133] Spurgeon, 'Witnessing better than Knowing the Future', p. 497.

[134] C.H. Spurgeon, 'The Personal Pentecost and the Glorious Hope' [preached 13 June 1886], *Metropolitan Tabernacle Pulpit* 32 (1886), p. 313.

[135] C.H. Spurgeon, 'Our Urgent Need of the Holy Spirit' [preached 7 January 1877], *Metropolitan Tabernacle Pulpit* 23 (1877), p. 16.

[136] M. Hopkins, 'What Did Spurgeon Believe?', *Christian History* 29 (January, 1991), p. 30. For a brief synopsis of Spurgeon's call for 'a high degree of holiness', see C.H. Spurgeon, 'What we would be', *An All Round Ministry* (Banner of Truth, 1965), pp. 244-45, 'Is it possible for believers to be perfectly holy on earth? ... we dare not set limits to the power of Divine grace, so as to say that a believer can reach a certain degree of grace, but can go no further. If a perfect life be possible, let us endeavour to obtain it ... We dare not straiten the Lord in this matter ... Let us aspire to saintliness of spirit and character. I am persuaded that the greatest power we can get over our fellow-men is the power which comes of consecration and holiness.'

the power of the Holy Spirit in the church of God if by her means the multitudes are to be gathered to the Lord Jesus'.[137]

THE CHURCH'S NEED FOR REVIVAL

Spurgeon's own references to the 1858–59 spiritual Awakening in the USA and other great revivals,[138] illustrates something of his personal hope and theological convictions that another powerful work of the Holy Spirit would be seen, perhaps in his generation. Given the two desperate needs for 'the revival of saints and the ingathering of sinners',[139] Spurgeon articulated a call for the 'bringing on of the latter-day glory',[140] something which was transmitted to Joseph Smale and many others at the end of the nineteenth century.

The nature of latter-day rain expectations emanating from the Pastors' College was, however, more anticipated towards the fulfilment of Daniel's prophecy in Daniel 12:4 – that 'many will run to and fro' and 'knowledge shall be increased'.[141] Characteristic of Spurgeon, eschatological anticipation was to be interpreted very much within the realm of the preached word. That is not to ignore the fact that Spurgeon does entertain the possibility of other miraculous phenomena accompanying a mighty move of the Spirit. For his high regard for the eternal power of the Spirit is aptly described in the following rhetorical question:

> If at the commencement of the gospel we behold the Holy Spirit working great signs and wonders may we not expect a continuance – nay, if anything, an increased display – of his power as the ages roll on?[142]

However, such Spurgeonic expectation of the Spirit's work in revival, although appearing unconditionally open to signs and wonders, actually requires careful qualifications. These will be set out here, as they in turn have a significant bearing upon Smale's response to the days of 'Pentecostal overflowing' post-Azusa Street.

---

[137] C.H. Spurgeon, 'Our Urgent Need of the Holy Spirit' [preached 7 January 1877], *Metropolitan Tabernacle Pulpit* 23 (1877), p. 13.

[138] C.H. Spurgeon, 'The Outpouring of the Holy Spirit' [sermon undated], in *Power for You*, p. 10.

[139] C.H. Spurgeon, 'Praying in the Holy Ghost' [preached 4 November 1866], *Metropolitan Tabernacle Pulpit* 12 (1866), p. 622.

[140] C.H. Spurgeon, 'The Power of the Holy Ghost' [sermon undated], in *Holy Spirit Power*, p. 48.

[141] Spurgeon, 'The Power of the Holy Ghost', p. 48.

[142] C.H. Spurgeon, 'The Pentecostal Wind and Fire' [preached 18 September 1881], *Metropolitan Tabernacle Pulpit* 27 (1881), p. 93.

Practical Signs of Revival

Given the need for the Holy Spirit to awaken dull, asleep and dead churches,[143] Spurgeon regarded a true revival to be 'a glorious reply to scepticism'.[144] This was especially the case during the period when Smale was a student at the Pastors' College. The Downgrade controversy[145] and subsequent contention with the Baptist Union of Great Britain had raised fundamental questions of doctrinal orthodoxy, and Spurgeon consequently opposed anything appearing to be 'modern theology' or practice.[146] As a result, Spurgeon's expectations of any work of the Spirit in revival anticipated

> such a miraculous amount of holiness, such an extraordinary fervour of prayer, such a real communion with God, so much vital religion, and such a spread of the doctrines of the Cross that everyone will see that the Spirit is poured out like water, and the rains descending from above.[147]

Taking this into account, along with Spurgeon's word-centred ministry, it is not surprising that the records of the Holy Spirit's outpouring in the 1830s under the ministry of Edward Irving were dismissed by Spurgeon at a stroke, as merely 'Irving's actings' or 'pantomimes'.[148] By implication, as far as Spurgeon was concerned Irving's 'glossolalia and prophetic utterances'[149] were a superficial challenge to the word of God, and evidence of the 'worldliness' of the church of his generation.[150]

For Smale there was an apparent progression in his understanding of revival. By 1897, he informed his new church at First Baptist Los Angeles that 'we are looking for a revival, and several signs of it are already with us'.[151] Smale then highlighted ten 'things that are the great factors promoting a revival', citing a list very much in keeping with his Spurgeonic heritage

---

[143] C.H. Spurgeon, 'The Abiding of the Spirit and the Glory of the Church' [preached 5 September 1886], *Metropolitan Tabernacle Pulpit* 32 (1886), p. 488.

[144] C.H. Spurgeon, 'Restoration of Truth and Revival', *The Sword and the Trowel* (December, 1887), p. 605.

[145] The 'Down-Grade' controversy of 1887–88 was precipitated by an article written by Spurgeon in which he condemned 'the tendency to theological vapidity', with ministers leaving out the atonement, etc. Such decline subsequently prompted Spurgeon's resignation from the Baptist Union. See Bebbington, *Evangelicalism in Modern Britain*, pp. 145-46.

[146] C.H. Spurgeon, 'Presidential Address', *The Sword and the Trowel* (June, 1888), p. 259.

[147] Spurgeon, 'The Power of the Holy Ghost', p. 49.

[148] Spurgeon, 'Restoration of Truth and Revival', p. 605.

[149] D.D. Bundy, 'Edward Irving', in Burgess and Van der Maas (eds), *New International Dictionary*, p. 803.

[150] Spurgeon, 'Restoration of Truth and Revival', p. 606.

[151] J. Smale, *Church Quarterly* (First Baptist Church Los Angeles, Dec 1887), p. 1.

First. Perfect harmony between yourself and every church member. Ephes. iv:31,32.
Second. A living soul. "Said I not unto thee that if thou wouldst believe thou shouldst see the glory of God." Expect to see souls saved, and all other things being equal, we shall see souls saved. How can we think that sinners will take God at His word if we don't. God means what He says every time. Hebrews xi:6.
Third. A God-possessed heart. This involves a separateness from sin and self, a daily surrender, holy conduct, love in us as a master passion for God, for our fellow church members and for lost souls, a full indwelling of the Holy Spirit. Psalm li:10-13.
Fourth. Unceasing prayer for the Spirit to move upon all hearts in the service. John iii:3.
Fifth. An unceasing knowledge of the Scriptures. Through the word and Spirit we come to know God. James i:18; 1 Cor. ii:11,12, and they that know their God shall be strong and do exploits.
Sixth. A painful consciousness that everybody out of Christ is lost. John v:11,12. Anxious saints make anxious sinners.
Seventh. A willingness and readiness to co-operate with the church in every spiritual project. A disposition to be anything, and do anything, and go anywhere for the glory of God. It takes more than one stick to kindle a fire. It took four men to bring the palsied man to Christ. Acts ix:6.
Eighth. Attendance at all the services unless you can render a reason for your absence which you know the Lord will accept. Heb. x:25; Acts iii:3; Luke iv:16.
Nineth. Being faithful to known duties. Acts iv:19, 20; Galatians i:15-17. Paul's life opened out so gloriously, and the churches were blessed so wondrously, because he was not disobedient unto the heavenly vision.
Tenth. Last, but not least, a daily habit of family table reading and prayer. Genesis xviii:19; Deut. vi:5-7.
These ten things will serve a mighty revival.[152]

Smale emulates his mentor's emphasis, sensitive to every move of the Holy Spirit's influence.[153]

Although not using the language of 'baptism in the Holy Spirit' at this point, Spurgeon does describe the perfect relationship between the believer and the Spirit occurring when 'we have reached a high state of sanctification when God the Spirit and our own inward spirit are perfectly in accord'.[154] Only then can believers truly 'pray in the Spirit'.[155] Spurgeon is recorded as emphasising that 'you cannot get out of the Church what is not in it. The reservoir itself must be

---

[152] J. Smale, *Church Quarterly* (First Baptist Church Los Angeles, December 1887), pp. 1-2.

[153] C.H. Spurgeon, 'Praying in the Holy Ghost' [preached 5 September 1866], *Metropolitan Tabernacle Pulpit* 12 (1866), p. 619.

[154] Spurgeon, 'Praying in the Holy Ghost', p. 619.

[155] Spurgeon, 'Praying in the Holy Ghost', pp. 613-24.

filled before it can pour forth a stream.'[156] It was for pastors like Joseph Smale to work out the pneumatological implications of this in their own contexts once they had left the Pastors' College.

College Assessment

As Smale concluded his College career, each tutor at the Pastors' College gave their personal, one-sentence, assessment of how student 'Smale, J.' had fared during his time under their tuition. The four tutors made the following comments concerning Smale.

James Archer Spurgeon:	'Of much promise'.
David Gracey, Principal:	'Powers of useful order; gives fair promise'.
Archibald Fergusson:	'Earnest enquiring spirit: a little soft manner; and average ability'.
Frederick George Marchant:	'Has much improved. Average ability'.

Settled at Park Road, Ryde, March 1890.[157]

Smale's First Church: Park Road Baptist Church, Ryde, Isle of Wight

During October 1889 Joseph Smale had preached consecutive Sundays with a view to becoming the next pastor of Park Road Baptist Chapel in Ryde on the Isle of Wight. The Regency town of Ryde, situated just seven miles from Queen Victoria's royal residence at Osborne House, was continuing to expand during the 1890s.[158] Park Road Baptist Church was formed in March 1866[159] as a breakaway group that had splintered from the main Baptist congregation in George Street, Ryde.[160] In order to comprehend aspects of Smale's new church's DNA, the seceding members had previously disapproved of numerous trivial matters which culminated in agitation over the pastor at George Street 'wearing a gown in the pulpit'.[161] Consequently, this second Baptist congregation had emerged. By 1870 they had constructed a chapel 'in an iron building'[162] costing 'about £1200', which could 'seat about 500 persons', with a basement providing 'a large room used for school, lectures and other

---

[156] Spurgeon, 'Our Urgent Need of the Holy Spirit', p. 14.

[157] *The Pastor's College Assessment Book, 1882–1891* (Spurgeon's College Archives, London), p. 159.

[158] *Ryde's Heritage: Our Town, Your Histories* (Ryde Social Heritage Group, 2008), p. 30.

[159] Christ Church (Baptist), George Street, Ryde, *Centenary Souvenir Handbook: 1848–1948* (n.d. [c.1948]), p. 13.

[160] *Ryde's Heritage: Our Town, Your Histories*, p. 52.

[161] *Ryde's Heritage: Our Town, Your Histories*, p. 52.

[162] *Centenary Souvenir Handbook: 1848–1948*, p. 13.

purposes'.[163] By February 1890 the following paragraph regarding Smale's settlement appeared in the local press:

> The Rev. Joseph Smale, of the Metropolitan College, has received the unanimous invitation of the members to become the pastor ... We understand that the gentleman has acceded to the request.[164]

Figure 7: Ryde, Isle of Wight, 1891.
Photograph Courtesy of Isle of Wight County Record Office

Post-ordination, it was evident that Smale faced two immediate challenges as he commenced his ministry in Ryde. First, there was the need to strengthen the work numerically and spiritually, for on numerous occasions the chapel had been given notice to quit the building in Park Road, and, in Smale's own words, 'the place was almost deserted'.[165] Secondly, to clear an outstanding debt of £300 on the building, following refurbishment over the previous decade. A previous pastor, the Rev. J Harrison, explained the necessity of the loans in order to transform the premises from 'a run for wild cats' to a 'beautiful school room', along with the addition of a baptistery.[166]

---

[163] *Kelly's Directory of the Isle of Wight* (1891), p. 124.
[164] 'Ryde', *The Isle of Wight Times & Hampshire Gazette* 20 February, 1890, p. 5.
[165] 'The Park Road Baptist Chapel', *Isle of Wight Observer* 17 May, 1890, p. 8.
[166] *Isle of Wight County Press* 16 August 1890, p. 3.

However, in time, Smale became aware of another, more insidious, challenge to the work at Park Road, which may explain why his pastorate on the Isle of Wight lasted only twenty-eight months. In his farewell speech, Smale described how he had faced the opposition of 'people in [the] church with whom no pastor could work, [and] elements so at variance with Christian principles that it was impossible to go forward'.[167] Sadly, given that no church records from that period exist,[168] it is impossible to analyse the implications of these comments further, other than to be able to sense the overall struggle Smale was facing.

Yet during his time in Ryde there were a number of other facets of life for the new pastor that reveal something of his emerging all-round ministry, even in the face of such opposition. These also help to illustrate elements of Spurgeon's influence as this young pastor embarked on life in his first church.

Shared Platforms

Within months of Smale's arrival on the island, the Rev. Edward Bruce Pearson, pastor of the other main Baptist church in Ryde (George Street Baptist Chapel), invited Smale to preach at their forty-first anniversary service.[169] The subsequent relationship between the two Baptist ministers in Ryde continued to be mutually positive, as seen by frequent interchange at church events. Indeed, Pearson complimented Joseph Smale at the end of his tenure that 'there had been no jealousy between the two Baptist churches during his [Smale's] ministry there'.[170]

According to Martin Light, Pearson exercised 'a very successful ministry' during the period Smale served at the struggling Park Road church.[171] Major events, ranging from annual weeks of prayer to the memorial service for Spurgeon were all held at the larger George Street Chapel.[172] But no records hint of any resentment that Smale may have felt by working in the shadow of Pearson and the 'great success which had taken place during Pearson's ministry'[173] at the other Baptist church.

In fact the reverse is true, because from the outset of his ministry Smale articulated a desire to work 'amongst other evangelical denominations *(applause)*'. Furthermore, Professor Gracey, Principal of the Pastors' College, speaking at Smale's ordination, 'congratulated the church and their pastor on

---

[167] 'Farewell of the Rev. J. Smale', *Isle of Wight County Press* 17 Sept 1892, p. 7.

[168] M. Light (member of Baptist Historical Society, Isle of Wight), letter dated 27 November 2002.

[169] *Isle of Wight County Press* 30 August 1890, p. 8.

[170] 'Farewell of the Rev. J. Smale', *Isle of Wight County Press* 17 Sept 1892, p. 7.

[171] Light, letter dated 27 November 2002.

[172] 'Memorial Service at Ryde', *Isle of Wight Times* 11 February 1892, p. 5.

[173] *Isle of Wight Times & Hampshire Gazette* 20 October 1892, p. 5.

the representatives of other denominations being on the platform'.[174] This endorsement from the training college, testifies to important influences in Smale's understanding of 'Christian charity' – that, in the words of Gracey,

> such an exhibition of Christian charity must be a source of great strength to Christianity generally in that town and neighbourhood *(applause)*. It must be a source of great hopefulness to them and to their minister especially, because it told him he could lean upon a wider constituency than his church for sympathy, prayer and fraternal help in the work to which he had put his hands.[175]

During his time in Ryde, Smale continued to work very comfortably with other Nonconformist denominations, as seen by the fact that within four months of his arrival he was invited to speak at the anniversary services of the Ryde Primitive Methodists. Adding a touch of humour (another characteristic of his mentor, Spurgeon),[176] Smale told the gathered congregation that the world could not do without the Baptist and Methodist communities, in the same way the world could not do without steam – given 'the Methodists supplied the fire and the Baptists the water *(laughter)*'.[177]

Smale then issued a clarion call, that 'all the nonconformist bodies in Ryde would work shoulder to shoulder; at present some were standing aloof, which was not right. They ought to sink those differences which tended towards disintegration, and magnify those views that tended to draw them nearer together.'[178] However, within the scope of newspaper accounts, the nature of such 'differences' and common 'views' was, unfortunately, not specified. But here there are important signs of an emerging ecclesiology which would develop and stretch as far as possible to encompass the word and Spirit that was ultimately witnessed in the lead up to events at Azusa Street. Though, of course, within the Ryde context such aspirations remained, by and large, embryonic.

Nonetheless, a development in Smale's pragmatic ecclesiology can be noted, because it signals the start of a significant shift away from the theologically narrower paradigm established under Spurgeon's influence while at the Pastors' College. Under the impact of the recent Downgrade controversy,[179] Spurgeon had required his students, including Smale, to sign a new statement in 1887, refuting any new theology containing notions of compromise of doctrine or adaptations to the 'ever-changing spirit of the age'.[180] The College Conference Minutes were formulated as follows:

---

[174] 'Baptist Ordination at Ryde', *Isle of Wight County Press* 17 May 1890, p. 6.
[175] 'Baptist Ordination at Ryde', p. 6.
[176] Spurgeon, *Autobiography*, 'Pure Fun', II, pp. 435-52.
[177] *Isle of Wight County Press* 6 September 1890, p. 7.
[178] *Isle of Wight County Press* 6 September 1890, p. 7.
[179] For more information on the 'Down-Grade' controversy, see note 145, p. 64.
[180] Nicholls, *Spurgeon*, p. 143.

We, as a body of men, believe in the 'doctrines of grace' – what are popularly styled Calvinistic views. We feel that we could not receive into this our union any who do not unfeignedly believe that salvation is all of the free grace of God from first to last, and is not according to human merit, but by the undeserving favour of God. We believe in the eternal purpose of the Father, the finished redemption of the Son, and the effectual work of the Holy Spirit.[181]

Although Smale was encouraging partnership in the gospel among other Nonconformists in Ryde, he was not one to compromise the essentials of the Christian faith. A broader, almost 'non-denominational' strain of Baptist identity shows signs of emerging in Smale's pastoral ministry from these early days at Ryde, and the core of his ministry remained Bible-based, committed in his own words to presenting 'the unadulterated truth'.[182]

Bible-Based Preaching

Endeavouring to identify the focus and motivation for elements incorporated in Smale's formation is presumed possible by means of correlating perspectives which are reminiscent of Spurgeon during the controversies of the previous decades. Both men were contending for doctrinal purity based on scripture, although it has to be recognised that Spurgeon's stance had national and international import, often dealing with denominations as a whole, whereas Smale was working in a local town context, where relationships and theologies were much easier to interpret. To illustrate the background behind much of their shared convictions, Spurgeon, writing in the year that Smale started as a student, had penned the following attack on modern heresies as sufficient reason to remain separate from new connections:

> the atonement is scouted, the inspiration of scripture is derided, the Holy Spirit is degraded into an influence, the punishment of sin is turned into fiction, the Resurrection into a myth, yet the enemies of our faith expect us to call them brethren and maintain a confederacy with them.[183]

Not all within their denomination were convinced by Spurgeon's polemic, but 'his influence remained particularly powerful among the Baptists through men trained for the ministry at his college'.[184] The fact that the spiritual tide of Britain was seemingly so far out increased the urgency for Evangelicals of every denomination to concentrate upon evangelism for the salvation of sinners, by agreeing the fundamental tenets of the gospel. Therefore, for Smale

---

[181] Nicholls, *Spurgeon*, p. 143.

[182] 'Baptist Anniversary at Newport', *The Isle of Wight County Press* 20 February 1892, p. 6.

[183] C.H. Spurgeon, *The Sword and The Trowel* (August, 1887), p. 379.

[184] Bebbington, *Evangelicalism in Modern Britain*, p. 146.

it was an applied emphasis that he placed upon 'the nobility of personal service', urging the study of the Bible to enable Christians to meet the social and political questions of the day.[185]

According to Smale's convictions, the emphasis on God's revelation through his holy word was the unequivocal foundation that alone could unite Christians across the churches. So it was that Smale linked to a cross-denominational group in Ryde that attended various events, including 'The Bible Christians' anniversary meeting where he gave the address in 1891.[186] Interestingly, following the death of Spurgeon at the end of January 1892, Smale took the opportunity at his very next meeting to specify how he personally regarded the battle lines facing the 'Church in the world' as opposed to the 'Church Triumphant'. Expressing that 'there was a current of thought which was quite adverse to … the cardinal truths of revelation',[187] Smale continued by stating that Christ's church in the world 'should be a permanent protest to infidelity and to a life of sin'. Smale exhorted that 'the lives of Christians should be real and not such caricatures of Christian life as were only too evident around them … They were to prove both in business and home life that they were the better, brighter and nobler for being Christians.'[188]

Such brief newspaper synopses of sermons like those noted above naturally have limitations in establishing Smale's systematic theological positions. Suffice it to say that overall it appears Smale shared the same doctrinal and ethical basis of Evangelical faith as his mentor, Spurgeon.

In the course of a sermon in 1892, Smale paid public tribute to the life of C.H. Spurgeon. Coming just two weeks after Spurgeon's death, Smale affirmed his personal respect for Spurgeon, both as a man and his gift of preaching.

> That night they thought of one whom they called a friend to the churches of this land, as well as one who was regarded as the greatest preacher God had given to this age – Charles Haddon Spurgeon. They thanked God for the gift, and as God gave, God had taken away, and they would endeavour to have grace to say: 'Blessed be the name of the Lord'.[189]

Innovations

Visible signs of life and growth at Park Road Baptist Church were evident within months of their new pastor's arrival. Smale's creativity utilised opportunities afforded within the church calendar and without. The striking features of some of his innovations certainly caused interest and provoked

---

[185] 'Anniversary at Park Road Chapel', *The Isle of Wight Times* 5 March 1891, p. 5.

[186] 'The Bible Christians', *The Isle of Wight County Press* 24 October 1891, p. 8.

[187] 'Baptist Anniversary at Newport', *The Isle of Wight County Press* 20 February 1892, p. 6.

[188] 'Baptist Anniversary at Newport', p. 6.

[189] 'Baptist Anniversary at Newport', p. 6.

comment in the local press, such as 'the pastor may be congratulated in inaugurating a novelty so far as dissenting places of worship are concerned, in the town'.[190] This specific compliment referred to a flower service that Joseph Smale arranged for midsummer morning. Given that such novel ideas drew extensive comment in newspapers, a few further examples illustrate Smale's ability to find new ways of connecting his ministry of the preached word with his church's ministry to the local community, thus reinforcing the Spurgeonic influences upon his early ministry.[191]

Smale was astutely aware of the power of the local media's potential to make an impact locally. To that end the strategic emphasis of his early work concentrated upon a number of entrepreneurial ideas such as a regular magazine distributed to the locality, lectures, and social gatherings. A further observation from newspaper archives in the Isle of Wight, which, although seemingly superficial, does highlight an important facet of Smale's ministry as it develops over the decades. Basically, he knew how to utilise the local press, with evidence suggesting that Smale was adept at submitting regular press releases, given the regularity of church information appearing in the local papers compared to before his arrival. Further, on a number of occasions different newspapers reported events from Park Road Baptist Church using the same words and phrases.

'Sales of work' had typified a denominational attitude to combine fund raising and outreach. However, Smale set about creating another significant method of communication with the locality through the publication of a monthly magazine, entitled *The Park Road Baptist Visitor*.[192] The use of the printed word in magazine style is not surprising given the influence of Spurgeon's publishing house on a global scale. Certainly the content of Smale's effort in the first edition is described as 'of a high class character'. In the *Isle of Wight County Press* report, Smale's magazine incorporated 'an able and eloquent sermon [by Smale], of much literary merit'.[193]

Communication was at the heart of this venture. The magazine included positive information to share with the public, namely that the church's income over the past year had exceeded £300, and that church growth over the year was encouraging, as over '40 persons were added to the membership of the church'. The article concludes by stating that 'the magazine is well produced, and is calculated to be of great service in connection with the work of the church'. All

---

[190] 'A Flower Service at Park Road Chapel', *The Isle of Wight Times* 26 June 1890, p. 4.

[191] These examples of Smale's entrepreneurial projects suggest a subject requiring further research regarding the degree to which Spurgeonic influence impacted Evangelical methods of proclamation, outreach and publicity in the latter nineteenth and early-twentieth century.

[192] *The Isle of Wight County Press* 7 February 1891, p. 8.

[193] *The Isle of Wight County Press* 7 February 1891, p. 8.

such affirmations stand in stark contrast to the lack of mention of Park Road Baptist Chapel in newspapers prior to his arrival.

In February 1892, a variation of *The Park Road Baptist Visitor* magazine was published for the first time, called *The Park Road Pulpit*.[194] That title, with inevitable echoes of Spurgeon's more famous *Metropolitan Tabernacle Pulpit*, was to contain one of Smale's sermons every month.[195] A corollary of such initiatives demonstrates that, from the outset of his ministry, Smale exemplified a natural gifting for administration and organisation to enable ministry opportunities.

Evidence of Smale's organizational ability will be noted in subsequent chapters in a range of projects from church planting to starting a mission.[196] Perhaps it was something of Smale's innate bent for organisation that frustrated Frank Bartleman in 1905 just prior to the Azusa Street Revival in Los Angeles. One of Bartleman's severe criticisms[197] was that Smale was far too dependent upon, and constricted by, human organisation rather than allowing the Holy Spirit freedom to lead. Hence comments such as, the 'New Testament Church seemed to be losing the spirit of prayer as they increased their organisation'.[198]

Social Concerns

Following the example of his mentor, Spurgeon, Smale similarly responded to various social needs within the wider community, well beyond the confines of local church membership at Park Road Baptist Chapel. A couple of examples illustrate this, with links to London and within the Isle of Wight context.

Having left College Smale continued to support Spurgeon's own initiative at the Stockwell Orphanage. Within his first year of ministry in Ryde, Smale organised for a group of boys from the London orphanage to visit the Isle of Wight, which resulted in the sum of £30.10s.9d being raised for the ongoing work at the orphanage. In response to this generosity, Spurgeon wrote to Smale in what is the only extant direct correspondence between the two men. From Mentone, at Christmas 1890, Spurgeon wrote one of his characteristically brief notes,[199] which requires no further comment here, other than attributing

---

[194] *The Isle of Wight County Press* 13 February 1892, p. 6.

[195] The launch edition's message was entitled 'The Abiding Lord', a discourse based on the words 'Lo, I am with you always, even unto the end of the world' (Matthew 28:20). This particular sermon had, in fact, been Smale's New Year sermon for 1892.

[196] Smale began significant works in China (see chapter 5), as well as the formation of the Spanish Gospel Mission (see chapter 6).

[197] This is examined further in chapter 4.

[198] F. Bartleman, *Azusa Street: The Roots of Modern Day Pentecost* (Logos International, 1980), p. 31.

[199] Nicholls, *Spurgeon*, pp. 28-31, for examples of Spurgeon's written communications.

significance to Smale's organizational ability, and once more his personal acquaintance with Spurgeon himself.

> Dear Mr Smale,
> I am grateful both to you and to Mr Pearson. Please convey my thanks to your congregation and to all the generous helpers in Ryde by whom the grand sum of £30 10s.9d has been made up. To hosts, donors, chairmen, pastors, deacons, etc., hearty thanks from me, and may the blessing of the Father of the fatherless rest on them. I am not well, but I wish you well. God speed you richly.
> Yours very heartily,
> C.H. Spurgeon.[200]

Besides the natural bond between Smale and the work of his mentor, it is important to note that there were other social needs closer to home that Smale and his church also supported, such as the £3.10s. raised at the 1890 'Hospital Sunday' in Ryde.[201]

A second example presents a more local case, in which Smale took a public stand in support of the Sunday Closing Bill debated in Ryde during October 1891. At stake was the question of whether public houses should remain open on Sundays or not. To provide a sense of the tone of debate in one public meeting, owners of public houses were quoted as agreeing that they would be 'very glad indeed to close their houses on Sunday. They lived in a polluted atmosphere of beer, spirits and tobacco, and had no Sunday to look forward to.'[202] It would seem that Smale was a lone voice in that particular meeting, as somebody lamented the 'absence of clergy from the parish'.[203]

When Smale seconded the motion that a petition in support of the Sunday Closing Bill be signed and forwarded to both Houses of Parliament, he made the following three comments. First, he defended the other Nonconformist ministers who 'were kept away by other meetings'. Then, secondly, Smale issued a blunt challenge to the other church leaders to show more passion on such issues, stating, 'very little would be done in Ryde in this matter for a long time, unless they put more conscience into it; they were not at all enthusiastic on this vital question *(A voice: show your Christianity)*'. To the heckler, Smale replied that he 'endeavoured to do so by his life and work *(applause)*'. Finally, Smale expressed the broader hope that 'the time would come when Sunday railway labour would be done away *(A voice: and every chapel)*'.[204] Such debate provides a useful glimpse at another aspect of Smale at work in a secular

---

[200] 'The Stockwell Orphanage', *The Isle of Wight County Press* 3 January 1891, p. 6.
[201] 'The Ryde Primitive Methodists', *The Isle of Wight County Press* 6 September 1890, p. 7.
[202] 'Sunday Closing', *The Isle of Wight County Press* 10 October 1891, p. 7
[203] 'Sunday Closing', p. 7.
[204] 'Sunday Closing', p. 7.

milieu, on the cutting edge, where social concerns overlapped with his Christian principles for the welfare of society and community life.

Farewell Reflections

On Sunday 11 September 1892, Smale preached his final sermons at the Park Road Baptist Church to large congregations.[205] The following Tuesday evening a tea and public meeting were held, during which Smale was presented with a farewell cheque for £10 along with a travel bag,[206] and his mother, Ann, was given a handbag.[207]

However, his departure was marked by the conflicting emotions referred to earlier. The gratitude he expressed to the majority of members for their 'passionate devotion' was tempered by his righteous anger at those who had displayed only 'bad character'.[208] Claiming to be fearless in the 'face of any man', Smale publicly rebuked the group within the church who had 'cruelly deceived' him. 'Some had proved cowards, mean and selfish, and had shirked their responsibility, leaving him to struggle on with a burden on his shoulders that had well nigh crushed him to the earth *(shame!)*.'[209]

After twenty-eight months sacrificial[210] ministry among the people, Smale's personal conclusions concerning the future of the work were that the church at Park Road should keep its doors open, except he urged the people to 'go as a body to George Street, and come there on Sunday evenings'. But he warned the work would never be carried on at Park Road if those in leadership positions were going to remain so. Such was the parting that even the positive record of tasks accomplished – membership increased and debt sizably reduced[211] – could not diminish Smale's sense of what might have been. 'Had he had the cooperation of the church as a whole, there would not have been a farthing of debt on the place.' But a minority who displayed a 'disposition to be kings' had obviously created insurmountable challenges for Smale to progress his ministry further.[212]

---

[205] *The Isle of Wight Times & Hampshire Gazette* 15 September 1892, p. 5.

[206] *The Isle of Wight Observer* 17 September 1892, p. 5.

[207] 'Farewell of the Rev. J. Smale', p. 7. Joseph Smale had been joined on the Isle of Wight by his mother and sister, Mary Hannah, sometime during his first year of ministry in Ryde. All three are listed as sharing the manse accommodation. See 1891 English Census: Place – Ryde, Hampshire; District 13; Entry 167.

[208] 'Farewell of the Rev. J. Smale', p. 7.

[209] 'Farewell of the Rev. J. Smale', p. 7.

[210] In Smale's own words, he had gone to Ryde 'being a young man with no liabilities ... [he] was prepared to make sacrifices, which he had done *(applause)*. He should have been hundreds of pounds better off if he had not come there.'

[211] The initial debt of £300 at the start of Smale's ministry was reduced to under £100 by the end.

[212] 'Farewell of the Rev. J. Smale', p. 7.

There are signs that one of the deceptions Smale felt, concerned the level of financial support for himself. With the evidence to hand, it would appear that after nearly three years with them Smale was frustrated by their inability to pay him adequately, or another pastor after him for that matter. Hence, Smale's conclusion that, 'they were not in a prepared state to ask a man to shepherd them, because they were not able financially to support a shepherd in a respectable manner'.[213]

Even if elements of his own church did not appreciate their departing pastor, a forward glance at Smale's later connections in Los Angeles, which also stretched across denominational lines prior to the Azusa Street Revival, illustrates an interesting parallel here. It should be particularly noted that even as a twenty-five year old, Smale was held in high esteem by the broader Christian community in Ryde. Although a brief pastorate, Smale had worked in partnership with other Nonconformist denominations. His self-assessment was that the Christians of the town had given him much 'confidence, esteem and love'. This certainly seems to be borne out by various tributes from other church leaders reported at his farewell, including this parting comment from the Rev. A.G. Short, the minister of the Sandown Baptist church:

> Smale's leaving would be a real loss to many of them … He would carry away with him the respect and esteem of a large number of Ryde Christians *(voices: hear hear)*.[214]

There is no evidence to hand as to how Smale made contact with his next church. Certainly it was not uncommon for students from Spurgeon's College to be recommended for Baptist pastorates in other countries. At the Newport Baptist anniversary just prior to Smale's departure, mention was made of four other scholars from their Sunday school who 'had passed the Metropolitan College, two of whom were now in America'.[215] Aware of the approval of those in that congregation who voiced that hearty '*hear hear*,' Joseph Smale left the Isle of Wight bound for new ministry in the United States of America.

---

[213] 'Farewell of the Rev. J. Smale', p. 7.
[214] 'Farewell of the Rev. J. Smale', p. 7.
[215] 'Baptist Anniversary in Newport', *The Isle of Wight County Press* 20 February 1892, p. 6.

CHAPTER 3

Smale's Preparation for Revival (1893–1904)

The Lone Star Baptist Church, Prescott, Arizona (1893–97)

Sailing from Liverpool on the ship *Etruria*, twenty-five year old pastor Smale arrived in America on 17 October 1892,[1] and began his second pastorate at Prescott in March 1893.[2] However, other than those few facts, there is no further information recording his relocation from the Isle of Wight to Prescott, the capital of the Arizona Territory. The cultural contrasts facing Smale between Britain and America, Ryde and Prescott, can only be presumed to have required immense adjustment for the young English pastor. What can be more precisely gauged is the mission context for this next phase of Smale's ministry, and the connexions and experience gained in Arizona prior to his call to Los Angeles.

Smale was part of a second wave of missionary minded pastors to arrive in Prescott. A Methodist missionary, the Rev. A.G. Reeder, had established the first church in the town in 1872, amid 'plenty of saloons and gambling halls for the thirsty Bradshaw miners and soldiers from nearby Fort Whipple'.[3] In her research into the early development of churches in Prescott, Florence Yount describes how much of the town's reputation in the late nineteenth century would have 'centred around Whiskey Row ... renowned for its fights and murders', the 'recent gold discovery' and 'the Apache Indians'.[4]

In this milieu, the first Methodist missionary Reeder was soon joined by a Baptist pastor, the Rev. R.A. Windes and his family, who, in August 1879 travelled '2,020 miles in a covered wagon drawn by a mule'[5] to establish the Lone Star Baptist Church in Prescott.[6] This pioneer Baptist work, inaugurated on 11 August 1880 with only five members, was named in recognition of 'the great Pentecostal revival of the Lone Star Mission among the Telugus of

---

[1] Ellis Island Foundation; American Family Immigration History Centre: Passenger Records, 1892 Arrivals.

[2] 'In Memorium: Obituary of Helena Dunham Smale', *Arizona Baptist Association Minutes* (1894–1895), p. 13.

[3] 'Prescott: A Century of Coexistence', *The Arizona Republic* 1 September 1979, Section C, p. 1.

[4] 'Prescott: A Century of Coexistence', Section C, p. 1.

[5] First Baptist Church Prescott, Arizona, *Eighty Years With Christ* (n.p., 1960), p. 3. This is a brochure which covers the years 1880–1960.

[6] The name 'Lone Star Baptist Church' was later changed (in 1934) to 'First Baptist Church Prescott'.

India'.[7] The 'Lone Star' name and Indian revival referred to are not without significance in a study analysing patterns of spiritual revival, because the background provides key insights into Windes' vision for the emerging Baptist work in Prescott. Comparison of how the 'Lone Star', as it was referred to, could expand into a constellation, so the 1840s pioneer Baptist missionaries among the Indian Telugus had prayed and worked painstakingly at great personal sacrifice, with the hope of future gospel expansion. Growth explosion eventually occurred dramatically, as historian Thomas Armitage records, citing how one Telugus church at Ongole formed in June 1867, with eight members, grew to more than 16,000 members by 1881; with 2,222 of them having been baptised in one day alone. According to Armitage, 'the Ongole Church had become the largest in the world'.[8]

With prayers and vision for a similar Pentecostal revival occurring in 'the driest spot on earth'[9] in Arizona, Pastor Windes and the church members at Lone Star Baptist, Prescott, immediately began ministry, sharing one Bible and one hymn book, owned by their pastor, between them. 'Revival spirit began to grow ... and about twelve or fifteen had professed faith and were baptised in a nice baptistry which the members had constructed in a nearby stream'.[10] Soon after they began their first building programme, 'erecting a $2800 building on Academy Hill', later relocated to South Cortez Street in 1884.[11] Following the two brief pastorates of the Rev. J.M. Green and the Rev. C.A. Rice, both from the 'Home Mission Society', Joseph Smale became the fourth minister in thirteen years to take on the pioneering Baptist work. This was the setting for church life and ministry when Smale arrived to begin his pastorate in October 1893,[12] with the church membership roll numbering forty-three.

The context of an emerging town like Prescott merits description to provide a portrayal of life as Smale would have encountered it upon his arrival in the Territory. Physically, with a population of 4,000[13] the town was tackling 'problems of developing water and sewer systems ... and the need for pavement of streets and sidewalks'.[14] Spiritually and culturally the church was engaging with the transience of a shifting population in a busy mining town and

---

[7] First Baptist Church Prescott, Arizona, *Our Early History* (n.p., [1955]), p. 3. This is the church's diamond jubilee brochure covering the years 1880–1955.

[8] T. Armitage, *A History of the Baptists: The American Baptists, Foreign Missions – Asia and Europe* (New York, 1890), http://www.fbinstitute.com/armitage/ch13.html, accessed 24 August 2006.

[9] 'Prescott: A Century of Coexistence', Section C, p. 1.

[10] First Baptist Church Prescott, Arizona, *Our Early History*, p. 3.

[11] First Baptist Church Prescott, Arizona, *Eighty Years With Christ*, p. 7.

[12] *Arizona Weekly Journal Miner* 25 October, 1893, p. 3.

[13] H.L. Sutton and P.H. Yeomans, *Our History, Our Heritage, Our Homes, Our Hopes* (First Baptist Church Los Angeles, 1999), p. 10.

[14] First Baptist Church Prescott, Arizona, *The Ninetieth Anniversary* (n.p., 1970), p.20.

the inevitable features of a town attempting to establish an infrastructure with businesses in their infancy. All of 'this made the pastors feel insecure. The salary was low, housing poor, and the church members few.'[15]

'Spiritually faithful during these years of testing'

This heading from the archives of these embryonic years at Lone Star Baptist Church, Prescott, is a useful banner to frame all that is known about Smale's ministry within the church's evolution. Of the few notable features of his four year pastorate were developments which were characteristic of his time at Park Road Baptist Church on the Isle of Wight, as well as every subsequent church he led. Within the scope of this chapter they contribute to the identification of pertinent factors to Smale's preparation, personal and ecclesiological, for the revival he would later experience in Los Angeles.

EVANGELISM AND MISSION

Within Prescott and the wider Arizona Territory, Smale trained a team from the church to go out on missions, for what they described as 'protracted evangelistic meetings', often for a few days at a time using covered wagons to cross the deserts and mountains.[16] Besides this, visiting evangelists were welcomed to Prescott and in 1894 Smale organised the first 'Missionary Society' at Lone Star Baptist, noted for its inclusion of 'men and women'.[17] The church records describe this as 'a layman's group' which 'was very faithful and active in different areas of the work'.[18] The group's objectives also 'included the study and discussion of the, then little known Mission fields and Missionaries'.[19] At one of the Arizona Baptist Association meetings in 1897, Smale was commended for his evangelistic initiative in organising street meetings; something their Association historian considered should be revived.[20] All such signs point to Smale's cluster of giftings being primarily as a missionary pastor-evangelist-teacher.

---

[15] First Baptist Church Prescott, Arizona, *The Ninetieth Anniversary*, p. 20.

[16] R.A. Windes, 'Early History of the Arizona Baptist Association' (n.d., hand written paper), p. 5.

[17] First Baptist Church Prescott, Arizona, *Eighty Years With Christ*, p. 11.

[18] First Baptist Church Prescott, Arizona, *The Ninetieth Anniversary*, p. 20.

[19] First Baptist Church Prescott, *Programme for the Historical Pageant of Arizona Baptists*, Scene 4 (18 May 1962).

[20] Windes, *Early History of the Arizona Baptist Association*, p. 5.

Figure 8: Lone Star Baptist Church, Prescott, c.1895.
Photograph courtesy of First Baptist Church, Prescott, Arizona.

CONTEMPORARY INNOVATIONS

A number of additions during Smale's ministry deserve mention, in part because they provide contextual descriptions of an emerging work, but also because each one indicates some important emphases for pastor and people. A resolution in a minute of the church's record book, dated January 1894, that 'whereas this Church building is lacking in the necessities of comfortable worship, that this Church, here and now, commit itself to the forward step of a new building, which shall be of a character worthy of its location in the beautiful city of Prescott',[21] produced numerous projects. Later in 1894 the first organ was purchased[22] and in 1896 electric lights were installed, thus enabling the church to host the Territorial Convention in that year.[23] Significantly different from Smale's experience of church finances at Ryde, was the fact that the Prescott church's budget excluded any contributions from bazaars or food sales.[24] The focus was predominantly on missionary work, and all such fabric alterations were regarded within the gospel mandate.

---

[21] First Baptist Church Prescott, Arizona, *The Ninetieth Anniversary*, p. 10.
[22] A Mason-Hamlin organ, price $700.
[23] First Baptist Church Prescott, Arizona, *The Ninetieth Anniversary*, p. 14.
[24] First Baptist Church Prescott, Arizona, *The Ninetieth Anniversary*, p. 20.

LECTURE TOURS

There was one aspect of Smale's wider speaking ministry that extended well beyond specifically doctrinal, or even Christian, orientated proclamation. During 1894 he embarked on a number of tours throughout the valley to 'deliver a series of temperance lectures',[25] 'a recital of one of Gough's Orations',[26] and a 'humorous' lecture about 'Life in Spurgeon's Seminary'.[27] *The Arizona Republican* newspaper described Smale as 'a speaker of great ability'[28] having 'earned a reputation for eloquence in Phoenix', and certain to attract large audiences.[29]

THE ARIZONA BAPTIST ASSOCIATION

'For twelve long years', since its formation in 1881, the 'Arizona Central Baptist Association' had not met[30] due mainly to the long distances and poor transportation within the Territory. However, in 1893 the network of likeminded Baptists was rekindled under the slightly altered name 'The Arizona Baptist Association'. Smale's involvement stands out, as already mentioned above in terms of his practical mission initiatives, but also his leadership role, as 'the association proceeded to elect ... Rev. Joseph Smale, of Prescott, for moderator'.[31] At various meetings during his four years at Prescott, he is recorded as leading Association services, praying, and preaching. On one occasion *The Baptist Evangel* judged that 'Brother Smale makes a good moderator, presiding in moderation'.[32] His preaching was also appreciated. Before 'a large congregation' assembled at The First Baptist Church of Phoenix, Smale preached the closing sermon on the text, 'Those things which are the most surely believed among us'. The report states, 'this was a most able and thoughtful sermon'.[33]

One other initiative warrants brief comment during Smale's time in this Association, namely the 'beginning of Baptist Youth Training'. Records of 1894 illustrate the emphatic 'importance of enlisting and training young people in Christian work and that the young people's work should be fostered and encouraged throughout the denomination in every Baptist church in the

---

[25] *The Arizona Republican* (Phoenix), 12 April 1894, p. 1.
[26] *The Arizona Republican* (Phoenix), 12 April 1894, p. 1. John B Gough (1817–86) was a temperance reformer, renowned in his day as an international celebrity throughout America and Great Britain.
[27] *The Arizona Republican* (Phoenix), 22 April 1894, p. 1.
[28] *The Arizona Republican*, (20 April 1894), p. 1.
[29] *The Arizona Republican*, (22 April 1894), p. 1.
[30] Arizona Baptist Association Minutes (1894–1895), p. 21.
[31] 'Arizona Baptist Association', report on meeting of 5 April 1895.
[32] 'Associational Jottings', *The Baptist Evangel* 1.22 (11 April 1895), p. 2.
[33] Arizona Baptist Association, report on meeting of 5 April 1895.

Territory'.[34] Smale later addressed this same subject in his sermon delivered at the young people's session of the Los Angeles Baptist Association in 1898.[35]

The degree of Smale's faithfulness in ministry within somewhat difficult settings – the limited resources and living in an 'inadequate apartment that was built on at the rear of the church'[36] – was incomparable to the year of testing that was his in 1895. First, however, some further biographical information is required.

Marriage to Helena Dunham

It is not clear how or where Smale met Helena Dunham, who previously had worked as a school governess in Worthing, England.[37] The fact that she sailed from Southampton to New York, arriving on 16 September 1893[38] and was married to Joseph Smale within five days (at Vincennes, Indiana, on 21 September 1893),[39] indicates their romance had started a year or more earlier, before he had left England for America. Upon their arrival as the newlywed Mr and Mrs Smale, Helena obviously endeared herself immediately to the people of Prescott, teaching a Sunday school class of young children, leading and speaking at church Bible study meetings,[40] and supporting Joseph as a 'beloved wife, wise counsellor, and [his] efficient helper'.[41]

However, after just thirteen months in Prescott, Helena Dunham Smale died on 29 January 1895, aged twenty-seven.[42] She had been ill for a few days following the birth and death of their first baby.[43] Perhaps with a hint of prophetic statement regarding what lay just ahead, Joseph Smale had commenced 1895 with his new year sermon entitled 'Divine Solutions to the Mystery of Suffering'.[44] This was in fact the last church service that Helena Smale attended.[45] Certainly, these were dark days for Joseph Smale, having

---

[34] First Baptist Church Prescott, *Programme for the Historical Pageant of Arizona Baptists*, Scene 6.

[35] J. Smale, 'Lessons in Personal Work', *The Pacific Baptist* 22.43 (24 October 1898), p. 8.

[36] First Baptist Church Prescott, Arizona, *The Ninetieth Anniversary*, p. 20.

[37] 1891 England Census, West Sussex, Broadwater, Worthing, RG12/836.

[38] Ship Name: *New York*, New York Passenger Lists, 1893, Microfilm Roll M237_618, Line 27, p. 11.

[39] Indiana Marriage Records Index (1845–1920), 21 September 1893, Knox County Indiana, Book C-13, OS Page 326.

[40] *Arizona Weekly Journal Miner* 3 January 1894, p. 6.

[41] 'In Memorium: Obituary of Helena Dunham Smale', p. 13.

[42] 'In Memorium: Obituary of Helena Dunham Smale', p. 13.

[43] *Arizona Weekly Journal Miner* 30 January 1895, p. 5.

[44] *Arizona Weekly Journal Miner* 2 January 1895, p. 7.

[45] Obituary Records, Sharlot Museum, Prescott, Arizona, p. 415.

buried his baby, then laying his wife to rest at Prescott Cemetery.[46] Both the secular newspapers and the Baptist records pay profuse tribute to the 'high esteem in which Sister Smale was held, both in her own church, and in the community at large'.[47] The *Arizona Weekly Journal Miner* provides a very detailed and moving account of the funeral service, reporting how all the Prescott pastors took part along with a choir, and the Rev. S.C. Davis of Phoenix Baptist Church preaching 'a very touching sermon'.[48] Paying tribute to Helena Smale, Davis linked her successful life and ministry previously in England with the enriching time, albeit brief, that she had spent among them in Arizona, describing

> those charming Christian graces which made her brief life, of thirteen months in Prescott, so potent for righteousness ... her class in Prescott will not forget her ardent devotion for their salvation.[49]

Joseph Smale, very naturally the 'sorrow stricken husband',[50] had to maintain ministry among the people at Prescott while far from his own native family and friends. In light of his bereavement it is noteworthy to add that a year later Joseph was joined by his own mother, Ann Smale, by then aged sixty-three, who left England to join him in Prescott.[51] In fact, Ann Smale would remain in America, alongside her son throughout all the significant events in Los Angeles which are central to this biographical study, right up to her death in 1911.[52]

During Smale's four years in Prescott, the Lone Star Baptist Church had grown from forty-three to 125 members, and with his growing popularity and noted speaking ability, his wider connexions had brought Pastor Joseph Smale to the attention of a prestigious church in Los Angeles.

First Baptist Church Los Angeles, California (1897–1905)

Late in 1897 First Baptist Church Los Angeles, was facing a time of considerable difficulty due to the illness and subsequent resignation of both their pastors. During the infirmity of its associate minister, the Rev. J. Herndon Garnett, and Dr Daniel Read (who died shortly afterwards),[53] the church called

---

[46] Plot 1/E – 80, Oddfellows Cemetery, Prescott, Arizona.
[47] *Arizona Weekly Journal Miner* 6 February 1895, p. 7.
[48] *Arizona Weekly Journal Miner* 6 February 1895, p. 7.
[49] 'In Memorium: Obituary of Helena Dunham Smale', p. 13.
[50] Obituary Records, Sharlot Museum, Prescott, Arizona, p. 415.
[51] Ship Name: *Servia*, New York Passenger Lists, 1896, Microfilm Roll M237_664, line 1.
[52] 'Deaths: Mrs Ann Smale', *Los Angeles Times* 30 January 1911, p. 118.
[53] 'Los Angeles Baptist Association Minutes: 1898' (Southern California Baptist Convention Minutes 1894–1904), p. 49.

Joseph Smale to leave Prescott temporarily, to supply their pulpit at $75 a month,[54] which he did for three months. Facing the considerable loss of two pastors in as many months, Smale described his own felt inadequacy regarding the 'strange providence' of God in being called to minister 'during the lamented absence of [their] beloved pastors'.[55]

'Smale was on the spot and available' and was swiftly called to become the fourth Pastor of First Baptist Church Los Angeles, though not unanimously.[56] Many of the ten percent of members who were against his appointment[57] were to remain vociferous opponents of Smale over the following eight years. This is an important fact that lies behind some of the contributory factors which created the context for revival at First Baptist Church Los Angeles, to be presented in the next section. In spite of minority opposition, Smale formally accepted the church's call to the pastorate on Sunday 30 January 1898, 'declaring the purpose of his ministry to preach Jesus Christ only'.[58]

To gain a cursory understanding of this church's DNA, it is profitable to start at the beginning with a brief resume. The eleven charter members who established First Baptist Church in 1874 were soon serving in a rapidly growing city, and by 1895 there were 'a dozen Baptist churches in Los Angeles and its suburbs'.[59] Indeed, in the early years church growth at First Baptist practically doubled every five years[60] in line with the city's population explosion,[61] primarily due to the large number of newcomers arriving in the Los Angeles area. The establishment of a sizable Sunday school, revival meetings, and numerous mission works[62] added to the membership of what soon gained a reputation as one of the eminent churches in southern California. It was not surprising, therefore, that the church possessed a growing optimism regarding her capabilities and opportunities. In a detailed analysis charting Protestant church development in Los Angeles, G.H. Singleton observes that First Baptist

---

[54] H.L. Sutton, *Our Heritage and Our Hope* (First Baptist Church Los Angeles, 1974), p. 22.

[55] For Smale's felt inadequacy at the call to First Baptist Church Los Angeles, see Smale, *Our Church Quarterly*, II.1, p. 1.

[56] 'At The Churches Yesterday', *Los Angeles Times* 24 January 1898, p. 5.

[57] Sutton and Yeomans, *Our History, Our Heritage, Our Homes, Our Hopes*, p. 10. Although in Smale's 'Open Letter' (3 September 1903), he refers to a specific number of twenty-one members opposing his appointment.

[58] 'At the Churches Yesterday', *Los Angeles Times* 31 January 1898, p. 10.

[59] Sutton, *Our Heritage and Our Hope*, pp. 5 and 16.

[60] Sutton, *Our Heritage and Our Hope*, p. 16.

[61] G.H. Singleton, *Religion in the City of Angels: American Protestant Culture and Urbanization Los Angeles 1850–1930* (UMI Research Press, 1979), p. 70. The population of LA more than doubled from 50,393 in 1890 to 102,479 in 1900.

[62] Singleton, *Religion in the City of Angels*, p. 17. E.g., First Baptist Church Los Angeles sponsored Chinese and Spanish mission works.

quickly became the 'primary agent' of interdenominational activity in the city during the 1880s.

> Most of the cooperative meetings and worship services were held there [First Baptist], and the congregation gave generously to Presbyterian, Methodist, Episcopal, and Congregational groups as well as to fellow Baptists, to aid in the construction of new church buildings.[63]

Figure 9: Los Angeles city view, 1884, with First Baptist Church (1884–98) in the middle distance. Photograph courtesy of the California Historical Society, Ticor/Pierce Collection.

Through the 1890s, 'excellent' attendances exceeded 100 at their weekly prayer meetings. The church actively supported missionary enterprises at home and abroad, to the extent that 'the church was reputed for its generosity throughout the entire denomination'.[64] As we have already noted, by the time of Smale's arrival in Los Angeles, First Baptist Church was already supporting other smaller struggling churches more locally, as well as the Chinese Mission's evening classes and the Berean Mission's industrial training school in the poorer part of the city.[65]

---

[63] Singleton, *Religion in the City of Angels*, p. 57. In 1887 First Baptist Church Los Angeles appointed an assistant pastor, A.W. Rider, to coordinate interdenominational activities.

[64] Sutton, *Our Heritage and Our Hope*, p. 19.

[65] Sutton, *Our Heritage and Our Hope*, p. 19. However, not every church project was successful. For instance, the hope of establishing a Baptist university which, according to the records, would be 'worthy of ourselves, worthy of our denomination

Mention of these facets of church life uncovers more than sample activities accomplished. By identifying some of the personnel involved in this pioneering phase of church life also provides an illustration of the composition of members, who were predominantly from the higher echelons of society. The membership list included many 'movers' and 'shakers' from the Los Angeles' upper middle class[66] who inevitably brought high expectations from their professional lives to bear upon church life and practice. Highlighting just five such prominent members who were to figure significantly in Smale's later life and ministry, were the likes of generous benefactor and hotelier Mr I.N. van Nuys, Professor Alonzo Potter (Head of the Fairfield Conservatory of Music), Professor Melville Dozier, surgeon Dr Henry Keyes, and capitalist Charles Keyser, whose daughter Smale married in 1898.

Inevitably, with few alternative attractions for the Los Angeles populace on Sundays,[67] as early as 1892 the church's sanctuary and adjoining rooms were proving inadequate for the growing numbers and ministries, and therefore a new building project was launched. Significantly, in contrast with the building that became the home of the Azusa Street Mission at 312 Azusa Street, First Baptist Church explained, with illuminative justification, that, 'while God would honor sincere and acceptable worship offered in a barn', the church felt it necessary 'that a due regard should be given to the reasonable demands of enlightened and cultured taste'. In addition, 'for several years the membership had been longing for better quarters, for more room, greater facilities for work, less disturbing noise from without, and comforts to which we could, with better grace, introduce and welcome strangers and new members'.[68] So by the time Smale became pastor he was preaching to large congregations which had necessitated the construction of their new building at 727 South Flower Street (see Figure 10), with seating capacity for 1,200 in the main sanctuary, extendable by a 'disappearing partition' to 2,000 when required.[69] This new building was opened at a dedication service 'to the service of God' on 10 April 1898, followed by a week of evangelistic meetings.[70] Statistics available at the end of his first year record that Smale had baptised fifty-six people, welcomed

---

and the age and worthy of the Master whom we serve', although realised in 1887, was unable to maintain viability and eventually closed within ten years.

[66] Personal Interview with C.M. Robeck, Jr, the Society for Pentecostal Studies Conference, Marquette University, Milwaukee, 13 March 2004.

[67] Sutton and Yeomans, *Our History, Our Heritage, Our Homes, Our Hopes*, p. 8. First Baptist Church Los Angeles also employed rigorous monthly 'covenant' obligations, requiring members to support the church in person and financially, or risk being removed from the membership roll.

[68] J. Smale, *Our Church Quarterly* II.1 (First Baptist Church Los Angeles, December 1897), p. 2.

[69] Sutton and Yeomans, *Our History, Our Heritage, Our Homes, Our Hopes*, p. 11.

[70] 'Dedicatory Services', *Los Angeles Times* 9 April 1898, p. 11.

195 new church members, making a total church membership of 791, and by all accounts it was still growing.[71]

Figure 10: First Baptist Church Los Angeles, 727 S. Flower Street, c. 1900. Photograph courtesy of the California Historical Society, Ticor/Pierce Collection.

On his arrival, Smale was quick to remind the church of two 'truths that must be kept to the front in all [their] thinking and planning'. Firstly, 'that God indeed is with the church', and, secondly, 'that without doubt He has a great spiritual work for the church now to do'.[72] He developed this theme, thus raising expectation, by stating unequivocal objectives which at the outset of his pastorate resonate with his developing *raison d'être* focusing on revival. Even a month prior to his induction, Smale exhorted the First Baptist congregation with this challenging statement,

---

[71] 'Los Angeles Baptist Association Minutes: 1898' (Southern California Baptist Convention Minutes 1894–1904), p. 49.
[72] Smale, *Our Church Quarterly*, II.1, p. 1.

We are looking for a revival, and several signs of it are already with us. Let us stand for conditions, that, instead of neutralizing, will hasten it to a floodtide of strength.[73]

'The great factors promoting a revival'[74]

Smale's clarity in elucidating his main teaching points on the subject of revival was helpful for the congregation then, but also advantageous to enable a contemporary analysis of his methodical approach over a century later. Symptomatic of Smale's prescriptive and organised style which Bartleman came to despise in 1906, Smale presented 'ten things' that 'will serve a mighty revival' and encouraged each member of the church graphically to personalise them by putting 'one on each finger and thumb as you begin each day, and put them in your heart as you retire each night'.[75] The ten key factors, along with supporting Bible references, are worth citing here in order to grasp the strength and shape of his revival teaching.

> First. Perfect harmony between yourself and every church member. Ephes. iv: 31, 32.
> Second. A living soul ... Expect to see souls saved, and all other things being equal, we shall see souls saved. How can we think that sinners will take God at His word if we don't. God means what He says every time. Hebrews xi: 6.
> Third. A God-possessed heart. This involves a separateness from sin and self, a daily surrender, holy conduct, love in us as a master passion for God, for our fellow church members and for lost souls, a full indwelling of the Holy Spirit. Psalm li: 10-13.
> Fourth. Unceasing prayer for the Spirit to move upon all hearts in the service. John iii: 3.
> Fifth. An unceasing knowledge of the Scriptures. Through the word and Spirit we come to know God. James i:18; 1 Cor. ii:11-12, and they that know their God shall be strong and do exploits.
> Sixth. A painful consciousness that everybody out of Christ is lost. John v:11, 12. Anxious saints make anxious sinners.
> Seventh. A willingness and readiness to cooperate with the church in every spiritual project. A disposition to be anything, and do anything, and go anywhere for the glory of God. It takes more than one stick to kindle a fire ... Acts ix: 6.
> Eighth. Attendance at all the services unless you can render a reason for your absence which you know the Lord will accept. Heb. x:25; Acts iii:3; Luke iv:16.
> Ninth. Being faithful to known duties. Acts iv: 19, 20; Gal. i:15-17. Paul's life opened out so gloriously, and the churches and the world through him were blessed so wondrously, because he was not disobedient to the heavenly vision.

---

[73] Smale, *Our Church Quarterly*, II.1, p. 1.

[74] Smale, *Our Church Quarterly*, II.1, p. 1.

[75] Smale, *Our Church Quarterly*, II.1, p. 2.

Tenth. Last, but not least, a daily habit of family table reading and prayer. Genesis xviii:19; Deut. vi:5-7.[76]

A few themes stand out in this 'How To' bring about revival guide, indicating the nature of Smale's own pneumatological understanding at this stage of his life. In fact, they are the early formulations of convictions that he would develop extensively over the next decade of his life and ministry. In particular, the quintessential 'word' and 'Spirit' paradigm that he was advocating consisted of a quintet of contours, namely, concerted prayer, relational unity, heightened expectation, full surrender and faithful service. These will be explored further in chapter 5, although they are illustrative here in presenting the chronological biographical map of Smale's unfolding life and ministry.

The scene was set for Smale to continue his style and thrust of ministry, which, as noted during his Prescott days, involved his priority of preaching and evangelism, innovative ideas, and the development of broader denominational ministry. However, with the demands and expectations of First Baptist being far superior to those at either of his previous churches, Smale was given the opportunity to face possibilities, as well as challenges, which would have been inconceivable at either Prescott or the Isle of Wight. These are each pertinent to understanding the significance of Smale's major catalytic role over the few years leading to the 1905–06 period of revival in Los Angeles.

'The power of the Spirit in action'[77]

As we have seen, Smale was an evangelist at heart. His evening services were always directed towards the 'unsaved'.[78] In addition, series of evangelistic meetings, normally lasting from one to four weeks were held twice a year, conducted by outside speakers at Smale's invitation. This strategy included eminent speakers such as D.L. Moody,[79] and those less well known such as 'The Boy Preacher', Jack Cooke.[80] At Smale's instigation, Cooke spoke daily at First Baptist for a month of meetings throughout January 1900, which 'from the first the Spirit of God was manifest'. Smale describes how 'twice each day the capacity of our building was taxed to the utmost to accommodate the throngs

---

[76] Smale, *Our Church Quarterly*, II.1, p. 2.

[77] 'Los Angeles Baptist Association Minutes: 1900' (Southern California Baptist Convention Minutes 1898–1904), p. 19.

[78] Sutton, *Our Heritage and Our Hope*, p. 24.

[79] Sutton, *Our Heritage and Our Hope*, p. 24. However, attendances were too large for the 2,000 capacity at First Baptist Church Los Angeles, so after two nights the remaining meetings were moved to 'Hazard's Pavilion'.

[80] First Baptist Church Los Angeles, *Church Bulletin* 21 January 1900. Jack Cooke was a thirteen year old from Manchester, England, who travelled with his father and brother.

which gathered to listen to the simple Gospel from one in whom God held undisputed sway',[81] inferring that the scope of mission extended well beyond the First Baptist congregation, incorporating other denominations from across the city. According to Smale's summary of this particular mission, he regarded statistics with a degree of caution stating that 'where the unseen hand of God operates, the good accomplished and the number of souls awakened into life can never be computed'.[82] He did, however, record the following results, recalling with wonder 'the power of the Spirit in action':

> 286 professed conversion, of which 80 were baptised and united with this church. 64 backsliders were reclaimed, and 158 unsaved ones were under conviction.[83]

'A spirit of unity has been happily manifest'[84]

The church growth and consolidation at First Baptist from 1898 to 1902 were the encouraging consequence of all that Smale was attempting to promote, made all the more conspicuous by the troubled waters that were starting to stir by 1903. The annual report for 1900 itemised some of the 'innumerable blessings' at First Baptist. First, Joseph Smale as pastor was commended for his dependence 'upon the power of the Spirit' as their 'under shepherd and spiritual guide'.[85] Secondly, 'a spirit of unity has been happily manifested'. Thirdly, 'the increase in numbers'. Fourthly, the financial situation of the church 'afforded [them] deep satisfaction'.[86]

Pentecostal Prayer Union of Southern California

Smale's concerted prayer focus prompted an ecumenical partnership in the direction of the Pentecostal Prayer Union of Southern California.[87] Although no information about this particular Union has been forthcoming, the name and shared objectives add weight to the argument that Smale was operating with a wider network of Christians towards the collective hope of Pentecostal outpouring. His participation at a prayer convention in May 1900, held under the auspices of this Prayer Union, records Smale as preaching on 'Prayer in Our Hymnology', an address that extolled songs for the people of God in every generation as 'the best way we have of expressing our joy'.[88] The salient point

---

[81] 'Los Angeles Baptist Association Minutes: 1900', p. 19.
[82] 'Los Angeles Baptist Association Minutes: 1900', p. 19.
[83] 'Los Angeles Baptist Association Minutes: 1900', p. 19.
[84] 'Los Angeles Baptist Association Minutes: 1901', p. 19.
[85] 'Los Angeles Baptist Association Minutes: 1900', p. 19.
[86] 'Los Angeles Baptist Association Minutes: 1900', p. 19.
[87] 'Prayer Convention', *Los Angeles Times* 18 May 1900, p. 114.
[88] 'Prayer Convention', *Los Angeles Times* 18 May 1900, p. 114.

here is not so much about Smale's topic, rather his emerging prominence and association at conferences involving Pentecostal and holiness components.

The Centennial Conference at First Baptist Church Los Angeles

To mark the commencement of the twentieth century, Joseph Smale arranged a centennial conference, held at First Baptist, with thirty churches of Southern California in attendance for 'a three days' session, marked by inspiring testimony and teaching, as well as earnest application'.[89] Consistent with his ability for entrepreneurial activities, Smale's 'fertile brain and kindly heart' devised the conference to begin on the final day of 1900, while the actual transition to the New Year and century was planned to coincide with a 'watch night service'. The *Los Angeles Times* describes how, with a sense of the dramatic, 'as the clock struck the hour of midnight, Mr Smale appeared in the baptistry with two converted Chinamen whom he baptised by immersion, into the Christian faith'.[90] Both the themes of the conference speakers, as well as the tenor of spiritual life evidenced at this turn of the century conference, denote a heightened expectation among the Baptist delegates in attendance that these were significant days for missiological and eschatological aspirations. Across the front of the platform a large arch contained the motto 'Occupy till I come', with echoes of earlier uses of this biblical slogan, especially within the evangelisation of the world movement typified by characters such as John Mott and A.T. Pierson.[91]

Complementing the global emphasis of the centenary conference was the visual impact created by 'flags of all nations'[92] draped from the balconies. The final day of the conference was a forward look entitled, 'The Gospel of the Twentieth Century', with one speaker, the Rev. W.B. Hinson, prophetically proclaiming, 'This century is going to be marked by the churches giving more prominence than ever before to the ministry of the Holy Ghost. Know ye not that your bodies are the temples of the Holy Ghost, says the Bible.'[93]

Following this conference, the commencement of 1901 also prompted Smale and the Los Angeles' Protestant churches to join the growing worldwide momentum by associated with the 'Week of Prayer' initiative. First Baptist, along with Methodists, Lutherans, United Brethren, and Congregational

---

[89] 'Los Angeles Baptist Association Minutes: 1901' (Southern California Baptist Convention Minutes 1898–1904), p. 18.

[90] 'Joyous Welcome to New Century', *Los Angeles Times* 1 January 1901, p. 11.

[91] D.L. Robert, *Occupy Until I Come: A.T. Pierson and the Evangelization of the World* (Eerdmans, 2003). See chapter 6 for a detailed analysis of the 1888 Centenary Mission Conference and the theological, social, and missiological implications of occupying the world for Christ while waiting for his return, pp. 145-76.

[92] 'Joyous Welcome to New Century', p. 11.

[93] 'Centennial Conference', *Los Angeles Times* 3 January 1901, p. 11.

churches, inaugurated what they termed 'The Forward Movement', with an attempt to 'make a strong effort to start the new century with a great revival of religion and to level, so far as possible, the barriers of denominationalism that have hitherto kept the church people from working in unison'.[94] Here the emphasis was on importing organised methods, such that the city was divided into districts, enabling churches within each area to meet together for concerted prayer, with the suggestion that the week of prayer be followed by 'an eight days revival service and this by visitation among the different denominations of the city'.[95] All such initiatives listed above help to portray the context of Smale's priorities and connections during the early years of his ministry in Los Angeles.

Evidence of Schism at First Baptist Church Los Angeles

Smale had taken charge of First Baptist Church which, at the beginning of his pastorate, was regarded by a contemporary Baptist historian as a church 'full of enthusiasm, with a united people and a new and beautiful house of worship [which] was a wonderful asset to the Baptist cause in Southern California'.[96] However, Smale was not intent on the Baptist cause *per se*. His pneumatological focus remained constant on what the word and Spirit were saying to the church. As early as 1903, and significantly not during the protracted daily prayer meetings of 1905, it was already becoming clear that increasing schism and inherent problems at First Baptist were de-stabilising the church. These troubles require in depth analysis in a moment as they explain the backdrop to subsequent events in 1905 which would ultimately lead to the separation of pastor and people.

As noted in the introduction, and repeated here by way of re-emphasis, the woeful inadequacy of any scholarly investigation into Smale's resignation has perpetuated the myth that Smale and his board divided solely because of the fifteen week revival at First Baptist during May to September 1905. But the evidence of both the church records and the local Los Angeles press clearly plot the progression of deep irrevocable cracks that had appeared within the church much earlier, arguably as soon as Smale's ministry had commenced in 1897 – the point made above, that from the outset in 1898 a minority of members simply did not want him as their pastor.

Given that this study is an analysis of Smale's biographical journey, interwoven with his pneumatological development, it is necessary to place the church conflicts that Smale experienced at First Baptist within the context for revival at a personal and city-wide level, especially as these were the

---

[94] *Los Angeles Evening Express* 4 January 1901, p. 12.
[95] *Los Angeles Evening Express* 4 January 1901, p. 12.
[96] 'Report of Committee on History of First Baptist Church Los Angeles' (Los Angeles Baptist Association, 1921), p. 9.

contributory factors pertinent to the revival transformation under scrutiny. Yet a legitimate question may be posed in this regard: to what extent may an individual's epistemological and spiritual depths of insight be truly known and accurately evaluated a century later? This is especially relevant in historical research, where available data may inevitably be limited by quantity and/or personal, autobiographical expressions of self-understanding and convictions.

Analysis of Historical Qualitative Data using 'Transformational Logic'

In mapping the context for Smale's preparation for revival there is, thankfully, ample qualitative evidence which points towards his eventual burnout in 1904. This may in turn be analysed with an attempt to detect incremental signs of transformational knowledge/understanding, impacted by Smale's experience during this period. However, a suitable method is required to focus and interpret the analysis of such data correctly. To that end, I have selected to utilise the framework of the late Princeton Professor, James E. Loder, who describes typical phases within the process of human development, which he describes as 'The Transforming Moment[s]'.[97] Pertinent to this analysis is Loder's phrase 'the logic of transformation'.[98]

Of course, other similar psychological and theological attempts to analyse the mystical journey of the individual soul also exist, each distinguishing numerous phases and models such as 'conversion, illumination, the dark night and union'.[99] For instance, in her 1911 classic work, *Mysticism: A Study in the Nature and Development of Man's Spiritual Consciousness*,[100] Evelyn Underhill describes a five-stage pattern in the psychological process of spiritual transformation: awakening to glimpse the divine; submission and purification; illumination with the divine by the divine; fall from grace – the 'dark night of the soul' experience; and the integration of the previous phases into the unitive state. However, while Underhill views transformation positively as a lifelong transformation of the whole person, I have opted for Loder's model because of his particular work on the concept of 'insight'. Central to any biographical study that is seeking to explore the depths of human understanding, particularly self-understanding, Loder's 'Christian'[101] framework interweaves psychology

---

[97] J.E. Loder, *The Transforming Moment* (Helmers & Howard, 1989).

[98] Loder, *Transforming Moment*, pp. 2-4.

[99] J.J. Suurmond, *Word and Spirit at Play: Towards a Charismatic Theology* (SCM Press, 1994), p. 157.

[100] E. Underhill, *Mysticism: A Study in the Nature and Developments of Man's Spiritual Consciousness* (Meridian, 1955).

[101] Loder, *Transforming Moment*, pp. 183-96. Loder's thesis regards Christ as the instigator of all convictional knowing. 'This is not an attempt to establish 'spiritual laws' to which the Holy Spirit must conform. It is rather an effort to focus, in propositional form, certain crucial themes that characterize a transforming encounter

and theology, establishing 'insight' as the common ground in diverse types of knowing events.

Therefore, instead of simply telling the Smale story, the facts may be analysed within Loder's phases with a view to framing Smale's preparation for revival. Pertinent to a biographical theological analysis, Loder's thesis importantly takes into account the presence of the Holy Spirit's dynamic work within to unobtrusively direct and shape 'every meaningful knowing event' at several levels of human experience. Consequently, Loder breaks the process of transformation into five logical phases: conflict-in-context; interlude for scanning; insight felt with intuitive force; release and repatterning; and interpretation and verification.[102]

Testing his hypothesis, Loder found that his five-step pattern 'was relatively consistent across many aspects of life including major scientific advances, ancient Greek insights, psychotherapy, poetry and other forms of "knowing" in the fine arts, social and cultural transformations, human development processes such as identity formation, and religious conversion, and other spiritual experiences'.[103] According to Loder, probing questions such as 'how the Holy Spirit teaches, comforts, afflicts, leads into "all truth" is largely a theological blank'.[104] His view of traditional theology argues that its propensity to concentrate on what to believe is at the expense of more difficult questions, such as, how one comes to believe what is theologically sound. There is, in Loder's opinion, all too often a tendency to turn most of the theological answers to how questions, into what, or worse still when they are simply 'relegated to the Holy Spirit'.[105]

By recognising the transforming presence and work of the Holy Spirit in any and every circumstance, it becomes possible to view the connection points between 'knowing' and the notion of 'insight' with what Loder describes as 'convictional knowing'.[106] To explain his assumptions further, Loder highlights the analogous relationship between the human spirit and the Holy Spirit as the key to convictional knowing. In this analogy there is both 'a likeness' and 'a difference'[107] enjoined where the divine Spirit and the human spirit converge. Drawing upon the words of 1 Corinthians 2:11, this is where Loder considers the spirit and Spirit meet in the process of transformation: 'For what person

---

with the Spirit of Christ' (p. 184). Loder refutes any notions that convictional experiences may be nurtured by 'any human effort [of self], spirits, or departed souls' (p. 185).

[102] Loder, *Transforming Moment*, pp. 3-4.

[103] D. Ratcliffe, 'Qualitative Data Analysis and the Transforming Moment', *Transformation* 25.2-3 (April/July, 2008), p. 116.

[104] Loder, *Transforming Moment*, p. 20.

[105] Loder, *Transforming Moment*, p. 20.

[106] Loder, *Transforming Moment*, pp. 93-122.

[107] Loder, *Transforming Moment*, p. 94.

knows a man's thoughts except the spirit of the man that is in him? So also no one comprehends the thoughts of God except the Spirit of God.'[108]

Smale's Conflict-in-Context

Having presented a brief summary of Loder's theoretical approach to the identification of key processes involved in transformational insight, it is appropriate to return to our main subject with a dimensional dissection of Joseph Smale's journey as pastor at First Baptist Church Los Angeles. As already mentioned, the early years for Smale at First Baptist appeared to be encouraging in terms of mission activity, church growth, and promotion of the factors that would lead to a revival. However, a few opponents had viewed Smale as far too young to occupy the First Baptist pulpit,[109] succeeding as he did the much older and venerated Dr Read. Yet actually it was not his age that precipitated the initial conflict. It was romance!

ENGAGEMENT, RESIGNATION, MARRIAGE AND SEPARATION

On 17 February 1898, less than six months after an elaborate official reception had been held in the church to welcome and install Joseph Smale as the new pastor at First Baptist, came the shocking and sensational announcement concerning his resignation.[110] Right at the close of business at a meeting of the church's advisory board, Smale 'called them again to order and tendered his resignation, stating as the reason, his approaching marriage to Miss Alverda A. Keyser, a member of his church, an enthusiastic worker in the YWCA, and the only child of the then well-known capitalist, Charles A. Keyser'.[111] According to newspaper reports the following day, this announcement of both his engagement and resignation had come 'as a complete surprise to all but one member'.[112] One newspaper also clarified Smale's rationale, that he believed 'in the old adage that a pastor's wedding or building of a new church entailed a split in the congregation. To avoid any such contingency he had taken time by the forelock, and handed in his resignation.'[113] The internal church politics that ensued, although described as a 'tempest tea cup', was all presented in the *Los Angeles Times* for public consumption.

Although it was 'a unanimous request' from the board that Smale should withdraw his resignation and be given five weeks leave of absence following the wedding, confusion was increased by a sentence in the public newspaper

---

[108] See also Romans 8:16; Phil. 2:12-13.
[109] Sutton, *Our Heritage and Our Hope*, p. 28.
[110] 'Pastor Resigns', *Los Angeles Times* 10 June 1898, p. 13.
[111] 'Pastor Resigns', p. 13. For a photograph of Alverda Keyser Smale, see *Los Angeles Times* 24 September 1902, p. A1.
[112] 'Resignation Withdrawn', *Los Angeles Times* 11 June 1898, p. 9.
[113] 'Resignation Withdrawn', p. 9.

that 'the matter will probably not be brought before the church, although there has been some talk of explaining the situation which was brought to the public notice somewhat unexpectedly'.[114] This type of anomalous statement in the press was to be a consistent feature of Los Angeles press attention, thus broadening the scope of internal church conflicts into the public domain for the remaining years of Smale's tenure at First Baptist. Who was responsible for such negative dissemination or the processes by which church information was passed to the local Los Angeles newspapers is not clear.

One can only imagine something of the turmoil and distress that the engaged couple experienced in the few weeks before celebrating their wedding on 27 June 1898. Apparently the occasion was 'an exceptionally charming affair' held at the home of the bride's father. It is not necessary here to describe the wedding service in detail, nor who was present, and what they were all wearing, and so on; other than to mention that a very detailed synopsis appeared in the *Los Angeles Times'* 'Events in Society' column,[115] a pointer to the fact that Smale was already established, by virtue of his ministerial position at First Baptist and then his marriage into the wealthy Keyser family, as a notable figure in Los Angeles public life.

Taking the name Alverda Keyser Smale,[116] there were few references to the newly married couple's joint public role in church or society. One exceptional instance being, 'Rev. and Mrs Joseph Smale entertained at dinner yesterday evening at their home, in honour of …'[117] The reason behind such silence was eventually clarified publicly a few years later, as the fight between Smale and his opponents gathered momentum in 1902. But given human nature and Los Angeles' propensity to know the private business of prominent figures, especially church ministers, one can at least presume speculation must have been rife when Joseph Smale and Alverda Keyser Smale separated after only eleven months of marriage, and Joseph went to live in his study at the church.[118] Although later statements at the time of divorce proceedings a decade later, in 1910, indicate that the couple 'agreed to seal their lips, and the public was never able to secure much information about the separation'.[119]

Indeed, no facts about their marital problems were known at the time in either the Los Angeles newspapers or church records, apart from one reference during a church members' meeting in September 1902, described as the 'Second Round of Lamentable Contest in First Baptist Church', where a motion was brought by Professor Tripp, as follows:

---

[114] 'Resignation Withdrawn', p. 9.
[115] 'Events in Society', *Los Angeles Times* 28 June 1898, p. 5.
[116] 'Real Estate Transactions', *Los Angeles Times* 13 September 1898, p. 12.
[117] 'Events in Society', *Los Angeles Times* 15 March 1899, p. 9.
[118] 'Given Decree For Divorce', *Los Angeles Times* 26 May 1910, p. II2.
[119] 'Pastor Smale Seeks Divorce', *Los Angeles Times* 16 April 1901, p. II1.

> I move that we proceed to listen to any complaints that may be made except such as pertain to any domestic trouble, infelicity or anything that concerns the pastor's relations. There was a loud and long chorus of seconds to the motion ... It was decided unanimously that the pastor's family relations should not be mentioned.[120]

However, it was clear that for some church members the unresolved marital status of their pastor was an important underlying cause of acrimony within the fellowship. A member commented to the press that 'one of the serious objections is the fact that Mr Smale is living apart from his wife. For this state of affairs he has never given an explanation to the church or its board, and we believe that a discord of this nature should not be overlooked.'[121] Although not the defining matter that would eventually divide the church, this personal and sensitive issue most certainly played a part in the unravelling process of Smale's pastoral relations.

A few later insights became clear at the divorce hearing in 1910, which help towards explaining the breakdown of the Smale marriage and are worth inclusion at this point. They reveal how Joseph had apparently been 'urging his wife to make a home for him; the wife, indicating by her actions that she cared more for her parents and her old ways than she did for her husband and pastor ...' Giving evidence, the Rev. Smale said, 'For the first two weeks, after returning from honeymoon, they lived at the home of her father, and the first thing he knew in regard to her change of heart was when he was presented with a bill for half of the family expenses. He then asked his wife to make good her agreement and leave home and live with him, but she refused to do so.'[122]

Obviously a critical pressure point, apart from the natural adjustments from singleness to establishing the marital home, involved their divergent view of Christian ministry. As can be seen in the evidence cited in court, this was exacerbated by Joseph Smale's stance for opening their home in the name of Christ, while Alverda refused to cooperate. According to one of his heartfelt letters written at the time of their separation, and later read out in the divorce proceedings, Smale wrote,

> I also want a home that shall be consecrated to Christ and His church. Where I am not denied rendering hospitality to God's servants when I feel that I am called upon to do so. All that I have belongs to the Lord, and I want my dear wife to feel the same touching herself and her possessions ... If you would only understand that I do not ask you to serve me personally, but to absolutely place yourself upon

---

[120] 'Pastor and His Foes Both Score', *Los Angeles Times* 20 Sept 1902, p. A1.
[121] 'Opponents of Smale Are Organizing', *Los Angeles Times* 21 Sept 1902, p. B1.
[122] 'Given Decree For Divorce', p. II2.

the Lord's altar and help me in the relation I sustain to the Lord's name and work, then your heart would rejoice where it is now heavy.[123]

One example of Smale's open home policy is worth mentioning in this regard. Viewed alongside what many respectable church members perceived as 'the queerest' family relations following their marital separation, Smale's mother Ann had also moved into her son's new home, followed by an incident in which Joseph took compassion upon a dysfunctional fourteen year old boy, Joe Morgan, who was in the county jail. Smale visited him in prison and negotiated custody of the boy, inviting him home to be looked after until such time as the boy's family relationships could be restored.[124]

Of significance for the purpose of plotting the inherent schism within the church, some commentators at the time were in no doubt that his 'mysterious family relations had much to do with the dissatisfaction'.[125] However, according to Smale, during the period of separation he was able to state, 'I can go through this world with my head up on the question of my domestic life.'[126] But regardless of that self assessment, his adversaries had in fact a growing list of complaints which were the subject of numerous church business meetings for the membership at First Baptist Church over the subsequent months. These growing hostilities and power struggles constitute the basis of this study, namely that a pattern of defamation and conflict contributed to Smale's preparation for revival by 1905.

A VOTE OF CONFIDENCE

With the resistance and opposition to his ministry increasing, Joseph Smale took the initiative in September 1903 by calling for a special church business meeting. In an open letter to the congregation at First Baptist Church, which was also published in the *Los Angeles Times*, Smale wrote,

> MY BELOVED PEOPLE:
> For nearly five years I have had the privilege of sweet fellowship with you. In many ways, down to the present moment, I have received the assurance of your pleasure to have me among you as your minister. When I settled in this pastorate, twenty-one of its membership, according to the vote then taken, were opposed to me. Some of them who have remained on the Church roll have never ceased their opposition, and in the course of time, by their agitation have secured sympathizers, until it is now represented that the disaffection is seriously widespread. Under such circumstances I cannot continue as your Pastor unless there is a decided demonstration by a vote of confidence, that the discontented do not express the mind of the Church.

---

[123] 'Given Decree For Divorce', p. II2.
[124] 'Boy Goes Free', *Los Angeles Times* 18 April 1902, p. A2.
[125] 'Pastor Smale Seeks Divorce', *Los Angeles Times* 16 April 1901, p. III.
[126] 'Church Trial Won By Pastor Smale', *Los Angeles Times* 23 Sept 1902, p. A1.

Therefore, to know whether you wish the present pastoral relations sustained, I, by authority of the By-Laws of the Church, do now call a Church business meeting for the decision of this question, to take place at the conclusion of the preaching service on Sabbath morning next, September 7th 1902.
Yours faithfully,
JOSEPH SMALE[127]

That meeting signalled the outbreak of 'Return Fire' according to the *Los Angeles Times*, with their header graphically presenting the 'Call for Trial of Pastor Smale – Warfare Breaks Out in First Baptist Church'.[128] But the heat and ferocity of the ensuing fire would indicate this was not a Holy Spirit fire. The board of trustees called for Smale, first, to 'establish the truth of the charges made in his communication to the church' (Smale's letter dated 3 September). Secondly, 'to hear, consider and pass upon the defense of the alleged "agitators" and "sympathisers" to the charges set forth in Pastor Smale's aforesaid communication'. Thirdly, 'to hear, consider and pass upon various complaints, together with the reasons therefore, of any and all members against Pastor Smale ... why the present pastoral relations should be at once discontinued'. Fourthly, 'to hear, consider and pass upon the defense of Pastor Smale to each and all of said complaints'.[129]

A special business meeting was duly called for 18 September 1902. The measured judicial process set out by the church trustees was to lead to the most destructive two years for the church, internally for the congregation as well as for Smale and his personal health. Herein is my contention that this phase of conflict-in-context needs to be recognised as just as valid a precursor to his ultimate resignation in August 1905 as the fifteen week period of daily revival prayer meetings, because to appreciate fully the depth of hostility and factional conflict is to identity the stage by stage decision making that emanated from Smale's evolving insight. Therefore, a synopsis of much of the 'warfare' at First Baptist during 1902–04 will be presented chronologically, by way of illustrating the background that lay behind Smale's struggles, which in Loder's terms could equally be described as the deepening 'void'.

'BUNCH OF COINCIDENTS SETS BAPTISTS AGOG' (18 SEPTEMBER 1902)[130]

Utilising a trail of headers, such as this one taken from the *Los Angeles Times*, it is possible to plot the movement of the debacle at First Baptist, while also proving the indirect involvement of the secular press in the church's affairs. A meeting under the auspices of the Baptist Social Union was called to be held at the Van Nuys Hotel. It did not escape the attention of the journalist who penned

---

[127] First Baptist Church Los Angeles, Church Records, Vol VII (1900–1903), p. 139.
[128] 'Call For Trial of Pastor Smale', *Los Angeles Times* 15 September 1902, p. 14.
[129] First Baptist Church Los Angeles, Church Records, Vol VII (1900–1903), p. 141.
[130] 'Bunch of Co-incidents Sets Baptists Agog: Are the Agitators Grooming a New Pastor?', *Los Angeles Times* 18 September 1902, p. 6.

this piece, who had 'noted that the members of the Social Union who come from First Church, are almost entirely composed of the persons who are numbered among the opponents of Pastor Smale. There may be no significance in this, but the suggestion seems quite natural.'[131] Mischief-making may not have been the primary intention, but it was pointed out that the guest of honour at the banquet was due to be the Rev. Robert Burdette, who was 'not at present tied to any particular pulpit'.[132] Without doubt the speculation added fuel to the fire of discontent, which would in fact lead to the reality of a new Baptist church being inaugurated within the year, namely Temple Baptist Church, with Burdette becoming pastor, and taking, with Smale's blessing, 100 (plus) members from First Baptist in the process.

'PASTOR SMALE'S TRIAL BUT BEGUN' (19 SEPTEMBER 1902)[133]

Smale encouraged as many members as possible to come to the church 'at 11am to continue till 3pm in fasting and prayer' prior to the special business meeting that had been called by the trustees. The corroboration of church records and the *Los Angeles Times*' accounts of this meeting provide an accurate and detailed 'trial' summary. The meeting began at 7.40pm, with 'only 250 out of a membership of 1100' present.[134] Having read his letter, dated 3 September, Smale continued by requesting that 'if anyone feels accused under that, I would like to have him stand'.[135] Five persons stood up. Then Smale asked all those who knew that there had been opposition to him in the congregation ever since he was pastor of the First Church to stand up. About a dozen rose their feet. Smale immediately 'made the claim that his charge was thereby sustained',[136] and he felt vindicated. However, it was not as simple as that, especially in a church where business procedures and points of order were argued about in minute detail. R.G. Haskell, the church clerk, records how 'interruptions became frequent, questions were fired at one another without any permission from the Chair'.[137] After pages of arguments from both 'agitators' and 'sympathisers' the meeting was adjourned 'close to midnight' to be continued the following evening.

'PASTOR AND HIS FOES BOTH SCORE' (20 SEPTEMBER 1902)[138]

Described as a 'lamentable contest', the pathetic scenes on the second night included the chair 'with tears streaming from his eyes' pleading with the

---

[131] 'Bunch of Co-incidents Sets Baptists Agog', p. 6.
[132] 'Bunch of Co-incidents Sets Baptists Agog', p. 6.
[133] 'Pastor Smale's Trial But Begun', *Los Angeles Times* 19 September 1902, p. A1.
[134] 'Pastor Smale's Trial But Begun', p. A1.
[135] 'Pastor Smale's Trial But Begun', p. A1.
[136] 'Pastor Smale's Trial But Begun', p. A1.
[137] First Baptist Church Los Angeles, Church Records, Vol VII (1900–1903), p. 145.
[138] 'Pastor and His Foes Both Score', p. A1.

congregation 'that he was rendering fair decisions', while 'nearly half of the audience ... were laughing at him'.[139] As the 'trial' proceeded, it would appear that those members in opposition to Smale grew in confidence and vehemence. Mrs Barton Dozier, the church collector (pictured in Figure 11), rose to her feet and 'read a lengthy paper setting forth reasons for the immediate discontinuance of our present Pastoral Relations'.[140] Over the following four and half hours the church battled their way through amendment after amendment. 'Women were weeping; men were shutting their fists and breathing hard and moving restlessly in their seats and the pastor himself showed the first visible perturbation of the evening'.[141] The Doziers were typical of 'about thirty members of the opposition' who spoke, which helps to gauge the scale of hostility felt towards Smale. Following the statement from Mrs Dozier quoted above, Dr Dozier later is recorded as complaining of Pastor Smale's 'two pronounced attributes: stubbornness and selfishness'.[142] Others called him 'narrow ... of too small calibre to hold such a prominent and influential position, not in sympathy with the young people, too desirous to rule everything and to have his hand in all the details of the church management, and that he is not all together a man of his word'.[143] Similar to the previous meeting, this one had continued until five minutes past midnight, when the call was made for a further adjournment. Smale concluded proceedings requesting that anyone else with additional complaints should speak publicly at the next meeting before he would then make his response.

Alongside these special business meetings, the opposition party within First Baptist actually formed a committee with the express purpose of organising their attempts to remove him from office as pastor. It was a blunt and public attempt, accentuating the autocratic and dictatorial aspects of his leadership. Describing their case, the newly formed opposition group made this unequivocal statement:

> Our objections to Mr. Smale are not of a personal character, although we find much to complain of in his personality ... We regard Mr. Smale as unsuitable and unfit to command the position at this time, and believe that the interests of the church and the cause of Christ call for his resignation, and the placing in his stead a different man.[144]

---

[139] 'Pastor and His Foes Both Score', p. A1.
[140] First Baptist Church Los Angeles, Church Records, Vol VII (1900–1903), p. 147.
[141] 'Pastor and His Foes Both Score', p. A1.
[142] First Baptist Church Los Angeles, Church Records, Vol VII (1900–1903), p. 150.
[143] 'Pastor and His Foes Both Score', p. A1.
[144] 'Opponents of Smale are Organizing', *Los Angeles Times* 21 Sept 1902, p. B1.

Figure 11: Deacons of First Baptist Church Los Angeles, 1900.
Photograph courtesy of First Baptist Church Los Angeles.

Whatever the rights and wrongs of Smale's personality and leadership acumen, the irony of this opposition towards Smale must be seen against the fact that First Baptist Church had actually been growing prolifically under his charge. Earlier in 1902, the church had celebrated Smale's fifth anniversary with specific mention of 'seven hundred new members in five years', so much so that 'the day was one of rejoicing at the prosperity and growth of the congregation in that time'.[145] But certainly the vocal minority opposing Smale were unimpressed with such statistics. They simply wanted Smale out, and were stressing the mounting 'united opposition' as evidence that it would 'be impossible for Mr. Smale to continue as pastor'.[146] The fact that he would remain for a further three years is obviously significant in light of the subsequent developments for revival at First Baptist and across Los Angeles in 1905 and beyond.

---

[145] 'Anniversary Sermons are Preached', *Los Angeles Herald* 6 Feb 1902, p. 10.
[146] 'Opponents of Smale are Organizing', p. B1.

'CHURCH TRIAL WON BY PASTOR SMALE' (23 SEPTEMBER 1902)[147]

An atmosphere of vitriol continued at the following special business meeting on Monday 22 September 1902, with the final few Smale opponents being given the chance to add their complaints. The record is insightful for its lack of theological and doctrinal reasoning; perhaps an encouragement to many a pastor who, although maintaining doctrinal orthodoxy, yet receives vehement objections of personal and circumstantial attack.[148] A similar biblical example would be the Apostle Paul when facing the vehement criticism of the Corinthian accusers (2 Corinthians 10:10). It is noticeable that they resorted to attack not his doctrine, but the Apostle's appearance being 'unimpressive' and his speaking ability 'amounting to nothing'. Against Smale, it appears from the available evidence that his complainants spoke in generalisations, referring in unquantifiable terms to 'the talk of the city', where 'hundreds of people were known not to enjoy his preaching, not because of any question of doctrine, but because of the general lack of deep thought'. The opponents also included inaccurate statements, stated boldly, yet clearly not true according to all the documents discovered. For example, it was stated that 'Mr. Smale is not an educated man, having never received a college, university or seminary training'.[149]

After all the opponents had spoken, Joseph Smale stood to defend his own position, taking the floor for the next two hours.[150] The clerk, R.G. Haskell, records the 'intense interest' among the audience and the 'perfect silence' apart from Smale's voice. Haskell also observed 'no indication of fear or extreme nervousness' about Smale's persona. Rather, he spoke to each person and situation one by one, 'going back at his opponents with such a bulk of scriptures in his defence and in denunciation of those who fought him hardest, that they found themselves with a hopeless case on their hands'.[151] So much so, that by the conclusion of the meeting, which ended at twenty minutes past midnight, Joseph Smale had won an overwhelming vote of confidence, calculated at twenty votes to one, vindicating him of the charges leveled against him.

It is difficult, if not impossible a century later, to assess accurately the interplay of Smale's character traits with the legitimacy of the opposition's accusations. Smale obviously regarded the negativity he was facing as spiritual

---

[147] 'Church Trial Won By Pastor Smale', *Los Angeles Times* 23 Sept 1902, p. A1.

[148] First Baptist Church Los Angeles, Church Records, Volume VII (1900–1903), pp. 153-54. The list of complaints included statements of personal attack, such as 'he is dictatorial, vindictive, selfish'; and others that were circumstantial, 'he failed to attend recent BYPU rally in this church'. There were also many generalizations, such as 'A good evangelist never makes a good pastor.'

[149] 'Church Trial Won By Pastor Smale', p. A1.

[150] 'Church Trial Won By Pastor Smale', p. A1.

[151] 'Church Trial Won By Pastor Smale', p. A1.

opposition, and there was possibly some validity in their accusation that 'he openly and publicly characterizes all who do not think as he does as non-spiritual, non-praying and non-Christlike'.[152] Smale certainly drew on images of spiritual warfare pervading their battles, as he emotively argued and cleverly integrated the doctrinal with the historical import of his role within First Baptist, closing his defence, 'amid tremendous cheering', with these words:

> I stand for the supremacy of the church within the church. You are deciding something tonight that will last a generation. It has been insinuated that this is not a doctrinal issue. I say that it is. Satan does not like a gospel preacher. Satan wants to take your pastor away from you. I have been called into question for preaching the atonement and the second coming of Our Lord. I tell you, my friends of the opposition that you have misunderstood me. It is the fate of good men to be misunderstood.
>
> There never was a more misunderstood person in all the world than Jesus Christ. I can better afford to be misunderstood than to be faithless.[153]

The strength of the vote, 226 in Smale's favour, with only thirty against,[154] must be taken as ample evidence that Smale's critics were not nearly as numerous as portrayed by the opposition party. Especially in light of a total church roll of 1,091 members in October 1902, these thirty active opponents were responsible for causing great chaos, but at least Smale had established their public identity.[155] As the meeting adjourned at half past midnight, the clerk records the closure very simply: 'Doxology. Hand shaking. Congratulations. Were the order of the hour.'[156] However, employing Loder's dimensional perspective at this juncture, it would appear that Smale had embraced the conflict at First Baptist in a way that he had not done with previous troubles experienced at Ryde or Prescott. He maintained an expectation that change was possible, and that this time he was required not to escape the hostilities, but that God was somehow at work in the difficult processes and that a transformed church was emerging.

'SMALE'S ASSISTANT ABOUT TO RESIGN' (26 SEPTEMBER 1902)[157]

Smale's vindication at First Baptist was further endorsed the following week at their annual church meeting when it was unanimously decided to increase his salary from $1,800 a year to $2,400.[158] However, later the same week came further revelations in the Los Angeles press that Smale's assistant pastor, the

---

[152] 'Church Trial Won By Pastor Smale', p. A1.
[153] 'Church Trial Won By Pastor Smale', p. A1.
[154] First Baptist Church Los Angeles, Church Records, Vol VII (1900–1903), p. 159.
[155] Sutton, *Our Heritage and Our Hope*, p. 29.
[156] First Baptist Church Los Angeles, Church Records, Vol VII (1900–1903), p. 159.
[157] 'Assistant About To Resign', *Los Angeles Times* 26 September 1902, p. A1.
[158] First Baptist Church Los Angeles, Church Records, Vol VII (1900–1903), p. 165.

Rev. W.C. Clatworthy was about to resign.[159] Pages 162-64 of the church records are missing, so it is not known whether mention of this incident occurred in the church business meetings of that week as well. But given previous patterns already stated, whereby sensitive church matters were mysteriously communicated to the *Los Angeles Times*, it seems no coincidence that Clatworthy's resignation was used to rekindle the disruption among the congregation. The terminology used in the article is suggestive of what in today's parlance would be described as 'leaking' information to the media.

> Rev. Mr. Clatworthy would not confirm this statement, which was made by several of his intimate friends, but it is taken for granted by those who are in the inside of affairs in the First Church.[160]

Whatever the origins of this information, the result caused further chaos for Smale and the church who thought they had just navigated the previous 'scandalous affair' safely. Clatworthy was joined by other defections from First Baptist, including 'two of the most prominent laymen in the Baptist denomination in Los Angeles', Prof. C.C. Boynton and Dr Barton Dozier,[161] as well as the Sunday school superintendent, F.B. Crosier, and young men's teacher, Dr F Parker.[162] Conversely, the membership records also show that twenty new members were welcomed into the fellowship by Smale the following Sunday (5 October 1902).[163]

'SWAY OF SMALE MUCH EXTENDED' (9 OCTOBER 1902)[164]

As the list of discontents leaving First Baptist Church started to grow, Smale's response was typical of his desire to maintain authority through structures, and illustrates elements of his controlling leadership style which is certainly consistent with the accusations later leveled by Bartleman. This was, it would appear, intrinsic to Smale's temperament and dictatorial approach. Thus, at the 6 October church business meeting Smale brought forward some significant changes to the constitution, 'to extend his control of the church affairs', which were all 'disposed of with little discussion and no opposition'.[165] Perhaps the church was fatigued following the previous few weeks' wrangling. But, as perceived by Smale's opponents,

> The very objectionable features most strongly urged against his work are the ones made stronger by the revision. The Superintendent resigned and there was great

---

[159] 'Assistant About To Resign', p. A1.
[160] 'Assistant About To Resign', p. A1.
[161] 'Assistant About To Resign', p. A1.
[162] 'Superintendent of Sunday-School Quits', *Los Angeles Times* 6 Oct 1902, p. 6.
[163] First Baptist Church Los Angeles, Church Records, Vol VII (1900–1903), p. 167.
[164] 'Sway of Smale Much Extended', *Los Angeles Times* 9 October 1902, p. A6.
[165] 'Sway of Smale Much Extended', p. A6.

trouble over what was claimed to be undue interference with the Sunday-School by the pastor. The amendments contemplate giving the church absolute jurisdiction and control over all of the branch organizations, which include the Sunday-School and Young People's Society. The Tuesday afternoon prayer meeting, which has heretofore been under the direction of others, is placed absolutely under the control of the pastor, and he will either conduct the services or name the person who does.[166]

Smale determined to exert his control on all remaining members who felt unable 'to come into harmonious relations with the Church', requesting that 'they withdraw their membership and unite with a Church with which they can labor in peace and happiness, and we desire that all such questions be settled before the beginning of the new year'.[167] Consequently, 'the hand of fellowship was withdrawn' from many as requested, but the manner in which it was accomplished was not satisfactory to everyone, as illustrated by D.K. Edwards'[168] response when the resignation of the church treasurer, C.L. Hubbard, was announced:

> D.K. Edwards arose to express his pain and regret that conditions existed to cause these excellent persons to leave our church, and he set forth the idea that they were <u>driven</u> from this church.[169]

The discussion that followed, as one member after another stood to agree or disagree with Edwards' comments, reveals that the depth and hurt still experienced by many members had not been expunged by simply revising the constitution or pruning the membership. People were still polarized and confused, and a web of accusation was being presented by the likes of Edwards, charging Smale and his administration with 'dark and concealed motives' which would return to entangle Smale again and again.

Smale's preaching themes will be specifically analysed in chapter 5, but, suffice to state now, as the church was emerging from the 'great chaos' Smale sensed that 'the hand of our God was stretched forth ... [and] the blessing came',[170] and Smale began preaching with titles such as 'How to Receive the Gift of the Holy Ghost'.[171] The void felt and experienced at First Baptist was being linked directly to a greater need for prayer and consolidation. Daily

---

[166] 'Sway of Smale Much Extended', p. A6.

[167] First Baptist Church Los Angeles, Church Records, Volume VI (3 December 1902), p. 176.

[168] D.K. Edwards is pictured in Figure 11, confirming he was one of the Board of Deacons at First Baptist Church Los Angeles.

[169] First Baptist Church Los Angeles, Church Records, Volume VII (7 December 1902), p. 179, emphasis original.

[170] Sutton, *Our Heritage and Our Hope*, p. 29.

[171] 'Brevities', *Los Angeles Times* 8 November 1902, p. 12.

prayer meetings were commenced, starting at 2pm,[172] and by 1903 it was remarked that 'the average attendance at our mid-week prayer services has never been larger'.[173] There were also a number of other insightful events, no doubt breaking the mould of First Baptist respectability, such as one baptismal candidate 'leaping and shouting because of his conversion' and 'several others expressed a desire to be new creatures in Christ'.[174] Seen in light of manifestations that would later be commonplace during the fifteen week revival in 1905, some leaping and shouting at this earlier juncture was deemed noteworthy by the church clerk and myself.

'OBJECTIONS MADE TO PASTOR SMALE' (5 FEBRUARY 1903)[175]

The pattern of church disputes at First Baptist Church continued monthly throughout 1903. In the economy of time and space these will not be presented in detail here, as the issues and nature of contentious debate were unremittingly typical of all Smale had experienced through 1902. The following newspaper headlines provide a hint of the accusatory nature of the ongoing antagonism within the church business meetings, and the adverse affect the accumulative toll was placing upon Smale's health. These were inevitably significant in explaining the dark night of his soul and the void that was so central to his transformational process. Each indicating their own story, some of the 1903 headlines ran as follows:

February 12 – 'Will Smale Stay There?'[176]
February 16 – 'Pastor Smale May Face Church Council.'[177]
February 26 – 'Pastor Smale Still Sick.'[178]
April 5 – 'That Smale Will Resign.'[179]
April 12 – 'The Unending Case Of Pastor Smale.'[180]
July 18 – 'More Than One Hundred Come From First Baptist Congregation.[181]
July 28 – 'Baptist Bickerings.'[182]

---

[172] 'Brevities', p. 12.

[173] 'Los Angeles Baptist Association Minutes: 1903' (Southern California Baptist Convention Minutes 1898–1904), p. 21.

[174] First Baptist Church Los Angeles, Church Records, Volume VII (21 December 1902), p. 181.

[175] 'Objections Made To Pastor Smale', *Los Angeles Times* 5 February 1903, p. 11.

[176] 'Will Smale Stay There?', *Los Angeles Times* 12 February 1903, p. 13.

[177] 'Pastor Smale May Face Church Council', *Los Angeles Times* 16 Feb 1903, p. 8.

[178] 'Pastor Smale Still Sick', *Los Angeles Times* 26 February 1903, p. 14.

[179] 'That Smale Will Resign', *Los Angeles Times* 5 April 1903, p. 11.

[180] 'The unending case of Pastor Smale', *Los Angeles Times* 12 April 1903, p. D7.

[181] 'More Than One Hundred Come From First Baptist Congregation', *Los Angeles Times* 18 July 1903, p. A1.

[182] 'Baptist Bickerings', *Los Angeles Times* 28 July 1903, p. 7.

November 6 – 'Baptists Hot For Naught – Smale and James Prominent in Futile Fight.'[183]

However, it should be recognised that as Smale commenced his seventh year as pastor at First Baptist Church Los Angeles in January 1904, and in spite of the numerous battles outlined above, he also had many more allies who were swift to illustrate the abundant evidence of God at work through his leadership. This they regarded as sufficient endorsement that their pastor was God's 'true ambassador' and that

> through his ministry, it has pleased God to give the Church a spiritual uplift; that it has pleased God to give to this Church a keener realization of its responsibility in dealing with the wickedness in our city; that He is leading us out into a great work in the establishment of a Down Town Mission.[184]

The church clerk added his prayerful desire that it may 'please God to spare Pastor Smale to this Church many, many years and may it be that his work among us is just beginning'.[185]

The culmination of all the internal disputes at First Baptist Church during 1902–04, resulted in a church vote and decision 'to extend Pastor Smale's vacation six months or for such time as he shall be fully recovered and [that we now] proceed to raise funds to meet his expenses for a trip abroad'.[186] 'A collection of over $1,000 was taken on the spot for this purpose.'[187]

Such a motion, arising from the untidy realities of schism and compassion in their church life, was the integral link to all subsequent events in Los Angeles. More so, it was significant in providing the evidence for this study that Smale actually travelled back to Europe (and the Holy Land) to recuperate, and not initially with any intent to visit the Welsh Revival. This makes the scholarly consensus concerning Smale's motivation, which is commonly found in much Pentecostal historiography, clearly redundant. It was simply not a case that 'when news about the Welsh Revival came to Los Angeles, Smale was

---

[183] 'Baptists Hot For Naught', *Los Angeles Times* 6 November 1903, p. 11.

[184] First Baptist Church Los Angeles, Church Records, Volume VIII (31 January 1904).

[185] First Baptist Church Los Angeles, Church Records, Volume VIII (31 January 1904).

[186] First Baptist Church Los Angeles, Church Records, Volume VIII (31 July 1904).

[187] 'At The Churches Yesterday', *Los Angeles Times* 1 August 1904, p. 6. In addition, First Baptist Church Los Angeles agreed to pay Smale 'the sum of $125.00 per month ... while absent on his vacation'. First Baptist Church Los Angeles, Church Records, Volume VIII (17 August 1904).

interested enough to travel to Wales to visit Evan Roberts and observe the revival firsthand'.[188] Rather, in the words of the church clerk, Henry S. Keyes,

> Pastor Smale being in ill health, the Church has taken great pleasure in providing for him a trip to England and the Holy Land, as an expression of our love and a just appreciation of his faithful ministry among us and we trust that he may speedily recover his health and again preach to us the pure gospel in the mighty power of the Spirit.[189]

As with the disciples of Christ walking the Emmaus Road,[190] so the concept of Smale travelling away from Los Angeles bears helpful resemblances regarding the pivotal stages of transformation posited by Loder. For as with the enforced time away from his pulpit through 1904, and all that necessitated this prolonged break, so Smale's sabbatical trip provided the time, context and content for 'Step 2' within Loder's process to commence, whereby Smale would gain insights and convictions which were to revolutionize his own life and the spiritual life of Los Angeles in the following year.

Smale's 'Scanning' and the Role of the 'Inner Teacher'

When Joseph Smale, accompanied by his mother, left for Europe on 27 August 1904, 'a large number of the membership were at the station to wish them a pleasant journey'.[191] Judging by the clues contained in his last sermon before his trip, it would seem that an internal 'scanning' process had already begun. Smale preached about the 'expectations' of all that a Christian should anticipate in this life, referring specifically to suffering which he regarded as 'essential to the maturing of the Christian life within us. You cannot find a man of God without his trials.'[192] And then, understanding a broad trinitarian framework to be operational in the life of a believer with faith, he stated,

---

[188] C.M. Robeck, Jr, 'Joseph Smale', in S.M. Burgess and E.M. Van der Maas (eds), *New International Dictionary of Pentecostal and Charismatic Movements* (Zondervan, 2002), p. 1074.

[189] First Baptist Church Los Angeles, Church Records, Volume VIII (15 September 1904). Also 'Los Angeles Baptist Association Minutes: 1904' (Southern California Baptist Convention Minutes 1898–1904), p. 25.

[190] See Appendix II for an elaboration of Loder's model using the Emmaus Road encounter with Christ as a biblical prototype of the 'Transforming Moment' within conflicts-in-context.

[191] First Baptist Church Los Angeles, Church Records, Volume VIII (28 August 1904).

[192] 'Rev. Jos. Smale in Farewell Sermon', *The Los Angeles Examiner* 22 August 1904, p. 10.

> A Christian has a trinity of evil to fight, but let him be of good cheer, for he has an almighty trinity of good with which to fight them. Over against the world the flesh and the devil he may put God the Father, Son and the Holy Ghost.[193]

An emerging theology of brokenness can be identified at points such as this, consistent with other precursors to revival in Pentecostalism as well as more recent charismatic waves. Namely, that prior to divine outpouring there is, by necessity, a breaking of the self evidenced in humbling, emptying and barrenness. This theme is dominant in Bartleman's first chapter, 'Trials and Blessings. Revival Begins',[194] referring to a catalogue of personal suffering and grief that Bartleman had similarly experienced. Smale significantly observed that,

> the best Christians are not strangers to depression. When I hear the teachers on the higher life say that to be full of the Spirit is never to have an unhappy feeling I must say I cannot reconcile the statement with the experience of the choicest saints of the Church of Christ.[195]

Examples of this include C.H. Spurgeon and the Apostle Paul, and then Smale points to the highest defence of his statement, namely Jesus Christ, 'who said "now is my soul troubled", and remember he who thus cried possessed the Holy Spirit without measure'.[196] Contrasting the example of deity in flesh with the experience of 'so many professing Christians', Smale itemised the three major reasons for unbelief and the paucity of full spiritual experience of the Holy Spirit among God's people as

> First, the disposition to rest in first experience.
> Second, self confidence. There is a spiritual pride which is often engendered by wealth of resource ... When you think much of what you are there is no room for the true life of Christ.
> Third, turning to the world is a snare that hinders the flow of spiritual life to the soul ... There is nothing that will so readily stultify Christian growth, make the soul materialistic and cause it to minimize sin, and harden the heart as unbelief. Christian life is by believing. And its fullness is experienced by abiding in Christ.[197]

At this point of Smale's journey, before the Welsh Revival, it is noted that in the midst of broken health and personal suffering he publicly maintained a robust theology of suffering as part and parcel of the 'normal' Christian life, providing the opportunity whereby the presence of Christ meets with the self-

---

[193] 'Rev. Jos. Smale in Farewell Sermon', p. 10.
[194] Bartleman, *Azusa Street*, pp. 1-12.
[195] 'Rev. Jos. Smale in Farewell Sermon', p. 10.
[196] 'Rev. Jos. Smale in Farewell Sermon', p. 10.
[197] 'Rev. Jos. Smale in Farewell Sermon', p. 10.

in-conflict and ignites the possibility, even expectation, for the heart to become 'strangely warmed'.[198]

Reappraisal of Smale's Tour to the Holy Land and Welsh Revival (1904–05)
The compelling evidence that Smale did not leave Los Angeles with the intent to visit the Welsh Revival *per se* is the blunt fact that he left America before the Revival in Wales had even commenced! The calendar dates support this, given that Smale sailed to Europe on 27 August 1904, while Evan Roberts, the catalyst for the Welsh Revival, only later 'went to Newcastle Emlyn in September 1904 to enter preparatory school. As already well documented accounts of the Welsh Revival state, Roberts thereafter dropped out of school sometime late in October of that same year to enter the revivalist ministry'.[199] Therefore, the timeline may provide the argument for divine providential purposes orchestrating Smale's need of a trip, as well as the timing being critical for his later connections with Wales, the significance of which will be discussed further below.

Sadly, unlike his later tour to China in 1907, no diary or journal of Smale's 1904–05 extended vacation can be found, although we know that on this trip he 'travelled extensively in Palestine and Egypt, as well as spending considerable time in England'.[200] But among the limited information located in First Baptist Church Los Angeles records and a few cables telegraphed to Prof. Dozier (and reported in the *Los Angeles Times*) are snippets which help to piece together aspects of his time away. The implicit assumption is made that, given the nature of a sabbatical, especially involving a trip with slower modes of transport, there were ample opportunities for rest and reflection.

Smale's itinerary began by spending time in England, visiting 'friends and relatives'. Then in November 1904 he left 'for Greece, Egypt, Palestine, Syria and the Holy Land'. Summarizing this section of the trip, Smale is recorded as stating, 'I was gone four months and a half, and had many and varied experiences as well as some thrilling adventures.'[201] Of biographical interest it is worth mentioning one of his anecdotes that included being thrown from his horse while travelling from Jerusalem to Damascus. Near the Pit of Dothan, he records how his 'horse stumbled and pinned me to the ground with one of my feet beneath his body. When I was dragged away I found my ankle badly

---

[198] Evoking John Wesley's famous phrase upon conversion.

[199] D.D. Bundy, 'Welsh Revival', in Burgess and Van der Maas (eds), *New International Dictionary*, p. 1189.

[200] 'Returned Preacher Talks of the Holy Land', *Los Angeles Times* 26 May 1905, p.III1.

[201] 'Happy Safe Return from Holy Land for Dr. Smale', *The Los Angeles Examiner* 26 May 1905, p. 10.

sprained, and was obliged to stay in Nazareth three weeks in consequence.'[202] However, ultimately it was not Smale's injuries that altered his itinerary so significantly but the serious illness of his mother, on which more will be said shortly.

Biblically significant is the 1905 'New Year Motto' that Smale selected and sent back to the First Baptist Church in Los Angeles, in time for their 8 January meeting: Galatians 2:20, 'NOT I BUT CHRIST'.[203] This is especially important given that this verse was to become the operational basis for much of Smale's teaching for the personal Pentecostal life and experience that would be advocated upon his return.

Back in Los Angeles during April 1905 the congregation at First Baptist were encouraged to join with other Christians to hear F.B. Meyer preaching at the 'Temple Auditorium'.[204] Even the *Los Angeles Times* extolled Dr Meyer as 'one of the greatest living expositors of holy writ',[205] and as such 'great interest is felt in his visit by people of all denominations'.[206]

Subsequently, it was Bartleman who articulated the link between the events in Wales as recounted by Meyer and the growing availability of individuals such as himself and perhaps others, whose 'souls were stirred' and who, at Meyer's meetings, pledged themselves 'there and then promis[ing] God He should have full right of way [with me]'.[207] In respect of the linear time scale, it therefore should be noted that Meyer's firsthand report of the Welsh Revival, alongside Bartleman's distribution of G. Campbell Morgan's pamphlet on the *Revival in Wales*,[208] as well as S.B. Shaw's book *The Great Revival in Wales*,[209] all predate the personal accounts given by Smale upon his return in May 1905. In Blumhofer's succinct assessment, 'the [Welsh] revival contributed to the specific context from which Pentecostalism emerged'.[210] Smale's personal and direct contact with the Revival in Wales was simultaneous to Meyer's proclamation in Los Angeles, and both were to prove decisive contributory factors in these causal links.

Of interest to Baptist history is that in early April 1905 Smale obtained permission from his home church to 'be granted the privilege to remain in England until after the World's Baptist Convention, and that the Clerk be instructed to send to him credentials to represent this church as a delegate to the

---

[202] 'Happy Safe Return from Holy Land for Dr. Smale', p. 10.
[203] First Baptist Church Los Angeles, Church Records, Volume IX (8 January 1905).
[204] First Baptist Church Los Angeles, Church Records, Volume IX (2 April 1905).
[205] 'Editorial Article', *Los Angeles Times* 9 April 1905, p. II4.
[206] 'Famous London Preacher Is In The City', *Los Angeles Times* 8 April 1905, p.17.
[207] Bartleman, *Azusa Street*, p. 7.
[208] Bartleman, *Azusa Street*, p. 10.
[209] S.B. Shaw, *The Great Revival in Wales* (Christian Life Books, 2002 [1905]).
[210] E.L. Blumhofer, *The Assemblies Of God: A Chapter in the Story of American Pentecostalism:* Volume 1. *To 1941* (Gospel Publishing House, 1989), p. 100.

said Convention'.[211] At this Congress in London, which staged the 'formation of the Baptist World Alliance (BWA)', Meyer emerged again as one of the key speakers, calling the whole event a 'veritable Pentecost'.[212]

However, a discrepancy appears between this request for extension and Smale's actual schedule, because the Baptist World Alliance Congress did not open until 10 July 1905,[213] by which time Smale had returned to Los Angeles and was deeply in the midst of the fifteen weeks of daily prayer meetings. Whereas it is only possible to surmise plausible reasons behind such a change of plans, one piece of information definitely has some bearing on the timing. Smale's mother, Ann, 'became dangerously ill' in London in early April 1905 while Smale was still in Jerusalem, and therefore he was 'summoned to London' immediately.[214] The fact that she recovered sufficiently and was able to sail from Liverpool back to New York on 10 May 1905[215] raises two possibilities regarding Joseph Smale's exposure to the Welsh Revival.

Either Smale visited Wales en route to the Holy Land at the beginning of his sabbatical vacation, or else he managed to experience a few days, perhaps in north-east Wales, on his return leg to Liverpool docks with his mother. The available evidence points towards the latter, in that not as much detail of his experiences in Wales is as available as Pentecostal historiography has reported. Although I could find no evidence that Smale ever met and corresponded with Evan Roberts, Robeck, among others, has stated that Smale 'developed a friendship with Evan Roberts, the leader of the Welsh revival'.[216]

My personal view, based upon the documentary evidence discovered, is that Smale came into contact with the Welsh Revival at the end of April-beginning of May 1905 on his way back to Liverpool docks, and consequently he did not spend as long in Wales as he would have wished or has been surmised. Considering his earlier request to attend the Baptist World Alliance Congress in July, the providential circumstances concerning his mother's sickness in April 1905 actually curtailed his trip in the Holy Land to the significant benefit of himself and the wider Christian world. This can be corroborated, I believe, by the fact that having initially planned to stay away from Los Angeles until late July-early August 1905, he actually returned earlier, but with the story of the Welsh Revival as his predominant message ready to share at his first service on

---

[211] First Baptist Church Los Angeles, Church Records, Volume IX (2 April 1905).
[212] I.M. Randall, *The English Baptists of the Twentieth Century* (Baptist Historical Society, 2005), pp. 50-51.
[213] Randall, *English Baptists of the Twentieth Century*, p. 50.
[214] 'Is Not Dead But Kicking', *Los Angeles Times* 8 April 1905, p. 17.
[215] SS Baltic, Passenger Records, Liverpool 10 May – New York 19 May, 1905.
[216] C.M. Robeck, Jr, *The Azusa Street Mission and Revival* (Nelson, 2006), p. 58. Robeck's extensive sources will be able to substantiate this upon publication of his forthcoming *magnum opus* about Azusa Street.

his arrival back at First Baptist, with all the elements of fresh discovery rather than experiences retold from seven months earlier.

The old saying that 'big doors turn on small hinges' could well be applied to this sequence of events, for, if my conclusions are correct, then Smale came into contact with the Welsh Revival as a result of his mother's illness and his enforced change of plans and timing. Even though my reappraisal of this trip is unconfirmed, one fact is certain, Smale returned as a transformed man, with new insights gleaned from his firsthand experiences 'as a Bible student ... [who] obtained a wealth of information and visited scenes I will never forget',[217] and this as a consequence of seeing God's hand at work so vividly in Wales. As one newspaper account, two weeks after his return, described the change in him, 'it is noised about that on his visit ... Rev. Joseph Smale caught the Pentecostal fire'.[218]

Smale's Return to Los Angeles: Prepared for Revival

Soon after F.B. Meyer sailed from America back to England on 17 May,[219] so Joseph and Ann Smale docked in New York and made the long journey across the USA back to Los Angeles, eventually arriving home on 24 May 1905. It had been a sabbatical of nearly nine months. One can but imagine the disappointment of some of Smale's opponents who, while remaining at First Baptist Church, had made it known publicly during his absence 'that they hoped he would not return to the pastorate'.[220] However, for the majority of church members the welcome home reception 'was the biggest affair of the kind the church [has] ever held'.[221] Smale had telegrammed ahead from Chicago, informing the church that his mother was 'returning with him in good health', and his topics for the following Sunday were 'in the morning he will preach on the Welsh Revival, and in the evening on "Calvary"'.[222]

On his return, Smale went to stay for several days at the home of Dr Henry S. Keyes, a 'prominent physician and surgeon and hospital president',[223] who would play a prominent role in events over the following year. Outlining his itinerary to journalists, Smale provided a range of insights covering the political and religious situation in the Middle East, in particular how 'the Turks have walled up the East Gate of Jerusalem, as they say the time is coming when the Christians will have possession of the City, but they declare that the streets will

---

[217] 'Happy Safe Return from Holy Land for Dr. Smale', p. 10.
[218] 'Pastor Smale Stirs 'Em Up', *Los Angeles Times* 8 June 1905, p. II5.
[219] 'News and Notes', *Los Angeles Times* 20 May 1905, p. II1.
[220] 'Bombs For Baptists', *Los Angeles Times* 9 September 1905, p. 11.
[221] 'Rev. Joseph Smale to Arrive Home Tomorrow', *Los Angeles Times* 24 May 1905, p. II1.
[222] 'Rev. Joseph Smale to Arrive Home Tomorrow', p. II1.
[223] Robeck, *Azusa Street Mission and Revival*, p. 84.

run with blood before they will submit'.[224] Also, prior to that first Sunday, he briefly spoke to *The Los Angeles Examiner* about his firsthand encounter with the Welsh Revival.

> I was greatly interested in the great revivals which are in progress in Wales, and shall give a series of talks next week about them. The wave of religious enthusiasm is sweeping the entire country and thousands of conversions are reported.[225]

All in all, Smale had returned prepared and expectant for revival. This correlates with Loder's point about synchronicity of events directing the scanning process through the void, towards discovery, or rediscovery, of roots of hope.[226] 'In simplest terms', Loder comments, 'scanning is an internal dialogue that finds and grows the hope that is already there by establishing a context of rapport and tracing down the roots of that hope in the realities of personal, social and cultural history ... Many people find a synchronistic conjunction of events, which directs the scanning process or sets it on its way.'[227]

Certainly there seems to have been a transformational logic to Smale's journey in which various facets had culminated within and without the preparation of God's 'Moses', to the extent that he was ready the moment he returned on 24 May to be the catalyst for a significant work of God in Los Angeles. Physically, Smale had returned 'rugged and bronzed from the exposure to the sun under the European skies, and greatly improved in health'.[228] Emotionally, he was rested, recharged and enthusiastic 'to be back in Los Angeles'.[229] Spiritually, he was the recipient of a measure of 'Pentecostal fire' with the desire for further outpouring, that he and his people might share similar experiences of God's revival dealings in Wales. Certainly, Smale was aware that the architect of revival, whether personal, local, national or international was, by definition, 'the initiative of the Holy'.

It is also important to recognise the timing of such synchronicity of events within a wider sphere, as also in May 1905 'a local revival had broke[n] out in a Methodist church in Pasadena, with two hundred professed conversions in two weeks'.[230] The time and context was similarly ripe for similar events to unfold at First Baptist. When the culture of the church's life on his return in

---

[224] 'Happy Safe Return from Holy Land for Dr. Smale', p. 10.

[225] 'Happy Safe Return from Holy Land for Dr. Smale', p. 10.

[226] Loder, *Transforming Moment*, pp. 100-103.

[227] Loder, *Transforming Moment*, p. 102. Loder illustrates this, linking the frequency of 'coincidence' as the catalyst for scientific discovery and religious illumination.

[228] 'Happy Safe Return from Holy Land for Dr. Smale', p. 10.

[229] 'Returned Preacher Talks of the Holy Land', p. 111.

[230] J.E. Orr, *The Flaming Tongue: The Impact of Early 20th Century Revivals* (Moody Press, 1973), p. 178.

1905 is examined in more detail, there was a far greater sense of unity, generosity and expectation waiting to greet Smale than had been so at his departure nine months previously.

First Baptist Church Los Angeles Welcome Smale Home: Context for Revival

'Scores of the members' belonging to First Baptist Church greeted Smale and his mother at 'the depot upon his arrival' in Los Angeles on Friday 25 May, and then they escorted the Smales to the home of Henry S. Keyes on Bonnie Brae Street.[231] The following day, 'the largest reception ever given in the history of the church was held at 7:45 to welcome Pastor Smale and his mother ... Probably five hundred people were present.'[232] The record of celebrations are an indicator of the high degree of support and welcome that the majority at First Baptist wished to extend to Smale on his return, and are cited here to portray something of the unified church life context which was on the verge of the most intense prayer gatherings the church had ever experienced. These also underscore their receptivity to the innovations Smale was about to introduce, although, as the next chapter will show, not everyone was enamoured with Smale's Pentecostal emphases. The account contained in the church records describes the strength of people's affection.[233]

---

[231] 'Happy Safe Return from Holy Land for Dr. Smale', p. 10.
[232] First Baptist Church Los Angeles, Church Records, Volume IX (25 May 1905).
[233] First Baptist Church Los Angeles, Church Records, Volume IX (25 May 1905):
The Social Hall at First Baptist was beautifully decorated with palms, smilax, roses, seventeen hundred and fifty carnations, and many other varieties of flowers.
Deacon S.I. Merrill presided ...
Deacon C.O. Adams delivered an address of welcome on behalf of the Board of Deacons.
Chas. H. Brown welcomed them on behalf of the Board of Trustees.
Deacon R.H. Haskell made himself famous as a Poet by reading a verse from a paper about six feet long describing the various incidents of the Pastor's journey and containing a welcome from the Sunday School.
Mrs. Sewell gave an address of welcome on behalf of the Ladies' Society.
Mr. A.A. Lawson spoke for the Young People's Society.
The Junior Union welcomed them through Jesse Phelps and Cord Miller.
Rex Harrington and Gladys Harrington gave welcome on behalf of the Primary Department.
On behalf of the Church, the Clerk presented Pastor Smale with a purse containing $150. in Gold.
At this point, Mrs Smale, the Pastor's Mother made a very feeling reply, followed by a reply from the Pastor, giving a brief description of his Journey and outlining his purposes for future service to the Church.
An address of welcome was then given by Juan Rios on behalf of the Spanish Settlement Mission which was followed by a representative of the Chinese

Understanding the deeper fabric of church dynamics at First Baptist illustrates that some of the essential constituents of any revival were in place on Smale's return, unity in particular. Also of significance in the clerk's description above is the mention of Smale 'outlining his purposes for future service to the Church'.[234] He clearly returned to Los Angeles with a framework in mind, which was put into action immediately that first weekend back with his planned decision to speak about the Welsh Revival, and in doing so draw parallels for Los Angeles.

Smale's method became identical to that employed by Evan Roberts and others over the previous seven or eight months in Wales. Rather than a preaching emphasis in revival meetings, Roberts had introduced the prominence of 'confession of sin and calling on the Holy Spirit', a point noticed by other emerging Pentecostal leaders as well, such as Alexander Boddy, who visited Wales in December 1905.[235] The four aspects that Evan Roberts considered necessary for revival, which became integral in all his meetings from their commencement in Loughor at the start of the Welsh Revival, were: confession of known sin; removal of everything doubtful; entire commitment to the Spirit; and public confession of Christ.[236] It was no coincidence, therefore, that the subject for Smales's first sermon back in the pulpit at First Baptist Church Los Angeles, would simply be an account of his experience in Wales. Instead of 'the ten great factors for promoting a revival' that Smale had emphasised upon his arrival in Los Angeles in 1897, these had been honed through his own personal experiences as well as his exposure to the theology and practices emanating from Wales. It was these insights that were uppermost in his mind as Smale outlined his purposes for future service to the church. The internal 'scanning' was complete within the framework of his sabbatical journey.

Inevitably, the process of transformation would continue amid different circumstances. It seems curious to be able to specify something so definitely, but with hindsight it appears clear, as this chapter has attempted to show, that the background events at First Baptist Church over the previous eight years were integral to Smale's preparation for the 1905–06 Revival in Los Angeles. The milieu at First Baptist would soon reveal irrevocable cracks that would necessitate the formation of a new church, namely the First New Testament Church. These events will be continued in the next chapter.

Mission and by H. Haskell on behalf of the Grace Mission.
Salads, sandwiches, coffee and ice cream were now served'.

[234] First Baptist Church Los Angeles, Church Records, Volume IX (25 May 1905).

[235] G. Wakefield, *Alexander Boddy: Pentecostal Anglican Pioneer* (Paternoster, 2007), p. 75.

[236] N. Gibbard, *On The Wings of The Dove: The International Effects of The 1904–05 Revival* (Bryntirion Press, 2002), p. 19.

'The Transforming Intuition of Christ'

A final point, however, is appropriate here in connection with Loder's framework discussed earlier. His third step, entitled 'The Transforming Intuition of Christ', develops the notion of receptivity to any convictional insights that Christ, by his Spirit, has provided. With this there is the willingness to embrace the unexpected, as witnessed by the two disciples on the Emmaus Road when their eyes were opened. The relevance of Loder's point to Pastor Smale and his people at First Baptist is that Smale had been freed from the confines of his context, and the majority of his people were about to be released that Sunday and in the subsequent fifteen weeks. In many respects, Smale had been released from his previous world, described earlier as a void, as well as from the 'self' that had left Los Angeles nine months earlier. As already mentioned, his chosen motto verse for 1905 was an apt description of the spiritual process he was experiencing and desired for his church; in full 'I have been crucified with Christ and I no longer live, but Christ lives in me'.

Forensically and pragmatically, the results of such a transformation are inextricably linked by Christ's resurrection power to free disciples from the confines of their old contexts; to opt for or against Jesus in a renewing direction. Inevitably, First Baptist Church members had also been undergoing a transformational process, and even in Smale's absence a consistent theme is identifiable. This can be identified the Sunday before Smale returned, for instance, where the visiting preacher, the Rev. J. Hudson Ballard, took as his topic, 'Secret of Spiritual Supply, or the Holy Spirit and a Surrendered Life'.[237] The following Sunday, 28 May 1905, Smale had rejoined his people with a renewed sense of direction, and entire commitment to the Holy Spirit, fully prepared and expectant for revival to commence immediately.

---

[237] 'Special Notices', *Los Angeles Times* 21 May 1905, p. IV1.

CHAPTER 4

Pentecostalism's 'Moses' (1905–06)

William Seymour and Joseph Smale: Towards a 'Promised Land'

As earlier chapters have identified, Joseph Smale's particular role and function within revival beginnings in Los Angeles has largely been a neglected strand of Pentecostal historiography. Therefore, the thrust of this chapter will explore the nature of Smale's 'Moses' role within the broader context of Pentecostal origins and theology, arguing that Smale's personal contribution demands a reappraisal of Frank Bartleman's account. Indeed, the 'Moses' analogy which Bartleman devised for Smale employs two trajectories – both Smale's moving forward, as he led many to the 'Jordan crossing'[1] (believing that Los Angeles was about to be 'shaken by the mighty power of God'),[2] as well as Smale's later retraction from the emerging Pentecostal movement.

Using the 'Moses' metaphor as Bartleman intended it for Joseph Smale inevitably concerns the joint themes of journey and destination towards the 'Promised Land' of Pentecostalism, rather than any insinuation of actual messianic status. Walter Hollenweger,[3] among others including C.M. Robeck, Jr,[4] and Jean-Jacques Suurmond,[5] highlight the movements and roles of the many traditions and individuals responsible for the emergence of the complex map that constitutes Pentecostal and Charismatic Christianity. Graphically, Hollenweger presents the macro version of this map to include roots stemming from African traditional religion, Catholicism and Reformation history, which later converge via the Black Oral Root[6] and Holiness Movement strands into

---

[1] F. Bartleman, *Azusa Street: The Roots of Modern-Day Pentecost* (Logos International, 1980), p. 46.

[2] Bartleman, *Azusa Street*, p. 20.

[3] W.J. Hollenweger, *Pentecostalism: Origins and Developments Worldwide* (Hendrikson, 1997).

[4] C.M. Robeck, Jr, *The Asuza Street Mission and Revival: The Birth of the Global Pentecostal Movement* (Nelson, 2006).

[5] J.J. Suurmond, *Word and Spirit at Play: Towards a Charismatic Theology* (SCM Press, 1994). See chapter 1, 'A Fusion of Two Traditions', pp. 3-19.

[6] Hollenweger, *Pentecostalism*, p. 18. He describes the 'Black Oral Root' as emerging within African American slave religion, involving oral liturgy, a narrative theology and witness, maximum participation, and the inclusion of dreams and visions into public forms of worship, and an understanding of the body/mind relationship, evident in the ministry of healing the sick by prayer and liturgical dancing.

what we now term the Pentecostal Movement.[7] Obviously within this larger chart are the micro and more specific cultural spiritualities and personalities, of which William J. Seymour is generally regarded as the 'Joshua' type individual who ultimately led the revival breakthrough into the Pentecostal 'Promised Land' experience with his congregation at Azusa Street. But because Smale was portrayed by Bartleman to have never fully entered that same destination he was accordingly designated the subsidiary 'Moses' role.

For the purposes of this chapter, a simple definition of the 'Promised Land' that came into view for Smale, Seymour, Bartleman, and others, was the full baptism of (or with/in) the Holy Spirit, although what that actually meant to each of the participants on the journey equated to different things at different times. Certainly it was not just a case of glossolalia. For example, according to Bartleman's definition, arguably the most important given that he was the first to use the 'Moses' and 'Joshua' imagery, by February 1906 those worshipping at First New Testament Church, including Bartleman and Smale, reckoned to have never 'heard of such a thing [tongues]'.[8] Whereas a few months later, although Bartleman found it 'strange' that 'Seymour himself did not speak in "tongues" until some time after "Azusa" had been opened',[9] he still recognised that particular culmination of events in Los Angeles as the breakthrough enabled by the Holy Spirit through 'Brother Seymour' leading the people over into the 'Promised Land'.

The aptness of 'Exodus' imagery with the sense of journeying towards this 'Promised Land' combines cultural, historical and theological aspects which need to be taken into account when examining Smale's own particular contribution. Although First Baptist Church Los Angeles was to a limited extent racially mixed, the predominance of white middle-class individuals who were accustomed to a respectable ecclesiological position within the Los Angeles church scene, by definition, distinguished their aspirations for a divine outpouring from the African-American congregation that gathered around Seymour. In essence, although their 'Promised Lands' both involved Holy Spirit revival, the motivations and aspirations were clearly different. Douglas Nelson's seminal thesis has highlighted the significance of William Seymour's African-American slave roots for the beginnings of Pentecostalism.[10] Countering the traditional caricature of Seymour as 'an old colored exhorter with one eye', Nelson pinpointed the white bias of reporters who 'used

---

[7] Hollenweger, *Pentecostalism*, p. 2.

[8] F. Bartleman, *Azusa Street: The Roots of Modern-Day Pentecost* (Logos International, 1980), p. 40.

[9] Bartleman, *Azusa Street*, p. 62.

[10] D.J. Nelson, 'For Such A Time As This: The Story of Bishop William J. Seymour and the Azusa Street Revival' (unpublished PhD diss., University of Birmingham, 1981).

sensationalism and ridicule to make lively copy for [their] newspaper'.[11] It was, in fact, the force of Seymour's holistic African spirituality background, combined with the Wesleyan holiness influences he experienced along his journey,[12] which propelled Seymour towards his 'Joshua' apostolic role and position.

However, there is no need for polarisation about such conclusions on Smale and Seymour, as we see in Bartleman's original verdict. Rather, portraying the facts within the broader social, religious and racial contexts of their journeys places both protagonists in their respective settings prior to the events that unfolded during 1905–06. It is against this background, therefore, that the spiritual tide of expectation was already heightening across the city by the time Smale returned from the Welsh Revival in May 1905. A chronological account of events will aid the conceptualisation of the journey that Smale and many of his church members made towards their 'Promised Land' from May 1905 onwards.

Preaching back at First Baptist Church Los Angeles for the first time since his extended absence, Smale took as his theme 'The Great Welsh Revival'.[13] Using the narrative recorded by the church clerk, Henry S. Keyes, and interweaving firsthand accounts from newspapers and Bartleman, it is possible to establish a sense of the movement, timing and significant facets of the emerging revival that broke out almost as soon as Smale returned. This can then be linked to Loder's third stage, 'Insight felt with intuitive force', which metamorphoses into the fourth phase, 'Release and Repatterning', which for Smale was eventually to find a greater sense of coherence and completion at First New Testament Church some four months later.[14] Loder describes this stage of the process as the time sooner or later when 'the ingenuity of the spirit will surprise and often delight us with a constructive resolution that reconstellates the elements of the incoherence and creates a new, more comprehensive context of meaning'.[15]

Fifteen Weeks of Daily Prayer and Praise Meetings

Smale's sabbatical coupled with his direct exposure to the Revival in Wales registered the necessary insight for him to return to Los Angeles knowing exactly what must be implemented for what turned out to be the next significant phase of his life and that of revival history. Given that this phase has been

---

[11] Nelson, 'For Such A Time As This', p. 82.

[12] William Seymour's journey is described in detail in Robeck, *Asuza Street Mission and Revival*, chapter 1, 'William J. Seymour: The Beginnings of Pentecostalism', pp. 17-52.

[13] First Baptist Church Los Angeles, Church Records, Volume IX (28 May 1905).

[14] J.E. Loder, *The Transforming Moment* (Helmers & Howard, 1989), p. 3.

[15] Loder, *Transforming Moment*, p. 3.

superficially, and even incorrectly, recorded in Pentecostal historiography, it will be presented here within the actual fifteen week framework of daily prayer meetings at First Baptist Church, giving dates and the significant observations of eyewitness accounts, thereby correcting the erroneous 'nineteen week' schedule often cited.[16] Furthermore, alongside the narrative of these unfolding events, while the 'voices' of participants are allowed to speak for themselves, there are important points of connection with parallel phenomena emanating from the Welsh Revival which provide abundant material for analysis.

Week One: Sunday 28 May – Saturday 3 June

The morning service on Sunday 28 May 1905 commenced at 11am and continued until 2.15pm. It was described as 'a remarkable service, long to be remembered'.[17] The sermon simply consisted of Smale's account 'of the great Welsh revival under Evan Roberts'.[18] According to the eyewitness account penned by the church clerk,

> At the close of the sermon, the Pastor invited all those who were not right or felt they wanted to get nearer to God to come forward and kneel; at least two hundred people came. Prayer was offered and there followed a general confession of sin and an asking of forgiveness from each other. The Spirit was strongly manifest.[19]

Immediately following that morning service Smale 'called for a series of meetings every night for a week'[20] at which different 'phases' of the Welsh Revival would be recounted. The next day, Monday 29 May, a prayer meeting was held in the afternoon, a feature which became a daily occurrence, and then in the evening 'Pastor Smale spoke about the conditions prevailing in Wales before the revival.'[21] Again, the clerk's note provides a simple fact and observation, noting that he was supportive of Smale and his emphases: 'There followed a prayer and praise service with many manifestations of the Spirit.'[22] On Tuesday 30 May Smale spoke in the evening on 'How the Welsh Revival started', and prayer and praise followed as on the previous evening. By Wednesday 31 May there was a significant development as Smale was unable to deliver the talk as announced when 'the Spirit led the meeting and no chance was given him [Smale]. The Spirit has come upon some of the membership in a

---

[16] C.M. Robeck, Jr, 'Joseph Smale', S.M. Burgess and E.M. Van der Maas (eds), *New International Dictionary*, p. 1074.

[17] First Baptist Church Los Angeles, Church Records (28 May 1905).

[18] 'Pastor Smale Stirs 'Em Up', *Los Angeles Times* 8 June 1905, p. II5.

[19] First Baptist Church Los Angeles, Church Records (28 May 1905).

[20] 'Pastor Smale Stirs 'Em Up', *Los Angeles Times*, (8 June 1905), p. II5.

[21] First Baptist Church Los Angeles, Church Records (29 May 1905).

[22] First Baptist Church Los Angeles, Church Records (29 May 1905).

remarkable way.'[23] From the very beginning the week one pattern of daily 'Prayer and Praise' meetings in the afternoons, connected to the evening meetings described above attracted large attendances from 'people from outside Churches',[24] testimony to the fact that the Holy Spirit was being 'felt' in every meeting. Added to the written accounts, it is worth highlighting the photograph in Figure 12, which provides the actual image of the sanctuary at First Baptist Church in which these daily services were held. Consequently, this picture in itself makes a unique contribution to Pentecostal history.[25]

During the evening service at the end of the first week, Smale was reported in the *Los Angeles Times* as telling his congregation that 'he did not care to commit the church to another week's services, but announced that he would be at the church each evening and those who desired might come and they would have meetings together'.[26] This information alone can be regarded as sufficient evidence that what was happening among the churches in Los Angeles may have been attributable to the Holy Spirit's orchestration, but the movement was gaining momentum with Smale as the human catalyst, which, within Loder's framework, can be regarded as operating with 'Insight felt with intuitive force'.

Weeks Two and Three: Sunday 4 June – Saturday 17 June

Similar events to those Smale had witnessed in Wales were increasingly evident thereafter. During the June communion service the next Sunday 'one of the members who had taken the bread came to the table and laid it down, following the act by a heart-melting confession of sin. A deacon who was called upon to pray got as far as "Our Father" and broke down.'[27] Echoes of Evan Roberts' prayer 'bend me! Bend me! Bend us'[28] were translated into the Los Angeles context of First Baptist Church, and 'sobs of convicted hearts were heard in various parts of the building' making it difficult for the distribution of the elements. Smale comments how 'it was a never-to-be-forgotten night'.[29]

At the end of the second week

---

[23] First Baptist Church Los Angeles, Church Records (31 May 1905).

[24] First Baptist Church Los Angeles, Church Records (10 June 1905).

[25] T.B. Welch, 'Preparing the Way for the Azusa Street Revival: Joseph Smale, God's 'Moses' for Pentecostalism', *Heritage* (2009), p. 26. This picture is published here for the first time, with the kind permission of First Baptist Church Los Angeles archives.

[26] 'Pastor Smale Stirs 'Em Up', *Los Angeles Times*, 8 June 1905, p. II5.

[27] J. Smale, *Our First Anniversary* (First Baptist Church Los Angeles, September 1906), p. 3.

[28] E. Evans, *The Welsh Revival of 1904* (Evangelical Movement of Wales, 1969), pp. 68-71.

[29] Smale, *Our First Anniversary*, p. 3.

Pastor Smale was to have preached on 'The Heavenly Home' but at the close of the first hymn sung by the congregation, one member remained standing and witnessed that she had been filled with the Spirit. Then in quick succession, followed testimony, prayer and praise until about 1:30. <u>The Pastor having no chance to preach</u>. A boy and girl were evidently converted.[30]

Figure 12: Joseph Smale standing on the platform inside First Baptist Church Los Angeles, 1898. Photograph courtesy of First Baptist Church Los Angeles Archives.

The parallels between these events in Los Angeles and those Smale had witnessed in the Welsh Revival are striking. The immediacy of signs and wonders observable render Elvet Lewis' description of the Welsh Revival applicable to the revival on both sides of the Atlantic, such that Roberts' name could be replaced with the name of Smale, and still remain a true record of these phenomena associated with revival:

When Evan Roberts made his appearance ... [t]he ground was already prepared for him: it was one of the places revived before the revival ... When the Sunday was over, each weekday became a fresh Sunday: morning, afternoon, evening, an

---

[30] First Baptist Church Los Angeles, Church Records (11 June 1905), emphasis original.

almost unbroken continuance of prayer meetings, the number of conversions rapidly growing and the character of many of them startling.[31]

On Sunday evening 11 June, two local pastors, the Rev. A.P. Graves and the Rev. Randall, 'were received on the rostrum by Pastor Smale and they participated in the meeting'.[32] The significance of their presence at First Baptist and their subsequent roles come within the sphere of public confession, for both pastors admitted to having 'done much to injure Pastor Smale and the Church'.[33] Graves had in fact written to Smale the previous week, a short but impassioned plea for forgiveness:

> Dear Bro. Smale:–
> I am glad to see so much evidence of God's presence with you and the Church. While I review the past, I am sorry that in word or act I should have grieved you. This I heartily confess. Will you kindly forgive me in the Lord? God bless you and yours,
> In Christ,
> A.P. Graves.[34]

The church clerk recognised these acts of confession as 'matters worthy of attention showing how the Holy Spirit is at work making clean the House of God'.[35] For as the public confession intensified so it became contagious, as this example printed in the *Los Angeles Times* reveals. It was uttered by an unidentified 'well known' person with 'deep feeling':

> 'I have been untrue to my vows to the church and have even gone so far as to pray while our pastor was across the ocean, that he might not be permitted to return. I now confess my sin and ask the forgiveness of God and of Brother Smale.' With this he walked forward to the chancel and took the pastor by the hand. It caught the crowd and it is said there were other doings of the same character.[36]

Examples of similar expressions of repentance and confession occurring in other revivals are numerous, but may briefly be demonstrated as a transcontinental phenomenon integral to revival. For instance, during the Welsh Revival and quoted in the *English Daily News*, the Rev. J.J. Morgan told of a member's admission that years before he had kept back the price of some tickets sold for the church. But with the Spirit's outpouring he was compelled

---

[31] H.E. Lewis, *With Christ among the Miners: Incidents and Impressions of the Welsh Revival* (Hodder & Stoughton, 1907), p. 79.
[32] First Baptist Church Los Angeles, Church Records (11 June 1905).
[33] First Baptist Church Los Angeles, Church Records (11 June 1905).
[34] First Baptist Church Los Angeles, Church Records (11 June 1905).
[35] First Baptist Church Los Angeles, Church Records (11 June 1905).
[36] 'Pastor Smale Stirs 'Em Up', p. II5.

to return the money and 'begged for forgiveness'.[37] Simultaneously, during the Mukti Revival in India (1905), accounts describe 'confessions of sin and repentances' throughout prolonged prayer meetings.[38] Similar occurrences are also recorded in the midst of Holy Spirit outpourings in South America. Taking just one example, from the emergence of Chilean Pentecostalism, it is recorded that during all night prayer meetings in 1909 'confessions and restitutions were made'.[39]

Revivals historian, J. Edwin Orr, provides an analysis of such intense public conviction of sin as evidenced in revivals which may helpfully be applied to the powerful scenes of confession experienced at First Baptist Church Los Angeles from the second and third weeks of the Los Angeles Revival. He observes,

> There seems to be no way of attributing such intense conviction to any human technique or device or method or influence of a powerful personality ... the movement simply attributed the work of conviction to the Spirit of God.[40]

Week Four: Sunday 18 June – Saturday 24 June

By all accounts, at the start of the fourth week the meetings had continued in similar vein.

> The power of the Spirit was intense. Nearly the whole audience remained to the aftermeeting. Large congregation present ... House was well filled. Remarks upon the Welsh Revival by Pastor Smale followed by a second meeting for prayers, followed by a third meeting for consecration. Several were converted during the Sunday services.[41]

Smale's sermon title for the Sunday at the end of the previous week was 'Cease from man, look to God'.[42] This was the same weekend that Frank Bartleman first attended one of the prayer meetings at First Baptist Church. Bartleman's account tallies with the church records, indicating that the 'vision, burden and desire' of the gatherings were identical with his own, and also in his estimation that 'God was present'.[43]

---

[37] S.B. Shaw, *The Great Revival in Wales* (Christian Life, 2002 [1905]), p. 60.

[38] A.H. Anderson, *Spreading Fires: The Missionary Nature of Early Pentecostalism* (SCM Press, 2007), p. 79.

[39] M.G. Hoover, *Willis Collins Hoover: History of the Pentecostal Revival in Chile* (Imprenta Eben-Ezer, 2000), p. 19. Hoover provides specific examples of such confessions and restitution.

[40] J.E. Orr, *The Flaming Tongue: The Impact of Early 20th Century Revivals* (Moody Press, 1973), p. 188.

[41] First Baptist Church Los Angeles, Church Records (18 June 1905).

[42] First Baptist Church Los Angeles, Church Records (18 June 1905).

[43] Bartleman, *Azusa Street*, p. 13.

As with the Welsh and Azusa Street Revivals, word of the meetings at First Baptist spread quickly. Smale later recalled how, even without publicity, the 'scenes such as are witnessed in Wales were repeated in our midst' causing people to assemble 'from far and near', including 'professing Christians, of whom were ministers and church officers, and were baptized in the Holy Ghost'.[44]

However, a peripheral observation concerning church life at First Baptist during this period, when the emphasis was naturally on the daily prayer gatherings, is the notable continuity of business meetings whereby aspects of pastoral life and business decisions were routinely administered. For example, a marriage ceremony was conducted, new members were welcomed, candidates were 'received for baptism', and 'it was voted to discontinue the services' of personnel employed at the church's Spanish Mission.[45] Perhaps herein exists one of the tensions that prompted Bartleman's criticism regarding the manner in which the prayer meetings were shaping. That is to say, the routines of First Baptist Church continued to display elements of its (over) organised life and structures even amid the outpouring of the Holy Spirit.

As the weeks passed Bartleman was increasingly concerned about the focus of expectations, critical that too much was Smale-centred instead of the fact that 'they must expect from God'.[46] Indeed, on three occasions Bartleman claims to have started the meetings off outside First Baptist, because the people were waiting for the preacher [Smale] to arrive, whereas in the Welsh Revival Bartleman points out how 'the meetings went on whether the preacher was present or absent'.[47] As with any autobiographical account, it is legitimate to question the motives and perspective of the author's self-understanding, given the inevitable human tendency of placing themselves at the centre of events. In Bartleman's case the personal pronoun is frequently employed during his accounts of these events:

> I started the service in the evening on the church steps, outside, while we were waiting for the janitor to arrive with the key.[48]
> I began to pray aloud and the meeting started off with power. It was in full blast when Brother Smale arrived.[49]
> I visited Smale's church again, and started the meeting. He had not yet arrived.[50]

Bartleman has already been challenged on the objectivity of his own account.[51] That said, however, he does provide some significant data, especially

---

[44] Smale, *Our First Anniversary*, p. 3.
[45] First Baptist Church Los Angeles, Church Records (7–20 June 1905).
[46] Bartleman, *Azusa Street*, p. 15.
[47] Bartleman, *Azusa Street*, pp. 13-19.
[48] Bartleman, *Azusa Street*, p. 13.
[49] Bartleman, *Azusa Street*, p. 14.
[50] Bartleman, *Azusa Street*, p. 19.

concerning the sequence of spiritual movement in the city. For example, the fluidity of attendance at a number of other prayer gatherings in Los Angeles during these weeks must be recognized. Besides attending First Baptist Church, Bartleman also visited 'Brother Manley's tent and fell at the altar' there.[52] Then later that night he went on to join 'Brother Boehmer' at the 'little Peniel Mission' to pray some more.[53] Significant to the centrality of the daily prayer gatherings at First Baptist Church during this period, Bartleman confirms the frequency of his visits to Smale's church, 'taking part in the meetings with much blessing'.[54] In fact, it has been Bartleman's firsthand descriptions of events there that have formed the basis for much understanding of the overall thrust of the fifteen weeks of revival meetings. They are worth inclusion here because he independently corroborates the evidence of the church records that June 1905 witnessed a crescendo of expectation throughout First Baptist and the wider Los Angeles scene that they were on the verge of a Pentecostal revival. The prevalent themes of Smale's personal expectations alongside the human–divine management of meetings are both observable in Bartleman's account.

> A wonderful work of the Spirit has broken out here in Los Angeles, California, preceded by a deep preparatory work of prayer and expectation. Conviction is rapidly spreading among the people, and they are rallying from all over the city to the meetings at Pastor Smale's church. Already these meetings are beginning to 'run themselves.' Souls are being saved all over the house, while the meeting sweeps on unguided by human hands. The tide is rising rapidly, and we are anticipating wonderful things. Soul travail is becoming an important feature of the work, and we are being swept away beyond sectarian barriers. The fear of God is coming upon the people, a very spirit of burning. Sunday night the meeting ran on until the small hours of the next morning. Pastor Smale is prophesying of wonderful things to come. He prophesies the speedy return of the apostolic 'gifts' to the church. Los Angeles is a veritable Jerusalem. Just the place for a mighty work of God to begin ... Pray for a 'Pentecost'.[55]

The extent to which Smale himself felt the meetings were 'running themselves' and how he perceived the expectations of the gathered congregations is unclear from the First Baptist records. Curiously, the local press reports contain no reference to the daily prayer meetings throughout the fifteen week period they ran. Therefore, relying solely upon Bartleman's verdict about Smale's role in the construction of the daily gatherings Bartleman

---

[51] Hollenweger, *Pentecostalism*, p. 185. Reference is made to Robeck's innovative research tracing the 'original Bartleman' behind all the layers of various editions of text.
[52] Bartleman, *Azusa Street*, p. 14.
[53] Bartleman, *Azusa Street*, p. 15.
[54] Bartleman, *Azusa Street*, p. 16.
[55] Bartleman, *Azusa Street*, p. 16.

was still emphatically supportive, showing how, up to this point at least, when Smale arrived at one particular prayer meeting, it was already in full swing, so he

> dropped into his place, but no one seemed to pay any especial attention to him. Their minds were on God ... All seemed perfect harmony. The Spirit was leading. The Pastor arose, read a portion of the Scripture, made a few well chosen remarks full of hope and inspiration for the occasion, and the meeting passed again from his hands.[56]

Weeks Five and Six: Sunday 25 June – Saturday 8 July

At the start of the fifth week Smale preached about unity in the body of Christ at both morning and evening services, taking as his text the verse in the High Priestly Prayer, 'That they may be one, even as we are one' (John 17:22).[57] The following Sunday he spoke about 'The Triumphal Life', five new members were accepted into the fellowship, and 'Grace Merrill was baptised by Pastor Smale'.[58] After that service, Smale explained to the church 'that a person desired to be baptised by him and that the person was not persuaded as yet that they should unite with a Baptist church'. Recognising the ecclesiological issues raised here for some in his membership which had the potential to unite or divide the church, Smale stated 'that he considered that he had his commission to baptize from the Lord and not from the church, therefore he desired to know if the church would grant him the use of the baptistry in which to baptise this person and if there was any objection he would administer the ordinance somewhere else'.[59] In terms of evaluating Smale's influence and approach at First Baptist over these weeks prior to his resignation, it is not insignificant that the vote indicated only three members to be against the baptism. It is indicative of the delicate ground Smale was treading that, although the motion was carried, 'the Pastor stated that unless those three persons came to him and gave their consent he would not make use of the privilege'.[60] Accordingly he baptised the person five weeks later at the Central Baptist Church Los Angeles.[61]

---

[56] Bartleman, *Azusa Street*, p. 20.
[57] First Baptist Church Los Angeles, Church Records (25 June 1905).
[58] First Baptist Church Los Angeles, Church Records (2 July 1905).
[59] First Baptist Church Los Angeles, Church Records (2 July 1905).
[60] First Baptist Church Los Angeles, Church Records (2 July 1905).
[61] First Baptist Church Los Angeles, Church Records (6 August 1905). It is noted that this matter of baptism and church membership was problematic for other Pentecostals also; for instance the emergence of Pentecostalism in Sweden around 1913 and the Baptist roots of Lewi Pethrus.

A defining moment occurred at the end of the fifth week of daily prayer meetings, which the clerk simply states was 'THE REVIVAL'.[62] The importance of such sources is that other 'voices' are heard for the first time. So, allowing the eyewitness narrative provided by Henry S. Keyes to describe his insights regarding the movement of God's Spirit up to this point, here is his account in full:

> It is with us! Glory to God. The Holy Spirit is doing a profound work in Zion. For years God's professing people in the bulk have been drawing nigh to Him with their mouth and with their lips have been honoring Him, but their heart has been far removed from Him, and now he is revealing to them the pathetic truth that their fear of Him has been a commandment of men. (Isa. 29:13) But from under that commandment he is now bringing them, and causing the wisdom of their wise men to perish. And this is the rich promise that he is fulfilling: 'They also that err in spirit shall come to understanding, and they that murmur shall receive instruction'. (Isa. 29:24) Let us continue to wait upon Him, for every day the deaf are hearing the words of the Book and the eyes of the blind are seeing out of obscurity and out of darkness. Soon God's glory shall burst forth upon the people, and the multitude of thy foes O church of the living God shall be like small dust, and the multitude of the terrible ones as chaff that passeth away; yea, it shall be in an instant, suddenly.[63]

Similar revivalist themes of deliverance and eschatological fulfilment as evident in Keyes' report were reinforced by Smale's sermon at the end of the sixth week, entitled 'Returning to the Lord'.[64] Amidst the spiritual tenor of such exhortation was First Baptist Church's ongoing need to maintain the structural business of church activity, one of the marked differences between this established church and the Holy Spirit organised fellowship soon to emerge at Azusa Street. The records indicate that 'a special collection' was necessary to 'raise at least $500' for general running expenses.[65] Perhaps what is more surprising, and adds weight to Bartleman's criticisms about the heavy church structures dominating First Baptist life, was that during the sixth week of the revival prayer meetings, a committee was established involving deacons Keyes and Dozier to 'present to the Church Amendments of the Constitution such as may be necessary in striking out the office of Treasurer of Benevolences'.[66] Although Smale is not mentioned in this regard, it would appear that constant attempts were being made by the board of deacons to maintain running the

---

[62] First Baptist Church Los Angeles, Church Records (2 July 1905), emphasis original.
[63] First Baptist Church Los Angeles, Church Records (2 July 1905).
[64] First Baptist Church Los Angeles, Church Records (9 July 1905).
[65] First Baptist Church Los Angeles, Church Records (5 July 1905).
[66] First Baptist Church Los Angeles, Church Records (9 July 1905).

organisational threads of church life, while at the same time, in Keyes' estimation at least, enjoying the season of spiritual revival.

Weeks Seven and Eight: Sunday 9 July – Saturday 22 July

Once more, Henry Keyes provides a theologically articulate narrative, acutely aware of the significance and longevity of the events that were occurring, along with a realisation that their revival significance required setting them within a timeframe as well as a wider setting. On Monday 10 July 1905, he writes,

> The Seventh Week of Prayer Services begins with the meeting at 3 o'clock this afternoon. We are thankful to God for the wonderful movement of His Spirit in our midst. Truly the glory of the Lord is settling down in Los Angeles. The intercession of those in fellowship is telling upon the indifference that has sadly prevailed towards spiritual things. We are seeing an awakening among those who have been but nominal church members. Souls that have never been converted but yet have had their names upon the roll of some church, are coming in penitence to the Cross and entering into real union with our Lord Jesus Christ. A great work of sanctification is also in progress. Sinners are being regenerated and some of the professing people of God who have been living selfish, vain, proud, and carnal lives are becoming separated and devoted to the will of God and are being made holy. Glory! Hallelujah! Ye that are the Lord's remembrancers keep not silence and give him no rest, till He establish and till He make (the) Jerusalem (of the Church) a praise in the earth.[67]

The patterns between these unfolding events at First Baptist and the Welsh Revival, as with later occurrences in early Pentecostalism, are striking. Although with each there was undoubtedly an underlying sense of divine initiative, the prayer gatherings organised and perpetuated by Smale indicated the human preparation and receptivity for all God was about to deliver. Characteristic of former apostolic days, as Jessie Penn-Lewis observes, 'the Spirit of God did not come first upon the multitudes, but *upon the company in the upper room*' as the precursor to Pentecost.[68] Keyes is keen to point out that the impact of these daily meetings was, or was going to be, broader than just First Baptist Church; Los Angeles was the beneficiary. The 'glory of the Lord' had descended tangibly yet defying full definition. Certainly the intensity of prayer and intercession was a common denominator within such an aura of glory, as was the submission to Christ focused around crucicentrism.[69] Mindful that the evidence of history can only attest to facts and voices rather than any

---

[67] First Baptist Church Los Angeles, Church Records (10 July 1905).

[68] J. Penn-Lewis, *The Awakening in Wales and Some of the Hidden Springs* (The Welsh Revival Library, CDRom), p. 31, emphasis original.

[69] D.W. Bebbington, *Evangelicalism in Modern Britain: A History from the 1730s to the 1980s* (Unwin Hyman, 1989), p. 14.

deeper qualitative analysis of the mystical emotions of such meetings, the 'results' of the prayer gatherings at this stage would appear to have been primarily for the renewal of the church. The eighth week began with Smale preaching on the theme 'Baptism of the Holy Spirit', with further prayer meetings advertised for 2.30pm and 7.45pm each day.[70]

Weeks Nine and Ten: Sunday 23 July – Saturday 5 August

It is not certain how widely the clerk's record was distributed, but Keyes continues to combine facts interspersed with a 'preachy' challenge.

> Answers to prayer, thick and fast, are coming from the throne, harbingers of the greater awakening for which daily we are looking. Let all the Lord's people wait upon Him. Consider the magnificent promises and the fact that we are dealing with a faithful God.[71]

Following this, a selection of verses are presented in the church records reaffirming the word of God concerning some of the Pentecostal promises that typically convey metaphors of water and fire:

> 'He shall come down like rain upon the mown grass; as showers that water the earth.'
> 'I will pour water upon him that is thirsty, and floods upon the dry ground ...'
> 'He shall baptize you in the Holy Ghost and in fire.'[72]

Smale had thus far successfully altered the direction of First Baptist Church's emphasis, through teaching and the experiential dimension of the daily prayer gatherings. It is, therefore, no surprise to note that the church's weekly advertisement in the *Los Angeles Times* was adapted by week nine to express Smale's vision for renewal, stating,

> The First Baptist Church of Los Angeles, 727-737 Flower St. is a fellowship for evangelical preaching, evangelical teaching, pentecostal life and pentecostal service. Pastor Joseph Smale 11a.m. and 7.45p.m.[73]

The labels 'evangelical' and 'pentecostal' certainly stand out as the only such references amid the other sixteen advertisements for Los Angeles churches listed in the paper that day, thus making First Baptist's impact across the city even more distinguishable. Regardless of whether or not these newspaper advertisements added impetus to attract wider participants at First Baptist is not

---

[70] First Baptist Church Los Angeles, Church Records (16 July 1905).
[71] First Baptist Church Los Angeles, Church Records (23 July 1905).
[72] First Baptist Church Los Angeles, Church Records (23 July 1905).
[73] 'Church Services', *Los Angeles Times* 29 July 1905, p. III.

clear. According to Bartleman, any results were primarily attributable to the Holy Spirit, though Bartleman recognised the power of newspaper copies, such as an article he himself wrote for the *Daily News* of Pasadena describing the scenes at Smale's church. The results were self evident as the First Baptist Church daily 'congregation represented many religious bodies'.[74]

Weeks Eleven and Twelve: Sunday 6 August – Saturday 19 August

After 'ten weeks of solemn waiting upon God' in the First Baptist Church sanctuary, the shared vision contained in their prayers and hope was further elucidated at the start of week eleven with the following clarificatory statement: 'Pentecost has not yet come, but is coming. Hundreds of believers have been filled with the Spirit.' Helpfully, the primary objectives of the protracted prayer meetings are spelt out at this juncture as fourfold.

First, for a Pentecost;
Second, for the infilling with the Holy Ghost of all Christian believers;
Third, a reversion of the Church of Jesus Christ to Holy Ghost administration;
Fourth, the conversion of sinners.[75]

Smale's focus at First Baptist Church was clearly crystallising by this eleventh week of protracted meetings. Yet there is a sense in which persistence in prayer and patience needed to be encouraged. The fact that the previous ten weeks had 'proven blessed weeks to all in continuous attendance' was noted, while there was a detectable sense at this stage that something new was required in order to 'break through'.[76] Obviously God had 'been saving [sinners] right along in our meetings, but we are looking for a general turning unto the Lord and we believe it is nigh at hand'.[77] The following week Smale was stressing the need to exercise 'quietness and confidence' because 'blessed are all they that wait for Him'.[78] Another pattern worthy of mention occurred in week eleven, when Smale extended an invitation to the Rev. A.S. Worrell from Kentucky[79] to give an address at the meeting for intercession. Understandably, the momentum required for maintaining a daily schedule of afternoon and evening meetings would test the human resources of any church leader. By the

---

[74] Bartleman, *Azusa Street*, p. 20.
[75] First Baptist Church Los Angeles, Church Records (6 August 1905).
[76] First Baptist Church Los Angeles, Church Records (6 August 1905).
[77] First Baptist Church Los Angeles, Church Records (6 August 1905).
[78] First Baptist Church Los Angeles, Church Records (13 August 1905).
[79] A.S. Worrell (1831–1908) later visited the Azusa Street Mission seeking his baptism in the Spirit, and then contributed to further advocacy of the Pentecostal movement, writing 'An Open Letter to the Opposers of This Pentecostal Movement'. See, W.E. Warner, 'Worrell, Adolphus Spalding', in Burgess and Van der Maas (eds), *New International Dictionary*, p. 1217.

thirteenth and fourteenth weeks other speakers were similarly invited to cover Sunday services and midweek meetings.

Whether the innocent desires of corporate prayer were being expressed, or perhaps a more specific human strategy was at work, but here the first articulation of a 'cry for a New Testament Assembly' is located, 'beginning with this First Baptist Church to make it an organisation after His own heart'.[80] The theological ramifications of their specific fourfold prayer subjects itemised above inevitably required emerging ecclesiological and missiological constructs. For to have church and mission activities overseen by Holy Spirit administration was to require a distinctly different shape than First Baptist Church had embodied previously. Of course, all this is symptomatic of tensions that arise between any old and new 'wineskins' inherent in the human organisations of a church discovering, or more accurately, allowing the Spirit freedom to work and bring about change.

Analysing the former and future anticipations which were operational at First Baptist, the clerk (presumably prompted by Smale's teaching input) records three dimensions that had clarified in their self-understanding by the eleventh and twelfth weeks of protracted meetings:

> 1) PAST: Their omission in the past that their church had awoken to the fact that they had 'not walked according to the pattern of life and service as laid down in the Book'.
> 2) PRESENT: That there were hopeful signs among them of a desire 'to have the Church administered by the Holy Ghost'.
> 3) FUTURE: A reminder that their mandate was 'the supreme work of all the Churches of Jesus Christ, to go and disciple all nations'.[81]

For First Baptist this was culminating in a concerted prayer that 'He, whose prerogative it is to send forth laborers, thrust them out from us, into not only China, but Japan, India, Burmah, Africa and the Islands of the Sea, and fill our hands with missionary service direct'.[82] Accordingly, all evidence at this time portrays missional activity within the scope of the revival at First Baptist, as 'two of our fellowship, godly, consecrated and Spirit-endowed, have intimated that they believe the Lord has called them to be missionaries in China. They hope to leave us in about two months from now.'[83] Interestingly, the immediate reaction of this missionary couple, and that of the church clerk, is their significant refusal to go and serve with a missions board.

Indeed, similar to the spontaneity of many early Pentecostal missionaries,[84] their natural 'Pentecostal' reaction seems to be a disregard of the established

---

[80] First Baptist Church Los Angeles, Church Records (6 August 1905).
[81] First Baptist Church Los Angeles, Church Records (6 August 1905).
[82] First Baptist Church Los Angeles, Church Records (6 August 1905).
[83] First Baptist Church Los Angeles, Church Records (6 August 1905).
[84] Anderson, *Spreading Fires*, p. 54.

patterns, allowing a swift response and a direct reliance upon God rather than upon any human institution. Intrinsic to this stance, as early as August 1905, was this endorsement by First Baptist Church:

> we rejoice to say they are not going forth under a Board, but will look to the Lord for their support ... He is assuming the administration, blessed be His name.[85]

This characteristic of Pentecostal mission activity and faith will be explored in more depth in the next chapter, as Smale continued to develop such missiological expressions of a revived church.

Weeks Thirteen and Fourteen: Sunday 20 August – Saturday 2 September

Some of the church business decisions taken during these weeks of daily prayer are worth citing because they reinforce the expressed 'desire to have the church administered by the Holy Ghost'. Two decisions in particular stand out as illustrative of a church that is aspiring to look for Holy Spirit organisation rather than reliance upon human structures.

First, on 23 August 1905, the church council, at Smale's instigation, recommended that First Baptist should vote to 'discontinue the services of Mr Wyckoff' the choir leader now that the Holy Spirit was leading the meetings.[86] This was agreed. Secondly, the church council recommended limiting 'the newspaper advertising of the Church meetings to five dollars per month'.[87] Although explicit reasons are not recorded, given that this was not a church that needed to save money[88] and congregations continued to be large, this decision may be interpreted as a desire to rely upon the Holy Spirit to bring people into contact with God through the church itself rather than any self-advertisement.

A brief overview of the church's weekly bulletin is also insightful at this juncture of emerging frenetic Pentecostal activity. On the front cover Smale included six verses of scripture under the heading 'The Thirteenth Week of Special Prayer' encouraging confidence to pray for everything and anything at the 2.30pm and 7.45pm services. The sermon theme for that Sunday was 'Divine Ownership'.[89]

Inside the bulletin sheet are the names and addresses of forty-two 'recent additions to the church' with the prayerful challenge underneath, 'May all the above be filled with the Holy Ghost. Let them remember that this is a

---

[85] First Baptist Church Los Angeles, Church Records (6 August 1905).
[86] First Baptist Church Los Angeles, Church Records (23 August 1905).
[87] First Baptist Church Los Angeles, Church Records (23 August 1905).
[88] First Baptist Church Los Angeles had, in the same month, agreed to purchase a 'lot 40x165 feet, situated on Anderson Street, for the sum of $800'. First Baptist Church Los Angeles, Church Records (9 August 1905).
[89] First Baptist Church Los Angeles, *Church Bulletin* (20 August 1905).

command. Ephesians 5:18.' And then, finally, at the right-hand bottom of the page are two 'Hymns of the Welsh Revival' printed in full.[90] On the back page there is the clerk's account of 'The Revival' as noted below, along with a challenge to 'bring your Bible every time you come to the meeting'.[91] There is also a 'Church Motto for the week', 'Ask me of the things that are to come: concerning my sons and concerning the work of my hands command ye me. Isa. 45:11.'[92]

As already noted, while the local newspapers record nothing of the 'Special Prayer' gatherings, the church clerk provides a further portrayal that something significant altered in week thirteen. In fact, this is the second time Keyes uses the underlined heading 'THE REVIVAL'. This paragraph was also printed in the Sunday bulletin for 20 August, where he continues to describe 'another week of gracious blessing' as follows:

> The Holy Ghost broods over every meeting. Phenominal [sic] manifestations of spiritual life appear in each gathering. A wonderful era is opening. The Church is moving into the will of God and the Spirit is convicting the unsaved of their sins. We are truly on the eve of a great work of God which will spiritually revolutionize Southern California. Glory to the triune Jehovah![93]

Bartleman independently corroborates Keyes' observations with his own recollections of the daily services at this point in time:

> testimony, prayer and praise were intermingled throughout the service ... If one is at all impressionable religiously they must feel in such an atmosphere that something wonderful and imminent is about to take place. Some mysterious, mighty upheaval in the spiritual world is evidently at our doors. The meeting gives one a feeling of 'heaven on earth,' with an assurance that the supernatural exists, and that in a very real sense.[94]

Regarding what members of the congregation were actually doing during these services, Bartleman again proves informative, albeit personal to his perceived role. He describes this as a 'ministry in intercession',[95] which on one occasion prompted 'groaning in prayer at the altar'.[96] Such manifestations were not understood by everyone at First Baptist, causing Bartleman to explain this incident and his understanding concerning the importance of such phenomena.

---

[90] The Love Song of the Revival (tune Ebenezer), and The Young and The Old (tune Rhos).
[91] First Baptist Church Los Angeles, *Church Bulletin* (20 August 1905).
[92] First Baptist Church Los Angeles, *Church Bulletin* (20 August 1905).
[93] First Baptist Church Los Angeles, Church Records (23 August 1905).
[94] Bartleman, *Azusa Street*, pp. 20-21.
[95] Bartleman, *Azusa Street*, p. 18.
[96] Bartleman, *Azusa Street*, p. 22.

At Smale's church one day ... the spirit of intercession was upon me. A brother rebuked me severely. He did not understand it. The flesh naturally shrinks from such ordeals. The 'groans' are no more popular in most churches than is a woman in birth-pangs in the home. Soul-travail does not make pleasant company for selfish worldlings. But we cannot have souls born without it ... And so with a revival of new born souls in the churches.[97]

Similar negative responses at First Baptist caused Bartleman to reckon that elements of the meetings were being conducted in the 'flesh'. However, this must be balanced against Bartleman's own restless personality and movement. As Robeck points out, Bartleman 'seldom remained at one address or in one church for very long'.[98] A reappraisal of Bartleman's role during these weeks reveals a number of shifts that he makes with regard to Smale and other holiness congregations in Los Angeles. During the earlier phase of blessing at First Baptist, Bartleman wrote articles to some holiness papers 'describing God's operations' and exhorting the 'saints everywhere to faith and prayer for a revival'. He confesses being prompted by a concern for 'the Holiness people, that they might not be passed by, and lose the blessing'.[99] Interestingly, whereas his initial fear was that the holiness churches might miss God's blessing because of what he perceived as their 'prejudice and pharisaism', he conversely felt that at first Smale's church represented 'the weakest' who were being brought to repentance and would 'go through to victory (referring to the work in the First Baptist Church, at Brother Smale's)'.[100] Yet within a few months he was attending a holiness camp meeting 'in the Arroyo' where God met him personally, although he was not impressed with much of the 'empty wagon' rattle in the camp. However, as we have already noted, by the latter weeks of the prayer gatherings at First Baptist, Bartleman was also increasingly critical of what he regarded as 'too much "religion"' in Smale's church.[101]

With the growing intensity of the daily meetings during the thirteenth and fourteenth weeks Smale invited further visiting ministers to speak, taking the evening service on Sunday 20 August as well as some of the afternoon prayer events. It is helpful to take the opportunity to gauge the momentum of this phase at First Baptist Church, which ultimately lasted nearly four months. The temptation of unwitting hagiography within a simplistic overview of such a protracted period can promote the sense that everything was progressing positively towards the anticipated revival. However, week fourteen is marked out by the church clerk as a point of considerable spiritual conflict as well as

---

[97] Bartleman, *Azusa Street*, p. 22.
[98] C.M. Robeck, Jr, 'Frank Bartleman', in Burgess and Van der Maas (eds), *New International Dictionary*, p. 366.
[99] Bartleman, *Azusa Street*, p. 18.
[100] Bartleman, *Azusa Street*, p. 18.
[101] Bartleman, *Azusa Street*, p. 23.

victory: 'Satan has been abounding, but God more so.'[102] Such events indicate something of the toll this journey was taking upon Smale and others. Nonetheless, the testimonies emanating from First Baptist continue to point to a significant move of the Spirit's power in their midst. In particular three aspects are highlighted as remarkable evidence that 'greater blessings await us. The world is going to know as never before the grace of God, and the gift of Pentecost is to be bestowed upon all the Lord's real people. Hallelujah!'[103] The aspects provided by these eyewitness accounts are:

> Agony of soul in intercession is being followed by times of refreshing.
>
> Zion's captives that have been held in bondage to evil are being set free by the operations of the Spirit of God and entering the glad experience of the more abundant life. Souls regenerate and unregenerate are being delivered from the life and spell of the world, the flesh and the devil. The scene is glorious.
>
> The presence and power of the Spirit were remarkably manifested in the meeting last evening. It was the first time in all my experience of fifty years that I saw souls seeking the altar without being invited, led there evidently by the Holy Spirit. It was a sermon of power and bore fruit abundantly. All praise to the blessed Trinity![104]

Although the nature of 'spiritual conflict' is not specified by the clerk in the church records, there is a suggested link between this and the next major issue that stirred hostility in the church business meeting during week fourteen. It began with a letter signed by ten First Baptist Church women, requesting that the church membership review the 'hasty' decision taken the previous week regarding dispensing of the services of the choir leader, Mr Wyckoff. In their own words, 'there is reason to believe that some of those present did not understand the recommendation, and did not vote upon it'.[105] Significant to the matter under analysis in this study is the role that tradition and organisation ultimately played in Smale's resignation from First Baptist Church. Also relevant to contemporary ministry is the nature of church disputes that, in my experience, have often involved musicians and church music. In their letter of 30 August 1905, these ten members of the church choir were clear in their ultimatum:

> If it be the purpose of the Church to retain the services of the volunteer chorus choir, its members request that the Church reconsider the said recommendation.[106]

---

[102] First Baptist Church Los Angeles, Church Records (27 August 1905).

[103] First Baptist Church Los Angeles, Church Records (27 August 1905).

[104] First Baptist Church Los Angeles, Church Records (27 August 1905), quoting a letter written to Pastor Smale, dated 23 August 1905.

[105] First Baptist Church Los Angeles, Church Records (30 August 1905).

[106] First Baptist Church Los Angeles, Church Records (30 August 1905).

Without knowing the full background of this church decision, it is impossible to accurately judge whether or not this decision by Smale and the church council was prompted by the spiritual renewal being experienced by First Baptist Church. Certainly by the way Mr Wyckoff is described as competent to work 'with the material at hand' indicates formalism to his approach, which may have seemed incompatible to the new direction Smale was leading the church. But this assessment cannot be proven conclusively.

What is evident is that the choir leader's dismissal revealed that deeper and older warring factions still existed as 'Professor Dozier spoke several times for the motion' [to reconsider the motion passed the previous week], while 'R.G. Haskell and Pastor Smale [spoke] against'.[107] Interestingly, many of the church choir signatories 'publicly stated that had they understood the situation, they would never have signed it and that after hearing the discussion they could not vote for it'.[108] It is conceivable that a 'hidden agenda' of Professor and Mrs Dozier had manipulated these choir members to call for a reconsideration of the matter, as further evidence of their negative feelings towards Smale and the prayer meetings became evident during the week that followed. Constitutionally, regarding the reconsideration of the choir leader's dismissal, Smale won the vote forty to eight; but the fault line beneath the surface at First Baptist had once again been exposed.

Week Fifteen: Sunday 3 September – Sunday 10 September

In light of this internal church dispute, it is perhaps no surprise that Smale's theme for his morning sermon the following Sunday was 'The Fleshly Life of the Modern Church'. With the background of frustration we have noted, the fifteenth week of special daily prayer and praise meetings commenced. By surveying the movement of this sequence of meetings it becomes clear that only at this late stage was any public criticism of the prayer gatherings forthcoming. This is also a major contradiction to the portrayal within Pentecostal historiography over the past century, namely, that Smale's entire board of deacons was unhappy with the direction in which he was leading the church, and that they consequently expelled him. As the following evidence will confirm, that was not the case at all. All of this reveals significant historical errors contained within Bartleman's account, and this becomes evident through the sequence of events of what happened next.

Deacon Dozier's Opposition: Wednesday 6 September 1905

The regular prayer time on this Wednesday evening was followed by a 'Business Session'. Two church members were receiving letters of transfer to

---

[107] First Baptist Church Los Angeles, Church Records (30 August 1905).
[108] First Baptist Church Los Angeles, Church Records (30 August 1905).

other churches, and there was one application for church membership. Then, according to the church clerk's record, came three voices of complaint.

> Deacon Dozier and Rev. Dean spoke against holding the special meetings for prayer. Mrs. Dozier also asked the Pastor if 'these people could not be made to remain away from the Wednesday night meetings so that we can have our own little family and the Pastor to ourselves'.[109]

Such objections seem relatively innocuous, in as much as that was all the clerk recorded of the matters brought to the public attention of the church that night. However, deacon Dozier felt this account in the church records was 'manifestly unjust', which subsequently prompted a two-page handwritten explanation later inserted into the minutes 'in the interest of the truth of history'[110] (after Keyes and Smale had left First Baptist Church).

In brief, Melville Dozier wished to challenge the Smale's methods which in his estimation 'had become the subject of controversy'. For that reason Dozier sought 'to ask the cooperation of a sufficient number of members to legally call a general meeting of the Church for the ___ [word unclear] of all questions which were destroying its peace'.[111]

> The comments made by myself and Rev. Dean was [sic.] to the effect that the confusion and noise that characterized the meetings were, in our judgement, out of place in the House of God, and were not an evidence of the workings of the Holy Spirit, nor conducive to spiritual growth, adding that, unless this feature of the meetings ... had better cease, for we thought they would do more harm than good.[112]

Dozier also took the opportunity to clarify the remarks his wife had made that evening, again indicative of the couple's dissatisfaction with Smale and helpful for illustrating their precise points of disapproval. Mrs Dozier had spoken

> to the effect that those members of the Church who were not in sympathy with the boisterous character of the meetings were deprived of the enjoyment of any prayer service of the week, as the meetings were held every evening of the week. She therefore suggested that, as a very large proportion of the audience who contributed to the unpleasant features of the meetings were of other denominations, they attend the services of their own churches on Wednesday

---

[109] First Baptist Church Los Angeles, Church Records (6 September 1905).

[110] M. Dozier, undated transcript in the hand of Melville Dozier. Inserted into First Baptist Church Los Angeles, Church Records (6 September 1905).

[111] Dozier, undated transcript, in First Baptist Church Los Angeles, Church Records (6 September 1905).

[112] Dozier, undated transcript, in First Baptist Church Los Angeles, Church Records (6 September 1905).

evenings, leaving the pastor and his own members to enjoy the regular prayer meeting service alone.[113]

Ironically, and importantly as a corrective to false impressions presented in well established Pentecostal histories, Melville Dozier (who incidentally is pictured directly at Smale's right hand side in the photograph of deacons at First Baptist Church, see Figure 11), along with his wife and a Rev. Dean, are the only three voices in the extant evidence who outspokenly condemned Smale and the nature of Pentecostal meetings which had continued for fifteen weeks. Inevitably, among such a large congregation there must have been other protestors as was inferred by Dozier, but none are actually identifiable from any of the archival materials. Therefore, the minimal force of this opposition must be recognised in light of the decision Smale was about to announce to the church the following Sunday.

Smale's Resignation: Sunday 10 September 1905

Smale did not in fact preach that climactic Sunday morning because he was meeting separately with his deacons, and so the address was given by a 'missionary from Burmah'.[114] Allowing first hand reports to describe the events of that day as they unfolded, 'at the close of the service Pastor Smale asked the members of the Church to remain for a business session. After prayer the meeting was called to order at 12:45A.M.[sic] Deacon R.G. Haskell was by vote made Moderator ... Deacon Merrill requested the Pastor to state the object of the meeting':

> The Pastor now stated that on Wednesday evening, August 30th, at the meeting of the Deacons, Deacon Dozier moved that a special meeting of the Church members be called 'to consider interests of vital importance' to the Church. This is in plain language 'To consider the Pastoral Relations.' This was voted down in the Board of Deacons. The Deacons desiring to prevent any further publicity of Church troubles, had held another meeting this Sunday morning at 11 o'clock, at which meeting they asked Deacon Dozier what his intentions were, and requested him to stop his opposition and fall in line with the Church. He still desired the Pastor to resign and said he was not in sympathy with the way matters were going on in the Church. (That is the character of the meetings that have been held for prayer twice a day for the past fifteen weeks.) He was then informed that they requested him to take his letter [of transfer] or that they proposed to give him one. The Pastor stated that he could not go on as Pastor and stand the continued opposition of Deacon Dozier and further Church trouble and they were to understand that when they voted they voted to give Deacon Dozier his letter or to accept his resignation.

---

[113] Dozier, undated transcript, in First Baptist Church Los Angeles, Church Records (6 September 1905).

[114] First Baptist Church Los Angeles, Church Records (10 September 1905).

> It was moved and seconded that Melville Dozier be given a letter to unite with any other Baptist Church.
> On motion of Deacon Merrill, duly seconded, it was voted to hear only Deacon Dozier and the Pastor and then vote upon the question, carried by vote of 103 to 16. Deacon Dozier then spoke followed by the Pastor. Deacon Dozier then spoke again.
> The previous question now being called for, it was put to vote, and <u>Melville Dozier was given a letter by a vote of 85 to 55</u>, many members not voting.[115]

In spite of Dozier's protestation that the vote was not legal and he would not accept it, as 'a vote from the whole church would only be sufficient to give HIM a letter' he then climbed on to the platform and called for thirty-nine other members to come and sign a petition to call for a 'notified Church meeting'. However, at that point the meeting was adjourned, and Smale, in spite of his latest victory, went home to deliberate his next course of action.

Consequently Smale began the evening service by announcing 'that this was his last service as Pastor of the Church', and then continued to lead 'a prayer and praise service, at the close of which, [he] asked the Church members to remain to accept his resignation'.[116] Frank Bartleman was present at First Baptist Church that evening, though his account, which has provided the Pentecostal storyline to date, is factually inaccurate.

Reappraisal of Bartleman's Account

Bartleman's portrayal of this sequence of events at First Baptist Church must now be understood in the light of the correct context and not the sweeping generalizations contained in his well known paragraph which has gone unchecked for too long.

> I went to Smale's church that night, and he resigned. The meetings had run daily in the First Baptist Church for fifteen weeks. It was now September. The officials of the church were tired of the innovations and wanted to return to the old order. He was told to either stop the revival, or get out. He wisely chose the latter. But what an awful position for a church to take, to throw God out ... They tired of His presence, desiring to return to the old, cold, ecclesiastical order.[117]

If Bartleman had been a church member at First Baptist Church, which would have entitled him to stay for the business meeting at the close of the service on 10 September 1905, he would have heard and seen a very different scene to the one he later reported. For both the tenor of Smale's speech as well as the true explanation of events stand in marked contrast to Bartleman's version. As

---

[115] First Baptist Church Los Angeles, Church Records (10 September 1905).
[116] First Baptist Church Los Angeles, Church Records (10 September 1905).
[117] Bartleman, *Azusa Street*, p. 26.

Smale announced his resignation, he is recorded as having to 'request his friends to accept it at once', which they did, many of them 'rising to explain that they did so only at the request of the Pastor'.[118] Smale then 'requested the members to hold together and not take their letters [of transfer], but to continue to strive for God's best'.[119] If Bartleman had understood something of the turbulent previous few years at First Baptist then maybe he would also have been more sympathetic with Smale's concern to protect the church and glory of God from once more being embroiled in church fights in the public gaze.

The church clerk, already noted throughout the fifteen week period as a fervent supporter of Smale, encapsulated his thoughts and those of 'the majority of this Church' as a 'great blow' to all 'who loved him as one of God's choicest Ambassadors'. Henry Keyes' warm commendation provides a useful firsthand assessment of Smale's ministry at the conclusion of his pastorate at First Baptist Church.

> He has been fearless in the preaching of the Word as it is in the Scriptures. He is a true and noble example of a Spirit filled servant in the will of his Master striving with untiring energy to do His full will and to establish a Holy Ghost Church to be ruled of the Spirit only in all things. Man may attempt to set his will up against God's for a short time but his end will be fearful to contemplate. We believe that God has a wonderful mission for our Brother Smale and we know that all Hell cannot prevail against the will of God ... May God have mercy on this Church for rejecting His anointed.[120]

Typically, the *Los Angeles Times* was swift to report Smale's resignation with the sensational title 'Bombs For Baptists',[121] recognising the church as 'a seat of war' with a long history 'of discord between pastor and people'.[122] This public report substantiated Bartleman's theory in part, by virtue of its two-page outline of all the previous internal schisms at the church. Furthermore, it went on to explain the role of four contributory factors in the ultimate demise of Smale's ministry at First Baptist. Summarising the data in this 11 September 1905 article, these factors may be classified according to, first, Smale's personality, which a minority of the membership found to be 'intolerable', accusing Smale of 'assuming sole charge' of meetings and running them as a 'tyrant in his church relations'.[123] Another accusation levelled against Smale claimed that he had exercised 'a high handed piece of injustice' with regard to his handling of 'the expulsion of Dozier'. Some 'leading members' privately

---

[118] First Baptist Church Los Angeles, Church Records (10 September 1905).
[119] First Baptist Church Los Angeles, Church Records (10 September 1905).
[120] First Baptist Church Los Angeles, Church Records (10 September 1905), emphasis original.
[121] 'Bombs For Baptists', *Los Angeles Times* 11 September 1905, p. 1.
[122] 'Bombs For Baptists', p. 1.
[123] 'Bombs For Baptists', pp. 1, 5.

accused him of being 'dictatorial' and wanting 'to have full sway as a leader'.[124] Unquestionably, for some opponents, such as the Doziers, Smale was regarded as a 'youthful, enthusiastic and determined' contrast to their preferred 'old conservatism' of the church.[125] This reference recognised that Professor Dozier had been one of the 'chief supporters of the organization' since its earliest days in the previous First Baptist Church building.[126] All of which helps explain how Smale's treatment of Dozier was regarded by a minority as a personality clash between the modern wild euphoria endorsed by Smale and the traditional respectability represented by Dozier.

Secondly, there was Smale's revival strategies. Smale's ability to innovate has already been noted in previous chapters. But following his resignation, opponents such as Dozier were swift to criticise a number of his evangelistic initiatives and methods of previous years, including the 'effort made by a mighty revival, when a boy preacher persuaded many to join the church, to retrieve the heavy losses in the membership'.[127] Curiously, this reference stems back to the extended meetings in 1900,[128] which, as we have seen, were not linked at the time to declining membership, in fact quite the opposite. Perhaps this is more indicative of a journalistic slant and/or the bias of agitators, rather than the accuracies of church membership records and Los Angeles newspaper accounts.

Certainly the revival meetings of the final fifteen weeks of Smale's tenure were the catalyst for the final round of internal schism. The manner in which the newspaper reported these merits description. During the period when Smale was away on his travels to the Holy Land and Europe, and Dr Thomas Baldwin was in charge, Smale's opponents 'spread the news that now the tension was broken' and 'an era of good things for the First Church was fairly begun'.[129] Again, in journalistic fashion, the metaphors of 'the sore [that] was almost healed' and 'a spirit of love and accord [that] had settled like a dove of peace over the congregation' were accentuated to describe the condition of the congregation upon Smale's return. His decision to instigate 'strange forms of worship' certainly made for good copy, and by linking Smale's encouragement and the welcome given to the 'Holy Jumpers' from across the city, alienated 'some of his best friends in consequence of the fanatical actions of these uncouth worshippers'.[130]

Conversely, there were those who rushed to Smale's defence, stating spiritual reasons rather than opposition about methods. For instance, some

---

[124] 'Pastor Smale Resigns', *Los Angeles Express* 11 September 1905, p. 2.
[125] 'Pastor Smale Resigns', p. 2.
[126] 'Pastor Smale Resigns', p. 1.
[127] 'Bombs For Baptists', p. 5.
[128] See chapter 3 above.
[129] 'Bombs For Baptists', p. 5.
[130] 'Bombs For Baptists', p. 5.

striking comments from his supporters claimed the 'devil was in them [his opponents]', and 'you are opposed to our pastor because he is filled with the spirit'.[131] But the extent of such negative fallout is not substantiated by the official church records, although a brief sentence in them suggests that the documentary evidence needs to be handled with a degree of caution, as we will see.

Thirdly, there was Smale's exertion of control. Another of Smale's opponents, Mr D.C. Adams, later claimed in the aftermath of Dozier's resignation that 'Pastor Smale kept all the records of the church and would not allow those opposed to him to investigate the books'.[132] This might seem consistent with the highly favourable reporting of the revival within the church records, although the following pertinent observations are worth stating. First, that the revival accounts during the fifteen weeks were penned by Henry Keyes, a public supporter of Smale and the revival phenomena, who as a well respected medical doctor and surgeon in Los Angeles[133] may be regarded as maintaining a reasonable degree of independence. Secondly, the weight of active support provided by the other deacons and members would corroborate the historical records preserved, regardless of any potential interference by Smale. Thirdly, given that Professor Dozier assumed the role of chairman of church business meetings from 13 September onwards, following Smale's departure he had ample opportunity to rewrite any of the historical records at every point, as indeed he did regarding the manner in which Keyes reported his aborted dismissal. But further alterations were not made.

This leads me to conclude that while Smale, given his personality and managerial eye for detail, probably did maintain extensive oversight of every aspect of church life, including the church records, the evidence of the church records, newspapers and Bartleman's account all clearly indicate that Smale's ministry at First Baptist had reached its logical conclusion by September.

Others factors indicate that Smale's resignation was calculated to expedite the revival, hence, fourthly, we need to take into account Smale's future plans. The evidence of some Smale protagonists indicates that although he had been manoeuvred into a corner with events that culminated in Dozier's opposition, nevertheless 'Rev. Smale's resignation is for an entirely different cause. They say their pastor is so full of the evangelistic spirit that he sees greater opportunities before him and that his resignation is but a part of his plan for broadening his work.'[134] Although it was initially muted that another 'branch of the First Church may be formed', comments given by a few supporters suggest that a degree of continuity was anticipated, and that Smale would 'at once take

---

[131] 'Bombs For Baptists', p. 5.
[132] 'Bombs For Baptists', p. 5.
[133] Robeck, *Asuza Street Mission and Revival*, p. 199.
[134] 'Bombs For Baptists', p. 5.

up revival work along the lines of the Welsh meetings'.[135] This newspaper comment agrees with Bartleman's feeling that 'perhaps the Lord was cutting Brother Smale loose for the evangelistic field, at least for a time, to spread the fire in other places'.[136] Though following a personal discussion with Smale, Bartleman adds that Smale 'did not see it so'.[137]

The *Los Angeles Times* reckoned there were 'about 100' members who would go with Smale to 'form the nucleus of a church' that would be able to embody Smale's 'revivalist' intent. The *Los Angeles Express* was even more adamant that 'a new congregation will be formed'.[138] However, Smale's immediate comment regarding the future was a denial of any such plans, claiming that the events of 10 September had been 'entirely unexpected' and consequently he had 'nothing in view'.[139]

Smale versus Dozier: The Core Issues

Taking into account all the information available at this pivotal moment in Smale's life and ministry, further observations warrant inclusion here in the interest of understanding the immediate impact of the Smale-Dozier fight on the revival history of Los Angeles.

Personally Smale obviously found great comfort from his two greatest supporters at this difficult time, taking refuge in the home of Henry Keyes[140] where, together with deacon R.G. Haskell, they discussed 'the dramatic incidents of the stormy Sabbath sessions of the church' until 'after 1 o'clock in the morning'.[141] The day after his resignation, Smale himself was reported by the *Los Angeles Times* as 'reclining at ease',[142] while lucidly explaining he 'did not believe that God intended me for another baptism of suffering such as I passed through just before my trip abroad'.[143] However, regardless of all the personalities and the insidious nature of their dispute, the on-going health of the daily revival services following Smale's departure from First Baptist Church is summarised as 'continuing from day to day, but the attendance was diminished'.[144]

---

[135] 'Bombs For Baptists', p. 5.

[136] Bartleman, *Azusa Street*, p. 27.

[137] Bartleman, *Azusa Street*, p. 27.

[138] 'Pastor Smale Resigns', p. 1.

[139] 'Baptist Boil Still 'Biling'', *Los Angeles Times* 12 September 1905, p. II10.

[140] H.S. Keyes home address was 1249 Bonnie Brae Street, noted for its close proximity to 214 Bonnie Brae Street, where William Seymour claimed 'The beginning of the Pentecost started in a cottage prayer meeting'. See W.J. Seymour, *The Apostolic Faith* 1.1 (September, 1906), p. 2.

[141] 'Bombs For Baptists', p. 5.

[142] 'Bombs For Baptists', p. 5.

[143] 'Pastor Smale Resigns', p. 2.

[144] 'Church Likely to be Split', *Los Angeles Express* 13 September 1905, p. 5.

The personal fight between the two 'principal' characters, Smale and Dozier, certainly added a focus and impetus to the ongoing sensationalised reporting in the newspapers, which provides further insights into the warring tensions provoked by Smale's ministry. Immediately after Smale's resignation the homes of both men 'were besieged all day ... by great numbers of their friends and supporters'.[145] The journalistic interest in both camps seems to have prompted a fair degree of considered reflection, pertinent to the case being presented here as to the motivations and theological understanding that lay behind these sensational events.

Perhaps surprisingly, Dozier spoke of his initial support for the daily prayer meetings following Smale's return. However, the central issue at stake, he felt, was the meetings 'failed to appeal to the bulk of the membership, though they excited much interest on the part of members of other denominations, "especially of such as make unusual pretensions to holiness"'.[146] Integral to his outspoken criticisms regarding the direction Smale was leading the church was Smale's 'persistent declarations in favor of an undenominational church, and his denunciations of the national and State missionary societies of the Baptist Church, and of the local Young People's Society and the Ladies' Aid Society'.[147] Dozier also argued that the 'causes of contention continued to exist and valued members have continued to drop out ever since'. How quantifiable such statements were is a difficult question, although certain evidence lends itself to support Dozier's points. There seems no doubt that the departure of 200 members from First Baptist to join Temple Baptist at its inception in 1903 may well have formed part of Dozier's case,[148] as well as Smale's conflict and near withdrawal from the Baptist Association in October 1903.[149]

Indeed, Smale's alternative convictions regarding the establishment of a non-denominational church can be traced within his dislike of church politics during the 1903 internal church and Baptist Association conflicts just mentioned. Ironically, the very criticism raised by Dozier, namely that Smale's desire was for an 'undenominational church', proved to be 'vociferously endorsed by the people of other denominations'[150] visiting First Baptist for the daily prayer gatherings.

With the benefit of hindsight, it is possible to critique such dialogue and recognise the polarisation of their two positions. Dozier, by conviction, was standing within the safety of his historic denominational structures, intent on preserving harmony by use of the church constitution and rulebook. For example, the point of reference selected by Dozier in his statement justifying

---

[145] 'Baptist Boil Still 'Biling'', p. II10.
[146] 'Baptist Boil Still 'Biling'', p. II10.
[147] 'Baptist Boil Still 'Biling'', p. II10.
[148] 'New Church is 'Temple'', *Los Angeles Times* 18 July 1903, p. A1.
[149] 'Baptists Sit On Bossism', *Los Angeles Times* 9 October 1903, p. 7.
[150] 'Baptist Boil Still 'Biling'', p. II10.

his position was historic and legalistic, citing past turmoil from September 1902, as well as questioning the appropriateness of a morning congregation to vote upon his future status as a deacon and member. Any sympathy that might have been forthcoming towards Dozier's defence, given there were only 150 members present that Sunday morning (out of a possible 800 members), was quickly dismissed by Smale because he perceived Dozier's angst as 'the same old struggle over again'.[151] Understandably, Smale had run out of patience and, therefore, he was quick to press home his ultimatum to the board: 'Either Prof. Dozier must fall into harmonious cooperation with the present administration of the church in all matters connected with its spiritual development, or else take his membership from the church, and if he will do neither, then my resignation goes before the church; and this question must be settled before the church this morning.'[152]

Smale, by all accounts, felt liberated by the action he had taken, springing his resignation 'at a time when no one anticipated such action'.[153] His methods were justified, he believed, because they were 'in the interests of peace'[154] and because they avoided a further 'packed meeting on [the following] Wednesday evening and this precipitated a long struggle'.[155] Further, because he was standing by his convictions that 'many new methods in worship' were permissible, that 'noisy worshippers were not [to be] restrained',[156] and church 'societies that are auxiliary to the church proper on the ground that there is no biblical authority for the formation of such bodies'[157] should be disbanded, the parting of the ways was inevitable. The culmination of his experiences amid the Welsh Revival had reinforced Smale's perception that 'the old conservatism of the church was a thing of the past'.[158]

A final integral issue for Smale that surfaced in defence of his decision to resign was his health. In the extensive interviews with Los Angeles reporters, Smale recalled the strain of past troubles at the church and how he had been 'broken in health'. However, a contradiction exists between Smale's claims that he was in need of rest to recuperate after meetings lasting 'every day for fifteen weeks',[159] that he had no immediate plans, and the fact that within three days he was holding a meeting at Burbank Hall for all those members who left First Baptist after him to 'discuss plans for organization' of a new church.[160]

---

[151] 'Baptist Boil Still 'Biling'', p. II10.
[152] 'Baptist Boil Still 'Biling'', p. II10.
[153] 'Baptist Boil Still 'Biling'', p. II10.
[154] 'Pastor Smale Resigns', p. 2.
[155] 'Baptist Boil Still 'Biling'', p. II10.
[156] 'Pastor Smale Resigns', p. 2.
[157] 'Church Likely To Be Split', p. 5
[158] 'Pastor Smale Resigns', p. 2.
[159] 'Baptist Boil Still 'Biling'', p. II10.
[160] 'Baptists Form A New Church', *Los Angeles Express* 13 September 1905, p. 4.

Meanwhile, within that same week, Melville Dozier 'was re-established by the will of the same people who had endeavoured to throw him out of the church'[161] the Sunday before.

The verdict of the two ardent Smale supporters, who were witnesses to all the issues and methods employed in the Smale versus Dozier struggle, provides useful testimony to complete this section, given that no supporters of Dozier are documented in any of the archives. Henry Keyes concluded,

> the whole trouble is with one man, and that is Prof. Melville Dozier. His attitude has been at all times contrary to the pastor. His influence has been at all times a disturbing element in the church life.[162]

Haskell also affirmed Smale's motive was inspired by 'securing peace and harmony in the church', consequently leading to Smale's departure as the inevitable outcome after years of wrangling. A similar verdict would surely have been agreed by both parties:

> Smale has no criticisms to make of anyone, no aspersions to cast. This is simply a condition toward which we have been trending for some time. It was inevitable ... When he [Dozier] refused to recognise the authority of the church, Rev. Smale stepped out in the interest of peace and harmony.[163]

Six months later, Smale would reminisce about the significance of the sequence of events over the fifteen weeks, describing the period at First Baptist Church as 'the roots in a profound revival'.[164]

The Board of Deacons Respond

Before the focus of this study moves on beyond life at First Baptist, it is also advantageous to add a postscript detailing the actual response of the board of deacons following Smale's resignation, which further contradicts the popular impressions of Pentecostal historiography.

With the exception of deacon Dozier, there was unanimous support for Smale among his other deacons. This was expressed a week after Smale's departure when the remaining six deacons wrote an open letter to the church membership, requesting their own 'letters of dismission [transfer]' also, and explaining the 'reasons which actuate us to the painful act of severing our relations from this body'.[165] On the 17 September 1905, the clerk read out this

---

[161] 'Split in Baptist Church', *The Los Angeles Record* 14 September 1905, p. 6.
[162] 'Bombs For Baptists', p. 11.
[163] 'Bombs For Baptists', p. 11.
[164] First New Testament Church Los Angeles, *Historical Number of the Bulletin* (18 March 1906), p. 1.
[165] First Baptist Church Los Angeles, Church Records (17 September 1905).

significant statement signed by deacons Merrill, Haskell, Walberg, Adams, Marsh, and Dawson, presenting their rational and unequivocal support for Smale:

> FIRST: We believe that God placed our late Pastor Joseph Smale over this Church and we can see no evidence of a Divine will in the termination of his pastorate, but rather every Spiritual sign points to a continuance of his work as the Pastor of this Church.
> SECOND: Our late Pastor stands in his teaching for all the revealed will of God as made known in the New Testament ...
> THIRD: In his recent preaching, our late Pastor has been accentuating truths that have received scant courtesy at the hands of our own Baptist people, and we regard Pastor Smale's strong emphasis of these truths as necessary in these days of moral and Spiritual laxity in Churches and individuals. These truths to which we refer are:
> The Headship of Christ over the Church
> The Holy Ghost administration of the Church
> The Baptism of the Holy Ghost for all believers.
> FOURTH: That Pastor Smale has but differed from our denomination as to methods of Church work which we believe that any Pastor in the denomination has the right to do, if he conscientiously believes that the adoption of his position will make it possible or the Holy Spirit to administer the life and service of the Church. In Pastor Smale's differences from the denominational methods he has based the advocacy of new methods upon New Testament life and practice, a claim which we feel we dare not summarily disregard lest we grieve the blessed Holy Spirit of God.[166]

The full transcript of the deacons' letter shows not only their fraternal love and support for Smale, but also the degree of maturity and mutual theological understanding that existed among the leadership at First Baptist. They shared a developed sense of emerging Pentecostal identity as they journeyed together, much of which would gain significance in the next phase of Smale's ministry as he attempted to construct a church fully open to Holy Ghost administration. This camaraderie is quite the opposite of the picture traditionally presented by Bartleman, and an encouraging antidote to Smale's potential feelings of rejection.

Quite logically, following Smale's resignation as pastor, all further material pertaining to Smale and the revival meetings immediately ceased in the First Baptist Church records. Although it is noteworthy to log that within a week of Smale's concluding Sunday, a list of 169 church members also resigned, 'to unite with any other Baptist Church'.[167] Included in this list, apart from the loyal deacons mentioned above, there were various individuals each important for their roles later in Smale's later life and ministry: Dr and Mrs H.S. Keyes,

---

[166] First Baptist Church Los Angeles, Church Records (17 September 1905).
[167] First Baptist Church Los Angeles, Church Records (17 September 1905).

Miss Lillian Keyes, Mrs Ann Smale, the Rev. Huen Ming Cho, and Esther Hargrave, who would later marry Smale in 1911. There was also a contingent from the Chinese Mission who withdraw amid the debacle, reducing the First Baptist Church membership to 697.[168]

First New Testament Church Los Angeles (1905–06)

Within eight days of Smale's resignation from First Baptist Church, the inaugural meeting of the First New Testament Church was convened on 18 September 1905 at Burbank Hall.[169] Given the momentum of the 'seceders', involving approximately 200 former members of First Baptist along with about forty from other churches,[170] Joseph Smale was encouraged to establish a new fellowship, referred to by Henry Keyes as 'the down-town church'.[171] The formal launch was held on Monday 18 September 1905, with Smale preaching his first sermon to the embryonic church, not as yet named 'First New Testament Church',[172] exhorting them to fulfil their calling 'to lead the city to righteousness'.[173] Then, on 22 September, they marked the legal inception of the organisation with ratification of a constitution,[174] with the following Sunday characterised by great rejoicing and enthusiasm among the charter members, as 'a committee was appointed to escort him [Smale] into the hall, and as he entered the congregation joined heartily in singing a familiar hymn'.[175]

Once again utilising James Loder's model of the 'Transforming Moment', this new era signifies the distinct culmination of Smale's 'Moses' journey with regard to Pentecostalism, particularly focusing his 'release and repatterning' stage and thus enabling considered 'interpretation and verification'.[176] For not only was the year September 1905 to September 1906 a high point in his personal ministry after all the lessons of preceding years, but it significantly runs parallel to and intersects with the emerging Pentecostal movement at Azusa Street. This enabled Smale to exercise his all important role, described by Robeck as 'providing advocacy in the early days of the revival'.[177]

---

[168] 'Seceders Go In Harmony', *Los Angeles Times* 18 September 1905, p. 14.

[169] First New Testament Church Los Angeles, *Our First Anniversary* (September 1906), p. 3. See Figure 13, which shows the external aspect of the Burbank Theatre where First New Testament Church Los Angeles originally met after the church's inception (September 1905). Such an image has not been identified in any Pentecostal histories.

[170] 'New Church For Smale', *Los Angeles Times* 14 September 1905, p. 14.

[171] 'Seceders Go In Harmony', p. 14.

[172] 'New Church Is Organized', *Los Angeles Express* 25 September 1905, p. 3.

[173] *The Los Angeles Record* 19 September 1905, p. 5.

[174] First New Testament Church Los Angeles, *Our First Anniversary*, p. 4.

[175] 'New Church Is Organized', p. 3.

[176] Loder, *Transforming Moment*, p. 4.

[177] Robeck, *The Azusa Street Mission and Revival*, p. 198.

Figure 13: Burbank Theater, Los Angeles, 1905.
Photograph courtesy of Los Angeles Public Library Photo Collection.

An appropriate methodology must, therefore, be adopted for this phase which presents both the narrative and facts as well as enabling a more accurate analysis of the intersection between Smale's pneumatological role and the broader Pentecostal outpouring in Los Angeles. To that end, Robeck's theme of Smale's 'advocacy' is selected alongside a linear outline of the First New Testament Church's history during 1905–06. Assuming a simple dictionary definition, that 'advocacy' is 'giving support for a cause or position',[178] an apt framework is thus created whereby Smale's own ministry and the organizational life of his new church may be presented in their revival context without any artificial constructs. Hence the 'Moses' role of Joseph Smale within the wider sphere of Pentecostalism may clearly be identified, in that during 1905 and the first half of 1906 he directly and indirectly proffered support and encouragement to the expanding movement of Holy Spirit outpouring in Los Angeles.

The reason why this methodology has been selected is in deference to Robeck's authoritative insight into the wider context surrounding Azusa Street. His recognition of Smale's early ambassadorial role is already well documented

---

[178] Encarta Dictionary: English (UK).

in his 2006 book, and therefore the 'advocacy' theme provides further room for elaboration within the confines of this study which focuses on Smale's pivotal role.[179]

Consequently, the remainder of this chapter will be devoted to tracing Smale's 'Moses' role, concentrating primarily on the shape of 'Pentecostal life and service' at First New Testament Church. Then in chapter 5 the specific model of Smale's pneumatology, ecclesiology, and missiological activity will be analysed in light of early Pentecostal patterns. Thankfully, this study has been enriched by Smale's considerable attention to recording details in the many pamphlets he produced, thus enabling a clearer understanding of his 'interpretation and verification' phase to be presented than previously. Furthermore, the fact that Smale had the opportunity to formulate a church from the metaphorical 'blank piece of paper' has provided the clearest view possible into his maturing convictions and insights.

Smale's Advocacy through Organization

Joseph Smale's considered reflection of the transition from First Baptist to the First New Testament Church was that 'almost as the suddenness of the twinkling of an eye the revival which had come down from heaven and settled [at First Baptist] was lifted by the Holy Ghost and transferred to Burbank Hall'.[180] For all the old ecclesiastical strictures left behind at First Baptist, it begged the question as to how Smale would use his freedom to initiate a new organization purporting to embody Pentecostal beliefs and practices. In fact, from the very beginning Smale affirmed his allegiance to Baptist principles, 'so far as they accord with the teachings of the New Testament'.[181] At the close of service on the first Sunday, Smale issued a statement setting out the intended 'repatterning' for all that the First New Testament Church should be:

> Firstly, that Smale himself should be 'guided by the Holy Ghost and according to the New Testament precepts'.
> Secondly, to confirm that he 'would not countenance auxiliary affiliations'.
> Thirdly, that to all intents and purposes he would 'continue to be a Baptist, but will follow a liberal policy in regard to the reception of new members'.[182]

---

[179] I am indebted to Mel Robeck for providing this paradigm for Joseph Smale's influence during my personal interview, The Society for Pentecostal Studies meeting, Milwaukee, 13 March 2004. Robeck's 'Smale' information has since been published in *The Azusa Streeet Mission and Revival*.

[180] First New Testament Church Los Angeles, *Our First Anniversary*, p. 3.

[181] 'Rev. Smale's Successor May Be Dr. W.B. Hinson', *Los Angeles Express* 26 September 1905, p. 14.

[182] 'New Church Is Organized', *Los Angeles Express* 25 September 1905, p. 3.

Six months after First New Testament Church's inception Smale, writing in the church's commemorative 'Historical Bulletin', articulated his convictions further with the header boldly stating, 'The great principles of our organized life'.[183] This is an interesting feature of Smale's formulaic approach to his organizational approach, comparable to his 'Great factors promoting a revival' paper when he arrived at First Baptist Church Los Angeles in 1897.[184] Although such developments in 1905 provoked severe criticism from Bartleman as he expressed his disappointment that 'the New Testament Church seemed to be losing the spirit of prayer as they increased their organization',[185] however, a year or so later another observer-participant, A.S. Worrell,[186] still identified First New Testament Church (along with Azusa Street) as one of four places he had visited in Los Angeles 'where the gifts have been bestowed'.[187]

In the short term, however, the structural core issues for Smale and his people had crystallized around three doctrines which he had also attempted to make integral at First Baptist Church: the headship of Christ over the church, which became the motto for First New Testament Church; the Holy Ghost administration of the church; and the baptism of the Holy Ghost for all believers.[188] The question to what extent it was or was not possible to organize 'Holy Ghost administration of the Church' did not seem to vex Smale in the slightest. In fact, the church itself actually claimed that by the end of their first year they had established freedom from 'all the man-made systems of religious life and service'.[189] No doubt this was in part a reaction against all that Smale regarded as 'the modern church sociable' which he had encountered at each of his previous churches and was to be considered obsolete under 'the intensely spiritual character' of a true church of Christ.[190] Given his wider ambition to train every member for 'complete Christian service', Smale's organic church model quickly developed. Within six months, he had formulated a well-ordered mix of evangelistic ministries among the Chinese, Spanish, and Mexican communities of Los Angeles; a Bible and missionary training school called 'The New Testament Training School'; organized dates for fasting and prayer; and more besides.[191] What is striking in all this was Smale's view that an

---

[183] First New Testament Church Los Angeles, *Historical Number of the Bulletin* (18 March 1906), p. 6.

[184] See chapter 3 above, 'The great factors promoting a revival'.

[185] Bartleman, *Azusa Street*, p. 31.

[186] Smale had invited A.S. Worrell to preach at First Baptist Church Los Angeles during the fifteen week revival meetings. See above.

[187] A.S. Worrell, 'The Movements in Los Angeles, California', *Triumphs of Faith* (December 1906), p. 257.

[188] First Baptist Church Los Angeles, Church Records (17 September 1905).

[189] First New Testament Church Los Angeles, *Our First Anniversary*, p. 3.

[190] First New Testament Church Los Angeles, *Our First Anniversary*, p. 6.

[191] First New Testament Church Los Angeles, *Historical Number of the Bulletin* (18 March 1906), pp. 5-10.

intrinsic relationship existed between conscious planning seen in the rapid development of organized church life and the spiritual element of Holy Spirit administration.[192]

Important Pentecostal distinctive connections emanated from these convictions at First New Testament Church, which obviously resonated with Bartleman and other visitors from Los Angeles, although Bartleman viewed the expression of church organization somewhat differently than did Smale. When Bartleman eventually established his own church, along with William Pendleton, known as 'Eighth and Maple Church' (also commended by A.S. Worrell as one of the four churches noted above),[193] a visitor recognised it as another place where members were baptised in the Holy Spirit and where 'Jesus is proclaimed the Head, and the Holy Ghost is His executive'.[194] The realistic observation being inferred that whether Smale, Bartleman, Seymour or any other church leader was in charge, such spiritual life and pneumatological convictions necessitate incarnation in a human frame and organization.

For Smale it was an attainable priority to develop his church along New Testament lines, whereby he categorically affirmed that

> One, and only One is Master here, verily Christ. There is no officialism lording it over God's heritage, neither allegiance or tribute paid to any sect or Missionary Board, nor any idolatrous denominational worship, nor traditions eating as doth a canker, nor worldliness to secure prosperity, not the human expedients of ladies and young people's societies for the support of the church, nor the fleshly, ungodly sociable to catch the people. Thank God, this First New Testament Church is a stranger to all the man-made systems of religious life and service ... free from all the bondage of creature religion, and separate from man-made schemes for the furtherance of the work of God.[195]

Yet having clarified the negatives of all that his church was not to be in terms of structures, Smale conversely informed members and observers what 'Holy Ghost administration' looked like according to his definition:

> [The Church] lives, most simply, to glorify God, and to have God glorified in this city and throughout the earth ... The household of God will walk in God's house, servants to Jesus Christ, filled with the Spirit ... The secret is prayer, and an individual and organic life strictly in accordance with the Word of God.[196]

---

[192] First New Testament Church Los Angeles, *Our First Anniversary*, pp. 5-6.
[193] Worrell, 'The Movements in Los Angeles, California', p. 257.
[194] Bartleman, *Azusa Street*, p. 87.
[195] First New Testament Church Los Angeles, *Historical Number of the Bulletin* (18 March 1906), p. 2.
[196] First New Testament Church Los Angeles, *Historical Number of the Bulletin* (18 March 1906), p. 2.

However, these facets of church life alone could arguably have been a sterile list of proper intentions, not dissimilar to the aspirations of many other Evangelical churches, then or since. Nonetheless, Smale sought to clarify the great principles of his church's organized life, requiring that a right 'motive in all church gatherings, or gatherings of the sectional life of the church, should be only the glory of God'. He continued, 'we are redeemed for the purposes of the Lord's will, and if we fulfil those purposes we will have no time for selfish pleasures, neither, if our hearts are right, will we have any disposition for them'.[197] Furthermore, Smale was clear that authority in all matters lay with himself and his church eldership, constituting separate offices for elders and deacons.[198] Smale stressed how the essentials to unity were bound up in all such 'provision as necessary to the effective leadership and equipment of the respective departments of our organic life be made by the Church herself, after such matters have been considered by the eldership'.[199]

One practical aspect which helps to illustrate Smale's approach regarding the 'spiritual' growth of an organically Spirit-led church may be seen in the processes he employed for church admissions. Anyone wishing to join the New Testament Church was invited to meet with the elders for half an hour on a Sunday at 7pm.[200] Smale comments, however idealistically, that

> one of the most hopeful features of our church life is in the fact that those who have united have ... professed, upon being examined by the eldership, that they were led to come among us by a deep conviction of the Lord ... May none of our people urge or even invite any one to join this church. We shrink from human additions even when the material is excellent. We are content with those whom the Lord sends us be they few or many.[201]

Such strenuous attempts to exercise human organization by means of divine power and guidance alone were the hallmark of this innovative church, and should not be deemed unspiritual.

Of course, the same was true of William Seymour and the Azusa Street Mission, who also had to try and organise structures and frameworks to nurture the revival there. A spiritual life and community requires conscious planning as well as the spontaneity of Spirit-filled activities. Robeck confirms how

---

[197] First New Testament Church Los Angeles, *Historical Number of the Bulletin* (18 March 1906), p. 5.

[198] First New Testament Church Los Angeles, *Historical Number of the Bulletin* (18 March 1906), p. 3.

[199] First New Testament Church Los Angeles, *Historical Number of the Bulletin* (18 March 1906), p. 5.

[200] First New Testament Church Los Angeles, *Church Bulletin* (22–19 April 1906).

[201] First New Testament Church Los Angeles, *Our First Anniversary* (September 1906).

Seymour was adept in moving 'the theological ideal of a priesthood of all believers from a theory into a reality':[202]

> Seymour surrounded himself with a capable interracial staff of women and men, many of whom volunteered their time. He conducted 'leaders' meetings on Monday mornings. These meetings served as times of prayer, of building mutual support, of teaching, and as strategy sessions. The revival he led required planning and forethought. His administrative skills have not yet been adequately explored.[203]

At First New Testament Church other aspects of church governance were also stipulated from the beginning, especially matters concerning giving and appropriation of church finances, allowing the fullness of the Holy Spirit to prompt all giving and distribution. For example, on Christmas Day 1905, the church demonstrated what Smale concluded was an 'extraordinary' offering for mission work. 'No one was approached and solicited FOR A CENT', 'no basket was passed' around, and yet the offering that morning totalled $3,000 as Spirit-filled believers 'flocked to the front and laid their gifts on God's altar'.[204] Smale's reminder to his people as well as the churches of Los Angeles was that 'it was in SEPARATED LIVES and upon consecrated hearts that the Lord WROUGHT TO THIS END'.[205] Such assertions by Smale illustrate his belief that organization of his, or any, church administered by the Holy Spirit would be recognisable in Los Angeles or anywhere for the following reasons:

> The church that will live unto God shall be a peculiar treasure to God ... He will make it a power. He will give to it phenomenal glory. He will impart to it the miraculous element ... He will increase it and cause the very ends of the earth to know its faith and love in its sacrificial life and gifts.[206]

Such specific convictions tally with the later teaching of the Apostolic Faith Mission, with their early instruction on money matters.

---

[202] C.M. Robeck, Jr, 'William Joseph Seymour', in Burgess and Van der Maas (eds), *New International Dictionary*, p. 1056.

[203] Robeck, Jr, 'William Joseph Seymour', p. 1056.

[204] First New Testament Church Los Angeles, *Historical Number of the Bulletin* (18 March 1906), p. 7.

[205] First New Testament Church Los Angeles, *Historical Number of the Bulletin* (18 March 1906), p. 7 (emphases original).

[206] First New Testament Church Los Angeles, *Historical Number of the Bulletin* (18 March 1906), p. 9 (emphases by Smale).

We let the Spirit lead people and tell them what they ought to give. When they get filled with the Spirit, their pocket books are converted and God makes them stewards and if He says, 'Sell out,' they will do so.[207]

In that sense, Smale's view of Spirit baptism was that God's people, individually and collectively, should be so filled with the Holy Spirit that God may speak and act through each believer and organized activity of the one church. The onus was on First New Testament Church to 'act in concert as one body in all things as far as possible'.[208] In these things, although inevitably some vestiges of Smale's former propensity to dominate and control continued at First New Testament Church,[209] there was an express commitment from the outset in September 1905 to develop church life by spiritual means only.

Smale's Advocacy through Demonstration of the Spirit's Power

Delving deeper into the specifics of First New Testament Church's busy programmes, it is possible to plot the many 'blessings' that Smale attributed to be proof of what God 'hath wrought!', explaining, 'not a day have we had of our organized life but we have received demonstrations of this'.[210] Such was the evidence in Smale's estimation of profound Holy Spirit activity that was apparent for all visitors to First New Testament.[211]

In December 1905 he catalogued some of these 'demonstrations' during their short existence at Burbank Hall, in which 'hundreds of souls have been specially wonderfully blest during the twelve weeks':[212]

(1)   The reign of the Lord over us
(2)   A pulpit free to declare the whole truth
(3)   A people free to receive the whole truth
(4)   A really spiritual church
(5)   A people who will let the Lord work as He pleases, when He pleases

---

[207] W.J. Seymour, 'In Money Matters', *The Apostolic Faith* 1.3 (Nov 1906), p. 24.

[208] Seymour, 'In Money Matters', p. 5.

[209] It is a notable trait with Smale that he was unable to keep his assistant pastors on staff for any reasonable duration, e.g., the Rev. Clatworthy at First Baptist Church Los Angeles, and Elmer Fisher at First New Testament Church Los Angeles.

[210] First New Testament Church Los Angeles, *Historical Number of the Bulletin* (18 March 1906), p. 6.

[211] It is noted that the Los Angeles newspapers do not report the demonstrations listed above, tending to concentrate on Smale's sermon themes only in the regular 'At the Churches Yesterday' column. Greater publicity resumed when the Revival manifestations became more dramatic at First New Testament Church Los Angeles in July 1906.

[212] First New Testament Church Los Angeles, *Historical Number of the Bulletin* (18 March 1906), p. 6.

(6) A people serving for the glory of God and not for carnal and sectarian display, or the praise and honor of self, or any other vain motive
(7) A scriptural unity
(8) Soul winning power
(9) A deep knowledge of the prayer life
(10) Every meeting achieving the sanctification of believers or the salvation of the lost, and most meetings accomplishing both
(11) A passion for a world's evangelization
(12) Numbers without the fleshly worldy effort to get and keep them.[213]

Building on the aforementioned, which Smale believed to be ample evidence of the Spirit's organisation among them, the movement of Holy Spirit activity started to intensify by January 1906 and was described as 'a perpetual revival'.[214] Attributing the occurrences during services to the 'quickening' and 'fire' of the Holy Ghost, one church bulletin describes the following scenes:

> A congregation last Lord's Day morning so carried away in the Spirit that the Pastor had no opportunity of preaching! The abounding testimonies, the spontaneous singing, the frequent intercession, and the altar work supplanted the regular sermon. This was indeed mightier preaching.[215]

Again, these services must be regarded in the light of a wider witness to Los Angeles Christians. The daily prayer meetings once more attracted visitors, uninhibited due to the removal of negative influences previously encountered at First Baptist. One stranger asked a church member 'when does this let out?' and received the reply, 'it goes on 365 days in the year'.[216] All age groups were represented at prayer sessions, typified by a seventy-six year old man who came forward with a 'dear little girl kneeling by his side and with open Bible pointing him to Jesus'.[217]

Correlating Bartleman's journey with these phenomena, it would seem that given his time frame that he was oscillating in his response to First New Testament Church. His criticism that the church was losing its prayerfulness as a consequence of increased organisation is interspersed with endorsement, such as the night of prayer at the New Testament Church, when 'during a deep spirit of prayer on the congregation, the Lord came suddenly so near that we could

---

[213] First New Testament Church Los Angeles, *Historical Number of the Bulletin* (18 March 1906), p. 6.
[214] First New Testament Church Los Angeles, *Historical Number of the Bulletin* (18 March 1906), p. 6.
[215] First New Testament Church Los Angeles, *Historical Number of the Bulletin* (18 March 1906), p. 6.
[216] First New Testament Church Los Angeles, *Historical Number of the Bulletin* (18 March 1906), p. 7.
[217] First New Testament Church Los Angeles, *Historical Number of the Bulletin* (18 March 1906), p. 7.

feel His presence as though he were closing in on us around the edges of the meeting'.[218] Then a paragraph later Bartleman claims 'they began to oppose my ministry at the New Testament Church', and, still later, 'I felt the New Testament Church was failing God'.[219] Although significantly, Bartleman remained in regular contact attending meetings at the church, by February 1906 he and six others were concluding an afternoon service at Burbank Hall when they 'seemed providentially led to join hands and agree in prayer to ask the Lord to pour out His Spirit speedily, with "signs following"'.[220] Although Bartleman acknowledges they were not specifying the gift of tongues at that point, their anecdotal evidence points to an increased sense of expectancy at First New Testament Church and elsewhere in Los Angeles that there was 'nothing to hinder its continuance in the purpose of God till Jesus comes'.[221]

Further manifestations of the Spirit's work at First New Testament Church during the period January to March 1906 require brief mention in order to illustrate the demonstration of revival already in progress at the time when 'God's Joshua', William Seymour, arrived in Los Angeles in February 1906.[222] Amid the intensity of the daily prayer times, there were descriptions of 'the fiery baptism of the Spirit' manifesting itself, 'making us feel as if it were but yesterday Christ had died and risen from the dead'.[223] There was 'much joy in the reclamation of backsliders'. On another afternoon a participant described the experience as akin to 'a people seated in the heavenlies. The place was ablaze with the divine glory.' 'A soul that had wandered came back with great joy, testifying that his load of sin was gone.' 'The evening meeting was so blessed that altar work went on in several parts of the hall, and many bore testimony to the renewing work of the Holy Ghost.' 'Some of us were kept so late dealing with souls that it was after midnight before we reached home.'[224] By March 1906, the regular prayer policy for the sick was clearly set out with instruction in the bulletin, inviting any who were sick to employ the James 5:14-15 injunctions to call the elders for prayer and anointing.[225]

Earlier sections dealing with the fifteen week revival at First Baptist Church have already shown Smale's willingness and desire to permit alternative expressions of worship in accordance with his publicized criteria for his church

---

[218] Bartleman, *Azusa Street*, p. 36.

[219] Bartleman, *Azusa Street*, p. 38.

[220] Bartleman, *Azusa Street*, p. 40.

[221] First New Testament Church Los Angeles, *Historical Number of the Bulletin* (18 March 1906), p. 6.

[222] Robeck, *The Azusa Street Mission and Revival*, p. 90.

[223] First New Testament Church Los Angeles, *Historical Number of the Bulletin* (18 March 1906), p. 6.

[224] First New Testament Church Los Angeles, *Historical Number of the Bulletin* (18 March 1906), p. 7.

[225] First New Testament Church Los Angeles, *Historical Number of the Bulletin* (18 March 1906), p. 11.

where Christ is actively head, and a church where the Holy Ghost is the chief administrator. By definition, these convictions opened up new possibilities, by and large prompted by Spirit led manifestations witnessed in Wales, but also the desire to create freedom for God to work as he willed. It is also important to recognise what Smale was teaching his people about the nature of true worship, while also noting the outworking in practice during these revival months.

On 2 April 1906, a day of fasting and prayer followed by a night of prayer was called at Burbank Hall.[226] This pattern was to be repeated every Monday through to July 1906.[227] The April prayer meetings were to herald a monumental month in the life of First New Testament Church and for Smale himself, as well as something of a synergy for other likeminded groupings, particularly at Azusa Street. On 8 April Smale continued preaching his Sunday series from 'The Song of Songs' with a sermon entitled 'Enraptured with Christ', accentuating the love of Christ towards his people as 'the profoundest thing in the universe'.[228] Typical of his content, he encouraged the congregation to look away from 'chilling and arbitrary' religion, 'made up of stern precepts and prohibition', and instead to know the Lord Jesus Christ, where 'you will find true religion … exhilaration, not depression; freedom, not bondage; joy, not sorrow; health, not sickness; life, not death'.[229] The reason for including these sermon notes here is their relevance to the demonstration of congregations enraptured by the Holy Spirit in the events that followed the next day.

'THAT NEVER TO BE FORGOTTEN NIGHT' (MONDAY 9 APRIL 1906)[230]

More than 200 Christians met at First New Testament Church at various points throughout Monday 9 April[231] for what was described as a 'never to be forgotten night'. Whereas the holiness prayer services which were concurrently held at 214 Bonnie Brae Street (the home of Richard and Ruth Asberry) have always been well documented in Pentecostal history, the details of this 'all night watch' at Smale's church have not been known to the same extent. The significance of Monday 9 April is the simultaneous outpouring of the Spirit at

---

[226] 'The City In Brief', *Los Angeles Times* 2 April 1906, p. 118.

[227] 'Rolling On Floor In Smale's Church', *Los Angeles Times* 14 July 1906, p. II1.

[228] 'At The Churches Yesterday', *Los Angeles Times* 9 April 1906, p. 16.

[229] 'At The Churches Yesterday', p. 16.

[230] First New Testament Church Los Angeles, *Our First Anniversary*, p. 9.

[231] There is some ambiguity in the 15 April First New Testament Church Los Angeles church bulletin report as to whether 'the revelation of our dear Lord last Monday' refers to the day of prayer and fasting on Monday 2 April 1906 or the following week, Monday 9 April 1906. On the basis that the church bulletin for Sunday 8 April (unavailable) would have reported such events from the Monday of that week suggests that it is reasonable to conclude that there was a further day and night of prayer and fasting on Monday 9 April during which these demonstrations of the Spirit power occurred.

Bonnie Brae *and* at Burbank Hall. Vinson Synan describes how, at the Asberry's home, 'Seymour and seven others fell to the floor in spiritual ecstasy, speaking in tongues'.[232]

Charles Shumway provides one of the earliest critical examinations of the precursors to the revival in Los Angeles with his thesis in 1919 describing how 'the meetings in the Asbury [sic] home grew in intensity, and in the emphasis which was being placed upon Acts 2:4'.[233] Jennie Moore was evidently 'seated on the organ stool' when Seymour announced that Edward Lee had been given the gift of tongues. Jennie Moore 'fell to the floor speaking in tongues, and in an instant most of the people in the room were similarly engaged'.[234] Shumway commented that 'her action served as the releasing key, or final suggestion, which they needed'.[235] However, although Shumway briefly describes the noise and demonstrative phenomena emanating from this outpouring, he makes no connections with unfolding events elsewhere in Los Angeles that night, that is, at First New Testament Church.

Also on 9 April, at the larger and hitherto unknown prayer gathering with Smale, a significant number of people joined 'before the Lord brought new glories to already surrendered and spiritually baptized souls'[236] in the following ways. There was 'holy Laughter', seemingly indescribable, other than the emphasis placed on the fact that it was 'holy' laughter, and the link with Psalm 126, 'Then was our mouth filled with laughter and our tongue with singing'.[237] There were also 'glad exclamations'. The report simply records anecdotal examples of phrases uttered, rather than any analysis, except that they were 'involuntary' expressions of joy, such as, 'Oh! This is rich', 'this is sweet', 'this is blessed', and 'Oh my! Isn't this beautiful'.[238] Then there were 'countenances'. Among the 100 plus who had stayed throughout the night, 'there were faces smitten with the very light of the throne' which was interpreted by Smale[239] as further evidence that the congregation were the recipients of 'heavenly experiences on earth'.[240] Interestingly, the anticipation of revival in view of these demonstrations of the Spirit's activity was referred

---

[232] V. Synan, *The Holiness-Pentecostal Tradition: Charismatic Movements in the Twentieth Century* (Eerdmans, 1997), p. 96.

[233] C.M. Shumway, 'A Critical History of Glossolalia' (unpublished PhD diss., Boston University, 1919), p. 115.

[234] Shumway, 'A Critical History of Glossolalia', p. 115.

[235] Shumway, 'A Critical History of Glossolalia', p. 116.

[236] First New Testament Church Los Angeles, *Our First Anniversary*, p. 9.

[237] First New Testament Church Los Angeles, *Our First Anniversary*, p. 9. All these references to events on 9 April were recorded in the 15 April 1906 First New Testament Church Los Angeles bulletin.

[238] First New Testament Church Los Angeles, *Our First Anniversary*, p. 9.

[239] The assumption is made that Smale was the author of such reports in the First New Testament Church Los Angeles bulletins.

[240] First New Testament Church Los Angeles, *Our First Anniversary*, p. 9.

to, in the church bulletin on Easter Day, as imminent. 'The Lord of Pentecost is about to open the windows of heaven upon our city. He will not withhold His power from a people who are determined to have Him glorified.'[241]

Accounts such as these firsthand witness recollections and insights into life at First New Testament Church during this earlier period in 1906 have not previously been reported in Pentecostal histories, and they illustrate the breadth of revival optimism across Los Angeles.

'THE GIFT OF TONGUES' (EASTER SUNDAY 15 APRIL 1906)[242]

What is well documented is the recognition that during Easter Sunday 1906, the intensity of prayer gatherings climaxed in an outpouring of the Spirit at Smale's church in Burbank Hall when, according to Bartleman, 'a colored sister ... spoke in tongues'.[243] Robeck has, to date, provided the most comprehensive account of all these interwoven strands of that monumentally defining Easter week, which for this section can best be examined up to the San Francisco earthquake of 18 April.[244] Recognising the African-American dimension of the prayer group that had gathered at the Asberry's home on 9 April,[245] it is significant to note that Jennie Evans Moore bridges both the Bonnie Brae outpouring and the First New Testament meeting on Easter Sunday by her participation in both. For even at Smale's church there was a demonstration of cultural integration, identified as evidence of the Spirit's presence.

On that Easter Sunday morning, Jennie Moore and Ruth Asberry both attended First New Testament Church and heard Smale preach on 'The Resurrection'.[246] At the close, according to Robeck's account of events, Smale presented the congregation with the 'opportunity to share a few testimonies'.[247] In response, Jennie Moore stood and described what had been happening at the Asberry's home during that past week, and concluded with the unequivocal announcement 'that "Pentecost" had come to Los Angeles'.[248] Having already taken a broader look at the heightening expectation within First New Testament Church, it is easy to appreciate how Moore's testimony connected with the congregation's own prayerful and excitable aspirations. What they were not prepared for, however, were the manifestations that followed, when Jennie

---

[241] First New Testament Church Los Angeles, *Our First Anniversary*, p. 9.

[242] First New Testament Church Los Angeles, *Our First Anniversary*, p. 10. As recorded in the 24 June 1906 First New Testament Church Los Angeles bulletin.

[243] Bartleman, *Azusa Street*, p. 43.

[244] Robeck, *The Azusa Street Mission and Revival*, pp. 60-81.

[245] C.M. Robeck, Jr, *Enrichment Journal* (Spring, 2006) [Assemblies of God], http://enrichmentjournal.ag.org/200602/200602_026_Azusa.cfm, accessed 28 Nov 2008.

[246] Robeck, *The Azusa Street Mission and Revival*, p. 74.

[247] Robeck, *The Azusa Street Mission and Revival*, p. 75.

[248] Robeck, *The Azusa Street Mission and Revival*, p. 75.

Moore ended by speaking in tongues. Although Smale does not refer back to this particular incident in his *First Anniversary Bulletin*, the significance was obviously not easily forgettable. Robeck describes the scene, how 'the place was electrified!', causing diverse reactions at the church that morning with some shouting praises, others who had been to the Asberry home meetings joining in by speaking in tongues, while others 'were so frightened they jumped for the doors'.[249] Bartleman's eyewitness account adds how 'the people gathered in little companies on the sidewalk after the service inquiring what this might mean. It seemed like Pentecostal "signs".'[250]

Just over two months later, the Sunday news sheet at First New Testament Church marked the anniversary of 'the first year, beginning May 27, 1905, of the manifestation of Pentecost in our city'.[251] Besides highlighting the timeframe and the broader impact of revival upon the wider Los Angeles populace, Smale described the second year in which they were living as occupied 'by more phenomenal glory'.[252] He also affirmed that 'some of our fellowship are being favored with the gift of tongues, for which we adore Him who is the God of gifts'.[253]

Bartleman concurred with the 'glory' referenced in Smale's description, with his verdict that

> the New Testament Church received her 'Pentecost' yesterday.[254] We had a wonderful time. Men and women were prostrate under the power all over the hall. A heavenly atmosphere pervaded the place. Such singing as I have never heard before, the very melody of Heaven. It seemed to come direct from the throne.[255]

This would seem consistent with other such 'singing in the Spirit' revival phenomena, which Seymour called 'the heavenly choir'.[256]

However, all was not harmonious, as the unfolding pneumatological events at Azusa Street, and in time various other sites around Los Angeles, seemed to create a competitive edge regarding the gift of tongues. Bartleman records how by June 1906 Smale had visited Azusa Street to track down members of his First New Testament Church who, following countless others from around the world, were starting to attend the primary location for 'Pentecostal' baptism at the Azusa Street Mission. 'Brother Smale invited them back home, promised them liberty in the Spirit, and for a time God wrought mightily at the New

---

[249] Robeck, *The Azusa Street Mission and Revival*, p. 775.
[250] Bartleman, *Azusa Street*, p. 43.
[251] First New Testament Church Los Angeles, *Our First Anniversary*, p. 10.
[252] First New Testament Church Los Angeles, *Our First Anniversary*, p. 10.
[253] First New Testament Church Los Angeles, *Our First Anniversary*, p. 10, quoting from the church bulletin of 24 June 1906.
[254] A reference to 21 June 1906.
[255] Bartleman, *Azusa Street*, p. 61.
[256] Synan, *The Holiness-Pentecostal Tradition*, p. 100.

Testament Church also.'²⁵⁷ While embracing the experiential aspect of Spirit baptism, Smale's theological stance differed from William Seymour's in one important matter, namely the relationship between Spirit baptism and the spiritual gifts. Smale explained to his congregation in July 1906 that while the baptism of the Spirit is

> necessary, according to the Scriptures, for sanctification ...; enduement [sic] with power from on high ...; for endowment ... These three blessings do not necessarily involve three baptisms. Cornelius and his household were *born again, sanctified, endued, and endowed, all on one meeting.*²⁵⁸

Further clarification was forthcoming as to Smale's position regarding glossolalia, with a bold heading: 'THE GIFT OF TONGUES IS NOT FOR EVERY CHRISTIAN'.²⁵⁹ Then, on the inside page of that same bulletin, Smale included a paragraph outlining his position regarding 'The Azusa Street Meetings':

> The Pastor still maintains a cordial attitude toward them, and will continue to do so as long as God's Spirit works in them. He has a love for every child of God, but is obliged to differ from some of the doctrinal positions taken by the leaders of the Apostolic Faith Movement. The positions to which he has taken exception will be deplored by all lovers of an entire Bible ...²⁶⁰

While Smale does not specify glossolalia as the main point of divergence with Azusa Street (given the practice was endorsed under Smale's leadership), he obviously believed this and possibly other aspects of their emphases to be the deviant consequence of 'spinning doctrinal theories because a majority of certain scriptures seem to favour such theories'.²⁶¹ Herein lay the theological nub of Smale's 'Moses' *modus operandi*. Tongues were not the only definitive evidence of Spirit baptism, according to Smale, who cited the proof that

---

²⁵⁷ Bartleman, *Azusa Street*, p. 54.

²⁵⁸ First New Testament Church Los Angeles, *Church Bulletin* (8 July–15 July 1906), p. 1, emphasis original. Smale's understanding of baptism in the Spirit with regard to sanctification and spiritual gifts is presented more fully in the following chapter. In brief, at this point in his life and ministry Smale viewed 'the gift of the Holy Spirit' as a deepening, experiential extension of the initial conversion-gift of the Spirit. Rather than promoting a theological framework of rigid and distinct stages, Smale interpreted the inherent processes of sanctification and Spirit baptism more ambiguously, incorporating an amalgam of Wesleyan and non-Wesleyan emphases.

²⁵⁹ First New Testament Church Los Angeles, *Church Bulletin* (8 July–15 July 1906), p. 1, emphasis original. See full text reproduced in Appendix III.

²⁶⁰ First New Testament Church Los Angeles, *Church Bulletin* (8 July–15 July 1906), p. 3.

²⁶¹ First New Testament Church Los Angeles, *Church Bulletin* (8 July–15 July 1906), p. 3.

'thousands of the Lord's dear people have been baptized in the Holy Ghost and in fire who never received the gift of tongues'.[262]

That stated, Smale, like many of his Pentecostal counterparts, was having to develop and recalibrate his theology on the move, amid the experiential signs and wonders of Spirit baptism. Smale's bibliocentric position is not surprising given his Spurgeonic roots. However, what does appear radical in terms of his heritage was his willingness to encourage the space and permission for the more overtly charismatic gifts to be exercised at First New Testament Church during this period. From June onwards, besides glossolalia being regularly practised within his church context, Smale also encouraged prophecy, exorcism of the demonic, prayer for the sick, and a heightened expectation of miracles.[263] He also continued to provide opportunity for public testimony, capturing something of the public verification of Holy Spirit work in human contexts, as the next section illustrates.

'HEAVEN TOO IS COLOR BLIND' (JUNE 1906)[264]

Other tangible demonstrations of the Spirit's power, interpreted as signs of heaven upon earth, were manifest in Los Angeles during these months of revival. Racial integration at Azusa Street during the summer months of 1906 has already been well documented with Bartleman's graphic description that 'the 'color line' was washed away in the blood' of Jesus.[265] However, the evidence of further primary materials discovered illustrate that similar racial harmony existed at First New Testament Church during these months also, which was particularly significant amid the racial divides of the social milieu of Los Angeles at the beginning of the twentieth century. Apart from verifiable data about racial identities drawn from membership and baptism lists, the best insight and use of 'color blind' language emanates from this example the church's first anniversary bulletin:

> A colored sister in giving her testimony in one of the services declared that she felt very happy amongst us. Said she, 'my daughter said to me the other night after we had been to one of your prayer meetings, "Mamma, those people down at the New Testament Church are color blind."' Our hearts exclaim, 'Hallelujah!' We have no prejudices on the ground of nationality.[266]

---

[262] First New Testament Church Los Angeles, *Church Bulletin* (8 July–15 July 1906), p. 2.

[263] Robeck, *The Azusa Street Mission and Revival*, p. 83.

[264] First New Testament Church Los Angeles, *Our First Anniversary*, p. 8. As recorded in the 3 June 1906 First New Testament Church Los Angeles bulletin.

[265] Bartleman, *Azusa Street*, p. 54.

[266] First New Testament Church Los Angeles, *Our First Anniversary*, p. 8, quoting from the church bulletin of 3 June 1906.

Furthermore, a Spanish man was serving on the diaconate and a Chinese man had been serving in the eldership at First New Testament Church until he was sent as a missionary to China. While these reports appeared in the 3 June 1906 bulletin, the timing of Bartleman's similar statement about racial unity noted above is uncertain. It allows for the intriguing possibility that it may have been this testimony and article at First New Testament Church that prompted Bartleman's own description. The similarity of terminology is obvious, though direct plagiarism cannot be proven. A reflective comment on this emerging racial identity within congregations such as Azusa Street and First New Testament Church is worth noting because a process was at work within these early Pentecostal congregations modelling a new identity.[267]

Besides Smale's congregational experience contributing to the emerging model of racial integration, his teaching also elaborated the basis for true church integration as a harmony which is not determined by 'the country in which we were born nor the color of our skin', but 'our unity is determined by our relation to Christ'.[268] Then, following a statement reminding his congregation that 'Heaven too is color blind, for it is written, "I beheld, and lo, a great multitude ... of all nations, and kindreds and people and tongues stood before the throne ..."', Smale concludes with a prayer of intent encompassing all that was being experienced, and the challenge for more: 'Let us make the life of earth like the life of heaven.'[269]

Smale's Advocacy through Identification with 'The Holy Rollers'

By July 1906, the experiential manifestations of 'heaven on earth' at First New Testament Church were increasing in number, intensity and extraordinariness. This was paralleled at Azusa Street, which, some concluded, was bordering on fanaticism to the extent that press articles were describing the escalating

---

[267] D.D. Daniels, 'God Makes No Differences in Nationality: The Fashioning of a New Racial/Nonracial Identity at the Azusa Street Revival', *Enrichment Journal* (Spring, 2006), [Assemblies of God], http://enrichmentjournal.ag.org/200602/200602_072_nodifference.cfm, accessed 16 June 2008. David Daniels comments how early Pentecostals 'looked beyond the racial divide of the era and reflected a racial vocabulary, symbolism, and vision that differed drastically from the dominant society of that day ... For some of the participants, the revival introduced a new racial/non-racial identity. The mere existence of this new identity was in itself the self-understanding of the emerging Pentecostal movement. It most likely became the framework that oriented the multiracial congregations and fellowships that dotted the nascent Pentecostal movement. To even imagine a way of worshiping and living that looked beyond the color line created space for power sharing, culture exchanges, and institution building between the various races.'

[268] First New Testament Church Los Angeles, *Our First Anniversary*, p. 8, quoting from the church bulletin of 3 June 1906.

[269] First New Testament Church Los Angeles, *Our First Anniversary*, p. 8.

sensational phenomena with headings such as 'Holy Rollers Plan a Slaughter of Innocents'[270] and 'Holy Rollers' Meetings Verge On Riot'.[271] Such reports certainly created a polarization among other established churches and leaders, dividing those who felt these were Holy Spirit authenticated revivals from those who were vehemently opposed to what they considered as deception and works of the devil. Interestingly, these have been the similar responses to the more recent 'Toronto Blessing', 'Pensacola' and 'Lakeland' revivals.[272]

A brief portrait of the broader Los Angeles spiritual scene during July 1906 will establish the importance of Smale's personal and church identification with, and endorsement of, Azusa Street and other burgeoning Pentecostal mission works emerging over those months. Harvey Cox explains that Los Angeles 'has always demonstrated a remarkably high tolerance for spiritual innovators, political cranks, and religious eccentrics'.[273] For all the city's tolerance, however, the message both Smale and Seymour were proclaiming to their respective congregations concerning the imminent arrival of the 'New Jerusalem', accompanied by signs and wonders, evoked severe opposition from two flanks: the daily newspapers, and the established city churches. In respect of both of these, Smale provided implicit and explicit ambassadorial support lending weight to the vulnerabilities of early Pentecostalism, that this new spiritual movement was to traverse denominations at many levels.

IMPLICIT AMBASSADORIAL SUPPORT

Mention has just been made of two provocative headlines from the *Los Angeles Herald*. Other papers reported similar descriptions, such as 'Wild Scenes' and a 'Weird Babble of Tongues', 'Holy Kickers Carry on Mad Orgies', and 'Whites and Blacks Mix in a Religious Frenzy'.[274] The stir caused by events at the Azusa Street Mission in particular was relentless and 'overwhelmingly negative',[275] although it did ironically serve to promote the congregation's presence and purposes free of charge.

The same was true, if to a lesser extent, for First New Testament Church, which was the subject of the *Los Angeles Times*' attention on 14 July 1906 under the well-known heading 'Rolling on Floor in Smale's Church', followed by the 17 July 1906 column 'Holy Roller Mad'. These articles have been used as the defining portrayal of the Spirit's outpouring at Smale's church, typical of

---

[270] 'Jumpers to Kill Children', *Los Angeles Herald* 20 July 1906, p. 1.

[271] 'Monrovians Ask Officers to Act', *Los Angeles Herald* 21 July 1906, p. 4.

[272] See M. Poloma, *Mainstreet Mystics: The Toronto Blessing and Reviving Pentecostalism* (AlaMira Press, 2003); D. Hilborn, *Toronto in Perspective* (Paternoster, 2001).

[273] H. Cox, *Fire From Heaven: The Rise of Pentecostal Spirituality and the Reshaping of Religion in the Twenty-First Century* (Da Capo Press, 1995), p. 51.

[274] Cox, *Fire From Heaven*, p. 59.

[275] Robeck, *The Azusa Street Mission and Revival*, p. 82.

the meetings held at First New Testament Church throughout this period, although curiously, as we have already noted, such journalistic accounts have prompted no subsequent analysis.

The following observations are noteworthy in respect of Smale's wider ambassadorial support of the Pentecostal movement. In particular, the strong experiential and fanatical component was witnessed in their worship at First New Testament as they 'worked themselves into a wild religious frenzy at a meeting last night in Burbank Hall'.[276] In terms of Pentecostal definition, Smale was already in the 'Promised Land'.

Likewise, according to the developing theology evident at such gatherings, the gift of tongues was linked to their missionary mandate, believing they were 'chosen of God to carry the gospel to the ends of the earth', with the announcement 'that the church members will become missionaries to heathen lands'.[277] Other phenomena, independently witnessed by the journalist, are also worth stating here in the interest of researching patterns within revivals past and present.

> Muttering an unintelligible jargon, men and women rolled on the floor, screeching at the top of their voices at times, and again giving utterance to cries which resembled those of animals in pain. There was a Babel of sound. Men and women embraced each other in the fanatical orgy.
>
> One young woman jumped from her seat, screaming 'Praise Him! Praise Him! Praise Him!' and then fell in a writhing fit of hysterical weeping prone on the floor. None of the worshippers went to her rescue. She became unconscious and was left for hours where she had fallen.
>
> Evangelist Boyd, asked by an outsider why he did not secure medical aid for the young woman, smiled and said: 'Oh, she'll come out of that all right; she has the power and the Lord is working with her.'
>
> Sitting on the front seat was a pretty young woman scarcely more than 18, who seemed greatly affected by the condition of the girl who had fainted. She was fashionably dressed. Suddenly she arose and began to cackle like a hen. Forth and back she walked in front of the company, wringing her hands and clucking something which no one could interpret.
>
> The leader explained that she was speaking a dialect of a Hindoo [sic] tribe. He said she would leave soon for India to teach the natives the gospel.
>
> Another woman testified ... 'I want you all to pray for him [my husband].'
>
> This was a signal for the whole company to come forward and fall prostrate around the platform. Women and men trembled and prayed, shouted and muttered ...
>
> Boyd kept urging the people, especially the women, to testify. When he had the company rolling on the floor the leader clapped his hands for joy and smiled.[278]

---

[276] 'Rolling on Floor in Smale's Church', p. II1.
[277] 'Rolling on Floor in Smale's Church', p. II1.
[278] 'Rolling on Floor in Smale's Church', p. II1.

These occurrences are cited here to demonstrate that such phenomena were not restricted to the events at the Azusa Street Mission, thus sustaining the argument that Smale was implicitly providing support for the wider Pentecostal movement. Greater impact was to follow on 23 July 1906, with the *Los Angeles Times* headers, 'Queer "Gift" Given Many', and subheadings, 'Burbank Hall Is the Scene of Strange Services', 'Gift of Tongues Is Visited Upon Several Women', and 'Hindu Priest Tells How He Was Converted'.[279] Here Smale and his congregation were pilloried by cartoon and article regarding the following observations of the reporter who joined the congregation 'so large that scores could find no seats and stood about the doors and along the walls in expectancy of miracles to come'.

> Besides speaking in unknown languages, some of the adherents of the First New Testament Church, as Smale calls his house of worship, sang in languages unknown to those about them ...
> The storm arose gradually and began to sway the congregation in the midst of Smale's sermon ...
> Last night the jabbering was general ...
> Miss Keyes [the daughter of Dr Henry S Keyes] herself was the first to speak in a foreign language last night. The pastor had asked for quotations from the scriptures which had first converted the members to Christianity, and after several in various parts of the hall had given them, Miss Keyes arose and articulated something in a high-pitched voice, which can hardly be described. She claims it is Arabic. It sounded much like the rapid chattering of a frightened simian ...
> The climax came when Mr. Smale announced that a Hindu priest had a word to say. A little black man majestically ascended the platform, and told how he had been converted to Christianity, and had received the gift of tongues in Los Angeles ... and in a tedious manner, he related how he had smashed the stone god he carried about with him and had been given the gift of English in one night.[280]

The derogatory tones of the journalist's article aside, it is significant to note that the greatest impression of the evening on this person were the 'types' of attendees at the service, as highlighted in the cartoon and the descriptive account that followed:

> whilst there was a restless air about the audience before the services began, a stranger estimating the character of the crowd would not have expected to see the prosperous-appearing, tastefully-dressed and cultured-looking assembly resolve itself to an old-fashioned revival meeting with all the accompaniments of loud wailing, bursts of song and prayer and shouting of 'Hallelujah'.[281]

---

[279] 'Queer 'Gift' Given Many', *Los Angeles Times* 23 July 1906, p. I5.
[280] 'Queer 'Gift' Given Many', p. I5.
[281] 'Queer 'Gift' Given Many', p. I5.

Figure 14: 'QUEER "GIFT" GIVEN MANY',
Los Angeles Times 23 July 1906, p. 15.

Besides further evidence here of all that was being claimed as substantive demonstrations of the Spirit's work, the implicit role of Smale as a well-known, established pastor of the prestigious First Baptist Church beforehand, and now leading a new congregation incorporating the 'respectable' at Burbank Hall cannot be underestimated. Having said that and considering the ferocity of the attack of the press, it must not be construed that Seymour requested support or alliances, for he did not. They had their own interpretation of events, as recorded in *The Apostolic Faith* newspaper.

The secular papers have been stirred and published reports against the movement, but it has only resulted in drawing hungry souls who understand that the devil would not fight a thing unless God was in it. So they have come and found it was indeed the power of God.[282]

However, the coverage given to Smale's ministry at this juncture is critical when it is noted on the same evening another Los Angeles paper, *The Evening News*,[283] printed a satirical cartoon on their front page mocking, for example, the excesses of the 'Holy Roller' Pentecostal types, denigrating the gift of tongues and participation of women. Whereas this portrayal attributed the activities of such 'sects' to the 'Summer Solstice', Smale's involvement may legitimately be considered an implicit 'voice' of counter-propaganda, thus corroborating his shared convictions with Seymour and others, that they were indeed experiencing manifestations of the latter days.

EXPLICIT AMBASSADORIAL SUPPORT

The other flank of opposition to the revival at Azusa Street revealed itself among many of the established churches in the city who belonged to the 'Los Angeles Church Federation'. Robeck explains how the Federation 'raised serious questions' about what they and many regarded as 'out-of-control fanaticism'.[284] Their President, the Rev. E.P. Ryland, had in fact visited Azusa Street 'at the request of his fellow ministers'. He reported his findings, explaining his belief that 'enthusiastic fanaticism is responsible for the claims of the Azusa Street worshippers'.[285] Ryland continued by dismissing the antics he had witnessed at Azusa:

> I heard one negro woman talk in what she said was a foreign tongue, but the language had no resemblance whatever to any that I had ever heard, and there was nothing to indicate that it was a language with any rules of construction. I had no doubt the woman was sincere, but she had worked herself into an excitement that made her irresponsible.[286]

This was the extent of Ryland's objectivity. Although he had visited Azusa Street to gain firsthand evidence, this must be regarded as symptomatic of the Federation's indiscriminate hostility towards the new movement. Ryland represented a formalised church constituency, which, when confronted by the extraordinary zeal and exploits at Azusa Street and First New Testament Church, found themselves forced to respond. By Ryland's own admission, the

---

[282] *The Apostolic Faith* 1.1 (September, 1906), p. 5.
[283] 'Summer Solstice Sees Strenuous Sects Sashaying', *The Evening News* 23 July 1906, p. 1.
[284] Robeck, *The Azusa Street Mission and Revival*, p. 83.
[285] 'Churches Aroused to Action', *Los Angeles Express* 18 July 1906.
[286] 'Churches Aroused to Action'.

orthodox churches were, in many cases, content 'enjoying the light they have received', whereas the 'new creeds' which were 'springing up here and there' involve workers 'who have set us a good example in missionary effort'.[287] Significantly, the causal link was extended specifically to identify Joseph Smale as one of the catalysts for the Federation's resurgence, given that 'Speaking with Tongues' had 'extended to the First New Testament Church in Burbank Hall. These and other demonstrations have aroused the Federation to action.'[288]

While awaiting their first planning meeting to develop appropriate strategies for action, the Los Angeles Church Federation's concerns were further reinforced by secular press reports outlining the radical and, worse still, suggesting criminal intent inherent in these emerging Pentecostal 'sects'. Portraying the 'Holy Rollers' as a radicalising group, the newspaper's 'investigative' piece made front page copy, explaining how members were considering emulating the Abrahamic sacrifice of Isaac scenario, with some 'advocating the slaying [of] one child from each household as a human paschal lamb to gain sanctification'.[289] What's more, the police marshal or deputy had to attend the meeting 'each afternoon or night ... to restrain the frenzy of the Rollerites if necessary'.[290] Recognising the power of the printed word, as well as the fact that Smale and his church were already guilty by association with such phenomena, the physiological interpretation posited by the *Herald* with this explanation of the use of 'tongues' would have inevitably heightened the negativity of the Federation.

> To have one's jaw twisted completely about and the tongue loosed during a trance-performance is what these people go through, during which they 'get a tongue'. These spasms are usually preceded by moans and wriggling and peculiar antics. Men and women have been on the floor rolling about at the meetings.[291]

By comparison, the media attention given to the Los Angeles Church Federation appeared markedly sane. Their strategy for a programme of mission throughout the summer was swiftly put in place following an open meeting on 24 July,[292] under the theme 'What May Be Accomplished for the Church in July and August'.[293]

However, three days before the hundred plus[294] church leaders met, Joseph Smale chose to communicate with the Los Angeles Church Federation

---

[287] 'Churches Aroused to Action'.
[288] 'Churches Aroused to Action'.
[289] 'Jumpers To Kill Children', p. 1.
[290] 'Jumpers To Kill Children', p. 1.
[291] 'Jumpers To Kill Children', p. 2.
[292] 'Week's Events in Churches', *Los Angeles Express* 21 July 1906.
[293] 'Church Workers To Meet Tonight', *Los Angeles Express* 24 July 1906, p. 12.
[294] 'Evangelists To Work In Summer', *Los Angeles Herald* 25 July 1906, p. 4.

leadership in an 'Open Letter' printed in the 23 July *Los Angeles Express*.[295] The thrust of his letter was a clarion call that 'the churches must cease their unholy rivalries, their living for carnal worldly display, [and] their glorying in denominationalism'.[296] Hence the explicit ambassadorial role identified here which, in Robeck's view, affirmed Smale as 'the ideal mediator between the Azusa Street Mission and the Los Angeles Church Federation'.[297] Smale's letter reveals a passionate concern that the Federation's endeavours should synchronize with all that God was already doing in the city with the anticipation that 'we are nearing a great Pentecost' which may be months or a year off, but it 'is a sure experience for our city, and every Christian should be prepared to welcome it'.[298]

The tensions underlying the motivation of the Federation, though widely reported, had been denied by their president, E.P. Ryland, stating, 'this effort must not be construed into a fight against the new creeds'.[299] Smale responded by affirming his 'joy that the new movements of God in our midst are exercising your minds and provoking them to a serious study of the noteworthy situation'.[300] He then continued to outline recommendations to the Federation executive, primarily calling for greater openness on their part and 'suspending criticism of that which we do not understand, for the Lord is verily in our midst in unprecedented activity and grace, and will bless those who do not grieve Him by taking sides with the enemy'.[301] In terms of his mediation, Smale itemised core aspects of commonality whereby he considered the 'conservative orthodox'[302] historic churches and the newer 'undenominationalists' (which he considered himself to be) might start to connect to share progress. First, Smale called for caution with regard to classification: recognising that what some called 'fanaticism' others affirmed to be a 'deep work of the Spirit of God in human hearts and lives'. Secondly, Smale called for discernment regarding manifestations: acknowledging that 'the devil is working and demon possession is multiplying. This is nothing new and ought not to be thought peculiar ... Let us not stumble over these diabolical manifestations and reject what is indisputably of the Holy Spirit.' Finally, Smale endorsed the Federation's call 'that churches be urged to "reaffirm their faith in fundamental principles"'. For Smale this would need to be more than a declaration of orthodoxy. 'No reaffirmation of truth will eject the devil who is strongly entrenched in modern

---

[295] 'New Testament Leader Writes Open Letter', *Los Angeles Express* 23 July 1906, p. 6.
[296] 'New Testament Leader Writes Open Letter', p. 6.
[297] Robeck, *The Azusa Street Mission and Revival*, p. 84.
[298] 'New Testament Leader Writes Open Letter', p. 6.
[299] 'Churches Aroused To Action'.
[300] 'New Testament Leader Writes Open Letter', p. 6.
[301] 'New Testament Leader Writes Open Letter', p. 6.
[302] 'Praying Bands For Churches', *Los Angeles Express* 25 July 1906, p. 6.

religious life. If the contemplated reaffirmation be made, is it to be followed up in practical illustrations in pulpit and pew?'[303] However, apart from raising these elements for dialogue, the bulk of Smale's open letter was prescriptive, offering his insights from twenty-five years of church life and ministry. His convictions, described as the 'supreme need of the hour if the churches are to be saved from taking sides against God in the present and coming manifestations of Himself among men',[304] were sevenfold:

1) The churches must have a fearless ministry, preaching nothing but the Word of God.
2) The churches must be called to a renewed prayer life, as the method of purging the 'worldliness, commercialism, higher criticism, and every form of sacrilege of which they have been guilty'.
3) The churches must address their admission to membership, allowing 'only the godly into their fellowship', whilst being 'patterns of godliness to all that come among them'.
4) The churches must first 'share in the fellowship of His [Christ's] sufferings', 'accepting the offence of the cross'. The coronation day will 'not be until our Lord's second coming'.
5) The churches must 'exalt in a most practical sense the headship of Christ', letting 'the modern church officialism cease controlling the house of God ... in direct antagonism to the simplicity of organized life for the people of God as laid down in the scriptures'.
6) The churches must 'cease their unholy rivalries ... their glorying in denominationalism' and 'must seek to do the things that please the Lord'.
7) The churches must allow 'a perfect freedom of action to the Spirit of God'.[305]

Smale concluded the letter, acknowledging that there were other good points of organized church life that could be discussed, and assuring readers that his sincere motive in writing was never to 'deal unfriendly thrusts'. But he wrote with the hope that others may share his experience, having 'labored in a denominational church, often in a Gethsemane of suffering', and may also experience the discovery of 'the simplicity of New Testament life'. Such was Smale's theologically articulate defence and challenge publicly stated for all to read.

The Los Angeles Church Federation continued to make plans to evangelise Los Angeles by implementing a two-year programme. This included establishing 'praying bands' to promote private and public prayer times, linked to 'street meetings', and the organization of the city into districts where all newcomers could be visited to 'ascertain their church preferences'.[306] Further

---

[303] 'New Testament Leader Writes Open Letter', p. 6.
[304] 'New Testament Leader Writes Open Letter', p. 6.
[305] 'New Testament Leader Writes Open Letter', p. 6.
[306] 'Praying Bands For Churches', p. 6.

cooperation between churches was envisaged with a Federation committee appointed to make plans for a city-wide 'religious crusade'.[307] Ironically, the hostile reaction evoked by Azusa Street and First New Testament Church actually culminated in greater unity and evangelistic activity among the established churches, although the Los Angeles Church Federation were quick to deny the journalist's assertions that their new found 'aggressive' momentum was in fact simply following 'the example of the sects which preach "strange doctrines"'.[308] It was obvious to all that the Los Angeles Church Federation had been impacted within three months by the revival at Azusa Street and First New Testament Church. Robeck observes another surprising angle, that although Bartleman 'failed to pen a single word about' this encounter between the churches of Los Angeles,[309] *The Apostolic Faith* paper did note that 'in California, where there had been no unity among churches, they are becoming one against this Pentecostal movement'.[310] Smale had played his advocacy role boldly within the ecclesiological intensity of the summer months of 1906, leaving some to speculate to what extent he might have fulfilled greater leadership within the emergent Pentecostal movement had it not been for the factors that caused him to withdraw prematurely.

Smale's Advocacy through Publication

One final section about Smale must briefly be included here, because the printed word was also a component within Joseph Smale's ministry and advocacy of the emerging Pentecostalism. As already illustrated in chapter 2, Smale was an innovator in the mould of his mentor C.H. Spurgeon, and had previously attempted the publication of sermons and pamphlets as a means of evangelistic outreach in Ryde and Prescott. By 1906, seemingly with more financial and personnel resources, Smale and thirty-six team members from First New Testament Church strategized with the publication and delivery of 'gospel' material to 'every unevangelized home in the city'[311] – by then a population of 228,298.[312] These booklets included a sermon, the 'third chapter of John's Gospel' and an 'outline of the current meetings of the Church'. Deaconesses were appointed to coordinate the distribution among districts, with the encouragement that others might wish to join the team and discover the

---

[307] 'Plan For Religious Crusade', *Los Angeles Express* 2 August 1906, p. 5.
[308] 'Plan For Religious Crusade', p. 5.
[309] Robeck, *The Azusa Street Mission and Revival*, p. 86.
[310] *The Apostolic Faith* 1.2 (October, 1906), p. 32.
[311] First New Testament Church Los Angeles, *Historical Number of the Bulletin* (18 March 1906), p. 8.
[312] Synan, *The Holiness-Pentecostal Tradition*, p. 85.

leading of the Spirit 'yielding a great harvest in the day of our dear Lord's appearing'.[313]

Also printed in the first six months of the church's life, were seven other sermons by Smale, including: 'Christian Baptism and Church Membership', 'Search me, O God', 'The Bread of Life', 'A Cake not Turned', 'The Secret of Happiness', 'The Gospel for the Age', and, most significantly for this study, a book containing seven sermons that Smale preached in the Autumn of 1905, entitled, *The Pentecostal Blessing*. These sermons will be analysed in the next chapter when we analyse Smale's developing pneumatology in his preaching ministry. But the relevance for this section is the illustration that Smale's advocacy of the work of the Spirit provided a parallel basis, in word and print, for all that would transpire at Azusa Street and other centres of Pentecostal revival in Los Angeles. His name and sermons were widely distributed, suggesting popularity in some quarters, attracting individuals to meetings and adding legitimization, should that have been necessary, to the whole movement. During this period letters were 'multiplying, daily, from all parts of the world, enquiring into spiritual conditions prevailing in this church [First New Testament Church] and city. The Lord's people, from near and far, are rejoicing in the outpouring of the Holy Spirit upon us and craving to be remembered by us before God.'[314]

In terms of Smale's 'Moses' motif and leadership capabilities, it seems plausible to stretch his designation to include the foresight that was to be an integral characteristic of Pentecostal publishing. According to Malcolm Taylor's thesis, 'Publish and Be Blessed', Seymour also 'had the prescience to realise that the key factor in publicising this new work of God was literature'.[315] Though never printing anything like the quantity of *The Apostolic Faith* papers that Seymour was to publish and distribute,[316] Smale likewise realised the enormous potential of the printed page, through advertisements, sermons and unsolicited news reports, good and bad. For example, promotions for Smale's writing can be found in a 'Christian Missionary Alliance' magazine,[317] advertising his article 'The Gift of Tongues', then published in 'Living Truths'.[318] Copies of his work *The Pentecostal Blessing* were being advertised by April 1906, with the endorsement that the book 'should be in the hands of all young Christians and those who are seeking the Baptism of the Spirit and

---

[313] First New Testament Church Los Angeles, *Historical Number of the Bulletin* (18 March 1906), p. 8.

[314] First New Testament Church Los Angeles, *Our First Anniversary*, p. 13.

[315] M.J. Taylor, 'Publish and Be Blessed: A Case Study in Early Pentecostal Publishing History 1906–1926' (unpublished PhD diss., University of Birmingham, 1994), p. 79.

[316] Robeck, *The Azusa Street Mission and Revival*, p. 88.

[317] *Christian and Missionary Alliance* (12 January 1907), p. 24.

[318] *Living Truths* VII.1 (January, 1907), pp. 32-43.

the Sanctified Life'.[319] Similar adverts inviting subscriptions for all his writings and published sermons available for order were regularly included in church bulletins.[320] More informally, 'the Pastor's Correspondence' solicited a request for the prayers of the First New Testament Church congregation, that 'the Spirit may guide the pen of Pastor Smale to write a divine message to all who are writing him for spiritual tidings and the mind of the Lord'.[321]

It is also useful to log the emerging network connections that were in existence from 1906–08. On 22 April 1906, following the San Francisco earthquake, Bartleman took 10,000 of his published tract, 'The Last Call', to First New Testament Church. The material 'seemed very appropriate after the earthquake' and so the workers at the church 'seized them eagerly and scattered them quickly throughout the city'.[322] In this tract Bartleman predicted 'one last "world-wide revival" before the Day of judgement', prophesying that 'some tremendous event is about to transpire'.[323] Similar connections are illustrative of the degree of cooperation in place across some of the churches in Los Angeles, though, as we have seen, not all networks were sympathetic to the emerging Pentecostal movement.

Amidst the ecstasy of the scenes described at Burbank Hall during 1905 and 1906, a sequence of events was to happen at First New Testament Church that would cause Smale's retreat from early Pentecostalism. Whether there was a specific 'Moses' moment when he decided to rescind his more palpable Pentecostal convictions, or whether this was a more gradual process cannot be categorically concluded. The evidence of the next chapter suggests that Smale continued to employ aspects of Pentecostal life and practice for a number of years thereafter.

---

[319] First New Testament Church Los Angeles, *Church Bulletin* (22–29 April 1906), p. 1.
[320] *Church Bulletin* (22–29 April 1906), p. 1.
[321] First New Testament Church Los Angeles, *Our First Anniversary*, pp. 13-14.
[322] Bartleman, *Azusa Street*, p. 49.
[323] Synan, *The Holiness-Pentecostal Tradition*, p. 87.

CHAPTER 5

Smale's Pentecostal Life and Service

This chapter takes as its premise the centrality of the doctrine of the Holy Spirit in shaping Joseph Smale's life and ministry. Following his return from the transformational firsthand experience of the Welsh Revival, Smale's new insights prompted the catalytic daily prayer gatherings in Los Angeles described in chapter 4. By July 1905 Smale had simultaneously introduced this illuminative statement in all church bulletins and newspaper adverts to describe the new *modus operandi* of ministry at First Baptist Church Los Angeles:

> The First Baptist Church of Los Angeles is a fellowship for evangelical preaching, evangelical teaching, *pentecostal life and pentecostal service*.[1]

Indeed, this phrase, abbreviated thereafter to 'pentecostal life and service', was then repeated on all published documents emanating from First New Testament Church also.[2] On the basis of that slogan's frequent usage between 1905 and 1908, this period may appropriately be categorized for the purposes of this chapter as Joseph Smale's Pentecostal phase.

Within those parameters, my objective is to analyse the specific form or 'shape of pneumatology'[3] evident in Smale's theology and practice during that period in particular. But as this biographical study has repeatedly recognised, any theological developments may only accurately be evaluated within the scope of the subject's broader life history. Therefore, it is worth recalling that a distinct pneumatological thread is evident in Smale from his Spurgeonic roots, as we have seen in chapter 2, right through to the last available evidence discovered within a sermon that Smale preached at a 'Union Conference of Christians' in April 1925, one year before he died.[4] For Smale, 'Pentecostal

---

[1] 'Church Services', *Los Angeles Times* 29 July 1905, p. 111. First Baptist Church Los Angeles, *Church Bulletin* (20 August 1905), emphases added.

[2] This header was used in all First New Testament Church Los Angeles weekly church bulletins discovered from 22 April 1906 until 15 November 1908, as well as First New Testament Church Los Angeles advertisements placed in local newspapers; e.g., *Los Angeles Times* 29 April 1906 until 12 October 1907.

[3] J. McIntyre, *The Shape of Pneumatology: Studies in the Doctrine of the Holy Spirit* (T&T Clark, 1997).

[4] J. Smale, 'A Message to Spirit-Filled Believers' (sermon 9 April 1925), *Truth: Earthly and Heavenly*, No. 2625, (1925/26), pp. 87-92.

Theology' was not an 'oxymoron'.[5] Similar to other early Pentecostal leaders, he had to classify and interpret ongoing experiences of the Holy Spirit at First Baptist and then First New Testament Churches. So while Smale was instantaneous in identifying this activity of the Spirit of God within the scope of 'Pentecostal life and service', the labels he adopted were in part anticipatory, preceding as they did even greater outpourings of the Spirit. The fusion between his own experiences and theological construction will also enable an accurate evaluation of the factors that led to Smale's ultimate withdrawal from this Pentecostal phase. Before examining any specific shape of Smale's pneumatological outworking, a few other introductory comments will provide a broader context for the analysis that follows.

A Plethora of Pentecostalisms

Recognising the validity of Smale's 'theological self-interpretation'[6] at this key point in revival history in Los Angeles corroborates the view that there was never one exclusive 'Pentecostal' profile which primarily emphasised glossolalia or other charisms. Rather, as Donald Dayton explains,

> even the formalized statements of belief and doctrine within Pentecostalism reflect an amazing variety, containing not only the classical and common doctrines of the Christian church usually amplified by various additions on Pentecostal distinctives – tongues, baptism in the Spirit, and so forth, but also often 'articles of faith' on such topics as foot washing, church property, the usefulness of camp meetings, and membership in secret societies or labor unions.[7]

Frank Macchia's detailed article 'Pentecostal Theology'[8] provides clarification for the purposes of definition in light of what will be argued concerning Joseph Smale's theology and practice. Macchia contends that 'it is impossible to speak of "a" Pentecostal theology' because the 'relationship between experience and doctrine is ... complex'[9] and there are so many aspects of Pentecostalism still requiring methodical reflection. Therefore, it is within the plethora of 'Pentecostalisms'[10] that Smale's Pentecostal life and practice is analysed in this chapter, noting the validity of his unique contribution among others. Of course,

---

[5] D. Jacobsen, *Thinking in the Spirit* (Indiana University Press, 2003), p. 2.

[6] Jacobsen, *Thinking in the Spirit*, p. 9.

[7] D.W. Dayton, *Theological Roots of Pentecostalism* (Hendrikson, 1987), p. 17.

[8] F.D. Macchia, 'Theology, Pentecostal', in S.M. Burgess and E.M. Van der Maas (eds), *New International Dictionary of Pentecostal and Charismatic Movements* (Zondervan, 2002), pp. 1120-41.

[9] Macchia, 'Theology, Pentecostal', p. 1123.

[10] C.M. Robeck, Jr, 'Taking Stock of Pentecostalism', *Pneuma*, 15.1 (1993), p. 45; also W.J. Hollenweger, www.epcra.ch/articles_pdf/Pentecostalisms.PDF, accessed 22 April 2008.

one of the pervasive assumptions of early Pentecostal leaders was that their own experiences and formulations were the correct ones,[11] and that the Holy Spirit would, somehow, ultimately create a new unity within the broader Christian church, even among such diversity. Moreover, the period in which Smale utilised the term 'Pentecostal' was, according to Allan Anderson, the phase in which 'Pentecostalism was in a process of formation that was not seen as a distinct form of Christianity at least until a decade after the revival'.[12] As the 'Moses' designation infers, Smale was, by then, not a participant.

Considering Smale's haste in introducing this taxonomy, in view of the deeper philosophical conundrum as to whether 'Pentecostal theology' or 'Pentecostal identity' comes first (eliciting different answers among Pentecostals), it begs the all important question regarding how and when Smale defined the meaning of being a 'Pentecostal' pastor and church. Providentially, given the primary documents discovered, identifiable patterns may be charted in his teaching and writings, as well as more generally in his organizational church strategies. Furthermore, given his pre-existing Spurgeonic theological framework and his prolonged preparation for revival, it is observable that at first Smale regarded the new classification of 'Pentecostal' as a continuum, and indeed a fulfilment, of God's work in history.

Finally, by way of introduction, it seems profitable to advise a cursory understanding of Smale's biographical movements during the period under investigation. This is provided with a chart in Appendix I. As stated, the nature of this study is documenting the hitherto unknown aspects of Smale's life and ministry for accurate historical record. However, the inherent danger now, by focusing predominantly upon the theological aspects and shape of his pneumatological convictions, is potentially one of losing clarity regarding his linear biographical plot. Aware of this tension, Smale's unfolding storyline will nonetheless be interwoven throughout the theological analysis that follows. Indeed, taking all the available primary evidence discovered, concerning Smale and the revival in Los Angeles from 1905 onwards, three dominant Pentecostal patterns emerge, namely with regard to his preaching, ecclesiology, and missiology.

The Shape of Smale's Preaching

By the summer of 1905, Smale believed that the 'Pentecostal' label appropriately described his identity and experience, as his doctrine of the Holy Spirit coalesced with the various manifestations accompanying the Spirit's outpouring during 1905–06. As we have seen, Smale had advocated the necessity of a personal Pentecost and revival over the preceding years. But the

---

[11] Jacobsen, *Thinking in the Spirit*, p. 11.
[12] A.H. Anderson, *Spreading Fires: The Missionary Nature of Early Pentecostalism* (SCM Press, 2007), p. 4.

pressing question in view of this study is to what extent Smale's preaching might be considered Pentecostal? Certainly his earlier doctrinal grasp of the Holy Spirit at work sits appropriately within the heritage of Reformed theology as exemplified by Calvin.[13] Interestingly, although Calvin has been described as 'the theologian of the Holy Spirit'[14] by virtue of the scope and depth of his doctrine of the Holy Spirit, there is recognition among some Reformed theologians that Reformed churches have subsequently remained unaware of Calvin's 'magnificent theology of the Holy Spirit',[15] by which a believer comes to know and 'enjoy Christ and all his benefits'.[16]

Consistent with Calvin's view that the Holy Spirit is the divine agent in bringing about subjective and experiential dimensions of faith, the dynamic consequences of the Spirit's outpouring in Los Angeles in 1905 ensured that Smale avoided a purely cerebral, cognitive and systematic approach to his theology.[17] Significantly, Smale had previously established a pneumatological framework for the sophisticated members at First Baptist Church and elsewhere, by drawing on the prevailing negative spiritual conditions of his day in order to accentuate the need for the Person and work of the Holy Spirit. This can be traced in his earlier preaching ministry at First Baptist Church, for example, when Smale started a 1901 sermon entitled 'The Spirit of God and You'[18] by itemising some of the common conceptions held by 'supposedly Christian minds' regarding the Holy Spirit:

a) One man regards the Spirit as but an influence.
b) Another whilst he speaks of the Spirit as a person, yet fails to magnify His office and work.

---

[13] See above chapter 2 n. 55 on Smale's self-professed Calvinistic convictions. See also, J. Calvin, *Institutes of the Christian Religion* (Westminster Press, 1960). The concentration of this study is upon Smale and his interaction with contemporary Pentecostal theologies inevitably precludes in-depth analysis of Reformed pneumatology *per se*. Introductory insights to Calvin's (and Karl Barth's) doctrine of the Holy Spirit are provided by Reformed theologian Hendrikus Berkhof, *The Doctrine of the Holy Spirit* (Epworth Press, 1965); see also J. McIntyre, *The Shape of Pneumatology* (T&T Clark, 2004), pp. 109-73.

[14] Carver T. Yu, 'Charismatic Movement, Postmodernism and Covenantal Rationality', M.W. Alston and M. Welker (eds), *Reformed Theology: Identity and Ecumenicity* (Eerdmans, 2003), p. 164. This statement about Calvin is attributed to former principal of Princeton Seminary, B.B. Warfield (1851–1921), who advocated a cessationist position in response to the revivalism in America during his lifetime.

[15] Yu, 'Charismatic Movement, Postmodernism and Covenantal Rationality', p. 164.

[16] Calvin, *Institutes* 3.1.1.

[17] Calvin's emphasis was such that 'the knowledge of *faith consists in assurance rather than in comprehension*', *Institutes*, III.2.xiv, as quoted by Yu, 'Charismatic Movement, Postmodernism and Covenantal Rationality', p. 164, italics his.

[18] 'At The Churches Yesterday', *Los Angeles Times* 13 May 1901, p. 7.

c) A third is without any convictions. The Spirit of God to him is scarcely more than a meaningless phrase.[19]

To all intents and purposes Smale emphasized pragmatic teaching about the doctrine of the Holy Spirit. Advocating theology in terms of a personal relationship between the Christian believer and the Spirit, this section of a sermon in 1898 demonstrates several important insights as to how Smale regarded the balance of structures and Holy Spirit empowerment.

> There is one thing especially of which we must be careful. It must not be to use the Lord, but to let the Lord use us. God is not our servant, but we are his, and we must therefore be under the direction of the Holy Spirit. And our first, middle and last word must be, 'Lord, what wouldst thou have me to do'. Be definite in your work and methodical, but let your definiteness and methods be the creation of the Holy Spirit.[20]

Smale's audience for such teaching, by his own definition, was the 'evangelical fold' which Smale increasingly felt needed untangling of all the personal and ecclesiological misconceptions that were inherent within their constituency. In that sense, it is clear that Smale was addressing a markedly different congregation at First Baptist than were other Pentecostal preachers and congregations for whom 'worship [and preaching] was something one did, not something one theorized about'.[21] But the significance of the example above substantiates the argument that Smale was consciously preparing the way for a Holy Spirit outpouring by way of his proactive pneumatological teaching.

A Four-Fold Gospel

Prior to 1905, with the exception of glossolalia terminology, the theological *loci* of Smale's Pentecostal pneumatology as exhibited in his preaching was generally similar in conceptualisation to other classic Pentecostals. In the main, his theology certainly incorporated what later came to be defined as the 'four-fold pattern' or 'four-fold gospel' to describe and explain 'the logic of Pentecostalism'.[22] These four common themes which found expression among early Pentecostals were salvation, baptism in the Holy Spirit, healing, and the second coming of Jesus Christ.[23] Dayton rightly points out that similar four-fold patterns were also advocated by other Christian traditions, in various

---

[19] 'At The Churches Yesterday', p. 7.

[20] J. Smale, 'Lessons in Personal Work', *The Pacific Baptist* 22.43 (24 October 1898), p. 9.

[21] G. Wacker, *Heaven Below* (Harvard University Press, 2001), p. 99.

[22] Dayton, *Theological Roots of Pentecostalism*, p. 21.

[23] A 'five-fold pattern' can also be traced, historically, with the additional theme of [entire] 'sanctification'.

combinations, originating from A.B. Simpson's 'four-fold gospel'[24] with his stress on Jesus Christ being our 'Saviour, Sanctifier, Healer, and Coming King'.[25] Similarly, Smale deployed his own four-fold combination of essential 'pulpit themes'.[26] Using slightly alternative terminology, he integrated elements of the above models by accentuating the following truths: 'justification by faith; the Spirit-filled life; sanctification; the second coming of Christ'.[27] Interestingly, 'healing' is conspicuous by its absence in Smale's schema.[28]

Smale was undoubtedly further advanced regarding the centrality of the Holy Spirit's work than his congregation at First Baptist Church Los Angeles and other local Baptist churches. Akin to the salvation and Spirit empowered aspects of four-fold patterns, in 1898 Smale had issued a clarion call for preaching with christological and pneumatological emphases as the 'need of the hour'.[29] In this he combined preaching 'made up of the doctrines of the cross', which necessitated being 'breathed by the Holy Spirit', and while not actually specifying a baptism of the Spirit, Smale does come close to such an implication, with a reference to the 'reign of the Holy Spirit in human hearts':

> It is not electrical shocks of oratory that give life to our churches. It is not a dilation upon current abuses and reforms that will draw our people to live the heavenly life or bring about the conversion of sinners. If we would present a gospel that measures human need, it must be the gospel of the blood – the shed blood of the Lamb of God; it must be the gospel too, of the reign of the Holy Spirit in human hearts.[30]

Before dissecting the major themes that shaped Smale's preaching further, it is helpful to reinforce the culmination of all these contexts that were merging during 1905–08. By pedigree, Smale was representative of the established 'Higher Life' preachers of his day – orthodox Evangelical, theologically educated, respectful social connections with legitimization from the masses and elite alike, evidenced particularly in his role as Pastor at First Baptist Church Los Angeles.

---

[24] A.B. Simpson was founder of the Christian and Missionary Alliance.
[25] Dayton, *Theological Roots of Pentecostalism*, p. 22.
[26] J. Smale, *The Pentecostal Blessing* (First New Testament Church Los Angeles, 1905), p. 34.
[27] Smale, *The Pentecostal Blessing*, p. 34.
[28] Although Smale omits any emphasis on 'healing' in his preaching, he did provide opportunities at First New Testament Church Los Angeles for prayer and anointing for healing. See below for the discussion of Smale on 'The Baptism of the Holy Ghost'.
[29] J. Smale, 'The State of Religion', *The Pacific Baptist* 22.48 (30 November 1898), p. 4.
[30] Smale, 'The State of Religion', p. 4.

Word and Spirit – Without the Play

Although his developmental journey in the things of the Spirit prior to 1905 was already immersed within the contexts just outlined, for Smale they were, however, in effect 'word and Spirit' without the 'Play'.[31] According to Jean-Jacques Suurmond's thesis, the important connection between the Spirit and the 'Play' is where individuals in the congregation actively embrace Pentecostal theology and preaching as part of their worship and community, thus marking the essential integration between the play of word and Spirit in bringing liberation and deepening of faith. Such spirituality is typical of those for whom 'in the beginning there was an experience and a testimony, then came an explanation in the form of a theological construct'.[32] Macchia summarizes the movement of various historical strands which eventually culminated in 'a "gestalt" of devotion in the Spirit to Jesus that reconfigured evangelical piety and gave Pentecostalism its Christological center as well as its theological cogency and direction'.[33]

Such strains of holiness teaching and Evangelical piety can also be identified in Smale's earlier teaching about the work of the Holy Spirit. This is presented as evidence for the foundational work Smale provided through his teaching regarding the work of the Spirit. For example, in 1898 he was preaching to young people in Los Angeles in relation to practical purposes and effective Christian living. This serves to illustrate the presence of important background themes in Smale's pneumatological development which were later restated during the Revival of 1905–06. But presented here as arguably word and Spirit without the play, Smale highlights the essentials for a Christ-centred, Spirit-empowered spirituality:

> A prepared heart: Separation from sin; separation from self; Separation from the world; Separation unto God.
> A knowledge and use of the Scriptures.
> A union between you and the Lord Jesus. You must have an experience.
> We must therefore be under the direction of the Holy Spirit.[34]

Smale's challenge at First Baptist Church Los Angeles, similar to many Reformed churches, was a need to challenge the tendency towards adopting a scholastic orthodoxy with regard to the work of the Holy Spirit. It was not simply a matter of affirming correct doctrinal propositions about the Holy

---

[31] This is an intentional adaptation of the title of Jean-Jacques Suurmond's book, *Word and Spirit at Play: Towards a Charismatic Theology* (SCM Press, 1994).

[32] J.D. Pluss, 'Azusa and Other Myths: The Long and Winding Road from Experience to Stated Belief and Back Again', *Pneuma* 15.2 (Fall, 1993), p. 192.

[33] Macchia, 'Theology, Pentecostal' p. 1123.

[34] J. Smale, 'Lessons in Personal Work', *Pacific Baptist* 22.43 (26 October 1898), pp. 8-9.

Spirit, but the desire for the Spirit's dynamic power and presence as a Person which is characteristic of Smale's teaching. Once again this is noteworthy by virtue of such emphases being presented by Smale over the decade prior to the 1905–06 Revival. In spite of facing many arduous church political problems, Smale desired tangible and powerful signs and wonders, and his teaching consequently provides valuable resources for the ongoing debate between Reformed and Pentecostal/Charismatic strands of the Christian church. His emphasis for any who were guilty of neglecting the Person and work of the Spirit was persistent, as the close proximity of these sermon notes indicates: 'you cannot communicate what you have not. You must have the blessing if you would impart it.'[35] Then a month later, also preaching at First Baptist Church, Smale issued this similar challenge:

> The truth is that a Christian is impossible without the spirit. We began the Christian life in the spirit, and if any man has not the spirit he is not of Christ. A true church of Jesus Christ is impossible without the spirit ... and Christian service is also impossible without the spirit. God would have me proclaim to you that the spirit for the Christian and the church is the one indispensible and all-sufficient blessing. Your every need and pleasure is comprehended in His responses to the human heart.[36]

However clear Smale's own theology of the Spirit was during the years of preparation for revival in Los Angeles, a further four years would pass before the 'gestalt' of devotion to the Spirit would encompass the majority of his church members.

Word and Spirit – At Play[37]

For Smale, that reconfigurement of word and Spirit ministry occurred during his first Sunday back in Los Angeles on 28 May 1905, and thereafter with the dramatic events at First Baptist Church, as a process continued over the subsequent fifteen weeks and on into life at First New Testament Church.

Together, as pastor and people, they were receptive to the spirituality Suurmond describes, which is best received by those who have gone through the 'school of anxiety',[38] having been 'broken so that they can accept without defensiveness God's gracious infusion of Godself into their lives'.[39] By the autumn of 1905 Smale embarked on a preaching series entitled 'The

---

[35] 'Rev. Joseph Smale Delivers a Notable Lecture', *Los Angeles Times* 12 April 1901, p. 12.

[36] 'At The Churches Yesterday', *Los Angeles Times* 13 May 1901, p. 7.

[37] Suurmond, *Word and Spirit at Play*.

[38] Suurmond, *Word and Spirit at Play*, p. 152.

[39] D. Jacobsen, 'Review: Word and Spirit at Play: Towards a Charismatic Theology', *Pneuma* 20.1 (Spring, 1998), p. 134.

Pentecostal Blessing',[40] presented to the newly formed First New Testament Church, clearly stating that his theology had been blessed and shaped through 'the hard school of life's experience' (events described in chapters 3 and 4).[41] Characteristic of Smale's convergent emphases on, first, personal practical Christian discipleship and, secondly, ecclesiological considerations, he established the intersection point to be found in a deepening Pentecostal experience of 'The Holy Ghost' referred to as 'The Gift' (Acts 2:38).[42] In his preface, Smale writes,

> No truth, more or even as important, can be considered by Christians today than that of the Holy Ghost. No other study if it be devoutly and prayerfully taken up can yield such blessed results to those who are exercised in mind about their own spiritual condition, and that of the Church of Christ ... A treatment of this subject of subjects is attempted in the hope of imparting a vision, where it does not exist, of the Holy Ghost as the one and all sufficient and divinely ordained Person, and inspiration, to meet the manifold needs of Christian souls individually, and in their corporate character of churches.[43]

Comparable to Spurgeon's preaching themes noted in chapter 2, whereby the Person of the Holy Spirit is regarded as the solution to the needs of any age by means of a 'Personal Pentecost' coming in 'wind and fire', so Smale's teaching consistently expands upon this understanding of the 'Pentecostal power of the Spirit'.[44] The immediacy of this hope is evident in much of his preaching content during the autumn of 1905, as this excerpt illustrates:

> God has a larger grace for this world than it has ever known. It is coming! It is coming! ... Oh let us be on the tiptoe of expectancy, 'for when the day of Pentecost was fully come, and they were all with one accord in one place, SUDDENLY there came a sound from heaven as of a rushing mighty wind, and it filled all the house where they were sitting'. I love to think of the suddenness of the Spirit's coming.[45]

Furthermore, as his mentor before him,[46] so Smale illustrated his teaching with cross references to previous revivals in America, particularly the figure of

---

[40] Smale, *The Pentecostal Blessing*. Seven sermons are incorporated in the book. I am indebted to Darrin Rodgers, Director of the Flower Pentecostal Heritage Center, for the discovery and receipt of this material at a critical point in my research.
[41] Smale, *The Pentecostal Blessing*, p. 3.
[42] Smale, *The Pentecostal Blessing*, p. 44.
[43] Smale, *The Pentecostal Blessing*, pp. 3-4.
[44] Smale, *The Pentecostal Blessing*, p. 50.
[45] Smale, *The Pentecostal Blessing*, pp. 50, 51-52.
[46] Spurgeon, *Autobiography*, II, p. 46, 'On the charge that those who hold Calvinistic views are the enemies of revivals, Spurgeon has this to say: "Why sirs, in the history of the church, with but few exceptions, you could not find a revival at all that

Jonathan Edwards. Arguably here Smale was intentionally using such patterns of history to raise expectations for a great work of Pentecost as well as depicting the nature of true revival in its 'glorious disorder'.

> Jonathan Edwards ... came to his pulpit with a closely written manuscript ... His subject, 'A sinner in the hands of an angry God'. He began reading it – think of it – and being near-sighted he held his manuscript close to his eyes. There were no gesticulations. He stood quietly in the pulpit reading, but as he read, Pentecost came, the people trembled, were terror-stricken with conviction. The scene was strange and sensational. Some fell to the ground, some swooned, some groaned, and others clutched the pillars of the church, lest – to use their own expression – 'they should slide into hell'. Oh, God can bring his blessings instantly.[47]

Given that this was preached in the midst of such phenomena occurring at First New Testament Church, which increased in intensity over the following year, these words formulate a powerful indication that Smale's preaching was anticipatory of 'extraordinary manifestations of the Spirit'.[48] The implication of this particular example also suggests that Smale believed there to be no inherent tension between prepared and written sermon texts and subsequent displays of Holy Spirit activity. This appropriately leads to consider the nature of Smale's rhetoric in light of other Pentecostal preaching of his era.

Smale's Rhetoric

Joseph Smale's preaching abilities, crafted under the supervision of C.H. Spurgeon and extensively cultivated over years of practice, were such that over time he became widely recognised as a gifted and anointed preacher in his own right. His sermon style was diagnostic in essence, typified by first setting out the nature of the given problem in his sermons, before then presenting the solution and remedies. Unlike other Pentecostal counterparts who often preached with spontaneity under the Spirit's anointing, Smale's homiletic tradition prompted carefully constructed outlines, very much Spurgeonic in form. For Smale, part of the Spirit's anointing was as evident in private preparation and writing, as it was in the public delivery. Inevitably, his challenge amid the revival at the prestigious First Baptist Church, and then First New Testament Church, was to communicate the realities of new wine within an acceptable rhetoric that was more akin to old wineskins.

Again, *The Pentecostal Blessing* is the most significant source for this aspect of pneumatological enquiry, because it is a treatise preached, written and published *during* the ongoing Revival in 1905–06, where word and Spirit

---

was not produced by the orthodox faith... Look at the wondrous shaking under Jonathan Edwards and others which we may quote.'

[47] Smale, *The Pentecostal Blessing*, p. 52.
[48] Smale, *The Pentecostal Blessing*, p. 61.

quickly came to be regarded as existing 'in a *mutual relationship*, not as a one-way street'.[49] Furthermore, indicative of an incremental shift in their corporate understanding, a synopsis outlining this 'Blessing' became a regular feature in all church bulletins printed during this period and up until 1908.

> The Pentecostal Blessing
> We hold that it is the duty and privilege of the believer to know the Holy Spirit as 'the promise of the Father' (Acts 1:4), elsewhere spoken of as 'The Gift' (Acts 2:38), an experience distinct from regeneration. The disciples knew not the Holy Spirit as 'the promise of the Father,' or in other words as 'The Gift' until the Day of Pentecost, therefore we speak of the Spirit as 'The Pentecostal Blessing,' necessary to the believer's sanctification, his knowledge of the fullness of God and his anointing for service.
> Scripture References – Isaiah 11:2; Luke 24:49; John 20:21-22; Acts 1:8; Romans 8:2; Galatians 5; I Cor. 2:9-12; II Cor. 3:18; Ephes. 1:17 to Ephes. 2:1-6; Ephes. 3:16-19; II Thess. 2:13; I John 2:20-27.[50]

In his preaching during this period, Smale was scathing about the deficient state of the contemporary church, especially in view of 'the Church of the Scriptures' which he presented in tabular form,[51] citing specific themes of 'need' in his exposition of 'The Church of To-Day'.[52] In Smale's estimation,

---

[49] J. Moltmann, *The Spirit of Life* (SCM Press, 1992), p. 3, emphasis original.

[50] Eg., First New Testament Church Los Angeles, *Historical Number of the Bulletin* (18 March 1906), p. 3. First New Testament Church Los Angeles, *Weekly Bulletin* (2–9 June 1907), p. 4.

[51] Smale, *The Pentecostal Blessing*, pp. 23-34.

[52] Smale, *The Pentecostal Blessing*, pp. 23-34. According to Smale, 'The Church of To-day' has various heads and masters. Has various creeds. Without spiritual freedom. Fettered by forms, ceremonies and customs.
  Capable of human explanation. Everything about its religious life ordinary and common place. Believes the day of miracles is past.
  Relies upon the natural and cultivated gifts of its preachers and choirs for its welfare.
  Lives for the praise of men. Worldly. Thirsts for a worldly good time.
  Quarrelsome, contentious, jealous, place hunting, position seeking; and these things are as true of the ministry as of the pew.
  Aims at a comfortable and inoffensive profession of Christ.
  Yields a preference to education rather than to works of evangelization.
  Doing many things which preclude its undivided attention upon and effectiveness in the great work of its life (in contrast with the Church of the Scriptures, in service pre-eminently at work spreading the gospel of salvation by a crucified Christ – Read the Book of Acts.). Boasting of what it does.
  Glorying in and striving to build up denominationalism.
  Filled with societies.
  The work of the minister: To discuss the topics of the day, to produce word painting sermons, to give stereopticon and other lectures, to make society calls, to

the greatest need of the church was repentance and cleansing at both personal and corporate levels, with 'the Holy Ghost'[53] presented as the one and only remedy to the decline of spiritual life. However, the didactic logic of Smale's preaching pushes the boundaries of theological particulars, calling for experiential dimensions to become integral for both the church and individual Christians, with tangible 'expression of a supernatural life'.[54] Such displays of the word and the Spirit in operation were presented as 'proof' in his preaching, pointing to evidence in his own church[55] as well as further afield with reference to the Mukti Revival in India.

> News comes to us of a revival in India, where there are extraordinary manifestations of the Spirit of God. A correspondent tells us that in singing, the converts wave their hands and jump and dance. They cannot restrain themselves in hymns expressing the love of God and their triumph over Satan.[56]

Significantly, Smale's predilection for needs-based preaching is identifiable in other Pentecostal preachers also, as Aldwin Ragoonath's analysis of early Pentecostal preaching highlights.[57] Critiquing the preaching of Charles Fox Parham, William Seymour, F.J. Lee, and C.H. Mason, Ragoonath demonstrates that all 'preached the full-gospel message; [and] started their sermon from the needs present in the audience … such as spiritual counterfeits'.[58] Beside this, the common emphases of such early Pentecostal preaching was 'apostolic (Parham's and Seymour's style), Christocentric, including the full gospel. A variety of homiletic principles existed side by side but expository preaching was the primary method of preaching.'[59] Accordingly, Smale's exhortation for divine experience was certainly consistent with the accent of these other Pentecostal preachers.

Regardless of each preacher's natural stylistic variations, as well as the obvious difference that Joseph Smale never advocated speaking in tongues, a

---

shine in social functions, to play the funny and humorous man, to interest people in the church.
Pulpit themes: minor moralities; principles of reformation; human philosophies of life;
patriotism; the poets; politics; men of today and yesterday; science and occasionally the gospel.
Prayerless, not withstanding its prayer meetings.

[53] Smale, *The Pentecostal Blessing*, p. 3.
[54] Smale, *The Pentecostal Blessing*, p. 39.
[55] Smale, *The Pentecostal Blessing*, p. 41.
[56] Smale, *The Pentecostal Blessing*, p. 98.
[57] A. Ragoonath, *Preach the Word: A Pentecostal Approach* (Agape Teaching Ministry of Canada, 2004), pp. 49-89.
[58] Ragoonath, *Preach the Word*, pp. 60-61.
[59] Ragoonath, *Preach the Word*, p. 69.

common emphasis in all early Pentecostal sermons intertwined the necessity for, first, true worship following regeneration, the experience of sanctification, and, thirdly, the indispensable baptism of the Holy Spirit. Attempting to elucidate Smale's own teaching and theology on these subjects in order to assess his understanding of the relationship between these stages of Pentecostal formation, the three categories can most accurately be presented using his own structures, in the same order that he preached such doctrines.

TRUE WORSHIP OF A TRIUNE GOD

Having established his grave diagnosis of the traditional Christian church, Smale presented a trinitarian pneumatology, promoting scripture's call to 'the worship of a Triune God – Father, Son *and Holy Ghost*'.[60] His assessment of the church's ineptitude was down to 'modern Christian worship' being 'very defective, vitally, fundamentally defective', which would not be reversed 'until God is recognized as Triune, and adoration be given *equally* to the three Persons'.[61] Smale's assessment of his contemporary situation was that the church had maintained worship of the Father and the Son, 'but scarcely a worship of the Holy Ghost',[62] which was to the detriment of Christian worship.

For the purposes of sermon illustration, Smale obviously felt sufficient confidence in the regained emphasis of Holy Spirit worship at First New Testament Church, to cite themselves as living proof of all that such worship entailed, with its potential to 'start revival fires in every place in the world'.[63]

> The secret of the profound spiritual movement there is in the fact that that church [First New Testament Church Los Angeles] has recovered the shamefully obscured and long buried truth of the Holy Spirit, and is opening its heart for the embodiment of Him ...
>
> We are worshipping the Holy Ghost. Note that, 'worshipping' the Holy Ghost, that is to say, adoring Him as God, but more, yielding the place that is given to Him by the Father and the Son. He is enthroned as the executive. They seek to give way to His office work. They desire Him to speak and work as He wills to be the Sovereign Administrator, and themselves as His servants. And this is just what is signified in the true worship of God.[64]

Smale's use of terminology here is significant, portraying the Spirit's personhood and work as something to be embodied that is both distinct while mutually relational with the Father and Son, full of a mystery incorporating revelation and human experience. Viewed against the general backdrop of Smale's own Reformed heritage, Luther, for example, had warned against

---

[60] Smale, *The Pentecostal Blessing*, p. 40, emphasis original.
[61] Smale, *The Pentecostal Blessing*, p. 40, emphasis original.
[62] Smale, *The Pentecostal Blessing*, p. 40.
[63] Smale, *The Pentecostal Blessing*, p. 41.
[64] Smale, *The Pentecostal Blessing*, pp. 41-42.

'radical subjectivity, of seeking inward experiences rather than allowing the Holy Spirit to come to them through the Word and sacraments'.[65] Herein is the kernel of historic tensions expressed in the Reformation controversies between the radical 'left wing'[66] pneumatologies of the 'Anabaptists'[67] and 'spiritualists',[68] against the 'word' orthodoxy of the mainstream Protestant reformers. Berkhof observes how 'the Catholics imprisoned the Spirit in the Church and the Protestants imprisoned it in the Word'.[69] Yet for Smale, while maintaining a high view of the supreme authority of scripture, his understanding of spirituality in general, and the nature and work of the Spirit in particular, was intrinsically receptive to subjective experiences, akin to Spurgeon's call for a 'Personal Pentecost' the possibility of which could be 'repeated in the heart of every believer'.[70]

One further observation concerning worshipping the Spirit as the 'executive' and 'administrator' bears clarification. Smale's integral view of the dynamic inter-relationship between the Spirit and the word was consistently evidenced in his preaching through plentiful scriptural references, quotations, and application.[71] Just as the historic Anabaptist pneumatological orientations differed from mainline reformers distinguishing between the 'outer Word' and the 'inner Word',[72] so the position of Smale was similar to that of early Anabaptists. As Karkkainen explains,

> The Anabaptists insisted that whoever has made the commitment to obedience and has the Spirit can read with understanding. Furthermore, far from being individualistic, they emphasized the importance of the community for the right

---

[65] S.M. Burgess, 'Holy Spirit, Doctrine of: Reformed Traditions', in Burgess and Van der Maas (eds), *New International Dictionary*, p. 764.

[66] V.M. Karkkainen, *Pneumatology* (Baker Academic, 2002), p. 55; section entitled 'The Anabaptist Vision of the Spirit', pp. 55-57.

[67] See Burgess, 'Holy Spirit, Doctrine of: Reformed Traditions', pp. 767-69, for information concerning 'Anabaptism' and 'Menno Simons (c. 1496–1561).' Exploration into Anabaptist pneumatology lies outside the scope of this study, but promises rich historical insight for further research.

[68] Burgess, 'Holy Spirit, Doctrine of: Reformed Traditions', pp. 767-68, for information on 'the spiritualists, who have a modern counterpart in the Schwenckfelder Church', and 'Thomas Müntzer (1488/9–1525)' who played a leading role as a 'revolutionary spiritualist'.

[69] H. Berkhof quoted in Suurmond, *Word and Spirit at Play*, p. 66.

[70] C.H. Spurgeon, 'The Personal Pentecost and the Glorious Hope' (preached 13 June 1886), *Metropolitan Tabernacle Pulpit* (1886), pp. 313-24.

[71] E.g., Smale's presentation of 'The Church of the Scriptures' contains fifty-three diverse Bible references, pp. 23-34.

[72] G.D. Badcock, *Light of Truth and Fire of Love* (Eerdmans, 1997), p. 89. The 'outer Word' was considered 'anything from Scripture itself to the words of Jesus', and the 'inner Word' involved the underlying principle of the 'outer Word' – but 'that principle apprehended subjectivity and inwardly, and thus by the power of the Spirit'.

understanding of revelation. In short, they claimed that the Spirit was operative in the church even though their opponents highly doubted it.[73]

This is relevant to our understanding of Smale's theology and practice at this juncture, given his teaching that 'The Gift' of the promised Holy Spirit was promoting a fullness of God that instigated individual and community transformation towards holiness. In Smale's own words,

> The pages of the Word confront us with the possibility and necessity of a holy life here and now ... Pentecost puts within our reach the power of holiness. 'God hath chosen you to salvation through sanctification,' and the method is 'the Spirit and the Word.' (II Thess. 2:14).[74]

Smale's preaching had this pneumatological vision that encouraged his hearers and readers to 'adore' and 'yield' to the Spirit 'for more, and *more*, and MORE, and MORE',[75] by believing the word for 'the God that lived at Pentecost is just the same today'.[76] Here Smale's connection with his reforming antecedents as well as his contemporary Pentecostal leaders was at its closest, for in advocating the potentiality to experience liberation in Christ via the Spirit, however subjective that may seem, he remained emphatic about word and Spirit centred worship. The primary intent amid the intensity of the Revival in Los Angeles was of course to return to apostolic preaching and worship, and not by prescribed methods but the adoration and obedience of worshipping the Holy Spirit *per se*, thus enabling him to move and work however he chooses.

SANCTIFICATION: AS A DISTINCT WORK OF GRACE

A second dominant theme arises in Smale's preaching during the first months of the newly established First New Testament Church, namely 'sanctification'. In fact his sermon title on New Year's Day 1906 was based upon the text

> 'God hath from the beginning chosen you to salvation through sanctification of the spirit and belief of the truth'. II Thess. ii. 13.[77]

Having raised the key question himself as to whether sanctification was immediate or progressive, Smale carefully explained that he considered it to be both.

> It is instantaneous, but by that do not understand that the full-grown Christian character is given to us in a moment; but there is such a thing as an instantaneous

---

[73] Karkkainen, *Pneumatology*, p. 56.
[74] Smale, *The Pentecostal Blessing*, p. 75.
[75] Smale, *The Pentecostal Blessing*, p. 48, emphases original.
[76] Smale, *The Pentecostal Blessing*, p. 51.
[77] 'At the Churches Yesterday', *Los Angeles Times* 1 January 1906, p. II3.

leap from bondage to liberty – an instantaneous leap from 'I cannot' to 'I can'; from weakness to strength and victory.[78]

These themes are further amplified in his printed sermons on 'The Pentecostal Blessing', advocating that the blessing known in conversion is not identical to the blessing experienced in Pentecost. That 'involves a second great work of grace'.[79] Using his own definitions, 'Regeneration is simply life' and 'Pentecost' (meaning a personal Pentecost) is 'the *fullness* and the *abundance of life*'.[80] Therefore, 'Pentecost and Regeneration are not one and the same thing.'[81] Smale then uses 'second blessing'[82] terminology with regard to the necessity and expectation of a further work of grace in sanctification that must follow the first blessing of regeneration. As to how this stage of Christian experience may be gained, Smale bluntly states, 'You cannot get at it by listening to one another, but if you listen to the Word you will be unerringly taught.'[83]

It is a point of their commonality for sound doctrine that such convictions advocating a purely bibliocentric focus were apparent among early Pentecostals, who also warned against the speculation and error of broader theological analysis, as asserted by *The Apostolic Faith*, 'We are feeding upon the Word which is revealed by the Holy Ghost – the whole Word and nothing but the Word.'[84]

Theological analysis is pertinent, however, on this point, especially with regard to Smale's ambiguous paradigms regarding sanctification and baptism in the Spirit. Perhaps not surprisingly given his Wesleyan *and* Spurgeonic roots, Smale adopts an integrative approach to Spirit baptism. This enables him to refer to a two-stage work of grace as cited above, while also regarding a personal Pentecost as the necessary corollary of sanctification. Inevitably, such terminology poses some difficulties when attempting to define the explicit nature of how and when the 'Gift' of the Holy Spirit is imparted in Christian experience. Needless to say the solution for Smale rested in an amalgamation of the Wesleyan view of sanctification as the prerequisite for Spirit baptism alongside the notion that Spirit baptism provides the impetus for intensifying sanctification and power.

Consequently, the logic of Smale's argument urged Christian believers to seek for their own Pentecost as the means of sanctification, incorporating the word and Spirit dimension in a deepening spirituality. Smale's challenge was

---

[78] 'At the Churches Yesterday', *Los Angeles Times* 1 January 1906, p. II3.
[79] Smale, *The Pentecostal Blessing*, p. 45.
[80] Smale, *The Pentecostal Blessing*, p. 45, emphases original.
[81] Smale, *The Pentecostal Blessing*, p. 45.
[82] Smale, *The Pentecostal Blessing*, p. 46.
[83] 'At the Churches Yesterday', *Los Angeles Times* 1 January 1906, p. II3.
[84] 'To the Baptized Saints', *The Apostolic Faith* 1.9 (September, 1907), p. 2.

Smale's Pentecostal Life and Service 175

both theological and practical, stating, 'if the only Christian experience that you have had is the new birth, then Pentecost awaits you'.[85] He continues with this rationale that the word must be believed that God has far more by way of 'abundant life' than a simple comprehension of the gospel by believing on the Lord Jesus Christ. This point is graphically illustrated by Smale's image of a traditional Chinese shoe for bound feet.

> If tradition and church beliefs have narrowed and circumscribed the truth of God into such a shoe, imprisoning your feet, then throw it away, and become shod with the preparation of the real gospel: 'I am come,' says Christ, 'that they might have life, and that they might have it more abundantly'.[86]

While promoting the need for personal sanctification combined with that sense of expectancy for a latter day outpouring of the Spirit, it is clear that Smale's theology regarding God's work of grace (in regeneration and sanctification) was commonly shared by other early Pentecostals and resonated with Wesleyan holiness emphases.[87]

Smale's desire could appropriately have been an identical expression of many Pentecostals, then and now, addressing the practical question, 'how to get the glory of God into the modern Christian and into the modern church'.[88] In true Smale style, he went further by outlining nine practical secrets for a person to obtain the Holy Ghost in Pentecostal fullness, whereby 'sanctification is inevitable in relation to the Holy Ghost':

i. Have done with sin
ii. Have done with self
iii. Have done with skepticism
iv. I will accept every manifestation of the Holy Spirit in others
v. I will receive whatever the Spirit determines as my life work
vi. I will obey unquestioningly and instantly every leading of the Spirit of God
vii. Listening to God
viii. Praying for the blessing
ix. Glorifying Christ.[89]

---

[85] Smale, *The Pentecostal Blessing*, p. 47.

[86] Smale, *The Pentecostal Blessing*, p. 47.

[87] There were some Pentecostal preachers, such as Phoebe Palmer, who propagated the belief that total eradication of the old sinful nature was a possibility for believers in this life. This was regarded not so much as a process, but a definitive moment in time, achieved by faith. Some referred to this as the 'second blessing'.

[88] 'At the Churches Yesterday', *Los Angeles Times* 27 November 1905, p. 16.

[89] 'At the Churches Yesterday', *Los Angeles Times* 27 November 1905, p. 16. Each of these points is elaborated in 'The Secrets of Pentecostal Fulness', in Smale, *The Pentecostal Blessing*, pp. 88-115. By way of comparison it is interesting to note William Seymour's similar statement in *The Apostolic Faith* magazines: (a) Teaching on

During the Welsh Revival, repentance of any unconfessed sin and doubtful habits, openness to obey the Spirit promptly, and public confession of Christ had also been the core of Evan Roberts' teaching. Therefore, the specific facets on Smale's list inevitably link again to the experience gained during his visit to the Welsh Revival some seven months earlier, which had further honed his understanding of the Spirit's work in enabling a person to make determined shifts of surrender away from sin and self, thus creating openness to the work of the Holy Spirit in freedom. Repentance was regarded as the key to this process of sanctification as stated by Smale, basing his teaching on Acts 2:28, whereby Peter taught that 'the sin-convicted should receive their gift ... after repentance and baptism':

> For observe, the Scripture of the Pentecost begins with a copulative conjunction. Look at what precedes it: '*Repent* and *be baptized* every one of you in the name of Jesus Christ for the remission of sins, *and* ye shall receive the gift of the Holy Ghost.'[90]

In this doctrine of sanctification, the potential for a life-changing experience of God was cast. Although Smale typically liked to teach with itemised points, such as the nine listed above, this was not in any sense intended as a theory or formula for spiritual transformation. Rather, as Anthea Butler has observed, Smale's theology combines an amalgamation of both the practical ingredients of holiness Wesleyan purity, as well as the 'higher life' requirement for power.[91] Indeed, the thrust of Smale's sermons contain this passion for holiness and power in the life of a believer which cannot be adequately appreciated without the third specific emphasis that Smale accentuated, namely Spirit baptism.

THE BAPTISM OF THE HOLY GHOST

Because Smale's primary intent was to establish an independent 'fellowship for evangelical preaching and teaching and Pentecostal life and service',[92] he was explicit in introducing his people to the Holy Spirit, and their individual and corporate need of Spirit baptism. His opening sermon delivered at First New Testament Church was based on John 20:19-22, entitled, 'Jesus in the midst.

Repentance – Mark 1:14, 15. (b) Godly Sorrow for Sin, Example – Matt 9:13. 2 Cor 7, 9, 11. Acts 17:30,31. (c) Of confession of Sins – Luke 15:21 and Luke 18:13. (d) Forsaking Sinful Ways – Isa 55:7. Jonah 3:8. Prov 28:13. (e) Restitution – Ezek 33:15. Luke 19:8. (f) And faith in Jesus Christ.

[90] Smale, *The Pentecostal Blessing*, p. 46, emphasis original.

[91] I am grateful to Anthea Butler for her helpful responses to my Smale paper delivered at The Society for Pentecostal Studies, Fuller Seminary, March 2006.

[92] First New Testament Church Los Angeles, *Our First Anniversary* (September 1906), p. 1.

Peace be unto you. As the Father hath sent me, even so send I you. Receive ye the Holy Ghost.'[93]

Furthermore, emanating from the sermons that Smale preached during the autumn of 1905, it is possible to construct a detailed account of his theology of the Spirit with regard to Spirit baptism. This again was established in the broader sweep of raising expectations for the fulfilment of 'latter rain' within the eschatological framework which Smale assumed to be the last days before Christ's imminent return. Linking the Old Testament prophecy of Joel with the Pentecost narrative of Acts 2, Smale proclaimed,

> The world has yet to know a latter rain, exceeding the moderately former rain, for it is written: 'I will pour out my Spirit upon all flesh,' a Scripture that has never yet been fulfilled ... As this dispensation opened with a remarkable effusion of the Spirit upon believers, may we not confidently look for a remarkable effusion of the Spirit upon believers whose lot is cast in the closing hours of the dispensation. Such an effusion is absolutely necessary just prior to our Lord's second advent.[94]

Certainly Smale's comments would have gained acceptance among all early Pentecostals who possessed that same expectation of the Lord's imminent return, thus heightening evangelistic and missionary zeal, the necessity for Spirit baptism, and the anticipation of signs and wonders. Herein a direct link between pneumatology and eschatology is identifiable during this phase of Smale's ministry, reinforcing his preaching which interpreted the four-fold gospel and unfolding events as signs of the gospel era coming to a climax. Drawing on the cosmopolitan complexion of Los Angeles, Smale likened his city to 'a modern Jerusalem from the standpoint of inhabitants'.[95]

Although by late 1905 Smale sensed that 'God is preparing the mightiest Pentecost ever known',[96] nonetheless he was quick to distinguish that any congregational experience of Pentecost must also be received by a personal Pentecost as the urgent prerogative of each believer. Quoting Acts 2:3, Smale illustrated how 'tongues, parting asunder, like as of fire ... sat upon EACH ONE OF THEM'.[97] The filling of the Holy Spirit was taught to be another essential aspect of God's 'gift of grace'.[98] Smale defined the 'baptism' as 'the Gift' coming down 'pouring forth from on high',[99] with the 'Pentecostal Blessing' filling every empty vessel. He continues,

---

[93] First New Testament Church Los Angeles, *Our First Anniversary*, p. 4.
[94] Smale, *The Pentecostal Blessing*, p. 49.
[95] Smale, *The Pentecostal Blessing*, p. 50.
[96] Smale, *The Pentecostal Blessing*, p. 50.
[97] Smale, *The Pentecostal Blessing*, p. 52, emphasis original.
[98] Smale, *The Pentecostal Blessing*, p. 54.
[99] Smale, *The Pentecostal Blessing*, p. 55.

> He [God] is wanting a ready people, but our readiness consists not in our activities, but in our silencing of the flesh life. We must come to the place where we are nothing, and where we can do nothing, and when we are there God will send a mighty deluge of divine grace and baptize the earth with the blessings of heaven.[100]

The underlying contention of this study is that such reflections and teaching from a man of Smale's calibre and standing were undoubtedly a significant contribution to the broader Christian scene in Los Angeles during this period. The fact that the Los Angeles newspapers printed synopses of his sermons, and that subjects such as sanctification and Spirit baptism were at the heart of his teaching during the Revival period of 1905–06, provide the theological framework that was attempting to interpret Pentecostal life and practice for individuals and churches. Smale's clarion call for power contained a robust warning of the fear that would accompany a 'mighty stir' of Pentecostal 'wind' and 'fire'.[101] With this challenge to every Christian to believe God means what he says when promising 'He shall baptize you in the Holy Ghost and in fire',[102] Smale presented God's intention for all Christian believers:

> When we live in weakness we are not living in the will of God. God intends us to be filled with life, with power, with fire, and to give us the sight of the world bending before the word of our testimony.[103]

The baptism of the Spirit was further expounded by Smale to incorporate the following three dimensions of Pentecostal life: 'The Sealing. The Earnest. The Anointing'.[104] The 'Sealing' was a reference to the Holy Spirit's stamp of ownership on an individual Christian, and the Romans 8:16 experience of witness that stems from Spirit baptism: 'The Spirit Himself beareth witness with our spirit that we are the children of God.'[105]

According to Smale's references to divine attestation of sonship, this experience was to be the foundation of Christian assurance, enabling 'through Him, a life of holiness, power and love wherein we may reproduce the character of Christ in thought, word and deed'.[106] But there was no reference to speaking in tongues as one of the necessary identifying marks of Spirit baptism. After all, Smale was presenting his theology of the Spirit to First New Testament Church some five months prior to the first instance of glossolalia in his church on Easter Sunday 1906.

---

[100] Smale, *The Pentecostal Blessing*, p. 57.
[101] Smale, *The Pentecostal Blessing*, p. 62.
[102] Smale, *The Pentecostal Blessing*, p. 63.
[103] Smale, *The Pentecostal Blessing*, p. 63.
[104] Smale, *The Pentecostal Blessing*, p. 66.
[105] Smale, *The Pentecostal Blessing*, p. 68.
[106] 'At the Churches Yesterday', *Los Angeles Times* 27 November 1905, p. 16.

Secondly, the 'Earnest'[107] was a forward reference to the full salvation Christians were to know in the future. It is insightful that there were theological tensions requiring interpretation even amid their heavenly experiences upon earth during 1905–06, such that Smale was teaching regarding some of the 'not yet' aspects of Kingdom life. Included in Smale's rhetoric about the 'Earnest' were the following 'coming wonders, blessings magnificent, baffling all description and even conception' of future and eternal things yet to be received:

Full salvation.
The inheritance incorruptible.
Delivered from the very presence of sin.
Wholly conformed to the divine image.
The exceeding riches of His grace in His kindness towards us in Christ Jesus.[108]

Thirdly, the 'Anointing' combined several features of the Spirit controlled life. Preaching from Ephesians 5, in Smale's estimation the necessity of being filled with the Holy Spirit produced the ability to live an ethical life together with a power to speak and witness boldly for Christ. In essence, such anointing impacted 'service performed under the power of the enduement and endowment'.[109] Pentecostal life was presented as a life of power, the Christian believer being inextricably filled with God, with all the potentiality for joyful 'holy and undying delight'.[110]

Drawing all these emphases in Smale's preaching together begs the question, to what extent was Smale typical of early Pentecostal preachers? Observationally, it is clear that others also shared a three-stage understanding of the Christian life and development. Taking William Seymour's account as a primary example, *The Apostolic Faith* routinely reported on persons who had been 'converted and sanctified and filled with the Holy Spirit, speaking in tongues as they did on the day of Pentecost',[111] and they held to this pattern as their central message throughout the duration of the Azusa Street Revival.

Another shared and perhaps even more significant public emphasis between Smale and other early Pentecostals became evident in response to the San Francisco earthquake of 18 April 1906. Whereas some of the established church leaders of Los Angeles immediately dismissed notions that this tragedy was divine judgement on a city,[112] Smale joined other Pentecostal preachers

---

[107] The archaic meaning of the word 'Earnest' refers to a down payment, or a token of something to come.

[108] Smale, *The Pentecostal Blessing*, pp. 69-70.

[109] Smale, *The Pentecostal Blessing*, p. 73.

[110] Smale, *The Pentecostal Blessing*, p. 81.

[111] 'Pentecost Has Come', *The Apostolic Faith* 1.1 (September, 1906), p. 1.

[112] As propounded, e.g., by Robert Burdette (Pastor of Temple Baptist Church), A.C. Smither (Pastor of First Christian Church), and C.C. Pierce (Pastor of Memorial Baptist Church). For a detailed description of responses to the 1906 San Francisco earthquake,

who interpreted the tragedy as God's 'wake-up call'.[113] In his sermon after the earthquake, Smale posed this question and comment (by inference directed to other church leaders), duly printed in the *Los Angeles Express*:

> Why have we been spared, while San Francisco has been destroyed? Do not tempt God by saying that it is its geographical position or the geological formation of the land upon which it is built. It is my solemn conviction that the only thing which has saved Los Angeles is the intense and abounding prayer life of many of the Lord's intercessors in this city.[114]

Frank Bartleman certainly concurred with Smale's position, producing a tract in response to the earthquake, which by 11 May had been printed 125,000 times.[115] As for the Azusa Street Mission, the apocalyptic significance of the earthquake on the very same day as the *Los Angeles Daily Times* had first publicised a report about their apostolic work, was deemed a further sign that the return of Jesus was imminent.

Although there is a notable omission of 'healing' references in Smale's preaching themes prior to 1905, the opportunity for healing does feature during the fifteen week revival meetings, with the opportunity advertised for Smale to visit the homes of 'the sick and afflicted'.[116] This would seem a more tenuous point of his connections with Pentecostal life and practice, given it was structurally arranged through the pastor and seemingly not encouraged within the church community by praying for one another. However, with the formation of First New Testament Church this had developed somewhat, into active prayer for the sick within church life, with instructions based upon James 5:14-15 to call the elders for anointing with oil, that 'the Lord shall raise him up'.[117] But overall it must be recognised that for Smale the healing for the sick component of ministry receives minimal attention, with no indication in his teaching or practice that healing *per se* was regarded as one of the signs of the imminent Kingdom of God.

The greater theological divergence between Smale and Seymour surrounded glossolalia as evidence of Spirit baptism.[118] The very first edition of *The Apostolic Faith* referenced 'Tongues as a Sign' to be expected as confirmation

---

see C.M. Robeck, Jr, *The Asuza Street Mission and Revival: The Birth of the Global Pentecostal Movement* (Nelson, 2006), pp. 77-82.

[113] Robeck, *The Asuza Street Mission and Revival*, p. 81.

[114] 'Sermons by Pastors', *Los Angeles Express* 30 April 1906.

[115] F. Bartleman, *Azusa Street: The Roots of Modern-Day Pentecost* (Logos International, 1980), pp. 51-52; Robeck, *The Azusa Street Mission and Revival*, p. 79.

[116] First New Testament Church Los Angeles, *Church Bulletin* (week beginning 29 August 1905), p. 4.

[117] First New Testament Church Los Angeles, *Our First Anniversary* (September 1906), p. 7.

[118] See Appendix III, for Smale's summary of his view on speaking in tongues.

of 'belief and baptism',[119] yet it did not prescribe that this was to be an essential experience for every believer. The nuance of Seymour's theological stance regarding tongues was simply that tongues were part of the full experience of baptism in the Holy Spirit, not an end in itself. Furthermore, throughout all thirteen editions of his magazine, Seymour taught on this subject, as well as matters of sanctification, and Spirit baptism, which illustrates that there were numerous points of connection between the theologies of the First New Testament Church and the Azusa Street Mission, not least the challenge for every Christian to seek and expect a personal Pentecost, and to be pure vessels ready for the filling of the Holy Spirit.

Having presented the major themes of Smale's preaching during the Los Angeles Revival of 1905–06 in particular, one final comment merits inclusion in this section. Despite the theological frameworks outlined above, it must be recalled that the patterns of revival in Wales and Los Angeles often dispensed with the preacher and preaching altogether! As Edith Blumhofer notes,

> Spontaneity and seeming disorder replaced promotion, scheduling, regular preaching, financial planning, and even systematic evangelistic outreach ... No one knew for certain who – if anyone – would preach.[120]

Although there are a few recorded instances of services at which Smale similarly dispensed with the sermon at the Spirit's instigation,[121] the overall sense of his preaching schemes and content during the first three years of the Revival indicates a concerted control of the pulpit.

The profile of Joseph Smale's pneumatology during this era of Pentecostal life and practice will now be explored in a different direction, examining the ecclesiological implications intertwined in the formation of 'a Holy Ghost church'.[122]

The Shape of Smale's Ecclesiology

It is a matter of debate within dogmatics as to whether one should correctly begin with the 'Spirit and the Church' or the 'Spirit and Mission'.[123] The two are so closely intertwined. However, the decision has been taken to commence with an examination of Smale's ecclesiology in relation to his Pentecostal life and service because it was the formation of new churches which provides the essential insights to the development of his pneumatological convictions and

---

[119] 'Tongues as a Sign', *The Apostolic Faith* 1.1 (September, 1906), p. 13.

[120] E.L. Blumhofer, *The Assemblies of God: A Chapter in the Story of American Pentecostalism:* Volume 1. *To 1941* (Gospel Publishing House, 1989), p. 101.

[121] First New Testament Church Los Angeles, *Our First Anniversary*, p. 3.

[122] Smale, *The Pentecostal Blessing*, p. 65.

[123] H. Berkhof, *The Doctrine of the Holy Spirit* (Epworth Press, 1964), p. 30.

practice. Thereafter, the missional outworking from the church framework and identity may then be analysed within distinct parameters for a third section in this chapter.

Although a number of research approaches are feasible in this sphere, such as utilising disciplines of anthropology, sociology, organizational studies, theology,[124] the documentary data available within the confines of this study are best examined through practical theological lenses with regard to Smale's ecclesiology (and later his missiology). With revival phenomena in general there are limitations to empirical methods being effectively applied to 'large-scale, unpredictable, historical phenomena',[125] particularly with regard to accurate analysis of data retrospectively. Therefore, the favoured method of practice is employed, because it considers the historical and organizational data available, with a rationale that enables any pneumatological perspectives to be discerned and evaluated. Further, in spite of more than a century's passing, it even offers the potential for practical application and reflection for twenty-first century churches.

The inevitable break from the established 'old wineskin' of First Baptist Church provided the ideal opportunity for Smale to formulate a new church, in September 1905, along Pentecostal lines whereby the 'Administrator of the life and service of the church is the Holy Ghost'.[126] Aptly called First New Testament Church, they immediately hired Burbank Hall – a pattern not dissimilar to other Pentecostal congregations who, as Wacker comments, 'particularly liked to take over the devil's warehouses – vacant saloons and dance halls ranked high on the list – to turn them into houses of worship'.[127] First New Testament Church's twelve month lease on the building involved sharing the facilities with 'iniquitous' theatre-goers, an aspect that eventually caused antagonism and confrontation with the church's denunciation that 'he who goes to the theatre is on the road to hell'.[128] However, in the short term the more pressing challenges for Smale and his people concerned their identity and organization as an embryonic Pentecostal movement.

---

[124] H. Cameron, P. Richter, D. Davies and F. Ward (eds), *Studying Local Churches: A Handbook* (SCM Press, 2005), pp. 13-26.

[125] W. Kay, 'Revival: Empirical Aspects', in A. Walker and K. Aune (eds), *On Revival: A Critical Examination* (Paternoster Press, 2003), p. 202.

[126] First New Testament Church Los Angeles, *Historical Number of the Bulletin* (18 March 1906), p. 2.

[127] Wacker, *Heaven Below*, p. 112.

[128] 'Curb Preacher Scores Theater', *Los Angeles Express* 1 May 1906, p. 7.

Pentecostal Identity

Significantly, the services at Burbank Hall became more experiential and emotional as the 'power of the Spirit so moved in the place'.[129] One account of dramatic scenes reminiscent of New Testament days was witnessed one night in July 1906, being widely reported and ridiculed in the Los Angeles press, requiring a 'burly policeman [who] strode across the room, forcing his way between a tangle of waving arms and jumping bodies' to intervene.

> A pretty girl, 16 years old, went raving mad at the meeting of the 'Holy Rollers' in Burbank Hall last night, where Joseph Smale, the pastor, has his First New Testament Church ... Beating her fists against the east wall of the hall, butting the plaster with her head, only to fall in a heap and writhe like a snake upon the floor, the young girl shrieked an unintelligible wail horrible to hear. Dancing in front of her as she stood and crawling about her as she squirmed, women screamed 'Devil come out!' Devil come out! Devil come out![130]

Quite contrary to Smale's own theological heritage, his visit to the Welsh Revival had prompted an important experimental phase as he 'explicitly embodied restorationist intent'.[131] 'Restorationism', as defined by Blumhofer, was the underpinning conviction that 'the presumed vitality, message, and form of the Apostolic Church'[132] could and would be recaptured. This had a particular bearing upon church identity and practice, with restorationist aspirations and expectations which can be summarized as including,

> The hope for perfection and the call for religious reform.
> Christian unity and simplicity.
> Their eschatological role as an integral part of end-times Christianity.
> Antidenominationalism, with the insistence that God had long since abandoned organized religion.[133]

In reality, the establishment of the newly organized First New Testament Church involved the relocation of many members from the First Baptist Church, which after all the strife of previous years provided them all the opportunity for a new and free expression of church, seemingly without denominational pressures or demands. Such freedom was evident with features of Spirit activity that were felt noteworthy, like 'heart melting confession of sin', 'two-thirds of the congregation were so wrought upon by God that the

---

[129] First New Testament Church Los Angeles, *Historical Number of the Bulletin* (18 March 1906), p. 1.
[130] '"Holy Roller" Mad', *Los Angeles Times* 17 July 1906, p. II14.
[131] Blumhofer, *The Assemblies of God*, p. 100.
[132] Blumhofer, *The Assemblies of God*, p. 18.
[133] See Blumhofer, *The Assemblies of God*, pp. 18-19.

church was transformed into the likeness of a revival enquiry room', and 'the services on weekdays were even more remarkable challenging description'.[134]

To this end, Smale's challenge for greater freedom and worship by honouring the Holy Spirit was consistent with his Reformed background and the centrality of the cross, while also identifiable with other emerging Pentecostal/holiness emphases. One example which draws together the eschatological convictions that were being stirred, especially through song, can be identified in Smale's quotation of Francis Bottome's Pentecostal hymn 'The Comforter has Come'.[135] There are also various examples of Smale (who was musical himself) teaching his Los Angeles congregation the hymns from the Welsh Revival.[136]

In terms of formatting a new church for Pentecostal 'life and service', Smale was certainly not reticent to define the framework for the new church, as within just three months he had established 'The Great Principles of our Organized Life'.[137] This was a constitutional charter that First New Testament Church adopted on 22 September 1905, with additions ratified on 1 December 1905, illustrating Smale's construction of all his important values and beliefs. What is striking in this is his view of the intrinsic relationship between the rapid development of organized church life and implicit Holy Spirit administration.[138] Three salient points of this formal declaration help to outline their perceived identity as a new church, and may be enumerated as follows.

THE HEADSHIP OF CHRIST AND HOLY GHOST ADMINISTRATION

The circumstances of the church's formation must be taken into account in that a continuum from First Baptist days was taking place. Those who were closest to Smale during the period of transition from First Baptist to First New Testament Church presumably discussed the ecclesiological aspects at stake, and let it be known publicly that Smale felt duty bound by his convictions and integrity to follow New Testament patterns of church government rather than denominational hierarchy. On this point, his loyal deacons issued this statement:

> Pastor Smale has but differed from our denomination as to methods of church work, which we believe that any pastor in the denomination has a right to do, if he conscientiously believes that the adoption of his position will make it possible for the holy spirit to administer the life and service of the church. In Pastor Smale's differences from denominational methods he has based the advocacy of new

---

[134] First New Testament Church Los Angeles, *Historical Number of the Bulletin* (18 March 1906), p.1.

[135] Smale, *The Pentecostal Blessing*, p. 61.

[136] First New Testament Church Los Angeles, *Our First Anniversary*, p. 14.

[137] First New Testament Church Los Angeles, *Our First Anniversary*, p. 6. This statement is referenced to the *Church Bulletin* of 10 December 1905.

[138] First New Testament Church Los Angeles, *Church Bulletin* (17 December 1905).

methods upon New Testament church life and practice, a claim we feel we dare not summarily disregard lest we grieve the blessed Holy Spirit of God.[139]

During May 1906, Smale clarified their objective, in that they were adamantly 'not in existence to build up denominationalism'.[140] While warmly affirming 'whatever is Christian in all denominations', Smale was pursuing a different and innovative model of 'New Testament churches of our type' being multiplied by 'the favour of God'.[141] He was resolute that there would 'be no denomination arising out of our organizations with any consent from us',[142] because to do so would 'put us back under the bondage from which we have been delivered'.[143]

Some description of Smale's earlier plans to implement organized models for revival and to 'organize an institutional' work as part of the First Baptist strategy in 1904, illustrates the shift in his own thinking over two or three years, brought about by Pentecostal revival. For instance, at the annual Baptist Convention of Southern California, held at Ontario in 1902, Smale had launched a 'comprehensive revival scheme for Southern California'.[144] But there was no reference to either the headship of Christ or the Spirit's orchestration of events. Similarly with the developing ministry of First Baptist Church in 1904, Smale had advocated 'an adoption of secular methods':

> The distinctively religious work consists of attractive services, well-organized Sunday Schools for the downtown little folk, pleasant Sunday afternoon meetings, and the encouragement of helpful associations, such as men's Sunday evening meetings with special features.[145]

The striking emphasis of these plans, amid the church strife in which First Baptist was embroiled during 1903–04, was Smale's desire to employ 'business' and 'secular methods', such that 'the finances will be placed in competent hands and managed on business principals'.[146] In retrospect, both examples are a marked contrast with Smale's later practice, accentuating 'Headship' and 'Holy Spirit administration' emphases which permeate Smale's teaching and explanation of church strategies during his Pentecostal phase.

Indeed, as one who had broken away from all his organizational moorings, Smale develops this point in regard of headship to criticise any denomination's propensity to 'exercise lordship over the individual conscience' by instituting 'a

---

[139] 'Seceders go in Harmony', *Los Angeles Times* 18 September 1905, p. 14.
[140] First New Testament Church Los Angeles, *Our First Anniversary*, p. 7.
[141] First New Testament Church Los Angeles, *Our First Anniversary*, p. 7.
[142] First New Testament Church Los Angeles, *Our First Anniversary*, p. 7.
[143] First New Testament Church Los Angeles, *Our First Anniversary*, p. 7.
[144] 'The City in Brief', *Los Angeles Times* 29 August 1902, p. 12.
[145] 'Clouds are Rolling Away', *Los Angeles Times* 8 January 1904, p. A3.
[146] 'Clouds are Rolling Away', p. A3.

mode of thought and service not always agreeable to the teachings of the Word and free action of the free Spirit of God upon the individual heart'.[147] Of course, the notion of spiritual freedom is not easily quantifiable and begs the question to what extent is it actually possible to 'organize' 'Holy Ghost administration of the Church' anyway? After all, even Smale's own actions had provoked Bartleman to criticize the measure of spontaneity at First New Testament Church. Conversely, the New Testament Church felt that by the end of their first year, they had managed to establish freedom from 'all the man-made systems of religious life and service'.[148] For Smale the clue to his practice may in part be interpreted by his activist attempt to create an independent, nondenominational church.

INTENSELY SPIRITUAL IN CHARACTER

Smale regarded a true church of Christ to be 'intensely spiritual in character'[149] by discovering what, in his estimation, was the 'secret of prayer and in individual and organic life strictly in accordance with the Word of God'.[150] Just as he was reacting against denominationalism, so there is evidence that his developing ecclesiology was being shaped by a reaction to what he perceived as the non-spiritual life of the 'modern church sociable'.[151] Ultimately, this amounted to the underlying selfish 'motivation' in 'all church gatherings', as Smale refuted the popular impression that 'the prosperity of the work [of God] is dependent upon young or old people getting together for a worldly or even for an innocent good time'.[152] This was spelt out to mean the utter rejection of a human mindset.[153]

That stated, Smale was swift to dissect what he perceived as the danger of human thinking further. In his judgment 'the introduction of human wisdom' had wrongly been

> Permitted and established in the house of God under the plausible pretext that God has given us intellects for reasoning, judging, ruling; intellects to plan and propose.[154]

The pragmatic corrective to this error, which incidentally Smale reckoned to feature in every church and denomination,[155] was for individual Christians and

---

[147] First New Testament Church Los Angeles, *Our First Anniversary*, p. 7.
[148] First New Testament Church Los Angeles, *Our First Anniversary*, p. 3.
[149] First New Testament Church Los Angeles, *Our First Anniversary*, p. 6.
[150] First New Testament Church Los Angeles, *Our First Anniversary*, p. 4.
[151] First New Testament Church Los Angeles, *Our First Anniversary*, p. 6.
[152] First New Testament Church Los Angeles, *Our First Anniversary*, p. 6.
[153] First New Testament Church Los Angeles, *Our First Anniversary*, p. 7.
[154] First New Testament Church Los Angeles, *Our First Anniversary*, p. 7.

churches to come really to know 'the mind of the Lord'[156] which, he argued, was only possible through waiting on God in prayer. Herein lay the underlying premise for Smale's emerging ecclesiology. The prerequisite for his church formation was, therefore, founded on a mix of intense prayer and taking appropriate decisions, which Smale considered were consequently deeply spiritual in character.

Because intense spiritual life was deemed to be the 'supreme need of the hour', Smale urged all local churches to cultivate patterns of prayer, such as they themselves were experiencing at First New Testament Church. In his open letter to the mainline denominations of Los Angeles in July 1906, he issued a clarion call to concerted prayer, replete with weeping, humiliation before God and confession of sins, as the 'method' by which the churches may 'be purged of their worldliness, commercialism, higher criticism and every form of sacrilege of which they have been guilty'.[157]

This case study of Smale helpfully poses questions that are relevant to ecclesiological considerations in the twenty-first century. For example, how subjective experiences of intense spirituality may be adequately framed in a local church context, especially with regard to the interplay of congregational prayer/waiting on God, and subsequent leadership decision making. Of course, sooner or later, structures, organization and power implementation are essential in any movement and require evaluation within a longer term framework. Typically, early Pentecostals were characterized by their lack of organizational affiliation, believing that organization always 'quenched the Spirit', although that did not prohibit routinization and the development of bureaucratic forms of institution. The divide could be recognised in diametrically opposing stances, as Blumhofer notes, 'while some believed that organization would jeopardize the restored apostolic faith, others thought that only organization could salvage it'.[158]

This is especially interesting in view of Smale's swift construction of a Pentecostal identity within his organizational theory, which he considered to be intensely spiritual in character. Summarizing this principle, perhaps somewhat idealistically, Smale stated,

> Only in the rightful recognition of our Lord do we come to know thoroughly a divine life and a divine system of service.[159]

---

[155] Smale explains that with all churches and denominations there will be some error, or some truth of the scriptures that is neglected, which ought to be emphasized. First New Testament Church Los Angeles, *Church Bulletin* (6 May 1906).

[156] Smale, *Our First Anniversary*, p. 7.

[157] 'New Testament Leader Writes Open Letter', *Los Angeles Express* 23 July 1906, p. 6.

[158] Blumhofer, *The Assemblies of God*, p. 174.

[159] First New Testament Church Los Angeles, *Our First Anniversary*, p. 7.

Within such a paradigm, Smale regularly reaffirmed the 'Headship of Christ' and the sovereignty of 'Holy Ghost Administration' at work within First New Testament Church by illustrating the many examples of 'the Lord's glorious presence' among them. In so doing, Smale was specifically attributing the dramatic growth and progress of his new church as significant signs pointing to the facts of Holy Spirit administration and intense spiritual power, whereby

> One, and one only, is Master here, verily Christ. There is no officialism lording it over God's heritage, neither allegiance or tribute paid to any sect or Missionary Board, nor any idolatrous denominational worship ... Thank God, this First New Testament Church is a stranger to all the man-made systems of religious life and service. It lives most simply, only to glorify God, and to have God glorified in this city and throughout the earth, and the record of these pages will demonstrate that all a church needs for its well-being is the favour of God, which it can have if the members of the household of God will walk in God's house servants to Jesus Christ, filled with the Spirit, free from all the bondage of creature religion, and separate from the man-made schemes for the furtherance of the work of God.[160]

Signalling that such distinctions between 'worldly' and 'spiritual' church organization were the core issues dividing denominational from newly formed Pentecostal churches, Smale argued for the 'visible church' to rigidly pursue 'the execution of His [God's] will in spiritual matters in the earth'.[161] But he realised that this principle of spiritual life needed some further elucidation in practice, and thus stated that

> it is the will of God that we act in concert as one body in all things as far as possible, we hereby resolve that all our department service in its important features be determined and sustained when we are assembled in business session as a Church.[162]

Consequently, the various departments that were required to embody this intensely unified spiritual life at First New Testament Church were numerous. Given their daily prayer regime, coupled with his ambition to train every member for 'complete Christian service', Smale's church model quickly developed. Within six months, he had formulated a well-ordered mix of evangelistic ministries among the Chinese, Spanish and Mexican communities of Los Angeles; a Bible and Missionary Training School – later called 'The New Testament Training School'; he had organized dates for fasting and prayer; and more besides.[163] The ironies of these structures, however, were his

---

[160] First New Testament Church Los Angeles, *Historical Number of the Bulletin* (18 March 1906), p. 2.

[161] First New Testament Church Los Angeles, *Our First Anniversary*, p. 6.

[162] First New Testament Church Los Angeles, *Our First Anniversary*, p. 6.

[163] First New Testament Church Los Angeles, *Historical Number of the Bulletin* (18 March 1906), p.8.

call for New Testament simplicity,[164] but according to Smale that meant simplicity within structures where he and his elders held sway and their centralised authority was not to be questioned![165]

Sooner or later, as Hollenweger has noted, 'Pentecostalism must deal with the tension between charisma and institution'.[166] Regardless of the spiritual life evident at First New Testament Church during this era, or Smale's interpretation of structures that he considered had been established as Spirit-ordained, such aspects are inherent in any ecclesiology. Smale's theology inadvertently provoked a debate among mainline churches in Los Angeles as to whether the evidence of the Holy Spirit's work was equally evident in the praying bands and revival crusades arranged by the conservative Church Federation during 1906–07, or conversely, as Smale and other Pentecostals proclaimed, that the phenomena they were experiencing demonstrated and verified the signs of God's coming Kingdom.[167] Although the relationship between Smale and the Los Angeles Church Federation was characterized by diametrically opposed ecclesiologies, their channels of communication remained open.

Towards the end of 1908, the president of the Los Angeles Church Federation, the Rev. E.P. Ryland, contacted Smale, warmly inviting him to participate in the Torrey Revival campaign being held, with a view to him joining the Church Federation thereafter. But Smale politely refused this invitation, explaining that

> my understanding as to the nature of the Christian ministry precludes me from being able to identify myself by membership with a movement of semi-political aims ... let me say that my services, should they be wanted at any time, in the preaching and teaching of the Word of God, are, consistent with my pastoral engagements, at the disposal of the Federation, to aid in the execution of its spiritual plans to bring Christ to the people.[168]

---

[164] 'New Testament Leader Writes Open Letter', *Los Angeles Express*, p. 6.

[165] First New Testament Church, *Historical Number of the Bulletin*, pp. 5-6. All departments were required to accept the authority of 'the Church herself, after such matters have been considered by the eldership'.

[166] W.J. Hollenweger, *Pentecostalism: Origins and Developments Worldwide* (Hendrikson, 1997), p. 258. See also a detailed presentation of the complementary nature of 'charisms' and 'institution' from a charismatic perspective, in Connie Ho Yan Au, *Grassroots Unity in the Charismatic Renewal* (Wipf & Stock, 2011), pp. 183-203. Thomas O'Dea, 'Sociological Dilemmas in the Institutionalization of Religion', *Journal for the Scientific Study of Religion* 1.1 (1961), pp. 30-39, has posited 'Five Institutional Dilemmas' which illustrate common tensions in all religious organizations, especially manifest between spontaneity and stability.

[167] 'Praying Bands for Churches', *Los Angeles Express* 25 July 1906, p. 6.

[168] First New Testament Church Los Angeles, 'The Torrey Meetings', *Church Bulletin* (15–21 November 1908), p. 1.

Some modern Pentecostal theologians have argued that a divide between the 'natural' and 'supernatural' in relation to the charismata establishes an unhelpful dichotomy.[169] Typically, the debate focuses around speaking in tongues and the problematic nature of defining the essence of Pentecostalism around a supernatural phenomenon which is not necessarily a shared experience for all Pentecostal adherents.[170] With regard to Smale's ecclesiology during the Spirit's outpouring of 1905–08, there was obviously ample evidence of extraordinary phenomena within his church and elsewhere, besides the more ordinary examples of everyday church business. Significantly, all aspects at First New Testament Church, natural and supernatural, seem to have been interpreted by Smale as key components of their Pentecostal life and service, having voiced his personal angst with the 'worldly' condition of the wider Church, for relying upon human methods rather than a waiting upon God in prayer. There was another practical feature of their new church identity that Smale was keen to stress from the outset, as further indication of Pentecostal blessing, namely New Testament patterns concerning church membership and financial giving.

NEW TESTAMENT CHURCH PRACTICES

Within the 1905 constitutional statement of the emergent First New Testament Church were two points for practical implementation, emanating from recognition of the headship of Christ and Holy Spirit Administration, and being intensely spiritual in character. Each concerned New Testament practices for 'the execution of all His will in spiritual matters in the earth'.[171]

Church Membership

Given the opportunity to depart from the formal ecclesiology at First Baptist Church Los Angeles, Smale quickly let it be known that he would 'continue to be a Baptist', but would 'follow a liberal policy in regard to the reception of new members'.[172] His expressed intent was, in all things, to be 'guided by the Holy Ghost and according to New Testament precepts'.[173] When the details for membership at First New Testament Church were published, they immediately received public attention in the *Los Angeles Times* under the provocative heading 'Immersion Unessential', describing Smale's decision as 'the first

---

[169] E.g., Miroslav Volf, J. Veenhof, and Jean-Claude Schwab. See Hollenweger, *Pentecostalism*, pp. 226-27.

[170] Hollenweger, *Pentecostalism*, p, 224.

[171] First New Testament Church Los Angeles, *Historical Number of the Bulletin* (18 March 1906), p. 5.

[172] 'New Church is Organized', *Los Angeles Express* 25 September 1905, p. 3.

[173] 'New Church is Organized', p. 3.

sensational announcement from a Baptist standpoint' to 'emanate from the new church formed by Rev. Joseph Smale'.[174]

The essence of Smale's decision was to shift church membership away from a formalised church roll, to the organic life of 'a regenerate church membership without the requirement of baptism for membership'.[175] Stating the aspects of this decision succinctly, Smale explained,

> We hold that immersion, while it is the duty of all the Godly, is not a test of fellowship with the Father. We regard the new birth as the door into the true church, and we welcome everyone applying for membership in the local body who gives evidence of being a child of God.[176]

Although several criticisms were reported from continuing members at First Baptist Church who resented what they perceived to be Smale's disloyalty to the Baptist cause, Smale was intent on formulating this new church objective of a covenant people bound by spiritual 'unity of all persons who are born again'.[177] This doctrine of the church was further defined by the occasion of their first anniversary, as Smale underscored their identity as part of the true visible church: 'what is true of the church as a whole is true of the church in its parts'.[178] Those whom 'the Father receives, we receive'.[179] The accepted criteria for any professing to belong to Christ and wishing to join the First New Testament Church was limited to those

> Who give such evidence of the new birth, being 'in Christ'.
> Who hold to the Headship of Christ and the Holy Ghost administration of the affairs of the church.[180]

It is interesting to observe that these stipulations for acceptance into church membership, as well as First New Testament Church's endorsement of baptism by immersion, were regularly printed in weekly church bulletins, as well as special documents commemorating anniversaries.[181] The core distinctives of Smale's church were clear for all to comprehend.

In practical terms, the infrastructure of the new church was quickly established. Anyone interested in discovering more about the matter of

---

[174] 'Immersion Unessential', *Los Angeles Times* 28 October 1905, p. II6.

[175] First New Testament Church Los Angeles, *Historical Number of the Bulletin* (18 March 1906), p. 5.

[176] 'Immersion Unessential', p. II6.

[177] First New Testament Church Los Angeles, *Our First Anniversary*, p. 4.

[178] First New Testament Church Los Angeles, *Our First Anniversary*, p. 4.

[179] First New Testament Church Los Angeles, *Our First Anniversary*, p. 5.

[180] First New Testament Church Los Angeles, *Our First Anniversary*, p. 4.

[181] E.g., First New Testament Church Los Angeles, *Our First Anniversary*, pp. 4-5; *Church Bulletin* (26 May to 2 June 1907), p. 4.

'Christian Baptism and Church Membership' was given a copy of Pastor Smale's printed sermon,[182] and then encouraged to 'have a talk with him upon the subject and arrange for the baptism'. Indeed, including their first baptismal service at Manhattan Beach on 9 October 1905,[183] Smale baptised a total of 101 believers in the first year at First New Testament Church.[184] The evidence that Smale retained his Baptist loyalties appears incontrovertible.

Evaluating these aspects concerning membership structures in light of New Testament precedent, the merits of Smale's conscious planning seems consistent with the Acts 2 model, whereby the early church joined together in worship and practical arrangements when the Holy Spirit came upon them. Certainly this would seem more practicable to attain in the short term where, as in Smale's case, there was a common expectation of possession by the Spirit, as well as unifying prayer for the Spirit, to administrate every dimension of individual and corporate church life.[185] But newly constituted churches energised by a unifying purpose, albeit the creation of the Spirit, eventually grow older, and it is the longer term analysis of behaviour that ultimately has to address to what extent it remains feasible for the Holy Spirit to be truly embodied in the life and structures of a local church.

Margaret Poloma has conducted a longer term sociological analysis regarding the Assemblies of God, to illustrate the historic dynamic that enables newly arranged communities to promote freedom of charisma, but which eventually decline in line with 'the gloomy Weberian prognosis on the inevitable routinization of charisma'.[186] Inevitably, emergent congregations such as First New Testament Church appeared to have less to risk at first than established denominations.[187] But intrinsic to the matter of church membership was the catalytic role of Smale himself as pastor. The church membership increased to 394 by the end of their first year.[188] Grant Wacker proposes a plausible explanation as to why early Pentecostals survived in the first decade of their existence at all. This may appropriately be applied to Smale's function,

---

[182] First New Testament Church Los Angeles, *Historical Number of the Bulletin* (18 March 1906), p. 8.

[183] A photograph of Smale with the eleven he baptised on 9 October 1905 is printed in editions of the *Historical Number of the Bulletin* (18 March 1906), p. 4, and *Our First Anniversary*, p. 1.

[184] First New Testament Church Los Angeles, *Our First Anniversary*, p. 1.

[185] J. McIntyre, *The Shape of Pneumatology* (T&T Clark, 1997), p. 219.

[186] M. Poloma, 'The Future of American Pentecostal Identity: The Assemblies of God at a Crossroad', in M. Welker (ed.), *The Work of the Spirit: Pneumatology and Pentecostalism* (Eerdmans, 2006), p. 148.

[187] Poloma, 'The Future of American Pentecostal Identity', p. 149.

[188] First New Testament Church Los Angeles, *Our First Anniversary*, p. 2.

because he too was able to 'hold two seemingly incompatible impulses in creative tension', namely the 'primitive' and the 'pragmatic'.[189]

Smale was creating a blueprint for Pentecostal life and service, and had the necessary profile and charisma to gather a cross section of followers together, holding out the prospect of (primitive) experiences of the heavenly, within a framework of pragmatic 'principles of our organized life'.[190] While the prayer, hope and expectation of a mighty Pentecost lasted, the membership at First New Testament Church was able to operate comfortably within the Pentecostal identity that these tensions were forging. But once the church structures and administration had started to mature (routinization), and from 1911 the membership had acquired land and built a new church sanctuary,[191] the Pentecostal implications for them as a congregation had already dissipated.

Church Finances

The matter of finance is explicitly included within 'The Great Principles of our Organized Life' at First New Testament Church which bear comment, even if it is impossible fully to evaluate it. Smale obviously felt strongly that the new church should be established on the basis of 'freewill offerings' supported by the church's 'prayer life'.[192] In fact, this conviction had led Smale into conflict during former days at First Baptist Church, as he insisted upon living by faith in such a manner that he 'had no promised or stipulated salary for his services'.[193] Any money given required administration by the church business meeting 'after such matters have been considered by the eldership'.[194] This rule was explained as a means of establishing unity as one body, thus centralising and enabling the 'organic life' of the fellowship to flourish.[195]

However, a missiological inference to the habit of giving which Smale encouraged among his congregation may be detected within a pivotal phrase regarding the stewardship of 'their means'. As the premise of First New Testament Church was their shared aim to emulate the pattern of early Christianity 'They realized and rejoiced in the missionary characteristic of that life ... that by their prayers and *their means*, that to the extent of their ability and opportunity, and the guidance of the Lord, the spiritually destitute places of

---

[189] Wacker, *Heaven Below*, p. 10. For a detailed explanation of 'primitive' and 'pragmatic' impulses, see pp. 11-14.

[190] Headings of First New Testament Church Los Angeles Constitutional Statement were 'The Church', 'Baptism', 'Membership', and 'The Pentecostal Blessing'.

[191] 'Dedication of First New Testament Church', *Los Angeles Times* 27 May 1911, p. I13.

[192] First New Testament Church Los Angeles, *Anniversary Bulletin* (First New Testament Church Los Angeles, 1908), p. 10.

[193] '900 Members now on its Rolls', *Los Angeles Examiner* 9 May1904, p. 4.

[194] First New Testament Church, *Our First Anniversary*, p. 6.

[195] First New Testament Church, *Our First Anniversary*, p. 6.

the earth should not lack a living voice to preach the Lord Jesus Christ, and a living hand to offer the people the Scriptures that make wise unto salvation.'[196] Such emphasis on giving for mission purposes leads naturally to the last major aspect of Smale's Pentecostal life and service.

The Shape of Smale's Missiology

Smale's pneumatology also shaped the mission endeavours of First New Testament Church during the phase of Pentecostal revival. It is well documented that the theological explanation for the phenomenal expansion of Pentecostal and Charismatic Christianity over the past century has been its intrinsic mission focus and power. Based upon the Acts 1:8 promise, the Holy Spirit comes to individuals as well as communities and releases an 'inward dynamic',[197] empowering Christians and churches to evangelise 'as a natural result of receiving the baptism of the Holy Ghost'.[198] Veli-Matti Karkkainen equates Pentecostalism as 'almost a synonym for mission and evangelization'.[199] To that end, the missional thrust of Joseph Smale and First New Testament Church was no exception.

However, while Smale's practice reflected the same missiological priorities to reach the 'ends of the earth' as quickly as possible with a shared premillennial eschatology, a number of contrasts with the Azusa Street model are evident. First, early Pentecostal absorption in mission generally resulted in a tendency for 'activism' rather than considered 'reflection', and a similar imbalance existed between the 'experiential' and 'cognitive'.[200] Of course, for some 'Spirit filled' missionaries, such as those from the Azusa Street meetings, there was a compelling theological reason that propelled them towards activism and experience. As Grant Wacker succinctly explains, their logic was impeccable and motivating:

> The Lord was coming soon, the heathen were perishing for want of the gospel, thus the Holy Spirit had given missionary tongues to the church as a speedy and practical means for meeting that need. Missionary tongues would hasten world evangelization by enabling partisans to bypass years of arduous language study.[201]

---

[196] J. Smale, *An Apostolic Journey in the 20th Century* (n.p., [1908]), p. 3, emphasis added.

[197] P.A. Pomerville, *The Third Force in Missions* (Hendrickson, 1985), p. 96.

[198] V.M. Karkkainen, 'Missiology: Pentecostal and Charismatic', in Burgess and Van der Maas (eds), *New International Dictionary*, p. 879.

[199] V.M. Karkkainen, 'Mission, Spirit and Eschatology', *Mission Studies* Vol. XVI-I (1999), p. 93.

[200] L.G. McClung, Jr, (ed), *Azusa Street and Beyond: Pentecostal Missions and Church Growth in the Twentieth Century* (Bridge Publishing, 1986), p. 47.

[201] Wacker, *Heaven Below*, p. 48.

With regard to Smale there was typically a leaning towards careful reflection and documentation in his planning and implementation, as will be demonstrated below.

Secondly, a key theological difference may be identified in that Smale proceeded in his mission strategy without the same endorsement of xenolalia (speaking in tongues as to enable the gospel message to be communicated in the foreign languages of their recipients).[202]

For Smale, baptism in the Spirit enabled Christians to regain 'soul-winning' power both locally as well as overseas. Within the first three months of the First New Testament Church's formation, Mrs M.E. Davis, 'an old woman but with true missionary zeal', came forward to offer herself as a missionary to go to Jerusalem immediately.[203] Further offers to leave for mission service followed, such that by Christmas 1905 First New Testament Church was already 'supporting two strong missions and five missionaries, and eight of its young people are preparing for foreign mission work'.[204]

This frenetic pace was accompanied by the steady development of other local mission activities in Los Angeles which Smale initiated during the autumn of 1905, enabled by his genius for organization, essentially managing to balance the five hourly daily prayer gatherings at Burbank Hall, with 'Street meetings, [where] homes are visited and places of employment ... and a mission band is organized to follow as the Lord leads'.[205] The mix of prayer and action were deemed to be evidence of Holy Spirit potency. The tangible fruits of Smale's practice may be seen in the portfolio of mission works emanating from First New Testament Church which, by March 1906, included a number of missions and various evangelistic initiatives.

A Chinese Mission

This ministry, 'located at the very gateway of Chinatown', served the purposes of mission as well as compassionate social care for Chinese citizens facing 'arrest or deportation from the United States government'.[206] Bessie Smith, the superintendent of this work, gave testimony to the power of God that had used some of their members 'in freeing four of our brethren from prison', while retaining their underpinning mandate to 'tell the heathen the glorious gospel of our blessed Lord'.[207] Significantly, there are several pneumatological references which corroborate the shared need felt by the workers in the different

---

[202] Anderson, *Spreading Fires*, p. 46.

[203] 'Indian is a Hustler', *Los Angeles Times* 9 December 1905, p. 17.

[204] 'Mission Money Comes Quickly', *Los Angeles Times* 26 December 1905, p. II2.

[205] 'Echoes of the Welsh Revival', *The Missionary Review of the World* (July 1906), pp. 482-83.

[206] First New Testament Church Los Angeles, *Our First Anniversary*, p. 11.

[207] First New Testament Church Los Angeles, *Our First Anniversary*, p. 11.

departments of missions. Perhaps not surprisingly within the orb of First New Testament Church life they use similar language:

> Oh for a Pentecost upon our Christian Chinese, that this important part of heathendom may be moved by the power of God! There are great opportunities for this mission, and we need the power of the Holy Ghost.[208]

A Spanish Mission

Significant to this study at a personal dimension, was the Spanish Mission, directed by Esther Hargrave who Smale later married in 1911. Purely in terms of mission enterprise, this superintendent was also recognising the hand of God's Spirit at work in providing 'a precious band of native workers He has raised up – for the unity and love that reigns among them. Surely 'tis the work of the Spirit'.[209] Smale's personal interest in Spanish gospel work was to prove an important link with Miss Hargrave and their future mission involvement in Spain as we will see in the final chapter.

Door to Door Tract Distribution

In February 1906, thirty-six members of First New Testament Church embarked on a door to door campaign aimed at 'every unevangelized home in this city'. Their method was to insert one of Smale's sermons into an 'attractive cover whereon shall be outlined the current meetings of the Church, and the back of which shall contain the third chapter of John'.[210] Their encouragement, as they visited homes in each district of Los Angeles, was to remain 'prayerful' and 'led by the Spirit'.[211]

Christmas Day 1905

During their Christmas day service Smale interrupted the praise service at Burbank Hall to invite giving to 'Christian Missions'. Both the church bulletin and the account in the *Los Angeles Times* record how the free-will offering was 'made with remarkable promptness',[212] as people 'flocked to the front (no basket was passed) and laid their gifts on God's altar'.[213] More than $2,600 was

---

[208] First New Testament Church Los Angeles, *Our First Anniversary*, p. 12.

[209] First New Testament Church Los Angeles, *Our First Anniversary*, p. 12.

[210] First New Testament Church Los Angeles, *Historical Number of the Bulletin* (18 March 1906), p. 8.

[211] First New Testament Church Los Angeles, *Historical Number of the Bulletin* (18 March 1906), p. 8.

[212] 'Mission Money Comes Quickly', p. II2.

[213] First New Testament Church Los Angeles, *Historical Number of the Bulletin* (18 March 1906), p. 7.

given, and when this was announced to the meeting, 'a member arose and volunteered to bring the sum up to $3,000'.[214]

This was explained to the church as a further example of 'the day of His power'.[215] Once more the theme of money and mission had demonstrated their 'spirituality without the admixture of worldliness; for the divine government of the Lord's Church as against the human government of it'[216] had prompted this significant amount of money to be given without any human solicitation. By their estimation and standards, this was an extraordinary confirmation of the Pentecostal blessing. Who needed mission agencies or boards when God was able to deal directly with his divinely resourced supply of funding and people? After just six months in existence amid such anointing and blessing, the mission impulse emanating from First New Testament Church was getting stronger and the flexibility of the church structures amid revival power was a potent combination.

City Tent Work

Similarly, as a consequence of a 'spontaneous' offering in July 1906, the church was also able to 'establish Gospel Tent Work'[217] in Los Angeles. Under the direction of their evangelist John Boyd, this was a tent based mission involving preaching services every evening except Saturdays.[218] The report after the first six weeks includes description that the blessing at Burbank Hall was spilling over to the tent mission, where also 'the Lord was manifestly present'.[219] Articulating a sense of 'victory', the evidence emerging from the tent meetings reported that

> Quite a number of the Lord's dear people have been richly blessed according to their testimony a few have been anointed and prayed for in order to the healing of their bodies, some have professed conversion, several have been reclaimed from their backsliding.[220]

Illustrative of the unity that Smale was seeking to display in their organic church life, it is interesting to note that evangelist John Boyd was also involved at the height of the Spirit's outpouring during the dramatic services at First

---

[214] First New Testament Church Los Angeles, *Historical Number of the Bulletin* (18 March 1906), p. 7. The Christmas Day 1905 offering eventually reached $3,227.

[215] First New Testament Church Los Angeles, *Our First Anniversary*, p. 9.

[216] First New Testament Church Los Angeles, *Our First Anniversary*, p. 7.

[217] First New Testament Church Los Angeles, *Church Bulletin* (8–15 July 1906), p. 1. They had hoped to purchase just one tent, but the $500 given enabled two tents to be acquired.

[218] First New Testament Church Los Angeles, *Our First Anniversary*, p. 11.

[219] First New Testament Church Los Angeles, *Our First Anniversary*, p. 11.

[220] First New Testament Church Los Angeles, *Our First Anniversary*, p. 11.

New Testament Church in July 1906, being the one who announced 'that the church members will become missionaries to heathen lands'.[221]

The Bible and Missionary Training School

However, another facet of church life must be considered by way of explaining this impact. First, Smale had commenced 'The Bible and Missionary Training School'[222] alongside the inauguration of First New Testament Church. It emerged from his conviction that as a church they were 'entirely in organic existence to magnify and publish the Word of God ... and that the one great work of the church of this age in the purpose of God is world-wide evangelization'.[223] The 'missionary motive' was specifically linked to the 'wondrous prayer life' that existed within the church, such that 'hearts whom God has touched are witnessing to a constraint of the Holy Spirit in the direction of world-wide missionary service'.[224] The *raison d'être* of the school was to equip men and women 'to open up the Word under the guidance of the Holy Spirit', with Smale's awareness that many might not be able to afford such training and, therefore, the church would look to support them however possible.

Having described these diverse mission responses, the most significant mission strategy emanated from the revival fires of First New Testament Church in March 1906. 'The elders and deacons met in the spirit of delightful harmony, and prayerfully sought the mind of the Lord upon possible mission work in China.'[225] A two-stage scheme developed, whereby two of their church members, Huen Ming Cho and Clyde Lewis, were sent for 'immediate missionary service in the fields in China where the gospel standard never has been planted'.[226] This was followed a year later, when, with the agreement of his church in Los Angeles, Smale travelled to China with the sole purpose of establishing a 'Gospel Mission'. His trip is well documented, thanks to a tract discovered at Yale Divinity School, entitled *An Apostolic Journey in the 20th Century*. Although Bartleman criticized Smale for too much organization at the Spirit's expense, Smale's interpretation of the mission work accomplished

---

[221] 'Rolling on Floor in Smale's Church', *Los Angeles Times* 14 July 1906, p. II1.

[222] Originally called The Bible School.

[223] First New Testament Church Los Angeles, 'Origin, Scope, Object of the New Testament Church Bible and Missionary Training School', *Anniversary Bulletin* (September 1908), p. 7.

[224] First New Testament Church Los Angeles, 'Origin, Scope, Object of the New Testament Church Bible and Missionary Training School', p. 8.

[225] First New Testament Church Los Angeles, *Historical Number of the Bulletin* (18 March 1906), p. 9.

[226] First New Testament Church Los Angeles, *Historical Number of the Bulletin* (18 March 1906), p. 9.

between 1906 and 1908 speaks for itself, demonstrating his perception that God was in the details of givers and gifts.

> Think of it, one church, which though its membership is about 525, its giving strength is confined to about 200, sent forth to China in the space of ten months and without resorting to personal appeals ... the sum of $3100, and there was contributed to home work by the church the sum of $8722.[227]

China New Testament Mission

Smale left Los Angeles on 21 January 1907,[228] and sailed, via Japan and the Philippines, before eventually arriving in Hong Kong on 25 February. The purpose of his trip was to ascertain where and how a Pentecostal extension of the spiritual life at First New Testament Church might be reproduced somewhere in China. It is important to stress, however, that the available evidence at no point suggests that this was to be a denomination or empire-building exercise. Similar to the pioneering and 'ecumenical' nature of early Pentecostalism in the first decade, Smale was willing to cooperate with anyone who would help establish a Pentecostal work. As Allan Anderson observes, 'Any denominations that existed or were subsequently created were incidental to the fundamental missionary and interdenominational and international nature of early Pentecostalism.'[229]

The narrative account regarding precisely how Smale pursued guidance for this project merits detailed description for two reasons. First, there is a need within Pentecostal historiography for more case studies to be discovered and recorded, because each example helps contribute towards the emerging storyline and networks. It aids explanation regarding the motivation behind the movement, while identifying characters and societies who contributed to the legacy of mission strategies that were deployed amid the imperialist culture of western mission. However, a word of caution regarding the documentary sources available in Smale's case is necessary, as with much western mission material, providing a reminder that many letters and church documents were ultimately intended to inform and stimulate further financial and prayer support. Within the faith culture of North American Christianity, permission to be honest about struggles and failures was implicitly withheld.

Secondly, with regard to Smale's exploits it is important to examine the matter of timing and practice. It is accepted that the first wave of 'Spirit baptized' missionaries started leaving the Azusa Street Mission by November 1906, fanning out to numerous American cities before heading to various parts

---

[227] First New Testament Church Los Angeles, *An Apostolic Journey in the 20th Century*, p. 7.
[228] J. Smale, *My Trip Around the World* (handwritten journal, 1907), p. 1.
[229] Anderson, *Spreading Fires*, p. 9.

of the globe, including China, Japan, and India.[230] Four months from the date of this published information, Smale was researching the various options for his own instigation of a new Pentecostal mission work. His journal illustrates a more cautious approach, while highlighting some of the various aspects emerging in his meetings with different mission works and personnel. For instance, upon arrival at a hotel in Hong Kong, Smale writes that 'the first one to be my friend' was 'an independent worker, formally connected with the "Revivalist" people of Cincinnati' who was also hoping to secure a building. Smale comments, 'I am impressed with Hong Kong as a fine opening for an English Mission Rescue work, a place also for missionary Home, Bible School and Orphanage.'[231] The intention of Smale's search for guidance was openness to the leading by the Holy Spirit in every encounter.

Smale also provides insights into the fluidity and transfer of mission workers already in China at this time, dividing especially along theological differences regarding the charismata. Meeting one worker who had developed an 'undenominational' mission work to the consternation of 'Baptists at home in the South', Smale describes how he ('Mr Todd') had been 'turned down because of his views on "healing"',[232] presumably meaning the endorsement of this practice in Holy Spirit power. Simultaneous to Smale's arrival, 'a revival work had begun ... the devil however was trying to upset it'.[233] Smale continues to describe an incident that he witnessed in Mr Todd's home, whereby 'a man under the power of evil whom the workers were holding down' was delivered through the power of 'earnest prayer'.[234] Other phenomena were reported to Smale, which he duly recorded in his journal, such that another 'man got on the floor and kicked and bleated like a sheep'.[235] On a later occasion, it was recorded that 'Satanic interference' was evident with 'demons working' to oppose various mission ventures, yet the testimony of their first year was 'a work also wrought of God'.[236]

Such anecdotes evoke no further comment or explanation in Smale's own report. However, Daniel Bays places such occurrences in helpful context for the ambitions of Smale and First New Testament Church. The phenomenon of Protestant 'revivalism' in China emerged at the beginning of the twentieth century following decades of 'arduous foreign missionary efforts over the previous sixty to seventy years'.[237] Characteristically, such outpourings in

---

[230] 'Spreading the Full Gospel', *The Apostolic Faith* 1.3 (November, 1906), p. 11.
[231] Smale, *My Trip Around the World*, p. 21.
[232] Smale, *My Trip Around the World*, p. 22.
[233] Smale, *My Trip Around the World*, p. 22.
[234] Smale, *My Trip Around the World*, p. 22.
[235] Smale, *My Trip Around the World*, p. 22.
[236] Smale, *An Apostolic Journey*, p. 18.
[237] D.H. Bayes, 'Christian Revival in China', in E.L. Blumhofer and R. Balmer (eds), *Modern Christian Revivals* (University of Illinois Press, 1993), p. 161.

China were 'reminiscent in tone and size of those of Finney and Moody' inevitably augmented, in Bays' estimation, by the '"internationalization of revivalist expectations" – in particular, the worldwide publicity given to the Welsh revival from 1904'.[238]

At the micro level, Smale was continuing his search for a mission location, and his 'guidance came about in a remarkable way for the church to give the gospel to a section of the unevangelized in South West China'.[239] Smale considered that he was sent on a 'Divine errand' 'across the Pacific', which necessitated 'separation from a dear and frail mother of 76 years of age, and the impossibility of hearing from her at frequent intervals'.[240] Upon arrival in China, and travelling with Ming Cho Huen (the missionary First New Testament Church Los Angeles had sent to China a year previously), they were attempting to 'explore virgin soil' with a view to 'avoid encroaching upon spheres chosen by the missionary societies'.[241] However, travel circumstances enforced debarkation at Pakhoi on 10 March 1907 (see Figure 15). Consequently, the evidence does not point to an exclusive mission work, rather Smale's change of itinerary afforded the opportunity to develop a 'spirit of confraternity ... between the Medical Mission of the C.M.S. [Church Missionary Society] and the solely evangelistic Mission of the C.N.T.M. [China New Testament Mission], and each is glad and grateful to God for the other's presence and service'.[242] Such natural and spontaneous ecumenical relationships were further evidence of Smale's Pentecostal life and service.

A German Missionary: A.H. Bach

On arrival at the home of a missionary couple, Mr and Mrs Bradley, Smale immediately 'learned of a remarkable [and recent] conversion of a German missionary in Pakhoi called August Hugo Bach'.[243] Smale's brief summary of

---

[238] Bayes, 'Christian Revival in China', p. 162. For more information on a later revival in 1908, see a synopsis of Jonathan Goforth's ministry, along with manifestations of the Spirit's activity, pp. 163-64. Significantly, the revivalist phenomenon in Manchuria included public confession of sins, expressions of desire for the Holy Spirit, tears, and deep emotional responses including groans and sobs, which were regarded as 'legitimizing it for all'. This revival was predominantly among Christian congregations and pastors.

[239] Smale, *An Apostolic Journey*, p. 1.

[240] Smale, *An Apostolic Journey*, p. 3.

[241] Smale, *An Apostolic Journey*, p. 4.

[242] Smale, *An Apostolic Journey*, p. 4.

[243] There is a copy of Bach's photograph printed in Smale, *An Apostolic Journey*, p. 15. The quality of the image is poor. However, Smale's account of hearing about, and meeting August Bach, recording his conversion, and references from other local missionaries, is presented in detail, pp. 4-12. Further biographical information about

Bach is noted here for its important contribution to later Pentecostal mission biography, as Bach later worked as a financial agent for the 'Pentecostal Missionary Union'.[244] In addition it provides firsthand evidence of the common theological denominators in the mission work established by Smale in China. Thirty-three year old August Bach

> Had been in Pakhoi many years. He was a German missionary! A missionary, but throughout his missionary career an unconverted man! Had never known the Lord. Had lived a rationalist. And the motive of his work, misnamed mission, was educational and political.[245]

Figure 15: Map of China from Joseph Smale's Journal, *My Trip Around the World,* 1907, courtesy of H. Stanley Wood (Pakhoi is marked on South Coast).

Bach has kindly been provided R.G. Tiedemann, including this excerpt from his draft manuscript, *A Reference Guide to Missionary Societies in China.*

August Hugo Bach, German missionary (male); born 30 June 1873 at Büdingen, Oberhessen, Hessen, in Germany, the child of Heinrich Peter Bach, and Margaretha Schmidt. Was appointed by the Kiel China Mission (KCM) and arrived in China on 18 October 1898 at Shanghai. Died 13 January 1921.

Married Anna Maria Hermann in Beihai (Guangdong) on 14 April 1900. She was from Basel and was sent to China by the CIM in 1896.

Had issue: Hermann Theodor Bach, born ca. 1902 and Mrs. Bach also adopted a Chinese girl, Katrina M. Bach, born ca. 1912.

[244] I am most grateful that my supervisor, Prof. Allan Anderson, made this link, connecting Bach and the Pentecostal Missionary Union in an email, 13 June 2006. Anderson writes, 'Bach is named in the PMU minutes for June 1914, as the one to whom funds were transmitted from London to send on to PMU missionaries. He was manager of a mission home in Peking called the Peking Home, seemingly for missionaries to stay in, as two young PMU missionaries, Frank Trevitt and Amos Williams, stayed there temporarily. Bach had to send funds on to them in the interior.'

[245] Smale, *An Apostolic Journey,* p. 5.

Through the joint witness of the Church Missionary Society and a specially arranged 'Torrey-Alexander Mission' which visited Pakhoi, August Bach came into direct contact with these 'revival singers'.[246] Significantly, by his own admission, he had also heard accounts of the Welsh Revival.[247] His version of his own spiritual experience at this point is revealing, as Bach discussed spiritual matters with Charles Alexander.

> I decided to have a talk with Mr. Alexander, but with a view to prove that he was wrong. We had the talk. Dear me, he is not a smart man ... but he is a man of God. He had a power I could not resist. It was the Holy Spirit.[248]

Following his conversion in January 1907, Bach wrote home to the committee of the Kiel China Mission, explaining that he had come to true faith in Christ and in future desired to 'preach and teach Jesus Christ and Him crucified'.[249] Therefore, he requested to 'reconstruct' the German mission 'upon an evangelical and evangelistic basis' or else resign his membership from the mission, because 'our old Lutheran Church excludes a priori such things as revivals, conversions, being filled with the Spirit and so on'.[250]

Ultimately it was Alexander's challenge for 'full surrender, nothing less' which prompted Bach to turn to Christ with dramatic effect.[251] As expected, Bach's dismissal was cabled from Germany,[252] yet his

> prayers were answered in a remarkable manner. The very next day there landed in Pakhoi the pastor of a church in Los Angeles, Cal., who was visiting the Orient for the purpose of establishing a mission in China along strictly soul-winning lines.[253]

In his journal, Smale asked, 'Did the Lord bring me to Pakhoi to have him [Bach] connected with the New Testament Church Mission of South China? This is the question I am now asking.'[254] Smale later stated that he felt 'the Lord brought me to Pakhoi at a significant moment in the history of this new convert', but with no inclination that he would 'pick up a worker while away'.[255] During their time together, Smale and Bach shared numerous answers

---

[246] Smale, *An Apostolic Journey*, p. 11.
[247] Smale, *An Apostolic Journey*, p. 11.
[248] Smale, *An Apostolic Journey*, pp. 11-12.
[249] Smale, *An Apostolic Journey*, p.5.
[250] Smale, *An Apostolic Journey*, p. 11.
[251] Smale, *An Apostolic Journey*, p. 12.
[252] Smale, *An Apostolic Journey*, p. 10.
[253] Smale, *An Apostolic Journey*, p. 10.
[254] J. Smale, *Pakhoi Journal* (handwritten journal 1907), p. 9.
[255] Smale, *An Apostolic Journey*, p. 5.

to prayer, including the provision of a 'Gospel Hall', and the joy on Easter Sunday 1907 as Smale baptized August Bach in the sea at Pakhoi.[256]

The provision of Bach for the New Testament Mission work in Pakhoi was estimated by Smale to be further evidence of Holy Spirit administration. Bach 'had the advantage of a five year's start in mission work in China',[257] and had been providentially prepared for Smale's arrival in China. At a theological level, Smale was heartened to discover that Bach had been taught by the Holy Spirit 'all these blessed things of revelation and made him exactly one with the New Testament Church in doctrine and practice', emphasizing Bach's endorsement of 'The Pentecostal Blessing' and that he would consequently 'teach the reception of the Holy Spirit as the gift'.[258] It is not surprising that at the end of his time in Pakhoi, Smale wrote,

> What a month! What precious striking apostolic leadings of the Lord. It will make a great page in Church History. How wonderful; How marvellous is our God. Hallelujah.[259]

In a pragmatic sense, Smale's experiences of God's leading during his 1907 trip to establish a mission in China was, to all intents and purposes, a mirror of some of the New Testament emphases that were considered integral to his mission strategy and ultimately Pentecostal restoration. As well as the 'felt' component experienced in his 'leading', Smale also maintained an articulate cerebral approach to his evaluation of the missiological challenges and philosophy facing mission workers in China. This is most clearly seen by the next phase of his tour, as Smale attended the China Centenary Conference in Shanghai.

China Centenary Missionary Conference

Smale attended this conference from 25 April to 8 May 1907 as an independent delegate, joining 1,170 other missionaries and interdenominational home board members, to celebrate the first century of Protestant missionary activity in China following Robert Morrison's arrival in 1807.[260] To appreciate the western bias of these Shanghai proceedings it is notable that, according to Smale, there were no Chinese delegates in attendance.[261] Furthermore, it must

---

[256] Smale, *An Apostolic Journey*, p. 16; *Pakhoi Journal*, p. 51.

[257] Smale, *An Apostolic Journey*, p. 7.

[258] Smale, *An Apostolic Journey*, p. 7.

[259] Smale, *Pakhoi Journal*, p. 55.

[260] K.X. Yao, 'At the Turn of the Century: A Study of the China Centenary Missionary Conference of 1907', *International Bulletin of Missionary Research* 32.2 (April, 2008), p. 65.

[261] Smale, *My Trip Around the World*, p. 34, though Figure 16 clearly shows some 'Chinese Pastors on [the] Platform'. Yao, 'At the Turn of the Century', p. 65, has

be recognised that for Smale to participate in a structured conference of this nature was an anathema to early Pentecostals. However, this conference (hereafter referred to as the Centenary Conference) possesses missiological importance for several reasons, presenting the felt challenges facing mission agencies at the commencement of a new century, as well as providing inspiration for the template later used in planning the World Missionary Conference in Edinburgh in 1910.[262]

Using extracts from Smale's journal, it is instructive to place his own analysis and concepts for the China New Testament Mission within the orbit of themes emanating from the Centenary Conference, which may in turn be evaluated within the wider currents of Pentecostal mission activity of that period. Smale records his pleasure at hearing from another delegate that there were 'four great conferences held in China yearly, for the deepening of spiritual life. He spoke of one having an attendance of 400 missionaries!'[263] Illustrative of the spiritual climate within and without the conference proceedings were a number of optimistic pneumatological addresses. The titles of these three sermons indicate the thrust of some theological matters under consideration:

'The preaching of the Gospel and the Ministry of the Spirit', by Mr Walter Sloan.
'The Fulness of the Spirit', by Rev. A.B. Leonard.
'Led by the Spirit', by Rev. James Barton.[264]

Reflecting upon Barton's sermon, Smale commented,

> Dr. Barton's was a very timely searching address. It delighted my heart ... He made a splendid application to the effect that Christ was with us. Was he to be welcomed or asked to depart; He is going to interfere with our business and strike the path of denominational schemes and our plans and purposes. Then he said the hardest thing I ever have heard bearing upon modern methods of ill doing. It was this 'the Home Mission Boards had been a [sic] greatest hindrance to foreign missions than anything on the foreign fields.[265]

---

concluded there were actually some Chinese delegates present, though they numbered fewer than ten.

[262] B. Stanley, *The World Missionary Conference, Edinburgh 1910* (Eerdmans, 2009), p. 27.

[263] Smale, *Pakhoi Journal*, p. 65.

[264] China Centenary Missionary Conference, *Addresses: Public and Devotional* (Methodist Publishing House, Shanghai, 1907), p. ii.

[265] Smale, *My Trip Around the World*, p. 35.

Figure 16: China Centenary Missionary Conference, Shanghai, 1907.
From *Records: China Centenary Missionary Conference*,
(China Centenary Committee, 1907), p. 161.

Figure 17: China Centenary Missionary Conference, Shanghai, 1907.
From *Records: China Centenary Missionary Conference*,
(China Centenary Committee, 1907), p. 624.

As a delegate, Smale was indirectly participating in some key discussions and decision making in the history of mission in China. The Centenary Conference optimistically voted, believing that 'a three-self church could be achieved within the foreseeable future'. As the conference chairman concluded, 'We have already in China a Church which in a substantial degree is already [sic], and which is perfectly able to be entirely, self-governing, self-supporting, and self-propagating.'[266]

Such a positive stance did not, however, take into account the inherent tensions and difficulties already noted by Smale in his journal. The model of mission being transported to foreign fields required jettisoning much of the cultural baggage of the 'mother' institutions. Smale endorsed the expressions of many at the Centenary Conference, stating,

> I was delighted in their definition of belief, the orthodoxy of their stand, their insistence that the Chinese Church shall not be tacked on to foreign boards or to a foreign church when it can walk alone. A strong sentiment was expressed that China should lead the way in the overthrow of the denominations of the old world.[267]

However, this antipathy felt towards denominational and organizational structures, which was a common conviction of Pentecostals and other mission agencies, was not consistently implemented in Smale's model to establish a mission based on the constitutional statement of the parent First New Testament Church Los Angeles.[268] Both constitutionally and pragmatically Smale and Bach implemented a programme in Pakhoi similar to the routines of church ministry at First New Testament Los Angeles, mainly incorporating prayer times with evangelistic services.[269] The timing of the Centenary Conference preceded the later debates of the 1920s and 1930s, which embroiled Chinese mission history in controversy over modernist-fundamentalist divides. In fact, as Kevin Yao states, 'the conference of 1907 can be considered the last major manifestation of the Protestant missionary consensus in China'.[270]

Arguably, such unity among denominational mission societies in China around 1907 was timely for Smale, impacting on his own thinking regarding pioneer mission innovation. The Centenary Conference called for 'considerable expansion of the educational, medical, and other social dimensions of mission enterprises'.[271] Smale and Bach felt obligated to form their work 'in the worst quarters of Pakhoi where gambling houses, Chinese hotels and brothels

---

[266] *Records: China Centenary Missionary Conference* (China Centenary Committee, 1907), p. 18.
[267] Smale, *My Trip Around the World*, p. 38.
[268] Smale, *An Apostolic Journey*, p. 25.
[269] Smale, *An Apostolic Journey*, pp. 22-23.
[270] Yao, 'At the Turn of the Century', p. 66.
[271] Yao, 'At the Turn of the Century', p. 66.

abound[ed].'²⁷² The China New Testament Mission also responded to the needs of 'hundreds of people [who] came into the town as fugitives'.²⁷³ On average, 250 people attended their meetings as a consequence, although 'it was hard work to keep them in order and to make our talk spiritual at the same time'.²⁷⁴

Figure 18: Joseph and Esther Smale at the China New Testament Mission, at a reception for Mr and Mrs W.H. Crofts, Pakhoi, China, November 1921.
Photograph courtesy of George Wood.

However, such entrepreneurial works should be offset against emphases which Smale declined to pursue. For instance, he was resistant at first to some of the conference calls, particularly the call for mission participation in education. In response, he curtly writes how he 'was not at all pleased. Keynote was education, the very note that is missing in the New Testament Church life. Which is right – the moderns or Paul?'²⁷⁵ Although by Smale's later return visit to Pakhoi in 1921, it is ironic that a school mission work had obviously been in existence for some years, led by Mr and Mrs W.H. Crofts (see Figure 17), until

---

²⁷² Smale, *An Apostolic Journey*, p. 18.
²⁷³ Smale, *An Apostolic Journey*, p. 19.
²⁷⁴ Smale, *An Apostolic Journey*, p. 19.
²⁷⁵ Smale, *Pakhoi Journal*, p. 66.

William Crofts returned to Los Angeles to join Smale at, the later renamed, Grace Baptist Church.[276]

The expansion and development of Smale's New Testament Mission property in Pakhoi merits further description, including a compound measuring

> 596 English feet on the south side, 600 feet on the west side, 713 on the north side and 477 feet on the east side. The entire piece of land is surrounded by a fine wall of burnt brick of the best quality, seven feet high and three section walls running across the compound cutting it off into building compounds. The buildings consist of a fair foreign house of eight rooms, and two big halls sixteen feet wide, with bath rooms, kitchens, store rooms and outhouses. There is a lower and an upper story. The boys school is a brick building on the east side of the compound and will seat one hundred students. The girl's school is on the west side and will seat 25 students. The church is just in front of the foreigner's house and is a good building, built for a printing office but now used for a church … It will seat three hundred people. Opposite the church is a small four room house built for the workers, preachers and teachers, to live in. This has a lovely guest hall, here the guest always gather to discuss the 'doctrine' or any other subject of the hour. At the gate there are two small rooms with the kitchen for the Chinese staff to one side of them. We have also three good wells on the place and a fine vegetable garden and other out houses.[277]

In addition the China New Testament Mission acquired two burial grounds as well as further mission properties in Yamchow and Liemchow.[278]

There is one final observation about Smale's deployment of mission personnel, especially in relation to his shifting Pentecostal perceptions. Having already noted the involvement of A.H. Bach and his later transfer to the Pentecostal Missionary Union (certainly by 1914), there is circumstantial evidence that suggests that Bach actually left Smale's mission as early as 1909. This unsubstantiated possibility is based on the timing of Bach's departure from Pakhoi, bound for Los Angeles, in June 1909.[279] Thereafter, Bach was replaced at the China New Testament Mission by Smale's loyal friend and former

---

[276] R.G. Tiedemann, 'Crofts, William Herbert (1884–1963)', in *Reference Guide to Missionary Societies in China*. I am indebted to Gary Tiedemann for providing this primary information from his research, email, 10 March 2009.

[277] W.H. Turner, *Pioneering in China (Illustrated)* (The Publishing House of the Pentecostal Holiness Church, n.d., [1928]), pp. 167-68. This description of China New Testament Mission's assets is located his chapter 'The Opening of a New Mission Station', pp. 152-70, describing the Pentecostal Holiness Church's acquisition of the China New Testament Mission compounds. I am indebted to Connie Au for discovering this information, email 8 April 2010.

[278] Turner, *Pioneering in China*, p. 168

[279] Tiedemann, 'Crofts, William Herbert (1884–1963)', in *Reference Guide to Missionary Societies in China*. See also his 'Bach, A.H. (1873–1921?)'.

church clerk, R.G. Haskell, who left First New Testament Church with his wife[280] for what transpired as two five-year terms of service in China.[281]

Furthermore, the reasons which prompted Bach's later links with the more overtly Pentecostal mission established by Cecil Polhill,[282] raises key questions regarding the divergent theological differences which were obviously emerging between Smale's notion of 'Pentecostal life and service' and other, more Pentecostal, missionaries and societies. Herein, for the final part of this chapter, an analysis of Smale's withdrawal from Pentecostalism will be presented in terms of his doctrine and practice.

Smale's Withdrawal from Pentecostalism

Bartleman's popularised explanation of Smale's withdrawal from Pentecostalism presents it as the result of disaffection with the more radical elements at Azusa Street during 1906, and the fact that Smale 'never received the "baptism" with the "speaking in tongues"'.[283] This simplistic version of events has generally been accepted within Pentecostal narratives, hence the endorsement of the 'Moses' motif. Consequently, until Robeck's 2006 work *The Azusa Street Mission and Revival*, there have been no analytic attempts to discover a more detailed reconstruction of Smale's retreat. This will be rectified here, building upon Robeck's work, utilising contemporary newspaper accounts and Smale's own writing during the period in question. What becomes clear is that while Smale continued to define the 1905–08 period as one of 'Pentecostal life and service', there were a combination of early circumstantial and theological factors which enforced Pentecostal patterns with a different, more independent and organized, expression than those evident at the Azusa Street Mission.

Circumstantial Reasons for Retreat: Smale and Keyes

> The devil did his worst, to bring the work into disrepute and destroy it. He sent wicked spirits among us to frighten the pastor [Smale] and cause him to reject it. But Brother Smale was God's Moses, to lead the people as far as the Jordan, though he himself never got across.[284]

---

[280] 'Farewell for Missionaries to China', *Los Angeles Times* 13 March 1909, p. II10.

[281] Tiedemann, 'Haskell, Richard Glenn (1865–?)', in *Reference Guide to Missionary Societies in China*.

[282] The Pentecostal Missionary Union was formed in January 1909, following Polhill's baptism in the Spirit in Los Angeles early in 1908. See 'Pentecostal Missionary Union', in Burgess and Van der Maas (eds), *New International Dictionary*, pp. 970-71.

[283] Bartleman, *Azusa Street*, p. 61.

[284] Bartleman, *Azusa Street*, pp. 61-62.

This was Bartleman's verdict, referring to an incident that occurred at First New Testament Church in the summer of 1906. It involved the Keyes family who had, until then, been consistently loyal supporters and advocates of Smale's Pentecostal emphases, both at First Baptist Church and then First New Testament Church. Lillian Keyes, the sixteen year old daughter of Henry Keyes, President of the Emergency and General Hospital in Los Angeles, had received the gift of tongues at Azusa Street,[285] and was highlighted in *The Apostolic Faith* for being able to interpret a message about the return of Christ which had been delivered in an African dialect, for which the Holy Spirit had enabled a 'perfect accent'.[286] Most probably, in view of her family's social standing in Los Angeles, Lillian Keyes was also widely reported and disparaged in the local press for her Spirit-filled antics. For example,

> Miss Keyes herself was the first to speak in a foreign language last night ... Miss Keyes arose and articulated something in a high-pitched voice, which can hardly be described. She claims it is Arabic.[287]

Robeck has discovered further vital background information regarding Lillian Keyes around this same time, which helps to explain how the friendship between Smale and the Keyes became fractured. The sixteen year old had 'handed Pastor Smale a written prophecy claiming that he had grieved the Holy Spirit. Allegedly this rebuke had arisen because Smale had been too strict with those who wanted more freedom of the Spirit.'[288] Smale responded by writing to her parents, advising that Lillian had 'become a victim of fanaticism' and required 'deliverance from the work of the adversary'.[289] Robeck continues:

> Before Dr. Keyes could respond, however, Lillian delivered a second judgement – this one warning Pastor Smale 'to give up ambition in connection with his church work'. Once again Pastor Smale responded to this sixteen-year-old girl by addressing her parents in a letter. He expressed shock at her behaviour and implored the Keyeses to pray that she be delivered.[290]

When this happened a third time during a public service, Smale interrupted Lillian Keyes' attempt at any further prophetic statements, 'asking the people to ignore her as he led them in a song'.[291] However, Dr Keyes sided with his daughter, emphatically believing in her spiritual powers. When asked about her

---

[285] Robeck, *The Azusa Street Mission and Revival*, p. 200.
[286] 'A Message Concerning His Coming', *The Apostolic Faith* 1.2 (October, 1906), p. 24.
[287] 'Queer "Gift" Given Many', *Los Angeles Times* 23 July 1906, p. 15.
[288] Robeck, *The Azusa Street Mission and Revival*, p. 200.
[289] Robeck, *The Azusa Street Mission and Revival*, p. 201.
[290] Robeck, *The Azusa Street Mission and Revival*, pp. 201-202.
[291] Robeck, *The Azusa Street Mission and Revival*, p. 202.

credibility regarding speaking in tongues, he stated, 'there was no doubt whatever about the genuineness of her gift since her words have been interpreted and thoroughly proved'.[292] Joseph Smale was not convinced and remained vehemently opposed to Lillian Keyes. He would, no doubt, have concurred with Bartleman's description above, that these were 'wicked spirits'.

By September 1906, the impact of this schism between Smale and the Keyes family culminated in a church split as about fifty members of First New Testament Church followed Henry Keyes to form a new Pentecostal church.[293] The 'Comeouters', as they were colloquially termed in the press, immediately initiated numerous manifestations attributed to the Spirit's promptings. Not surprisingly, Lillian dominated services, described as even 'outrivaling the orgies conducted on Azusa Street'.[294] Dr Keyes himself announced that 'he had just been given the power to raise the dead', while 'several rolled on the floor in an ecstasy of bliss ...' believing that 'miraculous power is to be poured upon the band of men and women who have left Pastor Smale's church'.[295] A further curious evidence of spiritual gifting was also claimed, as Henry Keyes read to the new church an interpretation of 'hieroglyphics which he says he wrote when "possessed of the Spirit"'. This writing in tongues was allegedly a message from God, assuring them of 'the sanction of God to the movement' and promising 'prosperity to the little flock'.[296]

One further casualty in this rupture merits inclusion for the sake of logging Pentecostal historical networks. Elmer Kirk Fisher was Smale's associate pastor, having received his Spirit baptism at First New Testament Church during the earlier part of 1906.[297] However, as a consequence of Keyes' faction grouping around a desire for greater freedom, Fisher followed Henry Keyes. In time, this 'Comeouters' group established the 'Upper Room Mission' in Los Angeles,[298] which became one of the most prominent Pentecostal fellowships in Los Angeles, connecting directly with Azusa Street in Pentecostal mission and a shared stress on glossolalia as the biblical evidence of baptism in the Spirit, which Fisher fastidiously continued to maintain over the subsequent decade, even when the Azusa Street Mission relaxed its stance on the subject.[299]

---

[292] 'Young Girl Given Gift of Tongues', *Los Angeles Express* 20 July 1906.

[293] 'Both Sides Claim Victory in Church', *Los Angeles Examiner* 24 September 1906, p. 5.

[294] 'Claim Power to Raise Dead', *Los Angeles Times* 24 September 1906, p. II7.

[295] 'Claim Power to Raise Dead', p. II7.

[296] 'Claim Power to Raise Dead', p. II7.

[297] S.M. Horton, 'Elmer Kirk Fisher', in Burgess and Van der Maas (eds), *New International Dictionary*, p. 641.

[298] C.M. Robeck, Jr, 'Upper Room Mission', in Burgess and Van der Maas (eds), *New International Dictionary*, p. 1166.

[299] Robeck, 'Upper Room Mission', p. 1166.

Concurrent with these developments, it was reported at Smale's church that 'no one claimed to have the gift of tongues, and the pastor preached without interruption'.[300] Smale was moving in a different, more moderate Pentecostal direction, in line with the key mission objectives deployed since the beginnings of First New Testament Church in September 1905. There is no doubt that Smale would have embraced the Upper Room Mission's motto, 'Exalt Jesus Christ; Honor the Holy Ghost',[301] but their implementation of such doctrine in practice was simply diverging.

Theological Reasons for Retreat: Tongues and Disunity

Following the difficult experiences just outlined, Smale subsequently articulated his theological reflections in an article, 'The Gift of Tongues',[302] which provides the primary explanation for his withdrawal from the burgeoning revival movement and thus forging even greater independence as the New Testament Church. It can be demonstrated that personal circumstances and his theological rationale were interlinked in Smale's withdrawal.

Smale cited what he considered two 'erroneous lines of teaching' in connection with the Revival in Los Angeles. First, he refuted the notion that 'all Christians ought to be speaking in the tongues', and, secondly, that 'the Bible evidence of the baptism of the Holy Ghost is the power to speak in the tongues'.[303] His argument to substantiate these points was then developed in detail by looking at the semantics of various New Testament passages.[304] In summary, Smale remained critical of various interpretations of Bible words inferring 'all' shall speak in tongues, given 'there have been centuries when speaking in new tongues has been unknown in the church'.[305] Smale then levelled specific criticisms at the Pentecostal movement on this matter of tongues, providing a valuable theological critique from one who had been intensely involved as a participant in the Revival atmosphere of Los Angeles, but was beginning to adopt the position of an independent outsider.

> The effect, in the main, of the tongues in our city, instead of precipitating Pentecost as we had hoped, has been to remove what hopeful signs of Pentecost were known during the fall of 1905 and the early Spring of 1906. It broke the

---

[300] 'Claim Power to Raise Dead', p. II7.

[301] Robeck, 'Upper Room Mission', p. 1166.

[302] J. Smale, 'The Gift of Tongues', *Living Truths* VII.1 (January, 1907), pp. 32-40.

[303] Smale, 'The Gift of Tongues', pp. 34-35.

[304] Smale, 'The Gift of Tongues', p. 36. He suggests that Acts 2:4, Acts 10:46, and Acts19:6 require examination side by side with Acts 1:8, 1 Cor. 12:4-11, Gal. 5:22-23, Ephes. 5, 1 Cor. 13. Then 'there could have been no fooling of Christian people into the belief that the Bible evidence of the Holy Ghost baptism is the speaking in new tongues'.

[305] Smale, 'The Gift of Tongues', p. 36.

unity of the Lord's intercessors. It took the minds of many from the supreme work of the conversion of souls. It engendered strife, the factional spirit and division, and opened the door to fanaticism, hypnotism and spiritualism.[306]

Such an indictment begs the question to what extent Smale's vociferous comments were the direct result of the Lillian Keyes case. It appears so, for just a few months earlier Smale had endorsed total freedom during worship services, but by January 1907 he had catalogued a number of other aspects which were exhibited as distractions from the intentions originally shared at the commencement of the Revival in 1905.

> People professed revelations from God to cease their daily work ...
> The adversary so wrought his cunning work in what was originally a gift from God, that he occasioned a superstitious conception of the gift of tongues and nourished the conceit in some, that when they exercise their gifts they are the infallible oracles of God. The gift came to be regarded in certain quarters as superceding and transcending the office of teacher and the preacher ... Following a depreciation of the God-ordained office of preaching there resulted the concomitant evils of confusion, disorder and insubordination to Holy Ghost life in the assembly.[307]

In order to clarify his own position further, Smale had perceptibly retreated to the original vision for 'a deep humbling of the Lord's people before God', combined with joint prayer as providing the only viable means 'that alone would save the city from worse religious disasters'.[308] Furthermore, his blunt analysis of the broader church scene in Los Angeles by the end of 1906 provides a vital perspective of the Pentecostal movement during its earliest days as viewed from Smale's personal perspective. Substantiating his own developing theological convictions, Smale considered the divisions between church groupings regarding the matter of glossolalia to be detrimental to a coming Pentecost. Noting that he was writing these words in October 1906,[309] Smale elaborates upon his views, explaining that

> in the city there are already four hostile camps of those who unduly magnify the tongues, which prove that the tongues have not brought Pentecost to Los Angeles. When Pentecost comes we shall see the union of the Lord's people.[310]

---

[306] Smale, 'The Gift of Tongues', p. 38.

[307] Smale, 'The Gift of Tongues', p. 39. Here Smale linked his discovery to evidence that 'the same manifestations as take place in the meetings of spiritualists, were prevailing among us, such as shakings, babblings, uncontrolled emotions'.

[308] Smale, 'The Gift of Tongues', p. 39.

[309] Smale, 'The Gift of Tongues', p. 40.

[310] Smale, 'The Gift of Tongues', p. 40.

Seemingly with direct reference to the Henry and Lillian Keyes incidents at First New Testament Church, Smale states his theological and pragmatic position to therefore necessitate an approach of caution and discernment. This is the clearest expression of Smale's rationale for withdrawing from the emergent Pentecostal movement in Los Angeles.

> It has been made very evident during this year of 1906 that not even the Lord's people can be trusted with gifts to use themselves, and we are crying that the Lord will withhold the gifts of the Spirit until His people become so filled with God that there will be no danger of the flesh rising to glory in His blessing. We desire no manifestation of gifts, save only as He expresses a gift through us: then all will be well. The burden of the intercession henceforth will be, not the manifestation of gifts, but the manifestation of God Himself for the purpose of establishing His saints and bringing sinners to repentance.[311]

Chronologically, the timing of this explanation is pivotal to the developing shape of Smale's preaching, ecclesiology, and missiology from 1907 onwards. His theological reticence to completely open up charismatic 'celebration' and 'play'[312] to all participants (such as Elmer Fisher, the Keyes, and other critics) at this juncture ultimately enforced less 'dance' and more 'organization' at First New Testament Church. For Smale, the 'word and Spirit' balance inferred more order than for his Pentecostal 'Holy Roller' counterparts, whose demonstration of the Spirit's 'dynamic, surprising, innovative, unifying, and enthusiastic dimension of the game of theology'[313] could not be doubted. Presumably, Smale would have argued that his balance was equally as effective and liberating, believing the 'word' should always regulate the 'Spirit' dimension, and vice versa. Yet, as the Lillian Keyes incident demonstrates, Pentecostal praxis is not always that simple.

Summary

Having drawn all three strands together in this chapter, the extant evidence has enabled us to observe the incremental stages in Smale's own thinking and teaching about the Spirit alongside the Azusa Street Revival. These help clarify one of the fundamental questions of this study regarding the specific contributory factors which impacted Smale from within and without, thus casting him as the 'Moses' figure by which he has historically been recognised.

Smale's role regarding a Pentecost in Los Angeles was pioneering during the latter part of 1905 and throughout 1906; it was modified and tempered somewhat during the latter part of 1906 and until 1908; then from 1909 onwards the strap-line 'The First Baptist Church of Los Angeles is a fellowship

---

[311] Smale, 'The Gift of Tongues', p. 40.
[312] Suurmond, *Word and Spirit at Play*, pp. 84-97.
[313] D. Jacobsen, 'Review: Word and Spirit at Play', p. 136.

for evangelical preaching, evangelical teaching, pentecostal life and service', was removed altogether from both advertisements and church bulletins.[314]

During 1905–06, Smale certainly succeeded in raising expectations for an imminent Pentecost in Los Angeles, but he obviously felt the battle lines were drawn between 'the zeal in some quarters to combat the Scripturalness of this position [his own] by contending that every person knows the Spirit in conversion'.[315] Furthermore, he clearly differentiated between the blessing known in conversion and the 'distinct' blessing known in Pentecost. 'Regeneration is simply life. Pentecost is the *fullness and the abundance of life.*'[316] As such Smale was both promoting Pentecostal life and service, and also reacting to those who argued that Pentecost belonged to a past, completed, dispensation.

Basing his biblical argument on John 14:16, that the Spirit Comforter has been promised 'that he may abide with you forever', Smale cites New Testament evidence that in Acts 8 there was 'a Samaritan Pentecost', Acts 10 'a Roman Pentecost', Acts 19 'a Grecian Pentecost', each of which impacted both individuals and congregations. None of them occurred at the same time, and each of them was subsequent to the Jerusalem Pentecost. He goes further by stating the that the church has known many Pentecosts since then, and 'one is being experienced at this very time in the principality of Wales'.[317] His teaching was, by his own admission, aimed at raising expectations of a latter rain before the Lord's return.[318] The assessment of when Pentecost actually arrived remains a matter of tension between Smale and early Pentecostals. By September 1906, amid the explosion of spiritual life at Azusa Street, Seymour unequivocally exclaimed,

> Many churches have been praying for Pentecost, and Pentecost has come. The question is now, will they accept it? God has answered in a way they did not look for.[319]

For Smale, however, the circumstantial and theological factors outlined above inevitably curtailed his willingness to embrace the Azusa Street Revival in its entirety, arguably overseeing a parallel Pentecostal revival at First New Testament Church.

---

[314] The survey of primary documents includes all First New Testament Church Los Angeles weekly church bulletins discovered from 22 April 1906 to 15 November 1908, and First New Testament Church Los Angeles advertisements placed in the *Los Angeles Times* from 29 April 1906 until 12 October 1907. A similar 'box' advert in the *Los Angeles Times* 23 January 1909, omits the 'Pentecostal life and service' footer.

[315] Smale, *The Pentecostal Blessing*, p. 44.

[316] Smale, *The Pentecostal Blessing*, p. 45, emphasis original.

[317] Smale, *The Pentecostal Blessing*, p. 49.

[318] Smale, *The Pentecostal Blessing*, pp. 49-50.

[319] 'Pentecost Has Come', p. 1.

That stated, a curious question continues to lurk in the background as to Smale's own experience of Spirit baptism in a personal Pentecost he so boldly advocated. There is no doubt that the Comforter had been at work within Joseph Smale during his 1904–05 sabbatical tour of the Holy Land and Wales. In addition, there was absolute consistency regarding his teaching and own felt need for Pentecostal blessing for sanctification, knowledge of the fullness of God, and anointing for service. However, all that does not negate the criticisms levelled by Bartleman and subsequently others that although Smale was a catalytic figure in the Spirit's move through Los Angeles, he himself missed out when it came to glossolalia and other manifestations of full Spirit baptism. Viewed in these terms, Bartleman's dubbing Smale as 'God's Moses' appears to be a legitimate portrayal.

Although it is a fact that no record exists of Smale speaking in tongues *per se*, other weighty indications outlined above do reveal a greater openness to manifestations of the Spirit's power than Bartleman credits to Smale. For instance, Smale's description of 'That never to be forgotten night', 15 April 1906, is full of delight at the 'involuntary and glad exclamations' and the 'holy laughter'.[320] In June 1906 at First New Testament Church, Bartleman describes how 'men and women were prostrate under the power all over the hall. A heavenly atmosphere pervaded the place. Such singing I have never heard before, the very melody of Heaven. It seemed to come direct from the throne.'[321] In summary, over the summer months of 1906 it seems that Smale was ambiguous, by both sanctioning freedom in the Spirit, as well as adopting caution regarding all the Pentecostal life and service should entail.

In fact, this appears to have remained the nucleus of his pneumatological convictions for the remainder of his life and ministry, long after he dropped the 'Pentecostal' labels. Years later, in 1925, Smale preached a sermon one year before his death, entitled 'A Message to Spirit-filled Believers'.[322] The sermon contains very similar pneumatological emphases to his earlier preaching in the era just discussed. There is the presentation of urgent, deep personal need, and the promise of abundant provision by the Spirit for works of service. Yet he cautions the notion of 'degrading the "baptism of the Holy Spirit" by restricting it ... to a lingual exercise of the throat. The modern sinful and sectarian divisions among the people of God show the possibility of a baptism not of God.'[323]

Joseph Smale had fraternized with many of the early Pentecostals, advocated for the Azusa Street Revival in the local press, and ecumenically had shared

---

[320] 'Pentecost Has Come', p. 9. This was the same occasion at First New Testament Church where Jennie Moore spoke in tongues for the first time.

[321] Bartleman, *Azusa Street*, p. 61.

[322] J. Smale, 'A Message to Spirit-Filled Believers', in *Truth: Earthly and Heavenly* (No. 2625, for the author, 1925).

[323] Smale, 'A Message to Spirit-Filled Believers', p. 90.

speaking platforms with the likes of holiness teachers such as Carrie Judd Montgomery.[324] Amid the intensity of religious fervour in and around Los Angeles (c. 1906), many realised the necessity to discern which movements were of God and which were not, taking into account that inevitably there were margins of uncertainty. A.S. Worrell summed it up like this: 'We wish it understood that we do not stand for this whole movement, but only for that part of it that is of God; and so of the teaching.'[325] Smale would have agreed with those sentiments, believing he actually was pioneering authentic Pentecostal life and service.

---

[324] 'Christian Alliance Convention', *Triumphs of Faith* (Christian and Missionary Alliance Archives, January 1907), p. 11.

[325] A.S. Worrell, 'The Movements in Los Angeles, California', *Triumphs of Faith* (Christian and Missionary Alliance Archives, December 1906), p. 257.

CHAPTER 6

Conclusion

Smale's Post-Pentecostal Phase (1909–26)

Structurally, there appear to have been three general phases of ministry to Smale's life. His developmental years in preparation for revival have been covered in chapters 2 and 3. Thereafter, chapters 4 and 5 concentrated upon the revival years in Los Angeles, focusing on 1905–1908, with the bulk of available evidence enabling analysis of Smale's 'Moses' role, theology and practice. A natural question to ask in conclusion is, what happened to Smale after this Pentecostal phase of his life? Any biographical analysis would remain incomplete if no reference was made to the subject's remaining years of life and ministry.

In comparison with the extensive material already presented in conjunction with the revival period, sadly only minimal primary sources have been discovered for Smale's latter years. After 1909 his appearance in local newspapers were minimal, and few church records have survived. Nonetheless, the materials that have are adequate to summarize the key developments which track Smale's familial and geographical circumstances for this final phase. Indeed, the emerging facts within this section of his life's journey also serve to illustrate three of the dominant interlocking traits which characterise the complete life and ministry of Joseph Smale. By way of conclusion, these are presented describing Smale's conflicts at Hitherfield Road Free Church, London; Smale as a mission entrepreneur with the formation of the Spanish Gospel Mission; Smale as an independent pastor; and, finally, Smale as a Bible teacher emphasising the necessity of Spirit baptism within a word and Spirit dynamic.

Familial Circumstances: Divorce and Bereavement

As explained in chapter 3, some of the internal problems at First Baptist Church Los Angeles were the result of Smale's failed marriage to Alverda Keyser,[1] which resulted in their separation for twelve years including, most notably, during the revival period. Having been out of the newspaper headlines for a few years after the Pentecostal Revival experiences of 1905 and 1906, Smale once again became the subject of Los Angeles press interest under the heading

---

[1] 'Events in Society', *Los Angeles Times* 28 June 1898, p. 5.

'Pastor Smale Seeks Divorce: He would dissolve marriage that split church'.[2] A month later the non-contested divorce was granted on the 'ground of desertion'.[3]

The following year, on 29 January 1911, Smale's 'beloved mother' Ann died in her eightieth year.[4] Their mother-son relationship appears to have been genuinely close, as Ann Smale had accompanied Joseph Smale throughout his ministry, joining him at all his churches in Ryde, Prescott, and Los Angeles, besides travelling with him to Europe during 1904–05. Presumably Ann Smale had provided vital practical support and encouragement for her son as he exercised his intense pastoral ministry as a single man. Two weeks later Smale preached at his mother's memorial service which, for some reason (perhaps in the absence of First New Testament Church Los Angeles owning a building), was held back at First Baptist Church Los Angeles.[5]

Since First New Testament Church's formation in September 1905, Smale's congregation had continued to meet in hired halls awaiting construction of their first building, which was erected on the corner of Pico and San Julian streets and formally dedicated on 28 May 1911.[6] This was a pivotal moment for both pastor and people, as Smale used this occasion to close his ministry as pastor at First New Testament Church, as he 'celebrated the event' of their new church building 'by getting married and going to the Argentine Republic as a missionary. He will leave for the East on Monday in company with his future bride, Miss Esther Hargrave and they will be married somewhere in the East.'[7]

Marriage to Esther Hargrave[8]

Joseph Smale had known Esther Isabelle Hargrave since their days at First Baptist Church Los Angeles. Like many other members who resigned in the week after Smale,[9] Esther immediately joined the First New Testament Church

---

[2] 'Pastor Smale Seeks Divorce', *Los Angeles Times* 16 April 1910, p. II1.

[3] 'Given Decree for Divorce', *Los Angeles Times* 26 May 1910, p. II2. The newspaper account provides full details of Smale's attempts to encourage Alverda Keyser Smale to return, including numerous letters indicating that she did not share his desire for 'a home that shall be consecrated to Christ and His church, where I am not denied rendering hospitality to God's servants when I feel that I am called upon to do so'.

[4] 'Vital Record: Deaths', *Los Angeles Times* 30 January 1911, p. I18.

[5] 'Vital Record: Deaths', p. I18; 'Religious Brevities', *Los Angeles Times* 11 February 1911, p. I7.

[6] 'Dedication of First New Testament Church', *Los Angeles Times* 27 May 1911, p. I13. The significance of the church's address provides a significant clue which solves the last section of Smale's ministry at Grace Baptist Church from 1915. See below.

[7] 'Dedication of First New Testament Church', p. I13.

[8] Esther Isabelle Hargrave (1879–1958).

[9] First Baptist Church Los Angeles, Church Records, Vol. IX (17 September 1905).

in 1905, and soon became superintendent of the Spanish Mission in the Latin quarter of the city.[10] Prior to that Esther had graduated from Nyack College in New York.[11] According to their family oral history Joseph 'wanted to learn Spanish and consequently asked Esther to teach him. This led to courtship and then marriage.'[12] Their marriage and future service together was to be 'reconsecrated as missionaries',[13] stating their intention to 'leave for a short stay in England' before going 'to Spain to learn the language, and then depart for the Argentine Republic as missionaries'.[14]

Figure 19: Joseph and Esther Smale, c. 1911.
Photograph courtesy of George Wood.

Indeed, news of their marriage was 'cabled direct to the LA Times' from Topeka, Kansas, on 1 June 1911, simply stating they 'were married at the

---

[10] First New Testament Church Los Angeles, *Historical Number of the Bulletin* (18 March 1906), p. 10.

[11] G.L. Wood, recorded during an interview with his mother, about his grandmother, Esther Hargrave Smale.

[12] G.L. Wood interview.

[13] 'Pastor Smale's New Romance', *Los Angeles Times* 27 May 1911, p. II1.

[14] 'Bids Good-By at its Dedication: Founder of New Church Goes as Missionary', *Los Angeles Times* 29 May 1911, p. II7.

residence of Rev John Fazel here this evening'.[15] The Smales 'honeymooned in Niagara Falls'[16] and then travelled on to England. On arrival, Joseph Smale preached with a view to becoming pastor at Hitherfield Road Church, London, on 17 September 1911,[17] before leaving with Esther to 'spend the winter of 1911–12 in Northern Spain evangelising'[18] and presumably for Joseph the opportunity for some language study.

Conflict: Hitherfield Road Free Church, London (1912–13)

On their return to England in March 1912 Joseph Smale commenced his ministry, and was formally inducted as pastor of Hitherfield Road Free Church, Streatham Hill, South London, on 24 June 1912.[19] At the service, Smale explained that they were

> drawn to Hitherfield because of the spirituality, the philanthropy and sympathy of their beloved friend, Mrs. Donald Campbell ... For seven years he [Smale] had stood on interdenominational grounds. They wished to hail Hitherfield Free Church as a place for the rich and poor, for the erudite and for the ignorant, where all could meet in unity and fellowship.[20]

However, the pastorate was not to last long, 'contrary to the leaders' desire'.[21] Mrs Campbell had started the work at Hitherfield Road by building a chapel in 1907, with the motto 'All One in Christ Jesus'.[22] From the beginning the fellowship intended to be 'un-denominational in Church government and inter-denominational in Christian Fellowship', and as such was duly constituted in 1912, becoming known as Hitherfield Road Free Church.[23] Consequently, Smale was the first full-time minister, with the ministerial expenses being met 'mainly by Mrs. Campbell and her sons'.[24] Understanding that power base, especially in view of the church struggles Smale had encountered previously at

---

[15] 'Former Angelenos Wed', *Los Angeles Times* 2 June 1911, p. 15. The column also adds that 'Miss Hargrave is a niece of the Rev. John Fazel'.

[16] G.L. Wood interview.

[17] Hitherfield Road Baptist Church, *In His Service From 1907* (Hitherfield Road Church, London, 1987), p. 5.

[18] Hitherfield Road Baptist Church, *In His Service From 1907*, p. 15.

[19] 'Recognition Services', *Streatham News* 20 June 1912. The church used the occasion of Smale's induction to reconstitute Hitherfield Road as a 'Free' church. Mrs Donald Campbell removed the word 'Free' the following year, after Smale's departure, see Hitherfield Road Baptist Church, *In His Service From 1907*, pp. 14-15.

[20] 'Hitherfield Road Free Church', *Streatham News* 29 June 1912.

[21] Hitherfield Road Baptist Church, *In His Service From 1907*, p. 15.

[22] Hitherfield Road Baptist Church, *In His Service From 1907*, pp. 4-5.

[23] Hitherfield Road Baptist Church, *In His Service From 1907*, pp. 5, 15.

[24] Hitherfield Road Baptist Church, *In His Service From 1907*, p. 15.

Ryde and First Baptist Church Los Angeles, it is not surprising that conflict was soon apparent, and he 'tendered his resignation after only seventeen months with the Church'.[25] Smale and Campbell had clashed upon matters of church government as well as Smale's innovative proposal to relocate the church to a 'more accessible location to main traffic routes'.[26] As has been displayed throughout this study, such conflict was a characteristic feature of Smale's life and ministry. Nevertheless, utilising James E. Loder's scheme again,[27] the corollary of Smale's 'conflict-in-context' was a substantial beneficial outcome which, in the case of Hitherfield Road Free Church, resulted in the birth of a mission work to Spain.

Figure 20: Hitherfield Road Free Church, London, c. 1912.
Photographs Courtesy of Hitherfield Road Baptist Church.

---

[25] Hitherfield Road Baptist Church, *In His Service From 1907*, p. 16.
[26] Hitherfield Road Baptist Church, *In His Service From 1907*, p. 16.
[27] A brief critique of James E. Loder's framework is presented in Appendix II. The fact that a repeated cycle of 'conflict-in-context' (in London and Bristol) produced subsequent insights and transformation for Smale is regarded as further substantiating the validity of Loder's model to identify the role of 'insight' within the interplay of biography and theology.

Mission Entrepreneur: Spanish Gospel Mission[28]

While Joseph and Esther Smale were staying in northern Spain during the winter of 1911–12, they met a young Englishman, Percy Buffard, who was teaching English at a language school.[29] Buffard went to Spain 'with a sense of calling to missionary endeavours ... perceiving a lack there of authentic Christianity'.[30] Smale was impressed with Buffard and his 'mission zeal',[31] and subsequently, in 1913, while Buffard was studying at Regent's Park Baptist College, London, Smale 'arranged a meeting in the church vestry at which interested ministers and laymen agreed to the formation of the Spanish Gospel Mission'.[32] With his experience of pioneering new works, Smale immediately established a board of reference for the new mission, comprising F.B. Meyer, G.P. Gould and Sir John Kirk, while Smale fulfilled the role of honorary secretary and treasurer.[33]

Smale's conception of strategic mission possibilities is insightful. Bringing his international perspective to bear upon a campaign to promote support for the new mission, Smale stressed that

> Supporting the SGM could have implications for the proliferation of Protestantism far beyond the Iberian Peninsula. Smale explained that annually thousands of Spaniards emigrated to South and Central America, including Mexico. If many of them could be converted to authentic Christianity, he reasoned, a great impetus will be given to Missionary work in those countries.[34]

Almost a century later, having survived the Spanish civil war and numerous other problems and persecution, the work of the Spanish Gospel Mission continues. The foundational connections with Joseph Smale's contribution are an important element in mission history, as well as substantiating a vital aspect of the Smales' personal story and the couple's deep affection for the Spanish people.[35]

---

[28] I am indebted to Desmond Cartwright for directing me to Smale's pioneering work with the Spanish Gospel Mission.

[29] F. Hale, 'The Spanish Gospel Mission', *Baptist Quarterly* 40.3 (July, 2003), p.157.

[30] Hale, 'The Spanish Gospel Mission', p. 157.

[31] W.M. Pearce, *Don Percy* (Spanish Gospel Mission), p. 25.

[32] Hitherfield Road Baptist Church, *In His Service From 1907*, p. 15.

[33] Spanish Gospel Mission, annual magazines (1914, 1915, 1916).

[34] Hale, 'The Spanish Gospel Mission', p. 159.

[35] G.L. Wood, interview; H.S. Wood, email, 29 May 2008.

Independent Pastor: Unity Chapel, Bristol (1913–15)[36]

Following his resignation at Hitherfield Road Free Church, Joseph and Esther Smale moved to Bristol where he became pastor at Unity Chapel, listed in the *Bristol Directory* of 1915 as a 'Brethren' church.[37] For a pastorate which once again lasted less than two years, any church information gleaned may initially appear negligible, were it not for the significance of Unity Chapel as 'an interesting experiment in independent churchmanship in Bristol'.[38] This demonstrates further valuable insights into Smale's ecclesiology, as well as highlighting the network of relationships and associations he had cultivated in Britain.

Figure 21: Unity Chapel, Midland Road, Bristol.
Photograph courtesy of Alan H. Linton, from *The Harvester* 1.1 (1921).

Unity Chapel was situated in an industrial area of Bristol connecting primarily with the working class. For half a century, up until 1900, the church had expanded to the extent that average morning congregations numbered 255

---

[36] I am indebted to Alan Linton for aiding my research regarding Unity Chapel, Bristol.

[37] 'Unity Chapel, Midland Road', *Wright's Bristol Directory* (Kelly's Publishers, 1915), p. 787. Unity Chapel is now demolished, but the house where Smale lived (36 St Matthew's Road, Cotham, Bristol) remains.

[38] G.L. Higgins, 'Unity Chapel, St. Philip's Bristol (1850–1946)', *Evangelical Quarterly* 35.4 (October–December, 1963), p. 223.

and in the evening 590.[39] Prior to Smale's arrival, the chapel had been associated with prominent Evangelical figures in Britain such as George Müller, Major Tireman, G.H. Lang and the Rev. F.E. Marsh.[40] In fact, during the ministry of G.H. Lang (1900–08) two new principles were introduced which help to define aspects of the Unity Chapel 'Brethren' DNA by the time of Smale's arrival. They were

> i. The pastor should receive no stated salary ... but should be dependent upon the freewill gifts of the people. This practice had been followed for many years by Müller and Craik at Teignmouth and at Gideon and Bethesda Chapels, Bristol.
> ii. The usual method of settling church business by a majority vote, beside being held to be unscriptural, was impractical in that it led to dissatisfied minorities and should be replaced by the consent of an undivided church.[41]

Significantly, Lang's emphases resonated with Smale's own convictions concerning Christian ministry and church government. Having declined to 'accept a stated salary for his work at First New Testament Church',[42] and having sought to employ Holy Spirit leadership to gain a unanimous decision for all church decisions,[43] Smale was potentially well suited to the ethos of spiritual life that Lang had cultivated at Unity Chapel. In addition, the chapel had persisted to maintain 'vigorous evangelistic efforts'[44] in the locality, in particular hosting 'Western Counties Evangelization Conferences'.[45] To all intents and purposes, both Smale and Unity Chapel's ecclesiology was considered to embody 'The autonomy of the local church as did the early Independents, they practised believers' baptism, as did the Baptists, and at their

---

[39] Higgins, 'Unity Chapel', p. 228. Further details about Unity Chapel's history and context may be found in K. Linton and A. Linton, *I Will Build My Church* (Hadler, 1982), pp. 36-61.

[40] F.E. Marsh was the minister of Bethesda Baptist Church, Sunderland (1887–1905). Desmond Cartwright observes that 'Dr. Marsh's name crops up several times in later years, always as an opponent of Pentecostalism'. See Desmond Cartwright, 'Everywhere Spoken Against: Opposition to Pentecostalism 1907–1930', http://www.smithwigglesworth.com/ pensketches/everywhere.htm, accessed 3 June 2009. Marsh was, in fact, staying at A.B. Simpson's Christian and Alliance Missionary Home in New York at the same time that T.B. Barrett first read a copy of *The Apostolic Faith* (September 1906). Personal interview with Desmond Cartwright, Cardiff, 26 October 2004.

[41] Higgins, 'Unity Chapel', p. 229.

[42] 'Bids Good-By at its Dedication', *Los Angeles Times* 29 May 1911, p. II7.

[43] First New Testament Church Los Angeles, *Historical Number of the Bulletin*, p. 5.

[44] Higgins, 'Unity Chapel', p. 229.

[45] 'Evangelization Conference. Western Conference', *The Harvester* 1.1 (October, 1921), p. 12. This was formerly known as *Counties Quarterly*, established in 1901.

weekly Breaking of Bread there was liberty of ministry, as practised by the Brethren.'[46]

Furthermore, Lang also displayed an interest in the Pentecostal revival emanating from both Los Angeles and Sunderland, and he was certainly aware of Smale's past connections with what he described as the 'Tongues Movement'. Writing one book in 1913 entitled *The Modern Gift of Tongues*, and a further work around 1950, *The Early Years of the Tongues Movement*,[47] Lang cited Smale's role in the Los Angeles Revival.[48] Given that both Lang and Marsh were British critics of the Pentecostal movement, it is an intriguing subject of conjecture as to how Smale came to receive a call to the pastorate at Unity Chapel, and whether or not Smale ever spoke publicly regarding the dramatic pneumatological events he himself had experienced during the Revival in Los Angeles.

One final aspect of church life during Lang's tenure as pastor of Unity Chapel merits comment in view of Smale's succession five years later, and the subsequent brevity of his ministry. Lang considered some of the 'defects' at Unity to be 'particularly that gifts of ministry did not develop, nor spontaneity of worship. To this day the church is too weak to dispense with its fixed ministry and function healthily in the energy of the Spirit'.[49] Given the 'slow but steady decline' in church membership,[50] coupled with the onset of the First World War in 1914, the Smales had arrived at a pivotal stage in the church's history.

In fact, when the Smales announced their resignation and intention to return to the USA by the end of 1914, Unity Chapel decided 'there would be no formal pastorate' thereafter, 'but elders, suitably gifted and recognized by the church'[51] would carry out future leadership. Arguably, in terms of biographical analysis, there was another more personal factor which confirmed the Smales' decision to return to Los Angeles, namely the tragic death of their first child, Hargrave Smale. He died thirty-six hours after birth at the family home in

---

[46] 'Evangelization Conference. Western Conference', p. 233.

[47] Desmond Cartwright's research reveals further connections: 'When the Brethren writer G.H. Lang published his pamphlet *The Early Years of the Tongues Movement*, he had a set of *Confidence* loaned to him. [It is now clear that these were that same set that came from Mrs Penn-Lewis's set]'. See Cartwright, 'Everywhere Spoken Against', http://www. smithwigglesworth.com/pensketches/everywhere.htm, accessed 23 May 2009.

[48] G.H. Lang, 'The Early Years of the Tongues Movement', (c. 1950), see http://www.banner.org.uk/tb/lang.html, accessed 19 February 2004.

[49] G.H. Lang, *An Ordered Life* (Paternoster Press, 1959), p. 147.

[50] Higgins, 'Unity Chapel', p. 226. The church membership was about 200 during Smale's ministry.

[51] Higgins, 'Unity Chapel', p. 233.

Bristol[52] on 30 July 1914.[53] By 27 January 1915 Joseph and Esther Smale were aboard the ship *S.S. Haverford*,[54] preparing to sail back to America and the recommencement of ministry in Los Angeles.

Bible Teacher: Grace Baptist Church, Los Angeles (1915–26)

Aged forty-eight, Joseph Smale returned to a Bible teaching and pastoral ministry at Grace Baptist Church Los Angeles. Historically, this has generally been regarded as another new church congregation founded by Smale,[55] but the clue to its correct status appears to exist in the church's address. As noted above the new First New Testament Church building, which was dedicated the week before Smale left for England in 1911, was situated on the corner of Pico and San Julian streets. The first notice in the newspapers upon Smale's return to Los Angeles advertises Sunday services at 'Grace Baptist Church, Corner Pico and San Julian Sts'.[56] The inference herein being that the church altered its name, either while Smale was absent in England or immediately upon his return. The theological rationale behind the name switch may simply be deduced.

As stated, very little is known about the final decade of Smale's life, other than he maintained regular preaching at Grace Baptist Church, and numerous other events in Los Angeles by invitation, such as the 'YMCA Brotherhood', where he spoke on his favourite theme, 'Unrivalled Blessings'.[57] Only one brief account of church life has been located thereafter, with a sentence Smale sent to Unity Chapel Bristol in 1917: 'Pastor JOSEPH SMALE speaks in a recent letter of a great wave of blessing descending upon his church at Los Angeles. He also says in his letter, "We pray for dear Unity".'[58]

The one entire sermon that has been preserved from this era also resonates with the theme of blessing.[59] In isolation it would be unwise to develop any conclusions on the basis of just one published sermon. However, the subject content regarding the necessity for Spirit baptism for all Christian believers along with subsequent blessing is consistent with Smale's emphasis over a life-

---

[52] 'Hargrave Smale', Death Certificate, General Register Office, reference: 1914; Quarter – September; District – Bristol; Volume 6a; p. 8. For cause of death, the baby died of 'Meningeal Haemorrhage'.

[53] Hargrave Smale', Death Certificate, General Register Office, reference: 1914.

[54] Philadelphia Passenger Records: 1915 Departures.

[55] C.M. Robeck, Jr, 'Joseph Smale', in S.M. Burgess and E.M. Van der Maas (eds), *New International Dictionary of Pentecostal and Charismatic Movements* (Zondervan, 2002), p. 1075.

[56] 'Display Ads.', *Los Angeles Times* 27 March 1915, p. II9.

[57] 'Events Briefly Told', *Los Angeles Times* 6 April 1915, p. I10.

[58] 'Church Bulletin', *The Messenger of Unity Chapel* 1 (1917), p. 4.

[59] J. Smale, 'A Message to Spirit-Filled Believers', in *Truth: Earthly and Heavenly* (No. 2625, for the author, [1925]).

time of ministry, as has been illustrated throughout this study. In this sermon, 'delivered at a union conference of Christians in Los Angeles',[60] was robust teaching for Christians 'not go to the back door of our Lord's presence for blessings'.[61] Illustrating this by the account of the woman who had been bleeding for twelve years and approached Jesus from behind to touch his garment, so Smale was teaching that Jesus' 'dealings with her were on the lines of John 10:10, "I have come that they may have life and have abundance."'[62] The force of Smale's teaching on what seems to have been a favourite theme appears all the more pertinent given the proximity of this particular sermon to his death the following year. Although all 'Pentecostal' definitions are absent, there is similar intensity to this preaching in 1925 as exemplified during his Pentecostal revival phase. A couple of further excerpts will suffice to illustrate Smale's challenge and his developed position regarding a personal Pentecost.

> I say it soberly. I say it thoughtfully. Spirit-filled Christians can be strangers to the richest experiences of the personal Christ ... Let me say this upon the authority of Scripture, that if you have a real Pentecost, you have very little. 'The Acts of the Apostles' Christians were, by their Pentecost, filled for the work of evangelism. There was little else that was permanently their life. What a need there is to study the little words of Scripture. For example the prepositions, 'From' and 'To' – From faith to faith; from strength to strength; from glory to glory.[63]

His concluding theology of the Spirit had settled with the notion that 'There is no terminus in Christian experience', urging a baptism of the Spirit 'into thy love', 'into thy mind', 'into thy life', 'into thy will', 'into thy service'.[64] In essence, Smale was advocating that every Christian should 'hear Christ's word' and 'Let the Holy Spirit, Who is here to bless you, have His way with you'.[65]

The 'word' and 'Spirit' combination which was so evident within Smale's training at Spurgeon's College remained the constant through his life-long ministry, although his interpretative schema regarding Pentecostal dispensations and the nature of the church in the last ages did alter significantly during the latter years of his life. In fact, Smale's preoccupation with some fairly detailed and elaborate dispensational teaching prompted the self-publication of his own journal, *Truth: Earthly and Heavenly* (see Figure 22). To date, only three editions have been discovered, but as such offer limited scope for further investigation into Smale's analytic framework regarding the second advent. However, this would require synthesizing Smale's

---

[60] Smale, 'A Message to Spirit-Filled Believers', p. 87.
[61] Smale, 'A Message to Spirit-Filled Believers', p. 87, emphasis original.
[62] Smale, 'A Message to Spirit-Filled Believers', p. 87, emphasis original.
[63] Smale, 'A Message to Spirit-Filled Believers', p. 89.
[64] Smale, 'A Message to Spirit-Filled Believers', p. 91.
[65] Smale, 'A Message to Spirit-Filled Believers', p. 92.

diagrammatic concepts of 'Ano Spheres' and 'the Church of the Mystery' within a broader framework of dispensational teaching of that era.[66]

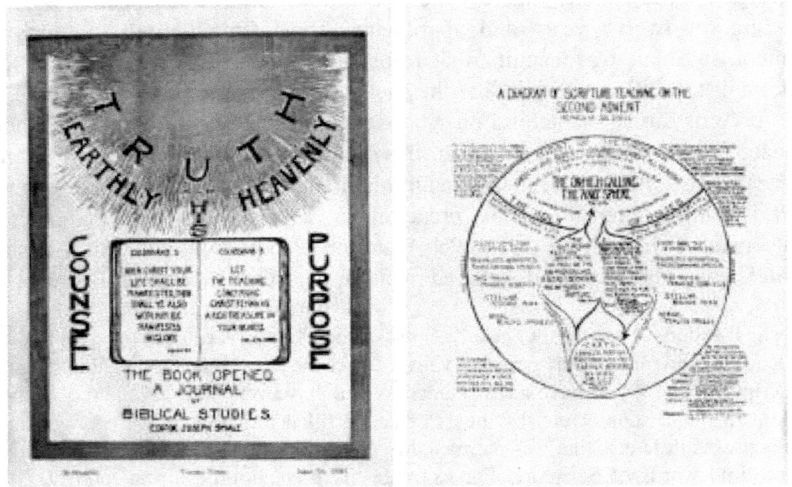

Figure 22: Front and back cover of *Truth: Earthly and Heavenly* journal, edited and self-published by Joseph Smale. Photograph courtesy of George Wood.

What was Smale's perception of the classic Pentecostal movement by the mid-1920s as he neared the end of his life? It is a legitimate question to pose and not easy to answer in detail. However, two significant clues exist, gleaned from the circumstances relating to Smale's relinquishment of the China New Testament Mission in 1923 to a Church directly influenced by the Azusa Street revival,[67] as well as evident in Smale's later pneumatological teaching.

First, by 1923 Smale was increasingly 'exercised over the problem of manpower for the C.N.T.M.' in Pakhoi, China, which prompted urgent 'cries to God' regarding 'the further welfare of [this] important service to the cause of Christ in China'. Early that same year, William Henry Turner of the Pentecostal

---

[66] The limited extant material and time constraints have prohibited further research into Smale's eschatology during his post-Pentecostal phase. Therefore, a decision was taken to leave this aspect for future analysis.

[67] Appreciation is expressed to Connie Au, Project Officer for the Hong Kong Christian Council, who directed me to these primary materials concerning the transfer of the China New Testament Mission to the Pentecostal Holiness Church.

Holiness Church[68] visited Pakhoi to investigate future outreach possibilities, and he was recommended to stay at the China New Testament Mission compound even though 'there were no foreigners there'.[69] Turner discovered that 'the mission had closed never to be reopened again under the old church [First New Testament Church Los Angeles]. All the property belonging to the church was now offered for sale. The Pakhoi compound alone for twenty-five thousand dollars Hong Kong currency, about fifteen thousand American, at that time.'[70] Turner describes his sense of God's guidance:

> Before I left Pakhoi the Lord spoke to me as plain as could be while praying for His direction for it had occured [sic] to me as rather a remarkable coincidence that at the very time we were preparing to come into these districts this mission of which we had never heard should be closed never to open again, and be offered for sale … Here, however, are the words the Lord spoke to us in prayer, 'I have prepared the way before thee, all of this will I give unto thee.'[71]

Written negotiations between William Turner in Pakhoi and Joseph Smale in Los Angeles followed during the summer of 1923, with both parties believing God was leading the transfer of mission work and property to this Pentecostal Holiness Mission.[72] Smale's willingness to sell the China New Testament Mission properties for just 'ten thousand dollars Hong Kong currency for the whole, and … [giving them] five years in which to pay',[73] was based upon his belief that the Pentecostal Holiness Mission were 'a people, banded together, to give a pure gospel message to the world and that an attitude of accommodation and sacrifice on our part is pleasing in the sight of the God'.[74] Smale's endorsement of this mission, with their Pentecostal statement of faith, continued, 'Our hearts overflow with gratitude, as we think of the probability of the work being sustained substantially advanced by such a thoroughly christian fellowship as that which you represent.'[75]

Secondly, with regard to evidence identified in his teaching, during a 1925 conference sermon, where Smale voices criticism against the tongues movement *per se*:

---

[68] H.V. Synan, 'International Pentecostal Holiness Church' in S.M. Burgess and E.M. Van der Maas (eds), *New International Dictionary of Pentecostal and Charismatic Movements* (Zondervan, 2002), pp. 798-801.

[69] W.H. Turner, *Pioneering in China* (Publishing House of the Pentecostal Holiness Church, 1928), p. 159.

[70] W. H. Turner, *Pioneering in China*, p. 160.

[71] W. H. Turner, *Pioneering in China*, pp. 161-162.

[72] W. H. Turner to J. Smale, 10 May 1923; Smale to Turner, 18 June 1923; Smale to Turner, 5 September 1923.

[73] W. H. Turner, *Pioneering in China*, p. 170.

[74] Smale to Turner, 5 September 1923.

[75] Smale to Turner, 5 September 1923.

> O let me plead that we do not degrade the baptism of the Holy Spirit by restricting it, or necessarily in relation, to a lingual exercise of the throat. The modern sinful and sectarian divisions among the people of God show the possibility of a baptism not of God which leaves one as but sounding brass and as tinkling cymbal.[76]

Such a dismissive statement is sufficient to confirm that twenty years after the Spirit's outpouring in Los Angeles, Smale had rejected the name and shape of early Pentecostalism. However, he was still advocating Spirit baptism as the divine means for explicit transformation to meet 'the universal need of the Lord's people'.[77] For Smale, tangible experiences and evidence of the Holy Spirit were not to be displayed by speaking in tongues, but rather in

> baptisms that take the kinks out of the human intellect, and the unkind unbrotherly, hateful criticisms out of man's soul; baptisms that sweeten relationships between man and man; baptisms that cement and glorify home and family life; baptisms that lead God's people to be faithful to the ordained responsibilities of life; baptisms that swing the human clear of the blighting selfhood of the natural man, baptisms that baptize with heavenly spiritual life.[78]

Inevitably, Smale's caricature of Pentecostalism in terms of glossolalia alone reflected a stance that indicates any rapprochement between their theology of Spirit baptism and his own was inconceivable. Following his early negative experiences[79] and the evident divisions among early Pentecostal groups, Smale had proceeded to fulfil the nuances of his 'Moses' motif, with the remainder of his life and ministry spent in a divergent direction to Pentecostalism.

A Baby Daughter: Esther Grace Smale

'Blessing' has already appeared as a major theme for Joseph Smale throughout his later years. One specific and most precious blessing was received on 1 October 1916, when a baby daughter was born to Joseph and Esther Smale, whom they named Esther Grace Smale.[80] Her young life was spent being nurtured in a mission-minded environment both at home and amid church life at Grace Baptist. When just four years old Esther travelled with her parents to China[81] on their return visit to the China New Testament Mission base at

---

[76] Smale, 'A Message to Spirit-Filled Believers', p. 90. Part of this quotation is also used in the summary of chapter 5 above.

[77] Smale, 'A Message to Spirit-Filled Believers', p. 91.

[78] Smale, 'A Message to Spirit-Filled Believers', pp. 90-91.

[79] A reference to the incidents with Henry and Lillian Keyes at First New Testament Church Los Angeles during 1906, documented in chapter 5 above.

[80] Esther Grace Smale (1916–2000). Personal interview with George Wood, South Pasadena, 14 March 2004.

[81] 'Large Party to Make Tour of the Orient', *Los Angeles Times* 25 July 1920, p. V8.

Pakhoi.[82] Some of these childhood memories have been passed on verbally to the next generation, although it must be taken into account that Esther was only ten years old when her father died. Nonetheless, Smale's grandsons, Stan and George, both fondly remember their grandmother relating incidents 'how God protected them as a family in China',[83] and her telling Bible stories 'with great charisma and drama' when putting them to bed as children.[84]

Final Assessment

For over a century Joseph Smale's epitaph within Pentecostal historiography has been the classic Frank Bartleman depiction that *'God found His Moses*, in the person of Brother Smale, to lead us to the Jordan crossing'.[85] This study has argued that an in-depth assessment of Smale's unique contribution as a forerunner to the Revival in Los Angeles has long been overdue. The significance of discovering previously unknown biographical and theological details about Smale's life and ministry has enabled new insights that would otherwise have remained hidden beneath the surface of the Azusa Street storyline.

Perhaps one of the most innovative and exciting aspects of discovery from this biographical 'dig' has been the impact of Smale's contextual preparation for revival. In particular two aspects of his spiritual formation are prominent. First, the Wesleyan 'rhythm of revival' permeating Cornish and Somerset life during Smale's childhood years, which is deemed significant for the parallel phenomena exhibited during the daily prayer gatherings in 1905. These deep emotional waves of spiritual fervour were integral to Smale's expectations and strategies throughout later revivals.

Secondly, a distinct 'Spurgeonic' root to Pentecostalism has also been identified. Given the role and function of C.H. Spurgeon and his London training college, it is little wonder that Smale, as a student, imbibed the potency of Spurgeon's church culture and Reformed theology which rigorously advocated preparation for revival for both pastor and people. The Spurgeonic emphasis on frequent prayer, teaching and work towards a personal Pentecost is clearly recognizable in the later ministry of Joseph Smale. Furthermore, Spurgeon's own methods were resonant with later Pentecostal emphases, especially with regard to his appeal that the gospel should cut across all class distinctions, particularly enabling the poor and uneducated. The common conviction shared by all early Pentecostal leaders was the underpinning belief

---

[82] See Figure 17.

[83] George Wood, telephone conversation on 14 June 2003.

[84] Stan Wood, email 29 May 2008. Their grandmother lived with them during her latter years.

[85] F. Bartleman, *Azusa Street: The Roots of Modern-Day Pentecost* (Logos International, 1980), p. 46, emphasis added.

that the Holy Spirit equipping is freely available for all Christians, activating Christ-centred teaching and works of power in mission at home and abroad. Indeed, through his voluminous pneumatological teaching and writing it could be argued that Spurgeon inculcated a great vision and expectancy for extraordinary signs and wonders with 'a season of glorious disorder'.[86] Certainly a detailed examination of Spurgeon's pneumatology would lead to some profitable future research possibilities.

However, in light of the 1905–06 Revival, the Smale evidence discovered and presented in this study has shown Bartleman's account to contain a degree of mythology regarding Smale. The triangulation of newspaper accounts and church records has prompted closer examination and correction of the Bartleman version in numerous aspects, thus enabling a more accurate picture of early Pentecostal and revival history. Consequently, the validity of a biographical approach has been endorsed by the uncovering of as much contextual data from Smale's life and ministry as has been possible. This has inevitably allowed Smale's 'voice' to speak again, providing dimensions to our understanding of Smale and Pentecostal roots which have until now been silenced by Bartleman's pejorative attitude to Smale.

Indeed, Bartleman's negative evaluation of Smale's ultimate failure in Pentecostal ministry certainly requires modification in light of Bartleman's own foibles. Cerillo notes how Bartleman was a 'fanatical antiorganizational man'[87] who obviously had a propensity for disillusionment with individuals and churches of all persuasions. Just as brashly as he criticised Smale for an over-reliance on human effort and organized structures, so Bartleman also condemned the Azusa Street Mission for erecting a sign on their building, identifying itself as an 'Apostolic Faith Mission'.[88] Transient throughout his own life, Bartleman remained critical of what he perceived as Smale's shortcoming regarding Spirit baptism. This criticism remained evident even years later when writing to Swedish Pentecostal leader Lewi Pethrus in 1913:

> Bro. Smale, like many others, did not get through to the 'Baptism' himself. Like Moses he led the people to the Jordan, but failed to cross over. However, he defended the experience for a time, but later in trying to lead his 'Baptized' people

---

[86] C.H. Spurgeon, 'The Pentecostal Wind and Fire', *Metropolitan Tabernacle Pulpit* 27.1619 (18 September 1881), p. 104.

[87] A. Cerrilo, 'Frank Bartleman: Pentecostal "Lone Ranger" and Social Critic', in J.R. Goff and G. Wacker (eds), *Portraits of a Generation* (University of Arkansas Press, 2002), p. 111.

[88] Cerrilo, 'Frank Bartleman', p. 111. See also C.M. Robeck, Jr, 'Frank Bartleman', in Burgess and Van der Maas (eds), *New International Dictionary*, p. 366. Although 'Bartleman attended a few prayer meetings led by W.J. Seymour ... he seldom remained at one address or in one church for very long'.

without the 'Baptism' himself, he failed to keep the victory and lost his self-control ... He died in Moab spiritually speaking.[89]

If Bartleman were to have had the final verdict on Joseph Smale based upon this assessment, then the 'Moses' motif would remain substantially condemnatory. However, the volume of original primary materials discovered about Smale's life and ministry necessitates caution regarding Bartleman's sweeping definitions of failure and success. Spiritual life and leadership are not always that simple.

The 'Moses' Idiom

As an alternative to the Bartleman version regarding Smale, the innovative findings arising from the research for this book have led to a more positive use of the 'Moses' epitaph. This new appraisal of Joseph Smale proposes that his 'Moses' designation may profitably be regarded as an idiom that represents all those who have experienced, or wish to experience, the power of God in revival, but feel, for whatever reasons, that they are still in 'Moab'. This too has pastoral and theological relevance for all who question the nature of Holy Spirit baptism; or who perhaps have previously identified with Pentecostal/ Charismatic theology and practice, but now find themselves out on the margins; or others who would like to experience increased divine power than previously; and for other Christian practitioners who attempt to harness spiritual power within earthly structures and organizations. In terms of building theological bridges and aiding ecumenical dialogue, Smale's 'Moses' idiom relates directly to both Reformed and Pentecostal/ Charismatic groupings.[90]

Furthermore, the 'Moses' idiom, as applied to Smale, allows for some of the untidy aspects of the broader Pentecostal story to be told with greater honesty – hopes, personality traits, church politics, power struggles, spiritual lessons, tears, hurts, organization, control, freedom, excesses, and so on. As Grant Wacker appositely comments,

---

[89] Typed letter from Frank Bartleman, Germany, to Lewi Pethrus, Sweden, 9 July 1913. I am very grateful to Desmond Cartwright for obtaining a copy of this letter.

[90] This research connects with personal observation from my own pastoral leadership in four churches over the past twenty years, where many in the congregations have longed for greater Pentecostal/Charismatic experience, finding regular and traditional forms of worship stultifying. Or, conversely, a sizeable number of Christians have joined our Baptist congregations, having left Pentecostal/Charismatic congregations after difficult and painful experiences. They are not necessarily dismissive of their past pneumatological experiences, but spiritually have found themselves in 'Moab' territory. Together, we are often seeking ways of working out spiritual life and expectation within a local church life setting that all too easily can become overly structured and cerebral. To that end, Joseph Smale's life story and the 'Moses' idiom offers a helpful frame of reference for constructive dialogue.

> To say that early Pentecostals merit our attention is not to say that the task is always pleasant. Even by their own standards they often proved petty and mean-spirited. In a way, though, that is precisely the point ... To the honest historian, the dead 'appear exactly as they were – every bit as odd as we are, as problematical, as difficult of access'.[91]

As painful as Smale's storyline is in places, there are many helpful and pertinent aspects emanating from his theology and practice which deserve reaching broader Christian constituencies. It is not only the construction of ministers' and leaders' formation that may provide inspiration and instruction, but also their diminishing role within a movement which can be just as educative. For Smale is among a plethora of (Pentecostal) leaders, then and now, who have experienced such a rise and decline in their popularity, power, and fame.[92] Therefore, sufficient attention should consequently be given to apparently regressive contours of spiritual formation such as afforded by the 'Moses' pattern, by virtue of its second-best connotations.

Inasmuch as all attempts to avoid the subtle dangers of hagiography have been observed in this biographical analysis, the substantial evidence presented also reveals that Smale's life and ministry followed patterns similar to those of many Christian leaders. Amid all the theological and ecclesiological crosscurrents in Los Angeles during the first decade of the twentieth century, Smale forged an independent way through the formalism of denominational life, and his leadership experienced the power struggles familiar to every church pioneer, minister and leader. In spite of having to contend with public accusation, insult and defamation, Smale persisted to facilitate Christian unity across Los Angeles, especially promoting gatherings to pray for a Pentecostal revival. Indeed, following his firsthand experience of the Welsh Revival, Smale's experimental openness for more of the Spirit's power and demonstration assisted a distinct and timely outpouring of spiritual life and fervour, which must be recognised as occurring prior to, and parallel with, the unfolding events at the Azusa Street Mission. To that end, this biographical and theological study contributes a necessary revision to Joseph Smale's inclusion in Pentecostal historiography.

Following a lengthy illness Joseph Smale died at home at midnight on 16 September 1926, aged fifty-nine.[93] Brief newspaper tributes publicly affirmed Smale as being 'widely known for the religious work which he conducted in

---

[91] G. Wacker, 'Early Pentecostals and the Study of Popular Religious Movements in Modern America', in M. Welker (ed.), *The Work of the Spirit: Pneumatology and Pentecostalism* (Eerdmans, 2006), p. 146. Wacker is quoting Peter Brown.

[92] E.g., Levi R. Lupton. See G.B. McGee and E.J. Gitre, 'Levi Rakestraw Lupton', in Burgess and Van der Maas (eds), *New International Dictionary*, p. 846.

[93] 'Rites for Churchman Tomorrow', *Los Angeles Times* 18 September 1926, p. II1. The Smale home was located at 1102 Magnolia Street, South Pasadena.

California during the past thirty years'.[94] Over eight decades since Smale's death, his 'Moses' idiom possesses a far richer legacy than that bland assessment in the *Los Angeles Examiner*. Smale embodied the multiple roots of Pentecostalism, by embracing what he considered to be a dynamic and supernatural power inherent in the 'Word' and the 'Spirit'. Arguably, the 'Moses' motif has the potency to cross denominations incorporating, and perhaps even reconciling, aspects of Pentecostal/Charismatic theology with emphases and heroes[95] within the Reformed tradition.

What became apparent in general discussions during the course of this research is how few church leaders (of various denominations) recognise Smale's name or know anything about his life and ministry.[96] Even Smale's own grandsons, Stan and George Wood, were not aware of the extent to which their grandfather was an entrepreneurial pastor, pioneering mission work in the USA, Europe, and Asia.[97] Therefore, Joseph Smale's story deserves wider circulation for both its emphasis on the work of the Holy Spirit in human lives as well as his strategic participation in the revival history of Los Angeles and Pentecostalism.

---

[94] 'Rites Tomorrow for Dead Pastor', *Los Angeles Examiner* 18 September 1926, p.17.

[95] The notion of Reformed 'heroes' would include individuals such as C.H. Spurgeon.

[96] Future research and publication of Smale's sermons would be welcome additions to scholarship.

[97] H.S. Wood and G.L. Wood, emails 29 May 2008. An interesting observation is that both Smale's grandsons, Stan and George Wood, are themselves missionary-pastor pioneers in their own right. H. Stanley Wood is an Adjunct Professor of Congregational Leadership and Evangelism at Fuller Theological Seminary, Pasadena, California, and an Adjunct Professor teaching church planting courses at Columbia, Memphis, Denver, and Pittsburgh Theological Seminaries. He is also the Executive Director of the Sower's Field, focused on the mission of 'new leaders for new churches'. George L. Wood has served as a pastor, and now works as a self-supporting missionary with 'Go Ye Fellowship', a sending mission organization based at the US Center for World Missions Campus in Pasadena.

Figure 23:
Joseph and Esther Smale's gravestones, Mountain View Cemetery, Altadena, California. Photographs courtesy of Paula Hinkel.

APPENDIX I

Joseph Smale Timeline

1826		Birth of John Smale (Joseph Smale's father)
1831		Birth of Ann Stephens (Joseph Smale's mother)
1867	7 July:	Birth of Joseph Smale (Cornwall, England)
1881	30 January:	Death of father, John Smale
1881	4 September:	Christian conversion of Joseph Smale
1887		Commenced training at the Pastor's College, London
1890	May:	Begins first pastorate, Ryde, Isle of Wight
1892	11 September:	Final Sunday at Ryde
1892	October:	Arrived in America
1893	March:	Begins pastorate at Lone Star Baptist Church Prescott, Arizona
1893	21 September:	Marries Helena Dunham (Vincennes, Indianna)
1895	29 January:	Death of wife, Helena Dunham
1898	January:	Accepts call to become pastor at First Baptist Church Los Angeles
1898	27 June:	Marries Alverda Keyser (Los Angeles, California)
1898–1902		Years of growth at First Baptist Church Los Angeles
1902–1904		Years of intense conflict at First Baptist Church Los Angeles
1904		Joseph Smale's health deteriorates amid ongoing church conflict
1904	31 July:	Extended sabbatical granted by First Baptist Church Los Angeles
1904	27 August:	Joseph and Ann Smale sail for Europe and they visit family and friends in England. Joseph continues on to Greece, Egypt, Palestine, Syria, and the Holy Land
1905	April:	Ann Smale becomes dangerously ill in London; Joseph has to return
1905	April–May:	Joseph Smale visits Welsh Revival on return to Liverpool docks

1905	28 May:	Joseph Smale preaches first sermon back at First Baptist Church Los Angeles on 'The Great Welsh Revival'
1905	29 May:	Fifteen weeks of daily prayer and praise meetings begin
1905	10 September:	Joseph Smale resigns as pastor of First Baptist Church Los Angeles
1905	18 September:	Inaugural meeting of First New Testament Church Los Angeles Meeting at Burbank Hall, as 'a fellowship for evangelical preaching, evangelical teaching, pentecostal life and service'
1905–06		Revival continues
1906	9 April:	Holy Spirit outpouring at Burbank Hall (and 214 Bonnie Brae Street)
1906	15 April:	The gift of tongues spoken at First New Testament Church by Jennie Moore
1906	14 July:	'Rolling on Floor in Smale's Church' (*Los Angeles Times* header)
1906	23 July:	'Queer "Gift" Given Many' (*Los Angeles Times*)
1906	September:	Henry S. Keyes and Elmer Fisher leave First New Testament Church to establish the Upper Room Mission, Los Angeles
1907	January:	Joseph Smale criticizes the gift of tongues and disunity among Pentecostal 'camps' in Los Angeles
1907	January:	Joseph Smale sails to China to establish a New Testament Mission
1907	March:	The China New Testament Mission begins, led by A.H. Bach
1907	April–May:	Joseph Smale attends the China Centenary Mission Conference
1910	May:	Joseph Smale divorces Alverda Keyser
1911	29 January:	Death of mother, Ann Smale
1911	28 May:	First New Testament Church dedicates new building
1911	1 June:	Joseph Smale marries Esther Isabelle Hargrave (Topeka, Kansas)
1911	June:	They travel to England
1911–12		They spend winter in Spain

Appendix 1: Joseph Smale Timeline

1912	March:	Joseph Smale begins pastorate at Hitherfield Road Free Church, Streatham, London (formally inducted on 24 June 1912)
1913		Joseph Smale establishes the Spanish Gospel Mission with Percy Buffard
1913		Resigns as pastor of Hitherfield Road Free Church
1913		Joseph Smale becomes pastor at Unity Chapel, Bristol
1914	30 July:	Baby son Hargrave Smale dies (thirty-six hours old)
1915	January:	Joseph and Esther Smale return to Los Angeles
1915	March:	Joseph Smale becomes pastor at Grace Baptist Church Los Angeles
1916	1 October:	Birth of daughter Esther Grace Smale
1920–21		The Smale family visit the China New Testament Mission, Pakhoi, China
1926	16 September:	Death of Joseph Smale, aged fifty-nine

APPENDIX 2

The Logic of Transformation

During the latter half of the twentieth century, there have been a number of influential works which address the impact of faith upon human understanding and development.[1] Primarily such approaches have posited theories employing psychology and theology as well as other disciplines.

James E. Loder's vocational and academic background is significant, combining his clinical training and Christian ministry in researching the relationship of Christian theology and psychiatric theory.[2] Consequently, my selection of his particular theory regarding the 'Transforming Moment' for use as a framework in chapters 3 and 4 enable Joseph Smale's biographical data to be presented and examined with the intentionality of identifying the incremental steps of his development and preparation for revival. Herein, Loder utilises the concept of convincing 'insights' as the common ground encapsulated in all human 'knowing events'.

Perhaps a historical case study of one such 'knowing event' can best illustrate Loder's thesis by briefly presenting 'the biblical prototype'[3] for the life-changing transformation and convictions that occurred within the two disciples on the Emmaus Road. The Luke 24 incident concisely reveals 'the patterned process by which the Holy Spirit transforms all transformations of the human spirit' in 'a four-dimensional knowing event initiated, mediated, and concluded by Christ'.[4] Drawing on Loder, as well as Donald Ratcliff's commentary on Loder's transformational logic,[5] the stages of this particular resurrection day event may usefully be segmented for the purposes of illustration as follows:

---

[1] S. Lownsdale, 'Faith development across the life span: Fowler's Integrative Work', *Journal of Psychology and Theology* 25.1 (1997), pp. 49-63. Examples cited include Jung (1958), Allport (1950), Piaget (1954), Kohlberg (1963), and Fowler (1981).

[2] James Loder completed his postdoctoral studies at Piaget's Institut des Sciences de l'Education in Geneva.

[3] D. Ratcliffe, 'Qualitative Data Analysis and the Transforming Moment', *Transformation* 25.2–3 (April/July, 2008), p. 118.

[4] J.E. Loder, *The Transforming Moment* (Helmers & Howard, 1989), p. 93.

[5] Ratcliffe, 'Qualitative Data Analysis and the Transforming Moment', pp. 116-33.

Step 1: Conflict-in-Context in Four Dimensions [D][6]

D1. The conflict takes place in the lived world of those involved (Israel, Roman occupation, threats from 'chief priests and rulers', etc.).

D2. The embrace of conflict, with the expectation of change ('I' cannot move beyond the area of conflict, yet the 'I' cannot escape it either. The possibility of new being persists, thus offering the potential of transformation).

D3. The 'void' as it appears to the two disciples that the potential for Jesus redeeming their world has come to nothing. (Darkness, disillusionment, total annihilation of their lived 'world', loss of faith, etc.; though still with a small element of hope).

D4. Turning to the holy, as they realise the conflict is related to God (their faulty expectations of Christ).

Step 2: Scanning begins and the Role of the 'Inner Teacher'[7]

D1. Christ, as 'the Stranger' enters the disciples' conflict and dialogue in disguise, to aid their personal scanning process. An outside initiative provides a sense of transformation that is continuous with the past, yet involving a radical change of those past conditions. Often based on 'leads' or hunches.

D2. The scanning of scripture provokes a sense within the internal dialogue that a breakthrough is possible, even imminent ('their hearts were warmed'). The dialogue between the presence of Christ and the self-in-conflict is the means by which God seeks to reopen the self to the transcendent, in order that it may become 'spirit'.

D3. Synchronicity of events directs the scanning process through the void, towards discovery of roots of hope (for example, see also John 4:16-30).

D4. The sense of the Holy within prompts turning outward toward the Holy beyond (noting it is the initiative of the Holy, working deeper than consciousness, which is able to bring about inside-outside reversal in the transformed person).

Step 3: The Transforming Intuition of Christ

D1. A decision is taken to request the 'Stranger' to stay, based upon their receptivity to the convictional insights he provides. Theirs is a willingness to embrace the unexpected.

D2. The moment when Jesus takes the bread (a sign of the cross and brokenness) blesses it, and breaks it, becomes for them a moment of realisation

---

[6] For the purpose of presenting Loder's dimensional outline, I have selected the abbreviations D1, D2, D3, and D4 accordingly.

[7] Loder, *The Transforming Moment*, p. 101. Augustine and Calvin refer to the 'Inner Teacher', not to be separated from the scriptures, but able to transcend their community 'relating them to it in a new way'.

– that change has been achieved ('No longer "I" who lives, but Christ within me', Galatians 2:20). Their eyes have been opened.

D3. The self, world, void and the holy are reconstellated by the nature of Christ, with the disciples freed from within the confines of their context – to choose for or against Jesus.

D4. Their experience, orchestrated by Christ, achieved a freedom for the disciples through the relationship established between the self and the holy.

Step 4: Release and Mundane Ecstasy

D1. They were still part of their world in conflict, but they have been redefined by Christ. He has indwelt and reconstructed them, so they have become part of his world.

D2. Their nature was transformed by the Holy Spirit, and they possess a new vitality, a sense of assurance and enthusiasm.

D3. The void that had been of their own making was reversed by the new creation experienced through the resurrected Lord.

D4. The Inner Teacher was now with them in a new way. The transparency of faith is now exhibited by the self to Christ and also toward the world as the creation of Christ's intention.

Step 5: Verification of Change

D1. The reversal of previous conflicts and their new convictions about the risen Christ verified by the transformation of other disciples in Jerusalem.

D2. New meaning through the eyes of faith, which in turn provides substantive changes personally and corporately.

D3. Verification occurs by being new people, with a shared intuition of Jesus as the Christ.

D4. The validity of the Emmaus experience was evidenced in the witness and transforming influence of their fellowship that found its unity and boldness in the continuing presence of the risen Jesus.[8]

Brief Critique of Loder's 'Transformational Logic'

While recognising that James Loder's theory of transformation derives from an explicitly Christian theological basis, it is also necessary to recognise some of its limitations. Firstly, the qualitative analysis of any subject (in this case Smale) depends on words – the words of both the subject and those connected by way of observation and comment. Each sample of such data requires careful analysis to ensure correct interpretation of any observable changes that become apparent.

---

[8] Loder, *The Transforming Moment*, pp. 97-122.

Appendix 2: The Logic of Transformation

Secondly, although accepting the five steps above as legitimate phases which enable transformational categorization, a deficiency may be identified (with Smale's case study, for example), in that it does not fully encompass the complete life story. Loder offers no category for a 'pre-conflict' phase and similarly no step for any final phase(s) allowing for the possibility of further, longer-term reflections.[9] There is just a danger, given the western bias of Loder and myself, that the frameworks employed are propagating a linear time frame of reference, whereas such continuities and discontinuities in a person's life may not always be as predictable or evident as the data suggests. Certainly it seems normative that one of the inherent problems with using any theoretical model is to assume that all aspects of real life will fit entirely the theory.

The strength of Loder's thesis, given his category of 'convictional knowing', allows scope within a Christian framework for the general work of God, and specifically the Holy Spirit to be incorporated. In contrast, this is a major weakness of James Fowler's 'steps of faith' treatise, which illustrates how a human analysis of life and faith patterns are problematic without adequate space or possibility for God's inclusion as a major premise of all transforming work. With regard to Joseph Smale, I propose that the interpretation of his spiritual transformation and theological understanding of revival demonstrates a development brought about by God at work, particularly through his circumstances, to the extent that Smale's theology and biography are integrally linked. Consequently the 'logic of transformation' is considered the best possible framework for analysing the transformation of Joseph Smale.

---

[9] Unless it is assumed that such later transformations continue within the confines of Step 5: Interpretation and Verification, and/or the cycle is repeated.

APPENDIX 3

'The gift of tongues is not for every Christian'

This teaching article, printed in a First New Testament Church Los Angeles Sunday bulletin, clearly elucidates Joseph Smale's theology of the Spirit with regard to glossolalia at the height of the Revival in Los Angeles during 1906. The core of his theology of the Spirit in terms of the spiritual gifts is presented in Smale's didactic style as below, with a robust appeal that scripture should settle the matter for each believer, though clarifying that 'no scripture is of private interpretation', but must be compared with 'every other scripture'.[1]

Read your Bible on the subject. Turn to 1 Cor. 12:4-11.

'To one is given by the Spirit the word of wisdom.' Note – the Scripture does not say, To all is given the word of wisdom.
'To *another* the word of knowledge by the same Spirit.' Note – the Scripture does not say, To all the word of knowledge.
'To *another* faith by the same Spirit.' Note – the Scripture does not say, To all faith.
'To *another* the gifts of healing by the same Spirit.' Note – the Scripture does not say, To all the gifts of healing.
'To *another* the working of miracles.' Note – the Scripture does not say, To all the working of miracles.
'To *another* prophecy.' Note – the Scripture does not say, To all prophecy.
'To *another* discerning of Spirits.' Note – the Scripture does not say, To all the discerning of Spirits.
'To *another*, divers kinds of tongues.' Note – the Scripture does not say, To all divers kinds of tongues.
'To *another* the interpretation of tongues.' Note – the Scripture does not say, To all the interpretation of tongues.

Let us not be wiser than the Word.
Do you stand for the whole Bible? Then don't tear out of it Acts 8:14-17, where there is no reference to the gift of tongues in the record of the gift of the Holy Ghost.
Thousands of the Lord's dear people have been baptized in the Holy Ghost and in fire who never received the gift of tongues.

---

[1] First New Testament Church Los Angeles, *Church Bulletin* (8 July–15 July 1906), p. 3.

'The Gift of Tongues' is not a blessing 'thrown in' to a Christian's experience. This is clear from 1 Corinthians 12:11. He who has it from the Lord, possesses it according to a divine and eternal purpose.

When the Apostle said, 'Do all speak with tongues,' he was not distinguishing between the merely justified and those who were Spirit-filled people in the Corinthian Church. This is clear from 1 Corinthians 12:11.

Remember the Scriptural phrase, 'in the last days,' refers to Apostolic times as well as to the twentieth century.

Christians, read your Bible and receive it in its fullness; then you will not define Scriptural experiences by unscriptural terms.

Let not those having the gift of tongues sit in criticism upon those who have not the same gift.

'Though I speak with the tongues of men *and of angels*, and have not LOVE, I am become as sounding brass, or a tinkling cymbal.'

The Corinthian Church had the gift of tongues, but its gifted members were not holy. Read the first Epistle carefully.[2]

---

[2] First New Testament Church Los Angeles, *Church Bulletin*, pp. 1-2, emphases original.

Bibliography

Abbreviations

ABHS	American Baptist Historical Society
ALC	Alan Linton Collection
ATS	Asbury Theological Seminary
BRL	Bristol Reference Library
CHS	California Historical Society
CMA	Christian and Missionary Alliance Archives
DCC	Desmond Cartwright Collection
FBC LA	First Baptist Church Los Angeles
FBC PAZ	First Baptist Church Prescott, Arizona
FNTC LA	First New Testament Church Los Angeles
FPHC	Flower Pentecostal Heritage Center
IoW CRO	Isle of Wight County Record Office
LA	Los Angeles
LAMB	Lambeth Archives, London
LAPL	Los Angeles Public Library
PHP	Paula Hinkel Photographs
SCHR	Spurgeon's College Heritage Room, London
SGM	Spanish Gospel Mission
SHMP	Sharlot Hall Museum, Prescott, Arizona
SPS	The Society for Pentecostal Studies
SRO	Somerset Record Office, Taunton
WBGA	Wiveliscombe Book Group Archive
WFC	Wood Family Collection
YDS	Yale Divinity School

Primary Sources[1]

Church Documents

Arizona Baptist Association, *Minutes* (1894–1895) [ABHS]
Brief History of the Wellington Circuit, 'Wiveliscombe' (Methodist Union, 1932) [SRO]
Christ Church (Baptist), Ryde, Isle of Wight, *1848–1948 Centenary Souvenir Handbook* (1948) [IoW CRO]
First Baptist Church, Los Angeles, *Church Bulletin* (Sunday 21 January 1900) [ABHS]

---

[1] The location of primary documents is indicated in parentheses.

———, *Church Bulletin* (20 August 1905) [ABHS]
———, *Church Records*, Vol. VII (18 April 1900–2 October 1903) [FBC LA]
———, *Church Records*, Vol. VIII (4 October 1903–28 September 1904) [FBC LA]
———, *Church Records*, Vol. IX (2 October 1904–19 September 1905) [FBC LA]
First Baptist Church, Prescott, *Historical Pageant of Arizona Baptists* (18 May 1962) [SHMP]
———, *Our Early History: Diamond Jubilee of the Founding of the First Baptist Church, Prescott Arizona* (1955) [FBC PAZ]
———, *Eighty Years With Christ: 1880–1960* (1960) [FBC PAZ]
———, *The Ninetieth Anniversary History of the First Baptist Church, Prescott Arizona: 1880-1970* (1970) [FBC PAZ]
First New Testament Church, Los Angeles, *Historical Number of the Bulletin*, (18 March 1906), [ATS]
———, *Church Bulletin* (22–29 April 1906) [ATS]
———, *Church Bulletin* (8–15 July 1906) [ATS]
———, *Our First Anniversary: Under the Headship of Christ*, (September 1906), [ATS]
———, *Church Bulletin,* (5-12 May 1907), [ATS]
———, *Church Bulletin,* (26 May - 2 June 1907), [ATS]
———, *Church Bulletin* (2–9 June 1907) [ATS]
———, *Church Bulletin* (26 April–2 May1908) [ATS]
———, *Church Bulletin* (28 June–4 July 1908) [ATS]
———, *Church Bulletin* (19–25 July1908) [ATS]
———, *Anniversary Bulletin: Three Years of the Right Hand of the Most High* (27 September 1908), [ATS]
———, *Church Bulletin* (25–31 October1908) [ATS]
———, *Church Bulletin* (15–21 November 1908) [ATS]
Hitherfield Road Baptist Church, *In His Service From 1907* (Hitherfield Road Church, Streatham Hill, London, 1987) [DCC]
Los Angeles Baptist Association, *Minutes* (Southern California Baptist Convention, 1898–1904) [ABHS]
Los Angeles Baptist Association, *Report of Committee on History of First Baptist Church LA* (1921) [FBC LA]
Sutton, H.L., *Our Heritage and Our Hope* (FBC LA, 1974) [FBC LA]
Sutton, H.L. and P.H. Yeomans, *Our History, Our Heritage, Our Homes, Our Hopes* (First Baptist Church Los Angeles, 1999) [FBC LA]
Taunton Methodist Circuit Historical Notes, D\N\tmc/7/2/1 [SRO]
Unity Chapel, *The Messenger* 1 (Unity Chapel, Bristol, 1917) [ALC]
Windes, RA, *Early History of the Arizona Baptist Association* (handwritten, c. 1900) [FBC PAZ]

College Records

The Pastors' College, *Discussion Minute Book* (1888–1889) [SCHR]
———, *Assessment Book* (1882–1891) [SCHR]

Correspondence and Personal Interviews

Anderson, A.H., email 13 June 2006
Au, Connie Ho Yan, email 8 April 2010
Blumhofer, E.L., email 20 May 2008
Bundy, D.D., personal interview, SPS, Milwaukee, 13 March 2004
Cartwright, D.W., emails and personal interview, Cardiff, 26 October 2004
Dunbar, B., letter and enclosures, 3 March 2003
Faupel, D.W., personal interview, SPS, Milwaukee, 13 March 2004
Light, M., letter, Isle of Wight, 27 November 2002
McBain, D., emails, November 2002–March 2003
Powles, J., emails, 12 February 2003, December 2006
Robeck, Jr, C.M., emails and personal interview, SPS, Milwaukee, 13 March 2004
Stevens, H., letter and enclosures, 12 November 2004
Tiedemann, R.G., emails and enclosures, March 2009
Wood, G.L., personal interviews, South Pasadena, and emails, March 2003 onwards
Wood, H.S., emails, 2004 onwards

Journals, Periodicals and Mission Booklets

The Apostolic Faith 1.1, 1.2 and 1.3 (1906), and 1.9 (September, 1907)
The Baptist Evangel, 'Associational Jottings' 1.22 (11 April 1895) [ABHS]
Christian and Missionary Alliance XXV.13 (7 April 1906), pp. 212-13; XXVI.25 (29 December 1906), p. 404
Confidence 2.11 (1909); IX.4 (April, 1916)
Hale, F., 'The Spanish Gospel Mission', *Baptist Quarterly* 40.3 (July, 2003), pp. 152-72
Higgins, G.L., 'Unity Chapel, St. Philip's, Bristol (1850-1946)', *Evangelical Quarterly* 35.4 (October–December, 1963), pp. 223-235
The Harvester 1.1 (1921) [ALC]
The Missionary Review of the World, 'Echoes of the Welsh Revival' (July, 1906), pp. 482-83 [FPHC]
Pearce, W.M., *Don Percy* (Spanish Gospel Mission, n.d.)
Smale, Joseph, 'An Apostolic Journey in the 20th Century: Relating the facts that led the First New Testament Church of Los Angeles to Establish a Gospel Mission in Southwest China' (n.p., [1908]) [YDS]

———, 'My Trip Around The World' (personal handwritten journal, 1907) [WFC]
———, 'Pakhoi Journal' (personal handwritten journal, 1907) [WFC]
———, 'The Gift of Tongues', *Living Truths* VII.1 (January, 1907), pp. 32-40 [CMA]
———, 'Truth: Earthly and Heavenly: A Journal of Biblical Studies', 2582, 2513, and 2625 (for the author, 1925–26) [WFC]
———, 'How we found Mr. Buffard' (Spanish Gospel Mission, 1913) [SGM]
Spanish Gospel Mission, Annual Magazine (1914, 1915, 1916) [SGM]
Triumphs of Faith, 'Christian Alliance Convention', 27.1 (January, 1907), p. 11
Triumphs of Faith, Worrell, AS, 'The Movements in Los Angeles, California', 26.12 (December, 1906), pp. 256-57

Newspapers

ARIZONA WEEKLY JOURNAL MINER
(25 October 1893; 3 January 1894; 2 January 1895; 30 January 1895; 6 February 1895) [SHMP]

ARIZONA REPUBLICAN
(12 April 1894; 20 April 1894; 22 April, 1894) [SHMP]

ARIZONA REPUBLIC
'Prescott: A Century of Coexistence', (1 September 1979), [SHMP]

ISLE OF WIGHT COUNTY PRESS [IoW CRO]
'Baptist Ordination at Ryde' (17 May 1890), p. 6
(16 August 1890), p. 3
'The Ryde Primitive Methodists' (6 September 1890), p. 7
'The Stockwell Orphanage' (3 January 1891), p. 6
'The Baptist Visitor' (7 February 1891), p. 8
'Sunday Closing' (10 October 1891), p. 7
'The Bible Christians' (24 October 1891), p. 8
(13 February 1892), p. 6
'Baptist Anniversary at Newport' (20 February 1892), p. 6
'Farewell of the Rev. J. Smale' (17 September 1892), p. 7

ISLE OF WIGHT OBSERVER [IoW CRO]
'The Park Road Baptist Chapel' (17 May 1890), p. 8, and (17 September 1892), p. 5

Bibliography 253

ISLE OF WIGHT TIMES AND *HAMPSHIRE GAZETTE* [IoW CRO]
'Ryde' (20 February 1890), p. 5
'Ordination Services at Park Road Baptist Chapel, Ryde' (15 May 1890), p. 4
'A Flower Service at Park Road Chapel' (26 June 1890), p. 4
'Anniversary at Park Road Chapel' (5 March 1891), p. 5
'Memorial Service at Ryde' (11 February 1892), p. 5
(15 September 1892), p. 5
(20 October 1892), p. 5

LOS ANGELES EVENING NEWS [LAPL]
'Summer Solstice Sees Strenuous Sects Sashaying' (23 July 1906), p. 1

LOS ANGELES EXAMINER [LAPL]
'900 Members Now on its Rolls' (9 May 1904), p. 4
'Rev. Jos. Smale in Farewell Sermon' (22 August 1904), p. 10
'Happy Safe Return from Holy Land for Dr. Smale' (26 May 1905), p. 10
'Both Sides Claim Victory in Church' (24 September 1906), p. 5
'Rites Tomorrow For Dead Pastor' (18 September 1926), p. 17

LOS ANGELES EXPRESS [LAPL]
'World Movement: Week of Prayer Will Be Observed' (4 January 1901), p. 12
'Pastor Smale Resigns – Baptists May Divide' (11 September 1905), p. 2
'Baptists Form a New Church' (13 September 1905), p. 4
'Church Likely to be Split' (13 September 1905), p. 5
'Dozier Wins Over Smale' (14 September 1905), p. 2
'New Church is Organized' (25 September 1905), p. 3
'Rev. Smale's Successor May Be Dr. W.B. Hinson' (26 September 1905), p. 14
'One Thousand Persons Are Reported Killed in San Francisco Earthquake' (18 April 1906)
'Sermons by Pastors' (30 April 1906)
'Curb Preacher Scores Theater' (5 May 1906), p. 7
'At The Churches Yesterday' (21 May 1906), p. II7
'At The Churches Yesterday' (28 May 1906), p. 16
'Church Census For City' (13 July 1906)
'Churches Aroused to Action' (18 July 1906)
'Young Girl Given Gift of Tongues' (20 July 1906)
'Week's Events in Churches' (21 July 1906)
'Church Workers To Meet Tonight' (24 July 1906), p. 12
'New Testament Leader Writes Open Letter' (23 July 1906), p. 6
'Praying Bands For Churches' (25 July 1906)
'Plan For Religious Crusade' (2 August 1906), p. 5
'Church Finds a New Home' (11 August 1906), p. 15

Los Angeles Herald [LAPL]

'Anniversary Sermons are Preached' (6 February 1902), p. 10
'Jumpers to Kill Children' (20 July 1906), p. 1
'Monrovians Ask Officers to Act' (21 July 1906), p. 4
'Creed-Makers Are Denounced: Latter Day Apostles Show Ingratitude' (23 July1906), p. 7
'Evangelists To Work In Summer' (25 July 1906), p. 4
'First New Testament Church', *Advertisement* (29 September 1906), p. 9

Los Angeles Record [LAPL]

'Split in Baptist Church' (14 September 1905), p. 6
'New Church Started' (19 September 1905), p. 5
'Grace Baptist Church', *Advertisement* (6 November 1915), p. 8

Los Angeles Times [LAPL]

'Y.W.C.A. Convention' (27 January 1895), p. 14
'Concluding Services of the Baptist County Association' (8 October 1897), p. 15
'Convention of the Santa Ana Valley Baptist Convention' (16 October 1897), p. 15
'At the Churches Yesterday' (24 January 1898), p. 5
'At the Churches Yesterday' (31 January 1898), p. 10
'At the Churches Yesterday' (7 February 1898), p. 6
'Events in Society' (18 February 1898), p. 5
'Dedicatory Services' (9 April 1898), p. 11
'At the Churches Yesterday' (25 April 1898), p. 6
'Pastor Resigns' (10 June 1898), p. 13
'Resignation Withdrawn' (11 June 1898), p. 9
'Events in Society', *Smale's Wedding* (28 June 1898), p. 5
'Real Estate Transactions' (13 September 1898), p. 12
'Events in Society' (15 March 1899), p. 9
'Prayer Convention' (18 May 1900), p. 114
'At the Churches Yesterday' (6 August 1900), p. 16
'At the Churches Yesterday' (13 August 1900), p. 18
'At the Churches Yesterday' (24 September 1900), p. 18
'Joyous Welcome to New Century' (1 January 1901), p. 11
'Centennial Conference' (3 January 1901), p. 11
'Home Industrial Society' (8 January 1901), p. 4
'At the Churches Yesterday' (11 February 1901), p. 5
'Compliment to Pastor' (24 March 1901), p. 12
'Joseph Smale Delivers a Notable Lecture' (12 April 1901), p. 12
'At the Churches Yesterday' (6 May 1901), p. 8
'At the Churches Yesterday' (13 May 1901), p. 7
'Baptists Convention Meets At Pomona' (14 November 1901), p. 15

'Boy Goes Free' (18 April 1902), p. A2
'The City in Brief' (29 August 1902), p. 12
'Call For Trial of Pastor Smale' (15 September 1902), p. 14
'The Kernel of the Smale Case' (16 September 1902), p. A1
'Bunch of Co-incidents Sets Baptists Agog: Are the Agitators Grooming a New Pastor?' (18 September 1902), p. 6
'Pastor Smale's Trial But Begun' (19 September 1902), p. A1
'Pastor and His Foes Both Score' (20 September 1902), p. A1
'Opponents of Smale are Organizing' (21 September 1902), p. B1
'Open Door at Smale Trial' (22 September 1902), p. 5
'Church Trial Won by Pastor Smale' (23 September 1902), p. A1
'Pastor Smale Gets a Raise' (24 September 1902), p. A1
'Smale's Assistant About To Resign' (26 September 1902), p. A1
'Superintendent of Sunday-School Quits' (6 October 1902), p. 6
'Sway of Smale Much Extended' (9 October 1902), p. 6
'Brevities' (8 November 1902), p. 12
'Pastor Smale Has The Call: 25 Members Asked to Come or Get Out' (29 January 1903), p. 5
'Eats Bread of Angels' (2 February 1903), p. 9
'Objections Made To Pastor Smale' (5 February 1903), p. 11
'Will Smale Stay There?' (12 February 1903), p. 13
'Pastor Smale May Face Church Council' (16 February 1903), p. 8
'Pastor Smale Still Sick' (26 February 1903), p. 14
'That Smale will Resign' (5 April 1903), p. 11
'The Unending Case of Pastor Smale' (12 April 1903), p. D7
'More Than One Hundred Come From First Baptist Congregation' (18 July 1903), p. A1
'Baptist Bickerings' (28 July 1903), p. 7
'Baptists Sit On Bossism' (9 October 1903), p. 7
'Baptists Hot For Naught: Smale & James Prominent in Futile Fight' (6 November 1903), p. 11
'Clouds Are Rolling Away' (8 January 1904), p. A3
'At the Churches Yesterday' (1 August 1904), p. 6
'At the Churches Yesterday' (22 August 1904), p. 13
'Famous London Preacher is in the City' (8 April 1905), p. 17
'Is Not Dead But Kicking; Smale's Mother is Seriously Ill' (8 April 1905), p. 17
'Editorial Article' (9 April 1905), p. II4
'The Message of Dr. Meyer' (19 April 1905), p. III1
'Planning a Reception' (11 May 1905), p. III1
'News and Notes' (20 May 1905), p. III1
'Special Notices' (21 May 1905), p. IV1
'Rev. Joseph Smale to Arrive Home Tomorrow' (24 May 1905), p. III1
'Returned Preacher Talks of the Holy Land' (26 May 1905), p. III1

'Pastor Smale Stirs 'Em Up' (8 June 1905), p. II5
'New Church is Temple' (18 July 1905), p. A1
'Church Services' (29 July, 1905), p. II1
'The Baptist World Congress' (13 August 1905), p. VI13
'Bombs For Baptists' (11 September 1905), p. 11
'Baptist Boil Still "Biling"' (12 September, 1905), p. II.10
'New Church For Smale' (14 September 1905), p. 14
'Seceders Go In Harmony' (18 September 1905), p. 14
'Immersion Unessential' (28 October 1905), p. II6
'New Testament Church. Chinese Evangelist Speaks' (25 November 1905), p. II6
'At the Churches Yesterday' (27 November 1905), p. I6
'Indian is a Hustler' (9 December 1905), p. I7
'At the Churches Yesterday' (18 December 1905), p. I9
'Mission Money Comes Quickly' (26 December 1905), p. II2
'At The Churches Yesterday' (1 January 1906), p. II3
'At The Churches Yesterday' (22 January 1906), p. I13
'At The Churches Yesterday' (26 February 1906), p. I6
'The City in Brief' (2 April 1906), p. I18
'At The Churches Yesterday' (9 April 1906), p. 16
'Church Services' (29 April 1906), p. II7
'Rolling on Floor in Smale's Church' (14 July 1906), p. II1
'"Holy Roller" Mad' (17 July 1906), p. II14
'Queer "Gift" Given Many' (23 July 1906), p. I5
'Claim Power to Raise Dead' (24 September 1906), p. I17
'Farewell for Missionaries to China' (13 March 1909), p. II10
'Pastor Smale Seeks Divorce' (16 April 1910), p. II1
'Given Decree for Divorce' (26 May 1910), p. I12
'Deaths: Mrs Ann Smale' (30 January 1911), p. 118
'Religious Brevities' (11 February 1911), p. I7
'Dedication of First New Testament Church' (27 May 1911), p. I13
'Pastor Smale's New Romance' (27 May 1911), p. II1
'Bids Good-by at its Dedication' (29 May 1911), p. II7
'Former Angelenos Wed' (2 June 1911), p. 15
'Display Ads., Grace Baptist Church', *Advertisement* (27 March 1915), p. I19
'Events Briefly Told' (6 April 1915), p. I10
'Large Party to Make Tour of the Orient' (25 July 1920), p. V8
'Deaths' (18 September 1926), p. I16
'Rites for Churchman Tomorrow' (18 September 1926), p. II1

STREATHAM NEWS (LONDON) [LAMB]
'Recognition Services' (20 June 1912)
'Hitherfield Road Free Church', *Report of Induction Service* (29 June 1912)
'Hitherfield Road Free Church', *Advertisement* (27 July 1912)

Smale Sermons

Smale, J., 'A Message to Our Church', *Church Quarterly* II.1 (December 1897) [FBC LA]

———, 'Lessons in Personal Work', *The Pacific Baptist* 22.43 (24 October 1898) [ABHS]

———, 'The State of Religion', *The Pacific Baptist* 22.48 (30 November 1898) [ABHS]

———, 'The People of God in this Age' (8 June 1903) [FBC LA]

———, *The Pentecostal Blessing* (First New Testament Church Los Angeles, 1905) [FPHC]

———, 'The Secret Rapture and the Second Coming of Christ' (First New Testament Church Los Angeles, 24 November 1907) [WFC]

———, 'Multi-Millionaires' (First New Testament Church Los Angeles, January 1908) [WFC]

———, 'The Greatest Truth I Know: After a Twenty-Five Years' Ministry; A Review of the Subject of the Baptism of the Holy Spirit in the Light of It' (First New Testament Church Los Angeles, 17 January 1909) [WFC]

———, 'Is the Church of the Fifth Chapter of Ephesians the Bride of Christ?', in *Forgotten Truths Reaffirmed* (Bible Fellowship Church, USA, n.d.) [FPHC]

———, 'A Message to Spirit-Filled Believers', in *Truth: Earthly and Heavenly* (No. 2625, for the author, 1925) [WFA]

Photographs

Burbank Theatre, *Building* (1905) [LAPL]

First Baptist Church Los Angeles, *Building* (Ticor/Pierce Collection, c. 1900) [CHS]

First Baptist Church Los Angeles, *Deacons* (1900) [FBC LA]

Hitherfield Road Baptist Church, London, *Buildings* (1907) [DCC]

Joseph and Esther Smale, *Portrait, China New Testament Mission, Journals* [WFC]

Joseph and Esther Smale, *Grave Stones* [PHP]

Joseph Smale, *Student Portraits* (1887; 1888) [SCHR]

Joseph Smale, *Portraits* (1898) [FBC LA]

Lone Star Baptist Church Prescott, *Building* (c. 1895) [FBC PAZ]

Los Angeles, *City View* (Ticor/Pierce Collection, 1884) [CHS]

Ryde, Isle of Wight, *Town View* (1891) [IoW CRO]

Unity Chapel Bristol, *Building* [ALC]

Wiveliscombe, *Abbotsfield Cottages, Wesleyan Chapel, School* (c. 1900) [WBGA]

Other

Assorted Birth, Marriage, Death Registers, UK and USA
English Census (1861, 1871, 1881, 1891, 1911)
Kelly's Directory, *Isle of Wight* (1891) [IoW CRO]
Kelly's Directory, *Bristol* (1915) [BRL]
Letter from Frank Bartleman to Lewi Pethrus, 9 July 1913
Los Angeles City Directory, 'Church and Places of Worship' (1908–30) [LAPL]
Obituary Records [SHMP]
Ship Passenger Records, *Etruria* (1892), *New York* (1893), *Servia* (1894), *S.S. Baltic* (1905),
Wright's Bristol Directory (1915–16)
http://www.genuki.org.uk/big/eng/Cornwall/Stokeclimsland/index.html#ChurchHistory, accessed 8 September 2008, 10 February 2009
The Bridgewater Mercury (2 March 1892), http://dbown100.tripod.com/Temp.html, accessed 9 March 2005
Guion, L.A., 'Triangulation: Establishing the Validity of Qualitative Studies', University of Florida, http://www.rayman-bacchus.net/uploads/documents/Triangulation.pdf, accessed 4 September 2004
World Alliance of Reformed Churches, 'Word and Spirit, Church and World Report', Pentecostal-Reformed Dialogue, http://www.warc.ch/dt/erl11/20.html, accessed: 1 August 2006)

Secondary Sources

Anderson, A.H., *An Introduction to Pentecostalism: Global Charismatic Christianity* (Cambridge University Press, 2004)
———, *Spreading Fires: The Missionary Nature of Early Pentecostalism* (SCM Press, 2007)
Anderson, A.H. and W.J. Hollenweger (eds), *Pentecostals after a Century: Global Perspectives on a Movement in Transition* (Sheffield Academic Press, 1999)
Anderson, R.M., *Vision of the Disinherited: The Making of American Pentecostalism* (Oxford University Press, 1979)
Armitage, T., *A History of the Baptists: The American Baptists, Foreign Missions – Asia and Europe* (New York, 1890), http://www.fbinstitute.com/armitage/ ch13.html, accessed 24 August 2006
Au, Connie Ho Yan, *Grassroots Unity in the Charismatic Renewal* (Wipf & Stock, 2011)
Badcock, G.D., *Light of Truth and Fire of Love: A Theology of the Holy Spirit* (Eerdmans, 1997)

Bartleman, F., *Azusa Street: The Roots of Modern-Day Pentecost* (Logos International, 1980)
———, 'With Other Tongues', *Confidence* 9.4 (April, 1916), pp. 63-66
Bayes, D.H., 'Christian Revival in China, 1900-1937', in E.L. Blumhofer and R. Balmer (eds), *Modern Christian Revivals* (University of Illinois Press, 1993), pp. 161-79
Bebbington, D.W., 'Culture and Piety in the Far West: Revival in Penzance, Newlyn, and Mousehole in 1849', in K. Cooper and J. Gregory (eds), *Revival and Resurgence in Christian History* (Boydell Press, 2008), pp. 225-50
———, *The Dominance of Evangelicalism: The Age of Spurgeon and Moody* (IVP, 2005)
———, *Evangelicalism in Modern Britain: A History from the 1730s to the 1980s* (Unwin Hyman, 1989)
———, 'Spurgeon and British Evangelical Theological Education', in D.G. Hart and R.A. Mohler, Jr. (eds), *Theological Education in the Evangelical Tradition* (Baker Books, 1996), pp. 217-34
Berkhof, H., *The Doctrine of the Holy Spirit* (Epworth Press, 1965)
Blumhofer, E.L., 'Alexander Boddy and the Rise of Pentecostalism in Great Britain', *Pneuma* 8:1 (Spring, 1986), pp. 31-40
———, *The Assemblies of God: A Chapter in the Story of American Pentecostalism:* Volume 1. *To 1941* (Gospel Publishing House, 1989)
———, 'Restoration as Revival: Early American Pentecostalism', in E.L. Blumhofer and R. Balmer (eds), *Modern Christian Revivals* (University of Illinois Press, 1993), pp. 145-60
———, *Restoring the Faith: The Assemblies of God, Pentecostalism, and American Culture* (University of Illinois Press, 1993)
Blumhofer, E.L., R.P. Spittler and G. Wacker (eds), *Pentecostal Currents in American Protestantism* (University of Illinois Press, 1999)
Bradley, J.E., and R.A. Muller, *Church History: An Introduction to Research, Reference Works and Methods* (Eerdmans, 1995)
Bundy, D.D., 'Edward Irving', in S.M. Burgess and E.M. Van der Maas (eds), *New International Dictionary of Pentecostal and Charismatic Movements* (Zondervan, 2002), pp. 803-804
———, 'Bibliography and Historiography', in S.M. Burgess and E.M. Van der Maas (eds), *New International Dictionary of Pentecostal and Charismatic Movements* (Zondervan, 2002), pp. 405-17
———, 'Lewi Pethrus', in S.M. Burgess and E.M. Van der Maas (eds), *New International Dictionary of Pentecostal and Charismatic Movements* (Zondervan, 2002), pp. 986-87
Burgess, S.M., 'Holy Spirit, Doctrine of: Reformed Traditions', in S.M. Burgess and E.M. Van der Maas (eds), *New International Dictionary of Pentecostal and Charismatic Movements* (Zondervan, 2002), pp. 763-69

Burgess, S.M., and E.M. Van der Maas (eds), *New International Dictionary of Pentecostal and Charismatic Movements* (Zondervan, 2002)

Calvin, J., *Institutes of the Christian Religion* (Westminster Press, 1960)

Cameron, H., P. Richter, D. Davies and F. Ward (eds), *Studying Local Churches: A Handbook* (SCM Press, 2005)

Carlile, J.C., *C.H. Spurgeon: An Interpretative Biography* (Religious Tract Society, London, 1933)

Cartwright, D., 'Everywhere Spoken Against: Opposition to Pentecostalism 1907–1930', http://www.smithwigglesworth.com/pensketches/everywhere.htm, accessed May/June 2009

Cauchi, T., 'The Apostolic Faith: Biographies on Principal Participants – Joseph Smale', CD-ROM (The Revival Library, 2004)

Cerillo, A., and G. Wacker, 'Bibliography and Historiography', in S.M. Burgess and E.M. Van der Maas (eds), *New International Dictionary of Pentecostal and Charismatic Movements* (Zondervan, 2002), pp. 382-405

Cerillo, A., 'The Beginnings of American Pentecostalism: A Historiographical Overview', in E.L. Blumhofer, R.P. Spittler and G.A. Wacker (eds), *Pentecostal Currents in American Protestantism* (University of Illinois Press, 1999)

———, 'The Origins of American Pentecostalism: A Review Essay of James R. Goff, Jr., Fields White Unto Harvest: Charles F. Parham and the Missionary Origins of Pentecostalism', *Pneuma* 15.1 (1993), pp. 77-88

———, 'Interpretive Approaches to the History of American Pentecostal Origins', *Pneuma* 19.1 (1997), pp. 29-52

Cheung, D., *Christianity in Modern China* (E.J. Brill, 2004)

China Centenary Missionary Conference, *Addresses: Public and Devotional* (Methodist Publishing House, Shanghai, 1907)

Court, L.H., *The Romance of a Country Circuit: Sketches of Village Methodism* (Henry Hooks, 1921)

Cox, H., *Fire from Heaven: The Rise of Pentecostal Spirituality and the Reshaping of Religion in the Twenty-First Century* (Da Capo Press, 1995)

Daniels, D.D., 'God Makes No Differences in Nationality: The Fashioning of a New Racial/Nonracial Identity at the Azusa Street Revival', *Enrichment Journal* (Spring 2006), pp. 72-76

Davies, R., A.R. George and G. Rupp (eds), *A History of the Methodist Church in Great Britain*, Volume 4 (Epworth Press, 1988)

Dayton, D.W., *Theological Roots of Pentecostalism* (Hendrickson, 1987)

Ellis, R.A., *Living Echoes of the Welsh Revival, 1904–5* (The Delyn Press, 1952)

Evans, E., *The Welsh Revival of 1904* (Evangelical Movement of Wales, 1969)

Farrington, S.M., *Wiveliscombe: A History* (Colden Publications, 2005)

Faupel, D.W., *The Everlasting Gospel* (Sheffield Academic Press, 1996)

———, 'Whither Pentecostalism?' *Pneuma* 15.1 (1993), pp. 9-27

Gibbard, N., *On the Wings of the Dove: The International Effects of the 1904–05 Revival* (Brynterion Press, 2002)

Goff, J.R., Jr., and G. Wacker (eds), *Portraits of a Generation: Early Pentecostal Leaders* (University of Arkansas Press, 2002)

Hacking, K.J., *Signs and Wonders Then and Now* (Apollos, 2006)

Hilborn, D., (ed.), *'Toronto' in Perspective* (Acute, 2001)

Hollenweger, W.J., *The Pentecostals* (SCM Press, 1972)

———, *Pentecostalism: Origins and Developments Worldwide* (Hendrickson, 1999)

———, 'Pentecostalisms', www.epcra.ch/articles_pdf/Pentecostalisms.PDF, accessed 22 April 2008

Hoover, M.G., *Willis Collins Hoover: History of the Pentecostal Revival in Chile*, (Imprenta Eben-Ezer, 2000)

Horton, S.M., 'Elmer Kirk Fisher', in S.M. Burgess and E.M. Van der Maas (eds), *New International Dictionary of Pentecostal and Charismatic Movements* (Zondervan, 2002), p. 641

Hunter, H.D., and P.D. Hocken (eds), *All Together in One Place: Theological Papers from the Brighton Conference on World Evangelization* (Sheffield Academic Press, 1993)

Irvin, D.T., 'Charles Price Jones: Image of Holiness', in J.R. Goff and G. Wacker (eds), *Portraits of a Generation: Early Pentecostal Leaders* (University of Arkansas Press, 2002), pp. 37-50

Jacobsen, D., *Thinking in the Spirit: Theologies of the Early Pentecostal Movement* (Indiana University Press, 2003)

———, 'Review: Jean-Jacques Suurmond, Word and Spirit at Play: Towards a Charismatic Theology', *Pneuma* 20.1 (Spring, 1998), pp. 134-36

Jones, C.P., *The Gift of the Holy Ghost in the Book of Acts* (Los Angeles: National Publishing Board of the Church of Christ [Holiness], 1996)

Karkkainen, V.M., 'Missiology: Pentecostal and Charismatic', in S.M. Burgess and E.M. Van der Maas (eds), *New International Dictionary of Pentecostal and Charismatic Movements* (Zondervan, 2002), pp. 877-85

———, 'Mission, Spirit and Eschatology', *Mission Studies* XVI-I.31 (1999), pp. 73-94

———, *Pneumatology* (Baker Academic, 2002)

Kay, W.K., 'Revival: Empirical Aspects', in A. Walker and K. Aune (eds), *On Revival: A Critical Examination* (Paternoster Press, 2003), pp. 187-204

Kelly, A., 'Wiveliscombe Congregational Church: A Brief History', http://www. wiveliscombe-congregational.org.uk/history.htm, accessed 19 July 2008, and 11 February 2009

Kim, M.Y., 'Reformed Pneumatology and Pentecostal Pneumatology', in W.M. Alston and M. Welker (eds), *Reformed Theology* (Eerdmans, 2003), pp. 170-89

Lang, G.H., *An Ordered Life: An Autobiography* (Paternoster, London, 1959)

———, 'The Early Years of the Tongues Movement: An Historical Survey and Its Lessons' (c. 1950), http://www.banner.org.uk/tb/lang.html, accessed 19 February 2004

Lawrence, B.F., *The Apostolic Faith Restored* (St Louis, MO: Gospel Publishing House, 1916)

Leonard, B.J., *Baptists in America* (Columbia University Press, 2005)

Lewis, H.E., *With Christ Among The Miners: Incidents and Impressions of the Welsh Revival* (Hodder & Stoughton, 1907)

Linton, K., and A. Linton, *'I Will Build My Church': 150 Years of local church work in Bristol* (Hadler, 1982)

Loder, J.E., *The Transforming Moment* (Helmers & Howard, 1989)

Macchia, F.D., 'Theology, Pentecostal', in S.M. Burgess and E.M. Van der Maas (eds), *New International Dictionary of Pentecostal and Charismatic Movements* (Zondervan, 2002), pp. 1120-41

MacGillivray, D. (ed.), *A Century of Protestant Missions in China (1807–1907), Being the Centenary Conference Historical Volume* (American Presbyterian Mission Press, Shanghai, 1907)

McBain, D., *Fire over the Waters* (Darton Longman Todd, 1997)

McClendon, J.W., Jr, *Biography as Theology: How Life Stories Can Remake Today's Theology* (Trinity Press International, 1990)

McClung, L.G., *Azusa Street and Beyond: Pentecostal Missions and Church Growth in the Twentieth Century* (South Plainfield, NJ: Bridge, 1986)

McCulloch, G., *Documentary Research in Education, History and the Social Sciences* (Routledge Falmer, 2004)

McGee, G.B., 'Pentecostal Missiology: Moving Beyond Triumphalism to Face the Issues', *Pneuma* 16.2 (1994), pp. 275-81

McIntyre, J., *The Shape of Pneumatology: Studies in the Doctrine of the Holy Spirit* (T&T Clark, 1997)

Moltmann, J., *The Spirit of Life* (SCM Press, 1992)

Morgan, J.V., *The Welsh Religious Revival 1904–5: A Retrospect and a Criticism* (Chapman & Hall, 1909)

Murray, I., 'Introduction', in C.H. Spurgeon, *An All-Round Ministry* (Banner of Truth, 1960)

Nelson, D.J., 'For Such a Time as This: The Story of Bishop William J. Seymour and the Azusa Street Revival. A Study of Pentecostal/Charismatic Roots' (unpublished PhD diss., University of Birmingham, 1981)

Nicholls, M., *C.H. Spurgeon: The Pastor Evangelist* (Baptist Historical Society, 1992)

O'Dea, T., 'Sociological Dilemmas in the Institutionalization of Religion', *Journal for the Scientific Study of Religion* 1.1 (1961), pp. 30-39

Orr, J.E., *The Flaming Tongue: The Impact of Early 20th Century Revivals* (Moody Press, 1973)

Penn-Lewis, J., *The Awakening in Wales and Some of the Hidden Springs* (Welsh Revival Library, CD ROM)

Pluss, J.-D., 'Azusa and Other Myths: The Long and Winding Road from Experience to Stated Belief and Back Again', *Pneuma* 15.2 (Fall, 1993), pp. 189-201

Poloma, M.M., *Main Street Mystics: The Toronto Blessing and Reviving Pentecostalism* (AltaMira Press, 2003)

———, 'The Future of American Pentecostal Identity: The Assemblies of God at a Crossroad', in M. Welker (ed.), *The Work of the Spirit: Pneumatology and Pentecostalism* (Eerdmans, 2006), pp. 147-65

Pomerville, P.A., *The Third Force in Missions* (Hendrickson, 1985)

Ragoonath, A., *Preach the Word: A Pentecostal Approach* (Agape Teaching Ministry of Canada, 2004)

Randall, I.M., 'Old Time Power: Relationships between Pentecostalism and Evangelical Spirituality in England', *Pneuma* 19.1 (1977), pp. 53-80

———, 'Mere Denominationalism – F.B. Meyer and Baptist Life', *Baptist Quarterly* 35.1 (January, 1993), pp. 19-34

———, '"Days of Pentecostal Overflowing": Baptists and the Shaping of Pentecostalism', in D.W. Bebbington (ed.), *The Gospel in the World: International Baptist Studies* (Paternoster Press, 2002), pp. 80-104

———, *School of the Prophets: 150 Years of Spurgeon's College* (Spurgeon's College, 2005)

———, *The English Baptists of the Twentieth Century* (Baptist Historical Society, 2005)

Ratcliffe, D., 'Qualitative Data Analysis and the Transforming Moment', *Transformation* 25.2–3 (April/July 2008), pp. 116-33

Records: China Centenary Missionary Conference (China Centenary Committee, 1907)

Robeck, C.M., Jr, *The Azusa Street Mission and Revival: The Birth of the Global Pentecostal Movement* (Nelson, 2006)

———, 'Joseph Smale', in S.M. Burgess and E.M. Van der Maas (eds), *New International Dictionary of Pentecostal and Charismatic Movements* (Zondervan, 2002), pp. 1074-75

———, 'William Joseph Seymour', in S.M. Burgess and E.M. Van der Maas (eds), *New International Dictionary of Pentecostal and Charismatic Movements* (Zondervan, 2002), p. 1056

———, 'Taking Stock of Pentecostalism: The Personal Reflections of a Retiring Editor', *Pneuma* 15.1 (1993), pp. 35-60

———, 'The Use of Biography in Pentecostal Historiography', *Pneuma* 8 (Fall, 1986), pp. 77-80

———, 'Upper Room Mission', in S.M. Burgess and E.M. Van der Maas (eds), *New International Dictionary of Pentecostal and Charismatic Movements* (Zondervan, 2002), p. 1166

Robert, D.L., *Occupy Until I Come: A.T. Pierson and the Evangelization of the World* (Eerdmans, 2003)

Roberts, B., *Biographical Research* (Open University Press, 2002)

Ryde Social Heritage Group, *Ryde's Heritage: Our Town, Your Histories* (Ryde Social Heritage Group, 2008)

Scotland, N., *Charismatics and the Next Millennium* (Hodder & Stoughton, 1995)

Shaw, S.B., *The Great Revival in Wales* (Christian Life Books, 2002 [1905])

Shumway, C.W., 'A Critical History of Glossolalia' (unpublished PhD diss., Boston University, 1919)

Singleton, G.H., *Religion in the City of Angels: American Protestant Culture and Urbanization Los Angeles 1850–1930* (UMI Research Press, 1979)

Smith, J.K.A., 'Teaching a Calvinist to Dance: In Pentecostal Worship my Reformed Theology Finds Its Groove', *Christianity Today* 52.5 (May, 2008), pp. 42-45

Spittler, R.P., 'Suggested Areas for Further Research in Pentecostal Studies', *Pneuma* 5.2 (Fall, 1983), pp. 39-57

Spurgeon, C.H., 'Praying in the Holy Ghost', *Metropolitan Tabernacle Pulpit* 12 (1866)

———, *Lectures to my Students* (Baker Book House, 1984)

———, 'Our Urgent Need of the Holy Spirit', *Metropolitan Tabernacle Pulpit* 33 (1877)

———, 'The Holy Spirit's Intercession', *Metropolitan Tabernacle Pulpit* 26 (1880)

———, 'The Pentecostal Wind and Fire', *Metropolitan Tabernacle Pulpit* 27 (1881)

———, 'The Abiding of the Spirit the Glory of the Church', *Metropolitan Tabernacle Pulpit* 32 (1886)

———, 'The Personal Pentecost and the Glorious Hope', *Metropolitan Tabernacle Pulpit* 32 (1886)

———, 'What We Would Be: An Address Delivered at the Conference of the Pastors' College Association', *The Sword and the Trowel* (June and July, 1886), pp. 253-59 and 337-43

———, 'The Holy Ghost and the Need of the Age', *Metropolitan Tabernacle Pulpit* 33 (1887), pp. 9-20

———, 'Restoration of Truth and Revival', *The Sword and the Trowel* (December, 1887), pp. 605-607

———, 'What we aim at in the Pastors' College', *The Sword and the Trowel* (May, 1887), pp. 205-11.

———, 'Annual Report of the Pastors' College', *The Sword and the Trowel* (June, 1888), pp. 316-36

———, 'Presidential Address at the First Conference of the Pastor's College', *The Sword and the Trowel* (June, 1888), pp. 257-65

———, 'What We Aim At: Address at the Commencement of the College Session' (September 1888), *The Sword and the Trowel* (November, 1888), pp. 568-74

———, 'Filling with the Spirit, and Drunkenness with Wine', *Metropolitan Tabernacle Pulpit* 35 (1889)

———, 'Peculiar Power in Prayer', *The Sword and the Trowel* (September, 1889), pp. 489-96

———, 'The Preacher's Power, and the Conditions of Obtaining It', *The Sword and the Trowel* (June; July; August, 1889), pp. 253-60, 349-57 and 413-21

———, 'Come From The Four Winds, O Breath!', *Metropolitan Tabernacle Pulpit* 36 (1890)

———, 'Witnessing better than Knowing the Future', *Metropolitan Tabernacle Pulpit* 39 (1893)

———, *Autobiography:* Volume 1. *The Early Years* (Banner of Truth, 1962)

———, *Autobiography:* Volume 2. *The Full Harvest* (Banner of Truth, 1973)

———, *Sermons on Revival* (Zondervan, 1958)

———, *Power for You* (Whitaker House, 1996)

Spurgeon, C.H., et al, 'Annual Report of the Pastors' College', *The Sword and the Trowel* (1886–1888)

Stanley, B., *The World Missionary Conference, Edinburgh 1910* (Eerdmans, 2009)

Stockley, T.I., 'Our Spiritual Life: Its Influence Upon Our Preaching', *The Sword and the Trowel* (July, 1886), pp. 586-90

Suurmond, J.J., *Word and Spirit at Play: Towards a Charismatic Theology* (SCM Press, 1994)

Synan, V., *The Holiness-Pentecostal Tradition: Charismatic Movements in the 20th Century* (Grand Rapids, MI: Eerdmans, 1971)

Taylor, M.J., 'Publish and Be Blessed: A Case Study in Early Pentecostal Publishing History 1906–1926' (unpublished PhD diss., University of Birmingham, 1994)

Tiedemann, R.G., *Reference Guide to Missionary Societies in China: From the Sixteenth to the Twentieth Century* (draft manuscript)

Turner, W.H. *Pioneering in China (Illustrated)* (The Publishing House of the Pentecostal Holiness Church, n.d., [1928])

Underhill, E., *Mysticism: A Study in the Nature and Developments of Man's Spiritual Consciousness* (New York, NY: Meridian, 1955)

Van der Ven, J.A., *Ecclesiology in Context* (Eerdmans, 1993)

Wacker, G., 'Are the Golden Oldies Still Worth Playing?: Reflections on History Writing among Early Pentecostals', *Pneuma* 8.2 (Fall, 1986), pp. 81-100

———, *Heaven Below: Early Pentecostals and American Culture* (Harvard University Press, 2001)

Wakefield, G., *Alexander Boddy: Pentecostal Anglican Pioneer* (Paternoster, 2007)

Welch, T.B., 'Digging Beneath Azusa Street: The Contribution of Joseph Smale within Pentecostal historiography', paper presented at Glopent Conference, Amsterdam, 27–28 April 2007

———, 'God's "Moses" for Pentecostalism: A Study of Baptist Pastor, Joseph Smale (1867–1926)', in J.H.Y. Briggs and A.R. Cross (eds), *Baptists and the World: Renewing the Vision. Papers from The Baptist Historical Society Conference, Prague, Czech Republic, July 2008* (Regent's Park College, 2011), pp. 152-65

———, 'God's "Moses" for Pentecostalism: Remapping the Smale-Trail', paper presented at SPS Annual Meeting, Fuller Theological Seminary, Pasadena, 23–25 March 2006

———, 'Preparing the Way for the Azusa Street Revival: Joseph Smale, God's "Moses" for Pentecostalism', *Heritage* 29 (2009), pp. 26-33

———, 'A Study of Baptist Pastor Joseph Smale', paper presented at Baptist Historical Society, Centenary Conference, Prague, 16–19 July 2008

Welker, M., (ed.), *The Work of the Spirit: Pneumatology and Pentecostalism* (Eerdmans, 2006)

White, H.W., 'Methodism Hereabouts', paper presented to the Wiveliscombe Historical Society, 15 February 2005

Yao, K.X., 'At the Turn of the Century: A Study of the China Centenary Missionary Conference of 1907', *International Bulletin of Missionary Research* 32.2 (April, 2008), pp. 65-70

Yu, Carver T. 'Charismatic Movement, Postmodernism and Covenantal Rationality', in Alston, M.W. and M. Welker (eds), *Reformed Theology: Identity and Ecumenicity* (Eerdmans, 2003), pp. 157-69

General Index

Adams, C.O. 96n
Adams, D.C. 125, 130
Alexander, Charles 203
Anabaptists 172
Anderson, Allan H. 161, 199, 202n
Anderson, R.M. 4
Apostolic Faith Mission 137, 234
Apostolic Faith Movement 145
Arizona Baptist Association 59
Arizona Central Baptist Association 61
Arkansas Baptist College 3
Armitage, Thomas 58
Asberry, Richard 141, 142, 143, 144
Asberry, Ruth 141, 142, 143, 144
Assemblies of God 2
atonement 29, 44n, 50
Au, Connie 230n
Azusa Street Mission 2, 3, 4, 5, 7, 8, 14, 15, 16, 18, 31, 41, 49, 66, 100, 110, 113n, 132, 134, 136, 141, 144, 145, 146, 147, 148, 150, 152, 154, 156, 157, 180, 181, 194, 199, 210, 211, 212, 216, 234, 236
Azusa Street Revival (1905–06) 1, 3, 4, 6, 12, 13, 17, 28, 35, 53, 56, 69, 107, 131, 138n, 161, 162, 165, 166, 168, 173, 178, 179, 181, 213, 214, 215, 216, 217, 219, 227, 233, 234, 246

Bach, August Hugo 201-204, 207, 209, 210, 240
Bach, Heinrich Peter 202n
Bach, Hermann Theodor 202n
Bach, Matrina M. 202n
Baldwin, Thomas 124

Ballard, J. Hudson 98
baptism 71, 107, 109, 146, 157, 191, 192, 226, 234, 235
baptisms 232
three baptisms 145
baptism in/with/of the Holy Spirit 3, 17, 29, 45, 100, 112, 130, 134, 138, 140, 142, 144, 145, 146, 157, 160, 163, 164, 171, 174, 176-81, 194, 195, 210, 212, 213, 217, 219, 228, 232, 234, 235, 246
Baptist Convention of Southern California 185
Baptist principles 133
Baptist Social Union 79, 80
Baptist Union of Great Britain and Ireland 1, 37, 44, 50
Baptist World Alliance Congress (1905) 92, 93
Baptists 1, 2, 3, 6, 7, 8, 12, 18, 21, 22, 27, 28, 36, 37, 48, 49, 50, 58, 61, 63, 65, 71, 123, 127, 130, 133, 164, 191, 192, 200, 235n
Barrett, T.B. 226n
Bartleman, Frank 1, 4, 5, 6, 16, 17, 53, 68, 85, 90, 92, 99, 100, 101, 106, 107, 108, 113, 116, 117, 119, 122, 123, 125, 126, 130, 135, 139, 140, 143, 144, 146, 147, 156, 158, 180, 186, 198, 210, 211, 217, 233, 234, 235
Barton, James 205
Bays, Daniel 200
Bebbington, David 22, 27, 37
Bell, E.N. 2, 3
Berean Mission, Los Angeles 65
Berkhof, H. 172
Bethesda Baptist Church, Sunderland 226n

Bethesda Chapel, Bristol 226
Bible and Missionary Training
  School, the 198-99
Bible Christians 51
bibliocentrism 174
Blumhofer, Edith 5, 28, 181, 183, 187
Boehmer, Brother 108
Bottome, Francis 184
Boyd, John 149, 197
Boynton, C.C. 85
Bradley, Mr 201
Bradley, Mrs 201
breaking of bread 227
Brethren 225, 226
Brown, Charles H. 96n
Buffard, Percy 224, 241
Bundy, David 8, 12
Burbank Hall, Los Angeles 128, 131, 138, 140, 141, 142, 143, 149, 150, 151, 153, 158, 182, 183, 195, 197, 240
Burdette, Robert 80
Butler, Anthea 176

Calvin College 9
Calvin, John 162
Calvinism 28, 50, 167n
Campbell, John 29, 30
Campbell, Mrs Donald 222, 223
Cartwright, Desmond 14, 34, 224n, 226n, 235n
Catholicism 99
Cauchi, T. 5, 6
Central Baptist Church Los Angeles 109
Cerillo, A. 234
cessationism 162n
charisma 189, 192, 193
charismata 190, 200
Charismatic Christianity 8, 9, 18, 99, 166, 194, 235
charismatic gifts 146
Charismatic Movement 6

Charismatic Renewal 1
Charismatic theology 235, 237
Charismatics 1, 2
China Centenary Mission Conference, Shanghai 204-10, 240
China New Testament Mission 11, 199-201, 208, 209, 230, 231, 232, 240, 241
Chinese Mission, Los Angeles 65, 96n, 195-96
Cho, Huen Ming 131, 198, 201
Christian and Alliance Missionary Home, New York 226n
christology 164, 165, 170
church membership 109n, 120, 146, 155, 157, 160, 190-93, 227
Church Missionary Society 201, 203
Church of Christ (Holiness) 3
Clatworthy, W.C. 85, 138n
Collard, Lukey 19, 20
Congregationalists 24, 28, 65, 71
conversion 29, 216
Cooke, Jack 69
Cox, Harvey 148
Craik, H. 226
Crawford, Florence 5
Crofts, Mrs W.H. 208
Crofts, William H. 208, 209
Crosier, F.B. 85
crucicentrism 111

Daniels, David 147n
David, Mrs M.E. 195
Davis, S.C. 63
Dawson, Deacon 130
Dayton, Donald 160, 163
Dean, Rev. 120, 121
discipleship 167
Downgrade controversy 29, 36, 37, 44, 49
Dozier, Barton 85, 91, 110
Dozier, Mrs Barton 81

General Index

Dozier, Melville 66, 119, 120, 121, 122, 123, 124, 125, 126, 127, 128, 129, 130
Dozier, Mrs Melville 119, 120, 124
Duke, David Nelson 17
Durham, William 5

ecclesiology 3, 9, 17, 26, 49, 109, 114, 133, 136, 156, 167, 181-94, 215, 225, 226
Edwards, D.K. 86
Edwards, Jonathan 168
Eighth and Maple Church, Los Angeles 135
Elim Pentecostals 34
English Mission Rescue, Hong Kong 200
Episcopalians 65
eschatology 43, 71, 110, 177, 183, 194
Evangelical piety 165
Evangelical Revival (Great Revival) 22, 23
Evangelical theology 37
Evangelicalism 3, 51, 163, 164
Evangelicals 5, 28, 50, 226
evangelism 37-39, 50, 59, 229
evangelists 37
exorcism 146

Farrow, Lucy 5
fasting 141
Fazel, John 222
Fergusson, Archibald 32, 33, 46
Finney, Charles 201
First Baptist Church Los Angeles 2, 4, 5, 6, 8, 12, 13, 14, 31, 37, 41, 44, 63-98, 100, 101, 102, 103, 104, 105, 106, 107, 108, 109, 110, 111, 112, 113, 114, 115, 116, 117, 118, 119, 120, 121, 122, 123, 124, 125, 126, 127, 128, 129, 131, 134, 138n, 139, 140, 151, 159, 162, 163, 164, 165, 166, 168, 182, 183, 184, 185, 190, 191, 193, 211, 215, 219, 223, 239, 240
First Baptist Church of Phoenix, Arizona 61, 63
First New Testament Church Los Angeles 3, 4, 6, 9, 11, 14, 15, 131, 132, 133, 134, 135, 136, 137, 138, 139, 140, 141, 142, 143, 144, 145, 146, 147, 148, 149, 150, 152, 153, 156, 157, 158, 159, 166, 167, 168, 171, 173, 176, 178, 180, 182, 183, 184, 186, 187, 188, 190, 191, 192, 193, 194, 195, 196, 197, 198, 199, 200, 201, 207, 210, 211, 212, 213, 215, 216, 217, 220, 226, 228, 231, 240
Fisher, Elmer Kirk 138n, 212, 215, 240
Fogelson, George 10
foot washing 160
four-fold gospel 163-64
Fowler, James 245

Garnett, J. Herndon 63
George Street Baptist Church, Ryde, Isle of Wight 46, 48
Gibbard, Noel 6, 7
Gideon Chapel, Bristol 226
Goforth, Jonathan 201n
Gordon, A.J. 8
Gould, G.P. 224
grace 28, 50, 51, 73
Grace Baptist Church, Los Angeles 209, 220n, 228-32
Grace Mission 97n
Gracey, David 30, 32, 46, 48, 49
Graves, A.P. 105
Green, J.M. 58
Guinness, Gratton 33n

Hacking, Keith J. 6

Harrington, Gladys 96n
Harrington, Rex 96n
Harrison, J. 47
Haskell, R.G. 12, 80, 83, 96n, 119, 121, 126, 129, 210
healing 163, 164n, 180
Hermann, Anna Maria 202n
Higher Life Baptists 8
Hinson, W.B. 71
Hitherfield Road Free Church, Streatham Hill, London 219, 222-23, 225, 241
holiness 42n, 173
Holiness Movement 99, 117
holiness teaching 8, 22, 42, 71, 165
Hollenweger, Walter 5, 99, 189
holy laughter 142
Hubbard, C.L. 86
immersion 71, 191
inspiration of scripture 50
intellectualism 27
Irving, Edward 44

Jacobsen, Douglas 2
Jones, Charles Price 3, 8
justification by faith 164

Karkkainen, Veli-Matti 172, 194
Keswick Convention 29
Keswick tradition 28
Keyes, Henry S. 12, 66, 89, 94, 96, 101, 110, 111, 112, 114, 116, 120, 123, 125, 126, 129, 130, 131, 150, 211, 212, 215, 240
Keyes, Lilian 131, 150, 211, 212, 214, 215
Keyes, Mrs H.S. 130
Keyser Smale, Alverda (née Keyser) 75, 76, 77, 239
Kiel China Mission 202n, 203
Kirk, John 224
Lakeland Revival 148
Lang, G.H. 16, 226, 227
Lawrence, B.F. 4

Lawson, A.A. 96n
Lee, Edward 142
Lee, F.J. 170
Leonard, A.B. 205
Lewis, Clyde 198
Lewis, Elvet 104
Light, Martin 48
Linton, Alan 225n
Loder, James E. 73, 74, 75, 79, 84, 89, 95, 98, 101, 103, 223, 242-45
Lone Star Baptist Church, Prescott, Arizona 37, 41, 57-63, 239
Los Angeles Baptist Association 38, 62, 127
Los Angeles Church Federation 7, 152, 153, 154, 155, 156, 189
Luther, Martin 171
Lutheran Church 203
Lutherans 71

Macchia, Frank 160, 165
Manley, Brother 108
Marchant, Frederick George 32, 46
Marsh, Deacon 130
Marsh, F.E. 226, 227
Mason, C.H. 2, 3, 170
McBain, Douglas 1, 6
Medhurst, Thomas 30
Merrill, Deacon 96n, 121, 122, 130
Merrill, Grace 109
Methodism 23
Methodists 22, 24, 49, 57, 65, 71, 95
Metropolitan Tabernacle 11, 12, 27, 29
Meyer, F.B. 8, 92, 93, 94, 224
millennialism 33n
Miller, Cord 96n
miracles 146, 246
missiology 9, 11, 14, 17, 26, 71, 114, 133, 182, 194, 215
mission 9, 11, 39, 59, 181, 182, 198, 199, 200
Montgomery, Carrie Judd 218

General Index

Moody, D.L. 29, 33n, 69, 201
Moore, Jennie 4, 142, 143, 144, 240
Morgan Joe 78
Morgan, G. Campbell 92
Morgan, J.J. 105
Morrison, Robert 204
Mott, John 71
Müller, George 33n, 226
Mukti Revival, India (1905) 106, 170

Nelson, Douglas 100
New Testament Church Mission of South China 203, 204
New Testament Training School, the (Bible and Missionary Training School) 188
Newport Baptist Church, Isle of Wight 56
Nonconformists 49, 50, 54
Nyack College, New York 221

open communion 9
ordinance 109
ordination 25, 28
Orr, J. Edwin 106

Palmer, Phoebe 175n
Parham, Charles Fox 5, 170
Park Road Baptist Church, Ryde, Isle of Wight 46-56, 59
Parker, F. 85
Pearson, Edward Bruce 48, 54
Pendleton, William 135
Penn-Lewis, Jessie 111
Pensacola Revival 148
Pentecostal Holiness Church 230, 231
Pentecostal identity 161, 183, 187
Pentecostal Missionary Union 202
Pentecostal Prayer Union of Southern California 70-71

Pentecostal theology 161, 165, 235, 237
Pentecostalism 1, 2, 3, 4, 5, 6, 7, 8, 9, 10, 16, 17, 18, 22, 25, 27, 28, 31, 35, 36, 88, 90, 92, 93, 99, 100, 106, 109n, 115, 119, 122, 129, 131n, 132, 133, 141, 143, 147n, 148, 149, 150, 153, 156, 158, 161, 163, 165, 166, 182, 184, 185, 188, 193, 194, 199, 200, 210, 212, 213, 214, 215, 218, 226n, 230, 232, 234, 235, 237
Pentecostalisms 160-61
Pentecostals 114, 146, 147n, 160, 161, 163, 173, 177, 179, 187, 189, 190, 192, 205, 236
perfectionism 42
Pethrus, Lewi 8, 9, 16, 109n, 234
Phelps, Jesse 96n
Pierson, A.T. 71
pneumatology 2, 3, 4, 5, 6, 7, 8, 9, 12, 17, 26, 28, 29, 31, 32, 36, 37, 38, 39-46, 50, 53, 68, 69, 71, 74, 86, 97, 100, 103, 105, 106, 107, 108, 110, 112, 113, 114, 115, 116, 123, 130, 132, 133, 134, 135, 136, 137, 138, 139, 140, 141, 142, 144, 145, 146, 148, 151, 155, 157, 159, 160, 161, 162, 163, 164, 165, 166, 167, 168, 169, 170, 171, 172, 173, 174, 175, 176-81, 182, 183, 184, 185, 186, 189, 190, 192, 194, 195, 197, 198, 200, 201n, 204, 205, 210, 211, 212, 213, 214, 215, 216, 217, 219, 226, 227, 228, 229, 232, 234, 235, 237, 246
Polhill, Cecil 210
Poloma, Margaret 192
Potter, Alonzo 66
Powles, Judy 11
prayer 9, 13, 25, 34, 44, 45, 68, 69, 72, 80, 96, 101, 102, 106, 107,

108, 109, 111, 113, 114, 115, 116, 119, 127, 140, 141, 146, 147, 155, 164n, 175, 186, 187, 240
preaching 9, 17, 25, 27, 36, 37, 51, 155, 157, 161-81, 216, 240
premillenialism 29, 194
Presbyterians 28, 65
priesthood of all believers 137
Primitive Methodists 49
prophecy 44, 146, 211
Protestants 172

Ragoonath, Aldwin 170
Randall, Ian M. 2
Randall, Rev. 105
Ratcliff, Donald 242
Read, Daniel 63, 75
Reeder, A.G. 57
Reformed churches 162
Reformed Pentecostalism 28
Reformed theology 162
Reformed tradition 9, 18, 166, 171, 235, 237
regeneration 171, 174, 175
Regent's Park Baptist Church, London 224
Regent's Park College, Oxford 1
restorationism 183, 204
revival(s) 6, 13, 22, 24, 28, 39, 43, 44, 57, 58, 59, 68, 72, 73, 75, 78, 79, 90, 99, 101, 104, 110, 111, 114, 117, 124, 125, 126, 129, 140, 142, 143, 144, 148, 157, 161, 167, 171, 181, 185, 200, 219, 227, 229, 233
  1814 Revival 23
  1858–59 Awakening 43
  1860 Revival 24
revivalism 162n
Rice, C.A.. 58
Rider, A.W. 65n
Rios, Juan 96n

Robeck, Cecil M. Jr, 5, 7, 13, 14, 15, 17, 93, 99, 108n, 117, 131, 132, 136, 143, 144, 152, 154, 156, 210, 211
Roberts, Evan 4, 6, 89, 91, 93, 97, 102, 103, 104, 176
Rodgers, Darrin J. 15, 167n
Roman Catholics 172
Rotcher, Ernestine 12
Ryde Baptist Church, Isle of Wight 31, 37
Ryland, E.P. 152, 154, 189

salvation 50, 164, 179, 194
sanctification 29, 45, 145, 153, 164, 169, 171, 173-76, 181, 217
Sandown Baptist Church, Isle of Wight 56
Schmidt, Margaretha 202n
Scotland, Nigel 6
second blessing theology 175n
second coming 163, 164, 229, 230
Sewell, Mrs 96n
Seymour, William J. 4, 99-101, 126n, 136, 137, 140, 142, 144, 145, 148, 151, 152, 157, 170, 175n, 179, 181, 216, 234n
Shaw, S.B. 92
Short, A.G. 56
Shumway, C.M. 4, 142
signs and wonders 28, 41, 43
Simpson, Albert B. 29, 164, 226n
singing in the Spirit 144
Singleton, G.H. 64
Sloan, Walter 205
Smale (née Stephens), Ann 19, 20, 55, 63, 78, 92, 93, 94, 96n, 131, 220, 239, 240
Smale, Alverda Keyser 220n
Smale, Ebenezer 19
Smale, Elizabeth 19
Smale, Esther Isabelle (née Hargrave) 6, 11, 131, 196, 208, 220-22, 224, 225, 228, 240

General Index 273

Smale, Esther Grace 232-33, 241
Smale, Hargrave 227, 241
Smale, Helena (née Dunham) 62-63, 239
Smale, John 19, 21, 239
Smale, Mary Hannah 19, 21, 55n
Smale, Samuel 19
Smith, Bessie 195
Smith, James K.A. 9
Southern Baptist Theological Seminary 3
Southern Baptists 12
Spanish Gospel Mission 15, 107, 196, 219, 221, 223, 224, 241
Spanish Settlement Mission 96n
spiritual gifts 145, 246
spiritual transformation 73
spirituality 23, 27, 165, 174, 197
Spittler, R.P. 17
Spurgeon, Charles Haddon 7, 8, 11, 12, 22, 25, 26, 27, 28, 29, 30, 31, 32, 33, 34, 35, 36, 37, 38, 39, 40, 41, 42, 43, 44, 48, 49, 50, 51, 52, 53, 54, 90, 146, 156, 159, 161, 167, 168, 174, 233, 234
Spurgeon, James Arthur 46
Spurgeon's College, London (Pastors' College) 1, 2, 25-46, 47, 48, 56, 61, 229, 239
Stockley, T.I. 36
Stockwell Orphanage 53
Suurmond, Jean-Jacques 99, 165, 166
Swedish Baptist Convention 8
Synan, Vinson 5

Taylor, Hudson 33n
Taylor, Malcolm 157
Temple Baptist Church, Los Angeles 80, 127
tent work 197-98
Tiedemann, R.G. 202n
Tipton, Mr 22
Tireman, Major 226

Todd, Mr 200
tongues/glossolalia 7, 44, 142, 143-46, 149, 150, 152, 153, 160, 163, 170, 178, 180, 194, 210, 211, 212, 213, 214, 227, 232, 240, 246-47
xenolalia 195
Toronto Blessing 148
Torrey, R.A. 8, 29, 189
Torrey-Alexander Mission 203
Trevitt, Frank 202n
Tripp, Prof. 76
Turner, William Henry 230, 231

Underhill, Evelyn 73
United Brethren 71
Unity Chapel, Bristol 11, 225-28, 241
Upper Room Mission, Los Angeles 111, 212, 213, 240

van Nuys, I.N. 66

Wacker, Grant 182, 192, 194, 235
Walberg, Deacon 130
Warfield, B.B. 162n
Welsh Revival (1904–05) 4, 5, 6, 8, 35, 39, 88, 90, 91, 92, 93, 94, 95, 97, 101, 102, 104, 105, 106, 107, 111, 116, 126, 128, 159, 176, 183, 184, 201, 203, 236, 239, 240
Wesleyan holiness teaching 101, 175
Wesleyan Methodism 22, 24
Wesleyanism 7, 25, 28, 174, 176, 233
Western Counties Evangelization Conferences 226
Williams, Amos 202n
Windes, R.A. 57, 58
Wiveliscombe, Somerset 19, 20, 21
Wood, Esther Grace 11

Wood, George 10, 11, 30, 233, 237
Wood, Stanley 11, 15, 233, 237
word and sacraments 172
word and Spirit 28-29, 38, 45, 49,
  69, 72, 165-68, 174, 219, 237
World Alliance of Reformed
  Churches 9
World Missionary Conference,
  Edinburgh (1910) 205
Worrell, A.S. 113, 134, 135, 218
Wyckoff, Mr 115, 118, 119

Yao, Kevin 207

www.ingramcontent.com/pod-product-compliance
Lightning Source LLC
Chambersburg PA
CBHW061434300426
44114CB00014B/1674